MUSSOLINI AS DIPLOMAT

Montgomery in Europe: Success or failure
The Ghosts of Peace
The Failure of the Eden Government
Der Verfehlte Frieden. Englands Aussenpolitik, 1935–1945
The Drift to War, 1922–1939
Churchill as War Leader: Right or Wrong?
War In Italy: A Brutal Story
The Macmillan Years, 1957–1963: The Emerging Truth

MUSSOLINI AS DIPLOMAT

Il Duce's Italy on the World Stage

RICHARD LAMB

FROMM INTERNATIONAL
New York

First Fromm International Edition, 1999

Copyright © 1997 by Richard Lamb

All rights reserved under International and Pan-American Copyright Conventions. Published in the United States by Fromm International Publishing Corporation, New York. First published in Great Britain by John Murray (Publishers) Ltd, London, in 1998.

LIBRARY OF CONGRESS CATALOGING-IN-PUBLICATION DATA

Lamb, Richard.
     Mussolini as diplomat : il Duce's Italy on the world stage /
Richard Lamb.
       p. cm.
     Includes bibliographical references and index.
     ISBN 0-88064-244-0
     1. Mussolini, Benito, 1883-1945--Political and social views.
2. Italy--Foreign relations--1922-1945. 3. Italy--Foreign
relations--Great Britain. 4. Great Britain--Foreign relations-
-Italy. I. Title.
DG575.M8L34 1999
945.091'092--dc21

                                                     99-38378
                                                       CIP

10 9 8 7 6 5 4 3 2 1
Manufactured in the United States of America

Contents

Illustrations

The author and publisher would like to thank the following for permission to reproduce illustrations: Plates 1 and 10, Topham Picturepoint; 2, 4, 6, 7, 9, 11, 12 and 14, Getty Images; 5 and 8, Associated Press; 13 and 15, National Archives; 16, Massimo Borgogni.

Acknowledgements

TRANSCRIPTS OF COPYRIGHT material in the Public Record Office appear by kind permission of the Controller of Her Majesty's Stationery Office.

I give my warm thanks to the staff of the Public Record Office for their unfailing help and courtesy. Under the Waldegrave initiative a number of hitherto closed official files have been opened to me, for which I am grateful. I thank Dr Elizabeth Evans for help with research in the Public Record Office.

I thank the Librarian and the staff of the London Library, Chatham House Library, Royal United Services Institute Library, the City of Westminster Library, the United Oxford and Cambridge Club Library, the Wiltshire County Library and the Italian Cultural Institute Library for their invaluable help.

I have been fortunate in that many have spared time to help me, and I particularly thank: the late Richard Acland, Antonio Armellini, Tom Braun, Curtis Cate, Massimo Coen, the late John Colville, Gervase Cowell, William Deakin, Orietta Doria Pamphilj, the late Renzo de Felice, Mario Fini, Ivo Grippaudo, Peter Hoffmann, Kim Isolani, the late Gladwyn Jebb, Mier Michaelis, Klaus-Jurgen Müller, Ilio Muraca, Eric and Wanda Newby, David Newman, Will Podmore, Paul Preston, Frank Roberts, Giovanni Rossi, Alberto Santoni, Enrico Serra, Christopher Seton-Watson, the late Roger Sherfield, the late John Simon, Denis Mack Smith, Alfredo Terrone, Igor Uboldi, Antonio Varsori, and Eduardo Vistarino.

I am grateful to Grant McIntyre, Gail Pirkis and Elizabeth Robinson for their meticulous editing, and to John Mark and Joan Moore for secretarial help. I thank my wife for her patience over a time-consuming book.

Finally, I note that this is in part the history of my own times. I voted in the Oxford Union for the motion that in no circumstances would we fight for King and country. I was enthusiastic for the Peace Ballot, and hostile to the Hoare–Laval Pact which I now consider sound diplomacy. As a lover of Italy I was appalled at the way in which British policy threw Mussolini into Hitler's arms. The archives reveal the cowardice and prejudices of the British Cabinet in the late 1930s – a period from which few British statesman apart from Austen Chamberlain and Winston Churchill emerge with credit.

Atlantic Ocean

GREAT
BRITAIN
London

North Sea

DENMARK
Copenhagen

LATVIA

LITHUANIA

Dunkirk
Brussels
BELGIUM
Paris

NETHERLANDS

Danzig

E. PRUSSIA

Berlin

Warsaw

USSR

RHINELAND

GERMANY

POLAND

FRANCE

Prague

SWITZERLAND

Munich

Vienna

CZECHOSLOVAKIA

Bordeaux

PORTUGAL

Stresa
Milan

Locarno

Trieste

Budapest

HUNGARY

ROMANIA

Marseilles

Toulon

Madrid

SPAIN

Corsica

ITALY

Venice

Zagreb

Belgrade

YUGOSLAVIA

Bucharest

Black Sea

Adriatic
Sea

BULGARIA

Rome

Sofia

Balearic Is.

Gibraltar
SP. MOROCCO

Sardinia

Bari

Tirana

Istanbul

Mers-el-Kébir

Taranto

ALBANIA

Corfu

GREECE

Aegean
Sea

TURKEY

ALGERIA

Tunis

Sicily

Ionian Sea

Athens

TUNISIA

Malta

Dodecanese

Mediterranean Sea

Crete

Cyprus

0   200   400   600 kms

0   200   400   600 miles

Tripoli

Tobruk

Sidi Barrani
Alexandria

Suez
Canal

Europe, 1935

LIBYA

El Aghella

EGYPT

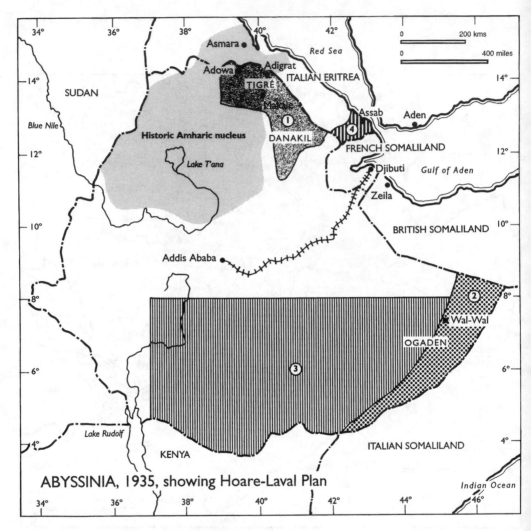

ABYSSINIA, 1935, showing Hoare-Laval Plan

1 Territory to be annexed by Italian Eritrea
2 Territory to be annexed by Italian Somaliland
3 Territory assigned to Italian economic influence
4 Territory and port assigned to Abyssinia

Introduction

THIS BOOK IS not another biography of Mussolini. It is a revisionist reassessment of the fluctuating relationship between Mussolini and Britain and, to a lesser extent, Mussolini and France. Much fresh evidence has become available with the most recent publications of Italian diplomatic documents, the voluminous researches of the late Renzo de Felice, captured Italian documents in the Public Record Office, and a recent book on Mussolini's Jewish mistress, Margherita Sarfatti. I have also included some material on Mussolini before he came to power.

Mussolini was not altogether an inhuman ogre. There was a sympathetic side to him, and until the mid 1930s the influence of Margherita Sarfatti tempered the brutality which was his chief defect. But for seventeen years he made preparations for war, and he ruthlessly consigned his fellow countrymen to heavy casualties in Abyssinia, Spain, and in the Second World War.

His popularity with ordinary Italians, particularly during his early years of power, cannot be overestimated. He had considerable personal charm and a hypnotic personality; large crowds filled the piazzas whenever he spoke, listeners raptly awaiting every word. His technique was superficial, flamboyant and vulgar, but it worked – though not always with people of taste and culture, who often abhorred him. He did much for Italian music, if not always altruistically.

Mussolini's principal weakness as head of state was that he based his decisions on whether they would increase his own popularity and that of the Fascist Party; the well-being of the Italian nation came only second.

With considerable efficiency he improved the civil service, and organized public works – new roads, schools, hospitals, irrigation, public buildings, etc. – which helped to raise the standard of living in towns. Yet his weakness for diverting state capital into flashy plans while ignoring fundamental economic problems meant that agriculture remained primitive. Corruption was allowed to flourish, but he

1

made peace between Church and State, and had some success in sub-
duing the Mafia. Had it not been for the Abyssinian war and his
alliance with Hitler, many Italians would regard Mussolini's rule as a
golden period in their history.

The theme of this book is foreign policy. Mussolini devoured the
reports of his overseas ambassadors and always had a sound knowledge
of what was going on all over the world. He had a passion for secrecy
and espionage, and uncovered many devious plans in foreign
embassies. However, in his final years he lost his judgement and lived
in a Cloud-cuckoo-land, succumbing to *folie de grandeur* and ignoring
the tragedies he had brought upon his nation.

Towards Britain his behaviour was that of a Jekyll-and-Hyde character. Apart from the atrocious Corfu episode of 1923, he aligned
Italian foreign policy with Britain's until the Abyssinian War in 1935.
He had ample reason to expect Britain to condone his invasion of
Abyssinia; hence it was a great shock to him when under the
Covenant of the League of Nations Britain took the lead over imposing economic sanctions on Italy. Once his conquest was complete he
tried to renew his friendship with Britain; only when his overtures
were spurned did he turn to Hitler, whom he disliked and feared.

Mussolini assumed power constitutionally in 1922. Summoned to
Rome by the King, he travelled by train – the March on Rome by
Fascist squads was largely a myth. British Conservatives hailed him
with joy as Prime Minister, seeing him and Italian Fascism as bulwarks
against the spread of Communism and ignoring the brutality of the
Matteotti murder (for which no evidence directly implicating
Mussolini has been found) and his persecution of anti-Fascists. On the
other hand, the British Labour Party and the Trade Unions became
vehemently opposed to Mussolini as a result of his suppression of the
Italian Trade Unions. His much-vaunted 'corporate state' amounted
to a government department replacing employers' and workers'
organizations, securing fixed prices and wage rates, and outlawing
strikes – which was a benefit to the Italian economy, much damaged
previously by inflation, frequent strikes and lock-outs. So incensed
were British trade unionists that the National Union of Railwaymen
threatened to refuse to operate Mussolini's train from Dover to
Victoria when it was thought he would come to London for the
signing of the Locarno Treaty in 1925.

His mistress, the intellectual Margherita Sarfatti, guided Mussolini
in his foreign policy during his first thirteen years of power. Pro-
British, pro-French and anti-German, she was until the Abyssinian

war his main advisor on international affairs, steering him away from aggrandisement and towards co-operation with France and Britain.

Immediately he came to power Mussolini was pitchforked into the world of international conferences. His first meeting with the British Foreign Secretary Lord Curzon at Lausanne in 1922 doubtless had its absurd moments, but between displays of bombast he took a sensible line over the Turkish–Greek dispute, and on his only visit to London shortly afterwards, for a Reparations Conference, he was persuaded to accept Britain's policy of opposing French occupation of the Ruhr.

When the assassination of General Tellini by Greeks in 1923 prompted Mussolini to bombard Corfu, British faith in him was shattered overnight, and it looked as though the League of Nations might impose economic sanctions. However Curzon and the French Premier, Jules Poincaré, were irresolute, and Mussolini compromised, so that the Corfu incident blew over; but not without inflicting grave damage on both the prestige of the League of Nations, and Mussolini's reputation.

At first there was doubt whether Mussolini would agree to the Locarno Pact of 1925. Briefly he contemplated the weird tack of seeking an alliance with Russia and Germany, directed against Britain and France. Guided by Margherita Sarfatti he changed course, and Italy's behaviour at Locarno was impeccable. A contributory factor was the friendship Mussolini had struck up with Austen Chamberlain, now Foreign Secretary, and Winston Churchill, Chancellor of the Exchequer. Both men spoke and wrote of him in glowing terms, a cordiality which angered the British Left, especially when it led Churchill to a generous settlement of Italian war debts.

Abyssinia's admission to the League of Nations in 1923 at French insistence was a disaster for Europe. Curzon wanted to concert plans with Mussolini to exclude her. The Foreign Office view was that as a country where slavery, gun-running and drugs were rife, they considered Abyssinia was unfit for membership. Robert Cecil, the Minister responsible at Geneva, contrived to ignore Curzon's instructions, and Abyssinia was admitted. In December 1925 an agreement between Austen Chamberlain and Mussolini virtually gave Italy a free hand in Abyssinia, with the British supporting plans for a railway to link Italian Somaliland and Eritrea which would mean an Italian military presence amid warring tribes. Mussolini accurately described the agreement as practically 'cutting Abyssinia in pieces'. While it has been largely ignored by historians, both this agreement and the admission of Abyssinia to the League of Nations were important contributory causes of the Second World War.

Mussolini cannot be criticized for his attitude to the abortive

Disarmament Conference which began in February 1932. Had France been as forthcoming as Italy, the rise to power of the Nazis might have been halted; the German people bitterly resented the military inferiority imposed by the Treaty of Versailles, and with support from Mussolini, the German Chancellor Heinrich Brüning tried to wrest from the Disarmament Conference a form of words which could be proclaimed for internal propaganda purposes as equality of arms for Germany. Success would have stolen Hitler's thunder and won votes in Germany, but while Britain and Italy supported Brüning, France and the 'Little Entente' would not give way.

Another severe blow to the German democratic parties in their fight against the Nazis was the Lausanne Reparations Conference of 1932, at which the French demanded and obtained a last tranche of reparations from Germany. Originally Britain had looked to wipe out future reparations with a 'clean slate' policy, and Mussolini approved; but weakly, Neville Chamberlain, Chancellor of the Exchequer, later the chief appeaser of Hitler, backed France. This was an important factor in the success of the Nazis in the elections of January 1933.

Mussolini's response to Hitler's accession to power was frigid. Believing himself to be the great statesman of the era, he resented suggestions of resemblance between him and the Führer. He would only agree that Nazism in Germany was like Fascism in Italy in that both were authoritative, collectivist and anti-democratic; he dismissed the Nazis' idea of a master race as 'arrant nonsense', and despised their anti-Semitism.

On 14 June 1934 the two dictators met at Venice. Mussolini's main concern was to warn Hitler to keep his hands off Austria. There was no meeting of minds and a bitter dispute ensued, with Hitler making fruitless demands for Nazis to be included in the Austrian government.

After Venice, Hitler persevered with plans for Nazis to infiltrate the Austrian government; Mussolini countered by sending arms to Englebert Dollfuss, the Austrian Chancellor, on condition that he conduct a one-party dictatorial government, and when Dollfuss visited Rome he was promised Italian military support in the event of a German invasion.

Relations between Mussolini and Hitler plunged when Dollfuss was assassinated on 25 July 1934 and the Nazis attempted to take over Austria. Mussolini reacted violently to the death of his friend, backing the right-wing Austrian government and ordering Italian troops to threatening positions on the frontier, so that Hitler was forced to abandon his coup. Mussolini's thwarting of Hitler in his first trial of strength indicated to the world that Italy held the balance of power in Europe; until 1942, it remained Hitler's sole failure.

Mussolini was still angry with Hitler when in March 1935 Germany revealed the existence of her illegal air force, and announced the introduction of conscription to raise a peacetime army of thirty-six divisions and 500,000 men, breaching the treaties of Versailles and Locarno. France and Italy delivered strong notes of protest in Berlin; Britain's was less forceful.

Mussolini's resistance to Nazi aggression culminated in his organization of a conference between Britain, Italy and France – the three victorious powers of the First World War – at Stresa on Lake Maggiore on 11 April 1935. The records of the Stresa discussions – much neglected by historians* – show Mussolini to have been more supportive of the French in their efforts to restrain Hitler than the British, who demurred at any suggestion of resolute action. The main issues at Stresa were Hitler's designs on Austria, and empowering the League of Nations to nip German rearmament in the bud.

Mussolini and Pierre Laval, the French Foreign Minister, argued strongly for a Central European Pact by which the smaller defeated powers of the First World War (Austria, Hungary and Bulgaria) would be freed from the Versailles restrictions and allowed to strengthen their armed forces *vis-à-vis* Germany. Mussolini declared that an *Anschluss* which left Germany in Vienna 'meant Germany on the Bosphorus and the revival of the Berlin–Baghdad drive'. Laval complained, accurately, that 'Britain had no intention of taking any part in the effective defence of Austria'. The British Foreign Secretary, Sir John Simon, could not deny this; his reply was that Britain would 'support' a Central European Pact but could not 'contract' into it.

Because of British intransigence, the final communiqué with regard to Austria was watered down to: 'The Three Powers recognized that the integrity of Austria would continue to inspire their common policy' – far weaker than Mussolini had intended when he proposed the conference.

As long as the Stresa Front held, however, Hitler was in a strait-jacket, unable either to attack Austria or to remilitarize the Rhineland – Mussolini had promised France that he would send aeroplanes and, if necessary, troops to help to throw the German army out if they entered the demilitarized Rhineland in violation of the terms of the Versailles Treaty.

At Geneva the French pleaded for a committee to be set up to consider League of Nations sanctions against Germany for her breach of treaties. Mussolini backed the French wholeheartedly, but Simon

---

* Notably by the late Professor Northedge in his book *The Troubled Giant, 1916–1939*, which is on most reading lists.

baulked. Still, to the world it seemed that a united front against Germany had been established; unfortunately, it proved the last time the three victorious powers of the 1914–1918 war were in agreement.

The deadly trap was Abyssinia. The British Foreign Office and Cabinet were well aware that Mussolini was contemplating an invasion of Abyssinia, but the matter was not discussed at Stresa, an extraordinary omission which has never been properly explained.

While Mussolini was making open plans to conquer Abyssinia, the British Cabinet were seeking a means of giving him what he wanted with the least possible damage to the League of Nations and without appearing to forsake Britain's obligations under the Covenant.

At the Palazzo Farnese in Rome in January 1935 Laval effectively promised the Duce a free hand in Abyssinia, both economically and militarily. Britain had always regarded Abyssinia as belonging to Italy's sphere of influence and, consequently, in Mussolini's eyes the British attempt to bar Abyssinia's entry to the League of Nations in 1923 and his agreement with Chamberlain of December 1925 loomed large. Mussolini was also conscious that Britain had not pressed for sanctions against Italy over Corfu (nor against Japan for her aggression in Manchuria), and had opposed the French demand for sanctions against Germany for illegal rearmament.

Then on 27 June there came a bombshell which shook the British government. The result of the 'peace ballot' held by the League of Nations Union revealed a vast majority in favour of the League's aims, in particular answering 'Yes' to the question whether, if one nation attacked another, the other states should combine to stop her. In these circumstances the Cabinet decided that Mussolini must not be allowed to get away with aggression in Abyssinia without obvious opposition from Britain, on behalf of the League.

On 3 October 1935 Italy invaded Abyssinia. The League declared Italy an aggressor, and preparations were made for the imposition of economic sanctions against her. In the General Election held on 14 November the Conservatives' main platform point was League of Nations sanctions against Italy, and they won a steam-roller majority. However, even while the election campaign was in progress, Sir Robert Vansittart (Permanent Under-Secretary at the Foreign Office) was negotiating with Laval in Paris for an agreement (known as the Hoare–Laval Pact) by which Italy would be offered annexation of a large slice of the Abyssinian Empire and economic control over the remainder. On 7 December the Hoare–Laval Pact was initialled in Paris. Mussolini was on the brink of acceptance, whereupon the Stresa Front against Germany would have been restored.

Unfortunately, the plan was leaked in Paris. Reaction in both

Britain and France was violent, and the government faced a storm of protest; Anthony Eden (Minister at the Foreign Office under Sir Samuel Hoare) suddenly turned against it, having previously minuted his approval. After a stormy Cabinet meeting Stanley Baldwin, the Prime Minister, decided to renege on the pact even though it had been approved by the Cabinet. Hoare refused to recant, and resigned. The opportunity to end the Abyssinian war and bring Mussolini back into the fold against Hitler was lost.

The League of Nations sanctions against Italy were ineffective. Only efficient oil sanctions and closure of the Suez Canal to Italian shipping could have produced results, but France refused to approve either and the United States, not a member of the League, continued to supply Italy with sufficient oil for her needs. Italian troops entered Addis Ababa on 5 May 1936, and Mussolini was hailed as a triumphant hero in Italy. Sanctions were called off.

Immediately Mussolini made overtures to Britain, and in the Foreign Office there were high hopes that the Stresa Front would be re-established. In March 1936 Hitler had remilitarized the Rhineland, in defiance of the treaties of Locarno and Versailles. The Baldwin government refused to help the French to throw the German troops out, or even to consider sanctions against Germany. Hitler was still militarily weak, and the last opportunity to stop him in his tracks was thrown away by British intransigence. The success of the Rhine operation greatly increased Nazi popularity: more than ever Britain and France needed Mussolini's support against Hitler.

In November 1936 Mussolini took his first definite step towards Hitler by signing the Anti-Comintern Pact (a treaty between Italy, Germany and Japan, designed to halt the spread of Communism; in his diary Ciano noted that it was 'anti-British'). He still hankered after the Stresa Front, but felt France would be more likely to accept his claims in Tunisia if he had German support. It was an ominous move. Eden's cardinal error, when he succeeded Hoare as Foreign Secretary, was to trust Hitler but to suspect every action of Mussolini's. There is strong evidence to suggest that with co-operation from Eden Mussolini could have been kept out of Hitler's camp and the balance of power in Europe preserved.

The Spanish Civil War which began in July 1936 proved a quicksand for British–Italian relations. The majority of the Conservative Party were on Franco's side, seeing him as a shield against Communism. Eden took a contrary view, however, and refused advances from Mussolini while Italy was sending volunteers to help Franco.

Mussolini's desire that Britain should grant *de jure* recognition of his conquest of Abyssinia became an obsession with him, and another stumbling block in British–Italian relations. Dino Grandi, the Italian Ambassador in London and an enthusiast for Anglo–Italian friendship, made friendly approaches to Eden, but came up against a brick wall over Abyssinia. At the same time, the Foreign Office feared that further cold-shouldering of Mussolini would drive him into Hitler's arms, and advocated the granting of *de jure* recognition. Baldwin, in his last months as Prime Minister, took little interest, but when Neville Chamberlain became Prime Minister in June 1937 he pressurized Eden to mend the bridges with Mussolini, realizing that Hitler was the more serious menace. Eden refused to agree with the Prime Minister that the Spanish Civil War was a side-show compared with the danger of German aggression, and was incensed by Mussolini's anti-British propaganda and his bombastic praise for the part played in Spain by Italian troops, submarines and aircraft. Neville Chamberlain wanted Eden to grant recognition of Italy's conquest in Abyssinia before the two dictators became even closer; he particularly feared lest Mussolini should consent to the annexation of Austria by Germany.

The disagreement between Chamberlain and Eden over Italy came to a head in July 1937 when Eden minuted that an agreement with Hitler might have 'a chance of reasonable life . . . whereas Mussolini is . . . a complete gangster'. Without telling Eden, Chamberlain off his own bat decided to write a personal letter to Mussolini; Mussolini's reply was encouraging, but with Eden still refusing to consider recognition of Italy's conquests in Abyssinia, conversations in Rome led nowhere.

In December 1937 Ivy Chamberlain, Austen's widow, was in Rome; after talking to Ciano and Mussolini she wrote to her brother-in-law, the Prime Minister, that Mussolini wanted a return to the Stresa Front, but that Eden's dislike of Italy was the stumbling block. Eden was infuriated by her meddling, even more so by his subsequent discovery that Neville Chamberlain was communicating with Grandi, secretly, behind his (Eden's) back. Then on 18 February 1938 Eden and Chamberlain had a stand-up row: Chamberlain wanted official talks with Italy at once; Eden refused, insisting they must await withdrawal of Italian troops from Spain.

Eden had no support in Cabinet, and resigned – not, as myth has it, because he was opposed to Chamberlain's appeasement of Hitler. He was replaced by Lord Halifax, whereupon talks began in Rome which led to the Easter Agreement signed on 16 April 1938. It was too late to save Austria: with Mussolini's connivance, Hitler had seized Austria on 11 March, opposed by neither Britain nor France. In a letter to his sister after the *Anschluss* Chamberlain declared that if he had had

Halifax at the Foreign Office instead of Eden when he wrote to Mussolini in August 1937, the *Anschluss* might have been prevented. He was right.

Unfortunately, the Easter Agreement made it a condition of *de jure* recognition of Italy's conquest of Abyssinia that Mussolini should first withdraw most of his troops from Spain. The unanswered question is whether, if Britain had waived her scruples about both recognition and Italian involvement in Spain, Mussolini would have abandoned Hitler. The British Cabinet was frightened of hostile public opinion if Italy's conquest of Abyssinia were recognized while Mussolini's help to Franco remained blatant, so that recognition was only granted in November 1938, after the Munich Agreement. As a result of the delay, Mussolini's attitude to Britain deteriorated.

Hitler paid a state visit to Rome on 2 May 1938, anxious to counter any good done to Anglo-Italian relations by the Easter Agreement, although relations between Hitler and Mussolini were clouded at the time by a dispute over the German-speaking Austrian minority in the Italian South Tyrol. During his visit Hitler informed Mussolini of his planned aggression against Czechoslovakia; Mussolini did not demur, but declined a military alliance with Germany when Hitler suggested it.

Hitler bluffed Neville Chamberlain into believing that his army would march against Czechoslovakia unless the Sudetenland was immediately ceded to Germany. At the last moment, Chamberlain made a plea to Mussolini to propose a peace conference and Mussolini exultantly agreed. Hitler at once transmitted his terms to Mussolini, who produced them at the Munich Conference, pretending they were his own. Weakly Chamberlain and the French Premier, Édouard Daladier, agreed to the German–Italian proposals, without consulting the Czechs. It was the high tide of appeasement.

Mussolini was hailed as the saviour of peace, and he revelled in his new reputation; in the House of Commons Chamberlain effusively thanked him for his role at Munich.

But Mussolini's intervention at Munich was a disaster. There is doubt whether war would have ensued if Hitler's bluff had been called (the German army could not have sustained hostilities against both the Czechs and the French, so that a plot by the German generals would probably have overthrown Hitler), but if war had broken out in September 1938 Britain and France would have been in an immeasurably stronger position *vis-à-vis* Germany than they were a year later. The Czechs had a strong and well-equipped army, with powerful fortifications on the German frontier (but not on the Austrian), and Russia was ready to intervene to help Czechoslovakia, whereas a year later she was on Hitler's side. While the bulk of the German army was attacking Czechoslovakia, the French could have pierced the German frontier and occupied the Ruhr. We know from evidence given at the Nuremberg Trials that in September 1938 the Siegfried line was 'nothing but a construction site', with only five divisions deployed to defend it. In September 1938 the Germans had only thirty operational divisions – a year later they had seventy-three: General Adam, who commanded the German army on the French frontier, noted in his (unpublished) memoirs that a war with Britain and France in 1938 would have been 'sheer lunacy'.

Nor did the year's 'breathing space' gained at Munich give Britain any advantage in terms of arms manufacture. Germany took possession of the giant Czech Skoda factory, which now manufactured arms for the Germans, instead of for the Allies, and Germany's own output exceeded the combined output of British and French factories. The view that Munich bought a valuable year which enabled French and British military strength to catch up with German is unsustainable.

After Munich, Mussolini had qualms about Germany dominating Eastern Europe and threatening his aspirations in the Balkans, and continued to baulk at a definite military alliance with Hitler. The British Ambassador in Rome advised that the only way to keep Hitler and Mussolini apart was to recognize Italy's position in Abyssinia, whatever the circumstances; although Italian volunteers were still pouring into Spain, Britain now granted *de jure* recognition: nothing had been gained by the six months' delay. Mussolini now went on to formulate demands against France over Tunisia, Corsica and Djibuti, threatening to join the German camp if they were not granted, and backed his demands with a vicious anti-French campaign.

Chamberlain and Halifax visited Rome in January 1939, and were well received by the Italian people. When Chamberlain put it to Mussolini that Hitler was rearming with a view to an aggressive war in the east or in the west, the Duce replied disarmingly (and untruthfully) that it was 'out of the question'.

The independent state of Czechoslovakia disappeared overnight when on 14 March 1939 Hitler, without consulting Mussolini, breached the Munich Agreement and occupied Prague. Chamberlain, counting on the good relations he thought had been established during his visit to Rome, asked Mussolini to intervene; this only produced a snub. However, although he supported Hitler, Mussolini was angry at not having been consulted, and particularly by the way Hitler's action devalued Munich, which he considered the pinnacle of his career. As a counter-stroke, he occupied Albania without consulting Hitler. Albania was already under Italian domination, but the invasion was ill-received in Britain, where it was thought that Mussolini was aping Hitler and his action was seen as a prelude to joint moves by Germany and Italy in eastern Europe. Britain and France gave guarantees to Poland, now obviously the next target for Hitler.

Diplomatic documents indicate that in the spring of 1939 Mussolini was wavering, not wanting to distance himself from Berlin but concerned to keep his options open with the British and French, and hoping to instigate another great four-power conference (without Russia) which would stabilize Europe and induce France to make concessions to Italy. The French Premier, Daladier, was antagonistic to Mussolini; the Foreign Minister, Georges Bonnet, less so: informal Franco–Italian negotiations began over Djibuti and Tunisia, and the question of Italian directorships in the Suez Canal Company. After a promising start they were terminated, much to Britain's disappointment, by a tactless but not ill-intentioned speech by Daladier to which the mercurial Mussolini took exception. There is no question, however, that whatever concessions France made to Mussolini at this stage might have been used by Italy as a basis for increasing her demands.

Mussolini reacted strongly when in the spring of 1939 Britain and France began negotiations with Russia (eventually superseded by a German–Soviet pact) for a military pact to save Poland. Overcoming his dislike of Hitler, in May 1939 he impulsively concluded the 'Pact of Steel', by which he was trapped into pledging that Italy would come to Germany's aid in the event of war. Mussolini was deceived by Hitler, who promised not to go to war for four or five years when in fact he had already instructed his generals to be ready to invade Poland in the autumn.

Hitler's threats against Poland increased during June and July. In a reply to a letter from Chamberlain, Mussolini stated that if war came over Poland, he would fight on the side of the Germans; however, he made no preparations for war, and was in a torment over the Pact of Steel. When Ciano went to Germany to see Ribbentrop on 11 August, Mussolini instructed him to tell the Germans emphatically that military action must be avoided, and that Danzig ought to be ceded to Germany after another international, Munich-style conference. Ciano was appalled to find the Germans determined on invasion.

Mussolini, alarmed by Italy's military weakness and in particular by the vulnerability of his northern industrial cities to bombing from nearby French airfields, oscillated between greed and fear. The German–Soviet Pact of 23 August was a bombshell for him; he intensely disliked Russia and Communism, and while he felt it put Germany into a stronger position, he now regretted his alliance with her. As an excuse to escape his commitment, he informed Hitler that he would only fight if Germany provided him beforehand with wheat, oil, steel and other materials – pitching his demands unsustainably high; instead, he would take military measures to immobilize 'notable' British and French forces. Mussolini was trying to evade war without denouncing the Pact of Steel. His message may have caused Hitler to delay his invasion of Poland for forty-eight hours.

Hitler told Mussolini that he could not meet his demands, and that he only asked Italy to pin down Anglo-French forces by propaganda and 'suitable military measures'. Horrified, Mussolini begged Hitler to find a 'political solution'. The British Ambassador in Rome reported that Italy would definitely not fight, and suddenly relations between London and Rome became cordial. Mussolini appreciated the way Britain kept him informed about negotiations with Germany while Hitler volunteered nothing; he sent word to London that he wanted to co-operate in a peaceful solution through another Munich-style conference. The Foreign Secretary, Lord Halifax, wrote to Mussolini stressing his faith in the Duce's ability to 'avert catastrophe'.

Whether Hitler ever genuinely considered a negotiated solution of the Danzig problem we will never know; suddenly, without informing Mussolini, he gave the order for German troops to attack Poland on the night of 30/31 August.

The British Cabinet refused to accept that war was inevitable, and pinned its hopes on Mussolini's intervention. Halifax persuaded Bonnet, the French Foreign Minister, to agree to Mussolini's request for a conference at San Remo, and Hitler asked whether he could be given until noon on 3 September to consider an armistice, and the Duce's proposed conference; probably he was only playing for time in order to delay British and French intervention on behalf of Poland.

Chamberlain and Halifax pleaded with the British Cabinet to wait until midnight of 3 September before declaring war. The Cabinet refused. Nevertheless, Halifax entreated Mussolini to persuade Hitler to withdraw his forces and agree to the San Remo conference. Ciano told Halifax that Hitler would never accept 'withdrawal' as a condition; whereupon Halifax again urged the Italian 'to try his best'. Ciano then firmly pronounced the whole scheme impossible.

At first Mussolini was far from giving unconditional support to Germany; he was disgusted by Russia's occupation of a large part of Poland, and by reports of Nazi atrocities against the Polish people. He doubted whether Hitler would win if he attacked France. Throughout the 'phoney war' the Duce vacillated between backing

Germany, staying neutral, and siding with the West. When a naval blockade deprived Italy of German coal imports by sea, he blew cold on the British. Seizing the opportunity, Hitler invited Mussolini to a meeting at the Brenner Pass, where he told the Duce of his plans to attack in the west. Mussolini was evasive when Hitler suggested that Italy should send twenty to thirty divisions to help Germany breach the Maginot Line.

After the German victory in Norway at the beginning of May 1940 Mussolini remained reluctant to throw his lot in with Germany; he still doubted a Nazi victory even as Hitler's armies rolled into Holland, Belgium and France, expecting another Battle of the Marne. Not until 30 May, when the British and French had been hopelessly defeated, did Mussolini plump for war. Until then, fearing lest he himself might fall victim to German's military strength, he wanted to be the organizer of a peace conference. But with the collapse of France, Mussolini itched to get his hands on the booty; he told Hitler the die was cast and he would declare war on 10 June.

Winston Churchill, now Prime Minister, authorized Halifax to say that if she remained neutral, Italy could appear at any peace conference on an equal footing with the belligerents. Halifax told the Italian Ambassador in London that the Allies would consider any proposals which might lead to peace, and even hinted that cession of Gibraltar and Malta might be contemplated. However, as soon as the British Expeditionary Force had been safely evacuated (minus equipment) from Dunkirk, Churchill set his face firmly against defeatism, while Mussolini turned down out-of-hand humiliating proposals from the French.

From the start the war was a disaster for Italy: her army made no progress on the French frontier; Mussolini longed for a military triumph in Egypt, but his forces were ignominiously beaten by the British; against Hitler's wishes he attacked Greece, where again he suffered defeat.

With his declaration of war Mussolini became vindictive against Britain, even offering troops and aircraft for Hitler's proposed cross-Channel invasion. Malta and Gibraltar were his foremost targets, but various plans for a combined German-Italian assault on Malta had to be postponed because of conflicting demands for petrol and troops for Libya. (A note of farce was introduced by Mussolini's suggestion that the water-buses of Venice should be used as troop transports.)

At the Casablanca Conference in January 1943 Roosevelt and Churchill agreed upon the formula of 'unconditional surrender' to be demanded of defeated opponents – but Churchill did not want to apply it to Italy. In 1940 and 1941 he had been in favour of offering anti-Fascist Italians 'soft' peace terms, even – surprisingly – of ceding Cyrenaica (Libya) to them. Eden, an implacable enemy of Italy, persuaded the War Cabinet in Churchill's absence that 'unconditional surrender' should apply to Italy as well as to Germany. This was a disastrous mistake: not only was Mussolini himself seeking a way out of the war, but the King and the anti-Fascists around him were plotting to topple the Duce and abandon the German alliance. With Italy down and out, this was the time for compromise. If there had been negotiations, plans could have been concerted for an unopposed Allied landing in Italy before German troops descended on the peninsula.

When Tunisia fell in May 1943, Mussolini realized all was lost. He tried to persuade Hitler to make peace with Russia and continue the war against the United States and Britain. When Hitler obdurately refused, Mussolini made overtures to Churchill, hoping to save Italy and on the understanding that he himself would be spared. There was no response. Overtures from anti-Fascists and the King were also ignored, so that the King's arrest of Mussolini on 25 July 1943 came as a surprise to Germans and Allies alike. Immediately German troops poured into Italy and when, after forty-five days, Italy made an Armistice with the Allies, the Germans were able to take over all the country apart from the tiny area already occupied by Allied troops.

When he was rescued by the Germans Mussolini at first wanted to retire into private life, but Hitler persuaded him to head a puppet Fascist government. Fearing that if he refused Italy would be subjected to barbaric treatment, like Poland, Mussolini reluctantly agreed.

By the spring of 1945 the British and American armies were entering Germany from the west, and the Russians from the east, while the Allied offensive to surge into the Lombardy Plain was unstoppable. Mussolini tried to approach Churchill, through Nicola Bombacci (a leading Fascist but a former trade unionist and a friend of Ernest Bevin, a member of Churchill's War Cabinet) and the Vatican, with the suggestion that once Germany was defeated the Fascist army should fight with the Allies against the Russians. No response came from Churchill.

For fifty years Italian newspapers have from time to time carried stories that Mussolini, when he was captured and executed, was carrying letters from Churchill, written in the concluding stages of the war and suggesting that the Duce should change sides. The evidence I have uncovered in the Public Record Office proves these stories to be untrue, as are the latest Italian claims that Mussolini was assassinated on the orders of Churchill.

The evidence is conclusive that once he had conquered Abyssinia,

Mussolini wanted to renew friendship with Britain. He both feared and disliked Hitler, and was intent on preserving Austria from the Nazis. The British policy of appeasing Hitler and opposing Mussolini was disastrous. Abyssinia and the Spanish Civil War were mere side-shows compared with Hitler's fanatical determination to use his enormously powerful armies for aggression. Unfortunately, Eden could never see this.

Mussolini would have been a slippery and treacherous ally, but in face of the Nazi menace his goodwill was essential for peace in Europe. Like all dictators, he was temperamental. His obsession with *de jure* recognition by Britain of the Italian conquest of Abyssinia may have been unreasonable, but the British Ambassador in Rome made it clear what a priority it was in Mussolini's mind – yet, because of public opinion at home, the Baldwin and Chamberlain governments delayed from spring 1936 until autumn 1938 before giving in. There can, surely, be little doubt that if this recognition had been granted in 1936, Mussolini would have stayed out of Hitler's arms. On such small things great events depend.

CHAPTER 1

Early Days and Rise to Power

BENITO AMILCARE MUSSOLINI was born in 1883 at Predappio near Forli in Romagna, on the southern edge of the Lombardy Plain. His father, a blacksmith, came from a decayed middle-class family and his mother was a school teacher. He was christened Benito after General Benito Juárez, who had headed the Mexican revolt of the 1860s, and Amilcare after the Italian socialist Amilcare Cipriani. Both his parents were strong Socialists; and although they were poor, they sent Benito to a fee-paying boarding school at Forlimpopoli, where the headmaster was the brother of the poet Giosuè Carducci. In July 1901, at eighteen, Benito left school with a diploma enabling him to teach in state schools. In July 1902, after teaching for a short time, he went off to Switzerland where he led almost a vagabond existence. Here he co-operated with Italian socialists who were trying to organize the underpaid Italian immigrant workers, especially those in the mill town of St Galle. At Lausanne he had the good fortune to make friends with Angelica Balabanoff, a prominent revolutionary Socialist from a well-off aristocratic Ukrainian family who had revolted against her class. She found Mussolini ill-dressed and unkempt, 'but full of enthusiasm with a completely undisciplined mind' and 'a hatred of oppression springing from his own sense of indignity and frustration, and a determination for personal revenge . . . he knew little of history or of economics or of socialist theory . . . No one could see in this bewildered and neurotic youth of twenty the man who was to rule Italy.'

Angelica became Mussolini's mistress. She was attracted by his youthful good looks and the bustling energetic mind which gave little thought to anything except politics. Her intellectual companionship worked wonders for him; she gave him innumerable books and pamphlets and arranged for him to go to stimulating lectures at the University of Lausanne. His political ideas matured fast. Nietzsche, with his revival of the heroic Roman superman, became Mussolini's favourite social theoretician. He quickly acquired a reputation as a writer for Socialist periodicals and as a speaker at Socialist meetings,

17

but when he organized a strike of building workers at Berne he was expelled from the canton. He was not a Marxist; the moderate Socialism of Giuseppe Mazzini, the hero of the Risorgimento, appealed more to him, with its ideal of abolishing both national frontiers and import duties.[1]

Meanwhile he had become a deserter, through failing to comply with his call-up papers for the Italian army; but when, in May 1903, King Victor Emmanuel III amnestied all deserters to celebrate the birth of the Crown Prince, Umberto, he decided to return to Italy and present himself for military service. He served the regulation two years and was discharged in September 1906, whereupon he took a job as a school teacher at Tolmezzo, an Italian-speaking town in the Friuli, then part of Austria. Dismissed for unruliness, he found another job at Oneglia on the Italian Riviera. Here he spent much of his time writing articles for Socialist periodicals which included venomous attacks on the Church. The police forced him to leave and he was later sentenced to a short term of imprisonment. However, he had created a reputation for himself as a Socialist writer and speaker, and he was subsequently offered the job of Secretary of the Chamber of Labour at Trento, again in Austrian territory, together with the editorship of their weekly newspaper.

At Trento Mussolini met the Socialist and Italian Nationalist Cesare Battisti (executed by the Austrians in 1916); he soon imbibed Battisti's doctrines, and furthered the cause of revolutionary socialism with fiery articles advancing claims for the Italian-speaking areas to be liberated from Austrian rule. The Austrians deported him and, returning to Italy with 'the halo of a martyred revolutionary', he was offered the post of Secretary to the Forli Socialist Party. There he edited a Socialist weekly, *La Lotta di Classe* (*The Class Struggle*). When the Russian minister Stolypin was assassinated Mussolini wrote that he deserved his fate, while in commenting on the London Sydney Street Siege of 1911 he declared that the victims, who were anarchists, 'were to be praised'. He also continued his attacks on the Church (which he later came to regret).

Never in his life did Mussolini show any interest in acquiring wealth. In January 1910 he married Rachele Guidi, a domestic servant without any money; she was a faithful wife, but incapable of rising in the world with him.

In September 1911 Italy declared war on Turkey after Austria had exposed Turkey's weakness by annexing Bosnia and Herzegovina. Giovanni Giolitti, the Italian Prime Minister, believed that Turkish-held Tripoli would be useful ground for Italian colonization, and the idea of an outlet for Italy's poverty-stricken surplus population in a former part of the Roman Empire had popular appeal. The Socialist Party was split over the war; Mussolini was strongly against. Here was an opportunity to assert his qualities of leadership. At Forli, aided by Pietro Nenni, a close friend, Mussolini led the workers in an attack on the railway station to prevent the movement of troop trains, and the line was blocked for three days. After cavalry had restored order Mussolini was arrested and sentenced to six months' imprisonment. His exploits at Forli gained him national renown, and he went to the Socialist Conference at Reggio Emilia in a blaze of glory. There he attacked the war virulently and became the rising star of the Socialist Party. A few weeks later he was appointed editor of *Avanti!*, the left-wing Milan daily paper. Luigi Barzini★ writes: 'At this period he was not only perhaps the most professional journalist of his day in Italy, but one of the best and most moving speakers in Italy, paying little attention to the logic and truth of what he said, provided it was energetic and stirring.'[2]

When the First World War broke out Mussolini was at first a neutralist, adamant that Italy should not fight beside Germany and Austria under the Triple Alliance. When the successful Anglo-French resistance on the Marne convinced him that Germany would eventually lose he suddenly changed course, becoming a vociferous supporter of Italian intervention on the Allied side: *Avanti!*'s editorial policy now shifted to support for the British and French. Detractors suggest that Mussolini was bribed, but the evidence is skimpy. However, when the Party Executive threatened to sack him if he continued to argue in *Avanti!* for Italian participation on the Allied side, he resigned and started a new paper in competition with *Avanti!*, entitled *Il Popolo d'Italia*. There is an element of mystery over how he obtained the capital for this new enterprise. Some historians claim that the money came not only from France and Britain, but possibly from Russia and the United States. However, the Foreign Office archives establish that foreign funds used to set up *Il Popolo d'Italia* came only from the French Embassy in Rome, and were channelled to Mussolini in Milan through Dr Filippo Malda of the Rome newspaper *Il Tempo*. Although Mussolini's was a Socialist newspaper, he received subsidies from rich industrialists who favoured Italy entering the war on the Allied side; the Italian government probably also gave funds.[3]

The thrust of *Il Popolo* was at variance with *Avanti!*'s. Instead of urging the workers to begin a class war against the injustices of capitalism, *Il Popolo* was strongly nationalist, appealing to patriots to com-

---

★ The best-known modern Italian journalist, whose book *The Italians* is a brilliant analysis of Mussolini's character and regime.

plete the Risorgimento by freeing Trieste and the Trentino from Austrian rule; in it, Mussolini now justified the Libyan war, which previously he had roundly condemned – a complete volte-face from the attitude which had landed him in prison in 1911. He obtained substantial support from vast numbers of irredentists who wanted all areas where the Italian language was spoken to be part of Italy, and in particular to expand Italy's frontiers at the expense of Austria.

With the foundation of *Il Popolo* Mussolini became a renegade Socialist in the eyes of Angelica Balabanoff, and she refused to speak to him. During his days at *Avanti!* she had been a great help, and the maturity shown in his leading articles was often due to her wisdom. Instead he fell under the influence of Margherita Sarfatti, one of Italy's leading art critics and a political journalist. Intelligent, and also rich and beautiful, with flaming red hair, she filled the gap in Mussolini's intellectual life brought about by Angelica's defection. He saw her daily at the office of *Il Popolo*: she was his constant companion, his political advisor, and his art director.

Il Popolo, describing itself as Socialist, first appeared on 13 March 1915. It became an immediate success with its polemic articles favouring war against Germany and Austria. It had considerable influence on Italian public opinion, which anyway was moving towards intervention with a gut feeling that this was a good opportunity to complete the Risorgimento and throw over the Austrian yoke in Italian-speaking parts of Austria.

Antonio Salandra, the Italian Prime Minister, entered into negotiations with the Allies and on 26 April 1915 concluded the Treaty of London with the French, British and Russians. In return for Italy's entrance into the war within a month, she was promised unspecified but important territorial gains in Turkey, the eastern Aegean islands and Africa and, specifically, the Trentino, Trieste, central Dalmatia and part of Albania. Many clauses of the Treaty were kept secret.

The harsh fighting on the Italian–Austrian frontier shocked Mussolini. He had deluded himself, as had Margherita Sarfatti, with the idea of a Garibaldi-style heroic war which would produce a quick victory and the liberation of great numbers of Italians. The reality of static trench warfare was quite different and, with a certain amount of justification, he blamed the hard slog of such a war on government inefficiency.

Mussolini was called up with others of his age group in September 1915, as a private in the *bersaglieri*. He rose to the rank of sergeant, but was ploughed in his officers' training course because of his strong political views. In the fighting Mussolini proved himself an 'exemplary soldier'; he survived close-contact battles with Austrian infantry despite being in constant danger (he claimed to have specialized in throwing grenades back at the enemy). Slightly wounded more than once, he eventually succumbed to typhus in February 1917; and returned to Milan, an invalid on crutches because of his shrapnel wounds and an exhausted man, in September. He had had enough of soldiering: he applied for his discharge in order to renew his journalistic activities. A new chapter in his life began.

When in 1938 Mussolini introduced Italy's anti–Semitic laws, he tried to eradicate all traces of his liaison with his Jewish mistress Margherita Sarfatti, although it was well known to the public. His son-in-law Ciano was instructed 'to tell the Italian press to ignore Margherita completely. Her public appearances were not to be reported and her name was not to appear in any Fascist publication.' In 1938 Margherita emigrated to South America, fearful of her fate should she remain in Italy. After the war she hid from the public gaze in apprehension of the opprobrium her association with Mussolini would generate. Little of her voluminous correspondence with Mussolini is available, and her career was shrouded in mystery until in 1993 two American historians, Philip Cannistraro and Brian Sullivan, published her biography, *Il Duce's Other Woman*, using both her papers and her published writings. From these they have reconstructed her long and close association with Mussolini, which came to an end in 1935.

Margherita Sarfatti's ascendancy over the Duce was much stronger than is generally realized. She was a moderating influence in both his domestic and foreign policy. She opposed violence, and was anti-Nazi, pro–British and pro–French. Her biography makes it clear that Margherita guided Mussolini so that, apart from the disaster of Corfu, he aligned his foreign policy with Britain until 1935. The authors describe her during this period as, appropriately, 'the uncrowned Queen of Italy'. During the Abyssinian crisis of 1935 her influence began to wane as she lost her sexual attraction for Mussolini, who was instead becoming enamoured of the stupid, pro-Nazi Clara Petacci – with incalculable, tragic consequences.

Mussolini's departure from the army in 1917 coincided with the death in action of Roberto Sarfatti, Margherita's son. Roberto was handsome and intelligent, with a charisma which would surely have led him to a successful political career. Both Mussolini and Margherita idealized his death as the symbol of the flower of Italian manhood dying for the sake of the nation, a bond which grew into a great love story.

Mussolini had had one affair after another with women to whom he was sexually attracted; he had also enjoyed the intellectual companionship of one plain but clever and witty woman, Angelica Balabanoff, and made her his mistress; he had never before fallen for a woman who combined great physical charms with a sparkling intellect. Like Lloyd George with Frances Stevenson, he became besotted with Margherita Sarfatti, and shared both his bed and his political counsels with her. Her husband Cesare was remarkably complaisant, perhaps because he relied on Mussolini to promote his own political career.

Soon after Mussolini's return to the editorial chair at *Il Popolo* came the news (24 October 1917) of the Italian disaster at the Battle of Caporetto. The commanding general, Cadorna, severely criticized the Italian troops for indiscipline and cowardice, but the Italian nation rallied, and despite abuse from the neutralists a strong new government was formed, under Vittorio Emanuele Orlando, with a firm resolution to continue and to win the war.

Mussolini devoted *Il Popolo* to a campaign for national unity and 'discipline' to encourage fiercer resistance to the Austrians. He demanded action against 'slackers', a new 'volunteer army', suppression of Socialist newspapers, and better treatment and pay for the army and navy.

Sir Samuel Hoare, who was to become British Foreign Secretary in the 1930s, was a senior staff officer in Italy with the British divisions sent to reinforce the Italians. Appalled at the scenes of disorder as the broken Italian army fled from the Austrians in disarray over the Isonzo river after Caporetto, and at the growing defeatism of the Italian press and politicians, he was told by a member of his staff that the person most likely to stop the rot was Mussolini. Hoare accordingly obtained authority from Whitehall to approach Mussolini, and British government money was used to subsidise *Il Popolo*. Mussolini was unconcerned when Hoare reminded him of this incident twenty years later.

Meanwhile Benito and Margherita, 'passionately and completely in love', found great satisfaction in *Il Popolo*, where they worked side by side; Margherita was also Mussolini's ghost-writer for many of his most pungent editorials about the importance of winning the war.[4]

Cadorna had been succeeded by General Diaz as Commander-in-Chief of the Italian armies, and his offensive across the Piave in October 1918 led to the capture of Vittorio Veneto and cut a wedge between the two halves of the Austrian army. The Austrians' military situation was hopeless when unexpectedly, on 27 October, as the German armies were reeling back in confusion before the combined French and British offensive in the west, an Austrian captain accompanied by two privates with large white flags crawled up a railway embankment near the Isonzo river and walked gingerly towards the Italian lines, bearing an official surrender note from the Austrian Emperor. The Italians were delirious with joy. Eight days later, after the fighting had ceased, Mussolini spoke before a huge crowd from the base of Milan's monument to the 1848 uprising against the Austrians. His reception was ecstatic.

> *Arditi!* Comrades in arms! I defended you when the cowardly Philistines slandered you ... The gleam of your daggers and the flood of your grenades will render justice to all the swine who wanted to halt the march of greater Italy. She belongs to you (*a voi*)!

'*A noi!* (To us!)' repeated the *arditi* (a band of young men recruited through *Il Popolo*), having been well rehearsed by Mussolini beforehand. He went on:

> Today the Italian flag flies from the Brenner to Trieste, to Fiume, to Zara, Italy of the Italians ... At home with victory we must achieve our other main war aim, which is the redemption of the workers.

The next day in *Il Popolo* Mussolini wrote: 'Every man who has fought and bled is superior to the rest ... the good have triumphed ... Peace has come to us as we planned; it is just.'[5]

Although *Il Popolo* had been launched as a Socialist newspaper, by the time the war was over in November 1918 it was singing a different tune. It condemned Marxism and class war and scoffed at the rule of the proletariat. Mussolini and Sarfatti together instigated an insidious campaign glorifying Mussolini's part in bringing Italy into the war and emphasizing the enormous territorial gains to which Italy was now entitled under the Treaty of London. More than any other country, *Il Popolo* claimed, Italy should insist on her right to 'a great imperial destiny, and territorial expansion should be the prime aim regardless of whether the rest of the world approves or not'.

The paper's editorials were contradictory. At times they championed the League of Nations, which at others they saw as an obstacle to Italy's territorial ambitions. Sometimes these leaders were Socialist in tone, at others they were Nationalist, with tilts at the monarchy followed by repudiation of republicanism. Mussolini was trying to be all things to all men in his search for a political creed which could sweep him to power.

By early 1919 Mussolini had convinced himself that parliamentary government in Italy was crumbling; and he was much impressed by the success of the Lenin coup in Russia. However, he managed both to toady to the industrialists, and to hint in private to Socialists that he might be at their disposal if they would support his pretensions to power. With Margherita's help he was showing considerable skill in riding two horses at once.

In March 1919 Mussolini launched the Fascist Party. At a small meeting in the Piazza San Sepolcro in Milan the formal political programme of his new party was issued. It bore little relation to the programme on which Mussolini later came to power. The early proposals included 'land for peasants', and workers' representation in factory management, nationalization of the arms industry and, thanks to Sarfatti, votes for women. 'Workers' representation' remained a cardinal plank in Fascist policy, but most of the other points were in time quietly discarded.[6] As important as the political formula were the *arditi*, who resembled the *Freikorps* of the same period in Germany. Mussolini quickly learnt that squads of armed men could be useful to an emergent political party.

By 1919 the Italian economy was in a bad way. There was little employment for the masses of soldiers being demobilized, and prices were rising fast. By January 1919 prices were six times those of 1915. There were food shortages and hunger was rife, while speculators prospered. The middle classes were resentful. Only the skilled workers were able to push their wages up to keep pace with inflation, by means of strike threats. Riots occurred in Milan and Turin.

In Paris, the Italian delegation to the Peace Conference fared badly. Woodrow Wilson had aspirations for the new Yugoslavia and would not grant Fiume to Italy, and in satisfaction of the secret clauses of the Treaty of London of 1915 (to which the Americans were not a party) Italy received only a frontier on the Brenner and Trieste – neither Fiume nor Dalmatia, nor part of Turkey, nor the Aegean islands. These were left to be settled later, and this failure to acquire extra territory made the Orlando government unpopular.

The General Election held in November 1919 proved a disaster for Mussolini and the Fascists. No Fascist deputies were elected, and Mussolini himself received a derisory vote. He had made the mistake of fighting on a left-wing and anti-clerical policy: the Socialists trumped his cards, while Milan was strongly Catholic.

In 1920 Italy underwent such severe disruption that it became barely governable. The middle classes were frightened of the strikes and violence. Workers occupied the factories, there were mutinies among the armed forces, and a general strike. When, in June, Giolitti replaced Francesco Nitti as Prime Minister, he faced an almost impossible task in restoring law and order.

Mussolini's opportunity came as, all over Italy, trains, barracks, banks and public buildings were attacked by mobs; local Soviets were proclaimed in worker-occupied factories, and control in some areas passed into the hands of Communists. Mussolini's Fascists now put themselves forward as the saviours of the country, claiming to be the only force capable of checking the spread of Bolshevism. They declared that violence must be met with violence, and attacked the Communists and strikers ferociously. This attracted support from the middle classes and the industrialists, and produced near civil war. Mussolini's recruitment of large squads of Fascists was helped by sub-scriptions from the wealthy, who saw Fascism as the only chance of stopping a Bolshevik-type revolution in Italy. Wearing black shirts and carrying the flag of the *arditi*, Fascist squads were for the most part made up of unemployed ex-servicemen and out-of-work youths; many were inspired by fervent patriotism, but there was also a hideous element of criminal types who were more interested in the money.

In near despair at his inability to restore order, Giolitti decided to co-operate with Mussolini in an electoral pact. After a relatively calm election on 15 May 1921 the Fascists obtained 35 seats; in Milan Mussolini was elected a deputy, obtaining 124,918 votes against his 4,800 in 1919. The new parliament met on 11 June 1921. In his maiden speech Mussolini attacked the Socialists and the government, and (taking a lesson from his humiliation of 1919) declared he was not anti-clerical. Soon after, on a vote of confidence, Giolitti's majority fell to 34, with the Fascists cynically ignoring the electoral pact which had given them a presence in parliament for the first time and voting against the government. Giolitti then resigned, and was succeeded by the Socialist Ivanoe Bonomi on 27 June 1921.

Meanwhile violence mounted; clashes between and outrages by both Fascists and Socialists occurred frequently, disrupting life, to the great inconvenience of Italian citizens.

Bonomi fared badly as Prime Minister. He was attacked for his weak foreign policy *vis-à-vis* France and Britain over Italy's claims to the Aegean islands of the Dodecanese and for territory in Africa; unemployment soared after major bankruptcies, which included the steel giants Ansaldo and Ilva and the giant Banca Italiana di Sconto, while in the United States Congress passed the Immigration Act of 1921, which reduced Italian immigration to a trickle. Bonomi responded with an expensive and impractical programme of public works which achieved little; despairing of restoring Italy's economic situation, he resigned in mid February 1922. He was succeeded by Luigi Facta, who proved extremely weak. His passivity encouraged the Fascists, by now virtually in control of many northern towns (but not Turin or Parma, which were Socialist strongholds), although Fascism was weak in Rome and the south. Mussolini was now proclaiming unfettered capitalism and, reassured by this, subscriptions flowed in for the Fascists from bankers and industrialists.

Margherita and Benito saw that the situation was developing fast, to their advantage. They planned a Lenin-like coup: with the government losing control over much of northern Italy, Mussolini prepared to take over. They toyed with the idea of mobilizing the Fascist militia for a march on Rome, to occupy the seat of government. Margherita dissuaded Mussolini from this plan, but they decided to keep up the threat of a Fascist attack on Rome to frighten Facta and the King, and the other political leaders. Simultaneously, Mussolini opened negotiations with both the Liberals and the Left for a share in government. He made offers to Facta, Salandra, Bonomi, Orlando, Nitti and Giolitti, and sent assurances to the King and the army chiefs that they had nothing to fear from Fascism if he became Prime Minister.

Facta, frightened by the threatened Fascist march on Rome, wanted to bring Mussolini and other Fascists into his government. His ministers, more resolute, decided to proclaim a state of siege, and to use the army to disarm the Fascists.

As part of his bluff, Mussolini published orders to the Fascist Central Council to mobilize the Fascist militia for the March on Rome. He knew well his Fascists would be no match for the army, and that if there was a clash they must be ignominiously defeated. But the militia made its preparations in earnest, which further intimidated Facta and the King. Salandra offered Mussolini five places in his Cabinet, should he become Prime Minister. Mussolini refused out-of-hand, and declared in Naples: 'The hour has struck. Either they give us the Government or we shall take it by falling on Rome.'

His bluff was never called. In the early hours of 28 October the Facta Cabinet approved a decree declaring a state of siege. It was drafted and printed immediately. All the prefects were warned, and at 8.30 a.m. posters began to be put up in Rome; but half an hour later, Victor Emmanuel refused to sign the decree, and the Facta Cabinet resigned. Mussolini was in an almost impregnable position once the King had refused to allow troops to be used against the Fascist militia. Victor Emmanuel still hoped that Mussolini would be content to be a junior partner in a Salandra, Orlando or Giolitti government, but Mussolini would accept nothing less than the premiership. On 29 October he wrote in *Il Popolo*: 'A complete victory is at hand through the almost unanimous will of the nation. The victory must not be mutilated at the last moment by coalitions . . . The new Government must be clearly Fascist.'

The King accepted the inevitable and asked Mussolini to fly to Rome to take over the government. Mussolini insisted that his appointment should be confirmed in writing, and went to Rome by train, arriving at the Quirinal Palace dressed in a black shirt on the morning of 30 October.

The King told one of his court, Vittorio Salaro Del Borgo, that he had been right to refuse to sign Facta's decree 'to save a Cabinet of poltroons', and that in his new Prime Minister he had 'really a man of purpose who will last some time and has the will to act and act well'. Squads of Fascists paraded in the centre of Rome, but the March on Rome was a myth; Mussolini, like Hitler, assumed power constitutionally.[7]

After Mussolini had given their Rome correspondent an interview on 30 October, *The Times* reported:

> The nationalist revolution is a lawful one since it succeeded without changing the regime and without derangement of the public services or private property . . . The impression created by the new Prime Minister is essentially one of strength . . . he smiles but rarely, speaks slowly and says little but without hesitation. His eyes are black and very expressive . . . he looks far younger than his 48 years and answers to the description 'A Napoleon turned pugilist'.

De Martino, the Italian Ambassador in London, was able to cable to Mussolini on 2 November that only the *Daily Herald* had commented unfavourably on the change in Italian politics, that most circles were taking their lead from the favourable article in *The Times* of 1 November, and that the City of London and the bankers were pleased by the accession to power of the Fascists.[8]

CHAPTER 2

Lausanne, London and the Ruhr: 1922

To UNDERSTAND THE international problems which confronted Mussolini as soon as be became Prime Minister, one must turn to the Anglo-Italian conversations held in London between 26 June and 7 July 1922, sixteen weeks before he came to power. The Italian government hoped for an advantageous agreement, which would help them electorally. There were eight meetings with the Prime Minister, Lloyd George (present on five occasions), and Arthur Balfour, deputizing for Lord Curzon, who was ill throughout.

The chief Italian representative was Carlo Schanzer, the Foreign Minister. He had asked Lloyd George for this meeting during the economic conference of European powers held at Genoa in April and May; he was hoping for a reconsideration of the economic situation in the Eastern Mediterranean, and a revision of the Graeco-Italian Treaty under which Italy, immediately after they had been granted to her by the 1920 Treaty of Sèvres, had agreed to give up the Dodecanese Islands: these were now coveted by the Italian government mainly to curry popularity with the voters. Sir Eyre Crowe, the Permanent Under-Secretary at the Foreign Office, commented:

> I confess to a deep-seated distrust of 'Italian formulas' . . . Italy is out to weaken and kill Greek influence and Greek trade all over the Mediterranean and at the same time to establish her own influence in the Balkans where she has the ambition to wield the power formerly exercised by Austria. In the pursuit of such a policy her hands will be much strengthened if she appears everywhere with British support at her back. At the same time this will not prevent her from playing us false and intriguing against British interests everywhere in the East as she has done consistently hitherto.[1]

After her 1912 war with Turkey, Italy had seized all twelve Dodecanese islands, including Rhodes, the most important; the majority of the population of these islands was Greek, not Turkish; at first the Greek population welcomed the Italians as liberators, but eventually came to find their rule more oppressive than that of the Turks. Following Turkey's defeat in the First World War, the Allies had forced her to accept the Treaty of Sèvres, which left to the Turks in Europe only Constantinople and the strip of territory up to Chatalja; internationalized the Straits; demilitarized the adjoining districts; established Greek administration in Smyrna for five years pending a plebiscite; ceded the Dodecanese islands to Italy; established an independent Armenia; and cut off all Turkey's Arab provinces. The treaty was signed by the Sultan, but Turkish nationalists rejected it and in the resulting war between Turks and Greeks the Turks were victorious.

Under Article 122 of the Treaty of Sèvres all the Dodecanese islands were ceded by Turkey to Italy, but under the Graeco-Italian Treaty of the same day, signed largely at British insistence,[2] the eventual return of the islands to Greece was guaranteed, except that Rhodes was to be retained by Italy for fifteen years. In London Italy, wanting to establish a strong naval base in the eastern Aegean to further her ambitions as a world power, hoped to secure British support in abandoning the Graeco-Italian Treaty and permanently securing as many as possible of the Dodecanese islands, disregarding their Greek population and proximity to Turkey. Italy also claimed economic advantages in Anatolia, and a mandate in other parts of the former Turkish Empire; and she wanted Jubaland (adjoining Italian Somaliland), to increase her African empire.

The British Admiralty strongly opposed Italian sovereignty over the Dodecanese; they considered that an Italian naval presence, particularly a submarine base, would prove 'a menace to our eastern communications'.[3]

A Memorandum sent by the British Foreign Secretary, Lord Curzon, to the Italian Ambassador in London (de Martino) on 10 February 1922 pointed out that although in 1912 the Italians had promised to surrender the Dodecanese to Turkey, by the terms of the Treaty of London (signed 26 April 1915) France, Britain and Russia had agreed that when the war ended Italy should receive 'entire sovereignty over the Dodecanese islands', and administration had remained in Italian hands during the war. However, the United States, who had not been a party to the Treaty of London, were strongly opposed to this on ethical grounds, and (according to Curzon) the Italians now had 'a moral obligation to implement the Graeco-Italian agreement' of 1912.

At all eight meetings in London Schanzer tried to secure some promise over the Dodecanese, but no concessions were offered by the British and the discussions were a failure from the Italian point of view; they gained nothing which would help them in the elections. During the discussions the Italians emphasized their opposition to Austria making economic agreements with Czechoslovakia or Yugoslavia, and that they favoured a customs union between Italy and Austria. They also stressed that Jubaland should be given to Italy as a colony.

Mussolini thus inherited the aftermath of a failed Anglo-Italian Conference, and a confused international situation in which Italy's post-war ambition to be a Great Power was being thwarted.[4] Within four weeks of becoming Prime Minister he was involved in the Lausanne Conference between Turkey, Greece, France, Britain and Russia, which began on 20 November 1922. The Conference took place under the shadow of the 'Chanak incident', which had nearly precipitated a war between Britain and Turkey, and led to the downfall of Lloyd George's coalition government.

It will be recalled that Turkish nationalists had rejected the Treaty of Sèvres, which resulted in war between the Turks and the Greeks. In the summer of 1922 the Turkish army routed the Greeks and drove them out of Asia Minor, and by mid September had reached the zone of Allied military occupation of the Straits. The Facta government, following the example of the French, immediately withdrew all Italian troops to the western shore of the Straits, which left the British alone, facing the Turks at Chanak. For a few days an Anglo-Turkish war seemed inevitable. On behalf of Italy Schanzer tried to mediate, while leaving no room for doubt that Italy would stay neutral. Fortunately the crisis ended when an armistice was signed at Mudanya on 11 October; a peace conference to revise the moribund Treaty of Sèvres was scheduled for 20 November in Lausanne.[5]

Meeting Mussolini on 1 November, Sir Ronald Graham, the British Ambassador in Rome, found him surprisingly well-informed and reasonable about foreign affairs. Mussolini asked if the Lausanne Conference could be transferred to an Italian town (preferably Capri), but did not press the point when Graham explained that it must be held in a neutral country, as promised to the Turks. After Graham had pointed out that otherwise Turkey would obtain excessive conces-sions, Mussolini agreed that the victorious Allies must present the same united front which had saved the situation at Mundanya – ignor-ing the fact that Italy had left Britain in the lurch at Chanak.

Mussolini told Graham he felt that relations between Britain and Italy were not as good as they might have been because of the failure of Schanzer's mission to London, regarded by Italians as a humiliation. In a good-tempered discussion Mussolini remarked that Schanzer had gone to London 'with a large basket under his arm which he had hoped to fill with plums without the trouble of picking them', and that this was not his (Mussolini's) method of doing business; he wanted the Schanzer negotiations resumed. Graham told him it should not be too difficult to reach a settlement over the Dodecanese, noting that 'if Italy considered the possession of any one of the islands as vital to her, this could probably be arranged', but pointing out that the majority of them had no economic value and would simply prove a drain, while a *beau geste* by Italy would be appreciated throughout the world.

Following his conversation with Graham on 1 November Mussolini, in a long personal note to Lord Curzon, which according to Harold Nicolson was 'very conciliatory', admitted that Italy was not free to settle the ownership of the Dodecanese unilaterally, and expressed Italy's willingness 'once more to examine the problem as a whole to arrive at a fresh settlement'.[6]

Graham told Curzon, who had stayed on as Foreign Secretary in the new Bonar Law government, that he was 'very favourably impressed' by Mussolini's reasonable tone and his sincerity. Mussolini had concluded the talk by saying that if the other Allies occasionally found Italy 'unreasonable and difficult', it was because of the deep sense of injustice felt by the Italian people at their post-war treatment; Italy considered she had been sacrificed, and that she had not obtained the fruits of victory to the same degree as the other Allies.[7]

Curzon had stipulated that the Lausanne Conference could not be held unless an explicit understanding was reached in advance that Britain, France and Italy should present a united front, and insisted that it should be subsequently maintained. Poincaré, the French Premier, agreed, and a joint telegram was sent to the Italian Prime Minister asking him to meet Curzon and Poincaré on the evening of 19 November before the Conference opened.

Mussolini's first appearance among world statesmen was bizarre. He was sure the French and British had come to an agreement without informing Italy. Poincaré and Curzon had had their trains linked for the long journey to Lausanne; arrived there, they learned that Mussolini was staying at Territet, on the Italian–Swiss frontier, and was insistent that they should dine with him there that evening. Reluctantly consenting, they found Mussolini surrounded by black-shirts, with a band playing the Fascist anthem 'Giovinezza'. Mussolini announced that he refused to attend the Conference at Lausanne unless a statement was issued that Britain and France regarded Italian interests in the Middle East as equal to theirs. Pioncaré and Curzon peremptorily refused to go as far as this. Mussolini was persuaded to agree to a press statement to be issued that evening to the effect that he, Poincaré, and Curzon

... had had a preliminary discussion in which they confirmed clearly their common purpose which was to come to decisions in a spirit of cordial friendship on the basis of *perfect equality* [My italics. R.L.] between the Allies on all the questions coming before the Lausanne Conference.[8]

Mollified by this, Mussolini accompanied Poincaré and Curzon to Lausanne the next day. He was badly briefed on the Turkish problems and took little part in the Conference. Indeed, he left before serious negotiations were under way, but ordered the Italian press to declare that his performance (really a non-performance) had been Italy's first diplomatic victory since 1860 because he had 'achieved a brilliant success in persuading the British to accept an increase in Italian colonial territory'. In fact, this had not been on the agenda, and was not discussed.

Although Mussolini did raise the vexed question of the perpetuation of Italian occupation of the Dodecanese with Poincaré and Curzon, all three sensibly decided that, as the immediate task of the Lausanne Conference was to bring about a settlement with the Turks, it would be better to leave the matter of the Dodecanese for friendly discussions between the Allies at a later date.[9]

Curzon was grateful to Mussolini for preserving the unity of the Allies, since this was helpful in dealing with Turkish claims to territory in Thrace ceded to the Greeks but reconquered by the Turkish army in the war. However, Curzon reported to the Cabinet that Mussolini 'knew next to nothing of the subjects and his agreement was procured with little difficulty to all the points in the Anglo-French programme'.

Harold Nicolson, who was part of the British Delegation, recorded how he was struck by the Duce's lack of ease in clothes which seemed too tight:

> Mussolini – a shade embarrassed by being thus confronted at his first diplomatic conference by such giants of the profession – chafes uneasily against his white stiff cuffs, rolling important eyes. He said little – '*Je suis d'accord*' was the most important thing he said. [His '*d'accord*' was very important, however, because it confirmed the unity of the Allied Front.]

Ivone Kirkpatrick, later to be Permanent Under-Secretary at the Foreign Office, relates that two members of the British delegation told him Curzon recognized in the 'somewhat awkward figure a politician who was likely to play a prominent role in Europe', and that 'he [Curzon] deployed, not without success, all his charm to captivate the dictator'. After his three days in Lausanne, Mussolini promised Lord and Lady Curzon he would write to them in English – after he had learnt sufficient.[10]

However, once back in Rome Mussolini exercised a baneful influence, threatening to rupture the Alliance unless Italy was promised a clearly defined slice of the mandated territories in the Middle East (Iraq, Palestine, Syria). He was on weak ground with his demands over the Middle East because in London in July Schanzer had approved the granting of a League of Nations mandate for Iraq and Palestine to Britain, and for Syria to France; all Schanzer had requested for Italy were commercial and economic advantages in the mandated territories. Curzon was justifiably annoyed with Mussolini for belatedly seeking to reopen negotiations on important matters now irrevocably settled. On one occasion on Mussolini's orders Garroni, the head of the Italian delegation, threatened to withdraw from Lausanne: according to Nicolson, Curzon told the Italian diplomat that he would not submit to blackmail, and that the Italians could withdraw, as Orlando had from Paris (in 1919), without disturbing the Conference at all.

Curzon then, again according to Harold Nicolson, described Mussolini as 'a dangerous demagogue, plausible in manner but without scruple in truth or conduct', and his attitude as 'a combination of the sturdy beggar and the ferocious bandit'. Nevertheless, in public three months later Curzon referred to Mussolini as 'a man of marvellous energy and a mailed fist' who had crushed internal disorder and restored Italy's prestige. This was just what Mussolini wanted to hear.[11]

An Allied Conference on German reparations was held in London in December 1922. Here there was bitter conflict between the British and the French. Germany was unable to raise a foreign loan to pay sums due to France, and in August Poincaré, to the horror of the British, proposed that if Germany did not pay, the French should take over the German customs, coal mines and state forests, and occupy the Ruhr militarily. Lloyd George, still Prime Minister, had refused to have anything to do with this plan. The value of the mark was falling, out of control, and he told Poincaré that nothing would be forthcoming except 'paper marks', and that the Allies would only be able to manage the forests and mines with the goodwill of German workmen, since the employment of forced labour was unthinkable; profitable undertakings might quickly become bankrupt, which would do nothing to solve the reparations problem. Lloyd George's views were shared by the more responsible French statesmen, and before Mussolini came to power Italy had supported Britain. Both Curzon and the new Prime Minister, Bonar Law, shared Lloyd George's opposition to French occupation of the Ruhr.

A big crowd greeted Mussolini at Victoria Station on 8 December 1922; London-based Fascists wearing black shirts sang Fascist songs.

The Times reported that 'Signor Mussolini has an air of authority and a dominating personality.' He immediately held a press conference at which he declared that he was not in favour of the French occupation of the Ruhr and 'we Italians are disposed to reduce reparations if our debts are reduced'.

However, in private Mussolini gave enthusiastic backing to Poincaré's extreme plan, and behind the scenes was violently anti-British, expressing the hope that the British Empire might break up and so open up the possibility of extending Italian influence world-wide. In public he quickly back-pedalled, pretending that he had always opposed French occupation of the Ruhr. Both the French and British delegations were disgusted with his oscillation.

At Claridges he behaved like a mountebank, complaining that the French delegation had been given more luxurious rooms than himself and organizing groups of blackshirts to greet him and sing 'Giovinezza' wherever he went. During his three days in London he had private meetings with the King and the Prime Minister, laid a wreath at the Cenotaph, and managed to issue six press statements. One press conference had to be cancelled because he was in bed with a prostitute. At this stage of his career he was erratic, refusing to be guided by the well-written briefs of the Italian Foreign Office; later he overcame this defect, and became an expert on European affairs. In December 1922 he was a demagogue, not a statesman, but he was quick to learn. Salvatore Contarini, in charge of the Italian Foreign Office, was pro-British, moderate and sensible; as the years went by Mussolini heeded him more and more.

The Times reported that his 'plan' was eagerly awaited, and Mussolini tabled a resolution for the London Conference proposing a reasonable solution of the reparations problem, suggesting that if the USA would give a quid pro quo (some remission of the debts of the Allies),

1.   the reparation debt from Germany should be reduced to 50 milliard gold marks;
2.   a moratorium of two years should be granted to Germany over the payment of the 50 milliard;
3.   to support the mark the German government should guarantee to obtain from their banks and industrial companies before 16 January a loan of 3 milliard gold marks.

Poincaré rejected Mussolini's solution out-of-hand.

Mussolini proudly told the King of Italy that his memorandum was the sole constructive plan put before the London conference, and that if the conference failed, it would not be Italy's fault; there is some truth in this.[12]

The conference adjourned to Paris, where Bonar Law published an alternative plan: it proposed a four years' moratorium (not two, as in Mussolini's proposal) and, after the four years during which Germany would pay nothing, reparations on a reduced scale. Poincaré rejected the British plan; *The Times* leader commented that '. . . the policy outlined by the Prime Minister was to treat our continental debtors with a generosity unparalleled in history.' When Poincaré refused to accept the plan even as a basis for discussion, Bonar Law said: 'It was a ditch no bridge could span.'

The Italian Foreign Office advised Mussolini that the four-year moratorium proposed by Bonar Law – as opposed to the two years suggested in Mussolini's plan – would place too much strain on Italy's ability to repay her war debts to Britain and the USA; they also emphasized that it would mean fewer shipments of coal and steel to Italy. They therefore advised Mussolini to oppose Bonar Law.[13]

On 9 January 1923 French troop trains poured over the frontier to occupy the Rhine; Belgian troops followed. It is clear from the Italian diplomatic documents that for a few days Mussolini, piqued by Bonar Law's lack of enthusiasm for his own plan, backed the French a hundred per cent, and took a strong anti-British line. He spoke of wanting to form a 'continental anti-British bloc' based on all-out support for Poincaré and opposition to Bonar Law, noting that 'a Continental bloc would be injurious to the British Empire'. He encouraged the Italian press to adopt a bitterly anti-British line.

Then, advised by Margherita Sarfatti to be moderate and shocked by the hostility to him displayed in the 13 January editions by the leader-writer of *The Times* and in other London national papers, Mussolini suddenly changed course. The extent of his volte-face is indicated by his declaration to the Council of Ministers on 16 January, reported as follows:

> He had sent engineers to the Ruhr because Italy could not remain aloof from control over a coal district fundamentally important for the economic life of Europe and Italy . . . no scheme for a continental anti-British bloc existed, and the Italians had never made such a proposal, and would not have done so because of existing relations between Italy and England.[14]

While working arrangements were being made for running the railways, for troop movements, coal deliveries, police matters and so forth, the British government did nothing to obstruct the occupation of the Ruhr; they also refrained from showing sympathy to Germany, from encouraging German resistance, and even from acting as advisors to the German government. There were numerous German protests to Britain at the illegality of the Franco-Belgian action, but these notes were only acknowledged by the British Foreign Office, never answered. During this period the British government were assiduous in maintaining good relations with Italy, and made no important moves without consulting Mussolini fully.[15]

On 12 January 1923 Mussolini told Sir Ronald Graham that he had serious misgivings about the French action. He compared it to Napoleon's march on Moscow – 'advance was easy, results nil, and retirement difficult'. He told Graham he had sent a protest to Paris, and that his advice to the French government was that they should arrive at an immediate economic agreement with Germany, and withdraw their troops.

Sir Ronald Graham wrote to Curzon from Rome on 15 January 1923:

> First news of British proposals at Paris produced as in France surprise amounting to indignation. In official circles they were described as showing cynical disregard of Italian interests . . . He [Mussolini] would welcome British participation in a deal but is anyhow determined that Italy shall not be left out of it. Hence [forth?] measure of Italian support however half-hearted is given to France.

The Foreign Office minute on this part of Graham's letter notes that it had been learned 'from an absolutely reliable source that Signor Mussolini had proposed to the French the formation of an anti-British bloc.' Graham continued:

> To understand the situation here one must remember that omnipotent as [he] is, his position is full of difficulty and some striking success in foreign policy is of vital importance to him. His courageous internal policy with its complete disregard of various interests and susceptibilities is rousing strong hostility, and he is having serious trouble with sections of his own followers. His moderate line on Adriatic question [Fiume] is equally unpopular. He must therefore recoup himself somehow and may at any moment spring surprise on us. In any case his foreign policy will be pure opportunism, and Italian friendship is on offer to highest bidder. My impression is that he would prefer to work with Great Britain, at a price. If we can give nothing he will turn to France. Failing France he may deal with Russia or Turks. It is a policy of sacred egoism carried to extremes. Possibly economic necessities of Italy and those of his own political position afford some extenuating circumstances.

Graham was right. In order to bolster his popularity at home, Mussolini was capable of wild U-turns. As has been seen, his wish for an 'anti-British bloc' was fortunately short-lived, and on the same day as Graham wrote his despatch the Italian Chargé d'Affaires in London was 'protesting' to a Foreign Office official (Sir Patrick Lindsay)

... against any suggestion that Italy was making a serious attempt to isolate Great Britain in Europe. Her action in regard to the Ruhr was due solely to the fact that the French might come to some industrial agreement with the Germans which might prove prejudicial alike to England and Italy. Signor Mussolini had always been in favour of the closest co-operation between Italy and Great Britain and no attempt at isolating us would be made.[16]

Lindsay had no doubt the message was based on specific instructions from Mussolini. From mid January 1923 onwards, Mussolini co-operated with Britain over France's occupation of the Ruhr.

The mark fell to 160,000 to the dollar on 1 July 1923; in August it was 1 million, and on 1 November 133 million. In Germany this produced not only widespread bankruptcies but also food shortages and unprecedented unemployment. The morale of the middle class and the working class was shattered as their savings were wiped out at a stroke; only a few industrialists and property owners prospered.

The Ruhr crisis reached its peak in August 1923 when the Cuno government elected in November 1922 was replaced by the Stresemann government. The new Chancellor called off the official campaign of passive resistance to the French, and lifted the ban on reparations deliveries to France and Belgium. Negotiations began for an agreed settlement. Ill-health had forced Bonar Law to resign as Prime Minister on 20 May 1923, and he had been succeeded by Stanley Baldwin, who had less sympathy than Bonar Law or Curzon with Germany's plight. With Curzon himself ill again, Poincaré and Baldwin met in Paris on 20 September and afterwards issued a communiqué stating that there was no 'divergence of views' between them; this was interpreted (perhaps falsely) to mean that Britain condoned all aspects of French policy in the Ruhr. It angered Curzon, reading it on his sick-bed, and he pronounced it to be a repudiation of his policy as Foreign Secretary, since he had continually expressed strong disapproval of the French occupation of the Ruhr.[17]

In January 1924 Ramsay MacDonald became Britain's first Labour Prime Minister, and acted as his own Foreign Secretary. A conscientious objector during the war, he believed earnestly that a reasonable solution of the reparations problem was the key to a prosperous Europe. Unlike Baldwin and even Curzon, he held to the Keynes theory, as endorsed by both Lloyd George and Bonar Law, that the victors of the war could not prosper while the vanquished suffered and starved. His settlement of the reparations question – with the help of the American Dawes Plan – was the high-point of MacDonald's career. Fortunately Poincaré, so bitterly opposed to any lenient treatment of Germany, had been succeeded by the scholarly and far less unyielding Édouard Herriot as Premier of France. In July the Dawes Plan, a new schedule of reparations payments conditional on the abandonment of the Belgian–French occupation of the Ruhr, was agreed by Britain, France, Germany and Italy, with Mussolini giving it full support.

CHAPTER 3

The Dodecanese, Corfu, and Abyssinia: 1923

In April 1923 a Foreign Office resumé of Anglo-Italian relations stated that only a week or so before coming to power Mussolini had been 'prophesying on public platforms the day when the Italian navy would be capturing Malta and otherwise inconveniencing the ramshackle British Empire'; however, his tone had changed when he assumed power, and 'relations with the Fascisti Government have been very much what they were with previous Italian Governments.'[1]

A highlight in Anglo-Italian relations was the visit of King George V and Queen Mary to Rome from 7 to 12 May 1923. Mussolini enthusiastically welcomed the visit, and had hoped (in vain) that Curzon would accompany the King and Queen. The attention paid him by King George greatly increased the Duce's prestige, but anti-Fascists were furious with the British government for sponsoring the visit, and also with the King for saying in public, when he bestowed the Order of the Bath on Mussolini, that the (Italian political) crisis had been overcome 'under the wise guidance of a strong statesman'. As Seton-Watson writes, 'The King's visit seemed to set the seal on Fascist Italy's respectability.'[2]

According to a despatch to Curzon from Sir Ronald Graham on 7 June 1923:

[The visit of the King and Queen] provoked an outburst of spontaneous enthusiasm which surprised as much as it gratified not only myself but other more experienced judges of Italian feeling. The personal impression created by their Majesties has been very great, and the whole visit has done much to strengthen the ties of that traditional Anglo-Italian friendship which may at times be strained or dormant, but is I sincerely believe deep rooted in this country . . . While the populace showed its enthusiasm, the Italian Government were anxious to give as much political importance to the visit as possible and there was genuine regret that your lordship was unable to accompany their Majesties . . . At the present moment we can count on a satisfactory measure of Italian co-operation and support.

But it must be remembered that Italian foreign policy is not based upon principles similar to those which actuate those of His Majesty's Government. It is frankly opportunist and egotistic. The Marquis della Torretta, as Foreign Minister, was constantly criticized for his unprofitable Anglophilism. The political reputation of Signor Schanzer was destroyed by the failure of his visit to London, and although it would be too much to say that he brought down the Facta Government with him, one may fairly assert that had he succeeded, it would have obtained a respite. Signor Mussolini will certainly not be willing to follow suit. He has proclaimed from the first, and has since emphasised, that his foreign policy will be in the sole interests of Italy and one of 'nothing for nothing'. At the present moment he is well disposed and is inclined, both from motives of sympathy and of interest, to work with us. The reason why he desires an early settlement of outstanding questions, more particularly that of Jubaland, is not so much owing to the intrinsic value of such a concession, in regard to which he has few illusions, as to the consideration that he can make play with it in internal politics, now bristling with difficulties for him, and justify a policy of friendship with Great Britain by pointing to concrete advantages as its immediate results.

Graham continued with a plea that the outstanding issues concerning Italy (Jubaland and the Dodecanese islands) should be resolved in Italy's favour as soon as possible; he asked for 'a more sympathetic attitude' from the Foreign Office so as to achieve a more stable Italian foreign policy and secure 'a measure of consistent Italian support'. He added that the Italian government regretted their precipitate rejection of the Bonar Law plan for German reparations in January, and were in an accommodating frame of mind.

Graham's advocacy of the cession of Jubaland to Italy did not find favour in the Foreign Office. In a Foreign Office memorandum of 4 April 1923 Harold Nicolson had noted that the ultimate disposal of the Dodecanese would be an integral part of a general settlement which would also include Jubaland, a view emphatically endorsed by Curzon.[3] Curzon considered that there was 'not the smallest reason for a *beau geste* to Italy' to coincide with the King's visit. Harold Nicolson minuted on 13 June that the 'right line lies somewhere between the extreme of emotional generosity and the extreme of irritable insistence, and to embark upon controversy regarding the existence of moribund Treaties would be both unprofitable and undignified.' When Miles Lampson (then a First Secretary) suggested 'meeting' the Italians over Jubaland and thereby securing the co-operation of Italy in the councils of Europe 'at the price of a few thousand miles of barren African scrub', Curzon again minuted his strong disagreement, stating that he did not believe that 'whatever price we pay to Italy we shall in return get her loyal support on any single question.

I wholly mistrust their Government from whatever party chosen . . . the Dodecanese question must be settled before we make the Jubaland concession.'

In the same minute, Curzon referred to Mussolini's activities in India; from secret sources the Foreign Office had learned that certain well-known Indian revolutionaries had been in contact with Mussolini in Rome, and that at an interview in Rome on 27 February Mussolini had informed the Indians of his aim to get rid of the economic domination of England and his intention 'ultimately to drive the English out of the Mediterranean'; he had assured the Indians, on behalf of the Fascist Party, that he would give them every assistance, but had explained that he must take precautions to avoid the Italian government being in any way compromised.

More publicly, Mussolini had decided to found an Indo-Italian commercial Institute with the help of the notable writer and patriot, Gabriele d'Annunzio, 'whose anti-British sentiments were well known'. In the Foreign Office letter to Graham giving details of Mussolini's intrigues, the Ambassador was warned that the life of the 'informant' would be endangered if his name was disclosed to the Italian government.

As was often the case, Mussolini was trying to run with the hare and hunt with the hounds, and the disclosure of his meddlings in India considerably influenced Curzon and his advisors in their distrust of him; Graham, as will be seen, was not similarly affected.[4]

Mussolini became impatient with Curzon's unforthcoming stance over Jubaland and the Dodecanese. Howard Kennard, deputizing for Graham during the Ambassador's absence on leave (he was later British Ambassador in Warsaw, in 1939), was told on 17 July 1923 by Salvatore Contarini, head of the Italian Foreign Office, that Mussolini wanted to 'proclaim the annexation of all the Dodecanese islands by Italy without any communication to Britain'. With difficulty, Contarini informed Kennard, he had persuaded the Duce not to take any 'hasty decisions'.

Nevertheless, two days later, on 19 July, the Italian Ambassador in London, Pietro Della Torretta, was able to record that Curzon could count on the support of Italy if there should be a complete break between Britain and France as a result of Poincaré's intransigence over reparations and the occupation of the Ruhr.[5]

Kennard's report of his conversation with Contarini led the Foreign Office to summon Della Torretta and remind him of Italy's undertakings, and of the direct British interest in the fate of the Dodecanese. In a lengthy minute dated 4 August 1923 Harold Nicolson commented:

. . . We should thus discard the feelings of irritation aroused by the turpitude, the persistently perfidious opportunism with which successive Italian Governments have tried to falsify this question . . . we are obliged to conduct business with them, and we can scarcely conduct business in a spirit of moral indignation. We must be wary and precise. I fear that in spite of the insistent temptation it will profit us little to be really disagreeable.

The naval balance of power in the Eastern Mediterranean is obviously not one which we can openly avow. Personally I doubt whether even from our own point of view it is of any overwhelming importance. An Italian naval base at Stampalia [in the Dodecanese] would doubtless be inconvenient . . . [but] it would not even in the view of the Admiralty be fatal.

We object to the Italians retaining all the [Dodecanese] islands partly because we regard it as a dirty trick, partly because we see no reason why these wholly Greek islands should be placed under Italy . . . If we give way to them they will trumpet the event as a diplomatic triumph. He [Mussolini] . . . may hope to obtain his diplomatic triumph . . . He may proceed to annex the islands on, or even before, the ratification of the Treaty of Lausanne.

Having thus got the cards in his hands he may as a mark of friendship to us surrender certain of the most valueless islands to Greece. He will then announce that he has behaved very generously and expect his *quid pro quo*.

The essential difficulty is that the Italians are established in the islands, and short of war we cannot turn them out. We can of course refuse Jubaland — but the result would merely be that the Dodecanese would become Italian and that Jubaland would remain rather aridly British. The solution would not be very satisfactory.

Curzon minuted on the Nicolson memorandum:

I do not agree . . . I cannot see the slightest reason why we should unnecessarily fight the battles of Greece . . . Of course we can hold back Jubaland in the event of a breach of faith and I think this would distress the Italians.[6]

This indicates that Curzon had changed his mind and was in the mood to give in to Italy over both the Dodecanese and Jubaland: it seemed as if the high hopes raised by the King's visit and Graham's despatch of 7 June were about to be realized. Alas, suddenly British–Italian accord tumbled from its new high into the abyss.

At the end of August 1923 an Italian officer, General Enrico Tellini, working with an International Boundary Commisssion party determining the frontier between Greece and Albania, was murdered on Greek territory. In retaliation Mussolini immediately ordered the bombardment of Corfu from the sea, causing civilian casualties, and occupied the island with Italian troops. Politis, the Greek delegate at

Geneva, was ordered by his government to bring the matter before the League of Nations as a breach of the Covenant, and also to refer it to the Council of Ambassadors, currently meeting in Paris to deal with subsidiary questions arising under the peace treaties, including the boundary between Greece and Albania.

The reaction of Lord Robert Cecil, the British Minister with responsibility for League of Nation affairs, was that the Italian aggression must be handled by the League: under the terms of the Covenant they should insist on Mussolini's withdrawal from Corfu, under threat of sanctions. However, after forty-eight hours the more realistic views of Lord Curzon prevailed (thus preventing a dress-rehearsal of the Abyssinian crisis of twelve years later).

Cecil's telegram to Curzon from Geneva on 1 September showed that he felt the League must bring Mussolini to heel:

> Action by Italy in occupying Greek islands appears to be clear breach of Article 15 of Covenant and exposes them to action provided for in Article 15 of Covenant [i.e., sanctions]; presumably HMG will desire me to do everything possible to uphold Covenant. Greek Government have finally asked for intervention of League of Nations.

The Foreign Office replied to Cecil that Curzon would need to know 'exactly where pressing for discussion of this dispute by the League would lead him'; this produced from Cecil:

> The Italian delegate hoped that you and France will declare the matter not within the competence of the League but must be dealt with by Conference of Ambassadors. There is, I am sure, no danger of such a deplorable decision as far as HMG is concerned, as any failure of League in this grave matter would do irreparable harm and perhaps lead to disintegration of League itself.

On 11 August Della Torretta had warned Mussolini that Lord Robert Cecil was an enthusiastic protagonist of the League ('*sostentore fanatico*'), always earnest to strengthen its prestige, so that he was bound to support a Greek appeal at the Council, for which there would be much press and public support in Britain. Unfortunately for Cecil's hopes, Curzon stood firm behind the Covenant only briefly, and then sought a solution outside the League.[7]

The British Ambassador in Rome, Sir Ronald Graham, was still on leave. On 2 September his deputy, Kennard, telegraphed to London, regarding the Corfu incident, that Italian foreign policy was 'in the hands of a man [Mussolini] who has no experience of statesmanship and who since he came to power has sought every opportunity of displaying to the world that Italy intends to play the role of a great power', and warned that any direct intervention might induce

Mussolini to take some rash and impulsive step which might greatly react on the people of Europe; he argued for the matter to be dealt with by the Council of Ambassadors in Paris and not by the League.

On the same day, Kennard wrote privately to Miles Lampson that '... this crisis is likely to be a very serious one and may even end in war ... Italy is in a dangerous mood and appears rather disposed to rush into wild adventures. Let us hope that no harm will come of the present one.' The next day, Kennard had an interview with Mussolini, who told him that the British press was unanimous in condemning the Italian action. The Duce stated that if British press extracts were allowed to appear in full in the Italian papers, there would be outbursts of indignation which might have serious results.[8]

Cecil informed Curzon that the view of the great majority of Council members in Geneva was that an act of war had been committed, and that the Greek representative had said Greece did not propose to resist militarily but preferred to appeal to the League; he suggested that 'the important point to bear in mind is that the effect of the failure of the League to settle this crisis would almost certainly be followed by a general exodus from the League of Nations by the smaller states.' Later on the same day another message from Kennard stated that he had seen Mussolini, who told him he was strongly opposed to the League dealing with the dispute; he (Mussolini) had added that he had always been strongly prejudiced against the League, but that he would accept 'action' by the Conference of Ambassadors.

Curzon was on the horns of a dilemma, and at first he inclined to Cecil's view, telling Della Torretta that Cecil had 'already received instructions to uphold the Covenant'. In this Curzon had been influenced by a further telegram from Cecil, reporting that opinion at Geneva was hardening 'in favour of a League solution' and informing him that he (Cecil) had 'had a private message from French that if Italian Prime Minister goes on he will have to face the rest of the world under the leadership of England without any support from France.'

Baldwin, holidaying as usual at Aix-les-Bains, at first agreed with Cecil, telling Curzon by cable:

> I approve entirely the language held by you to the Italian Ambassador. I regard attitude of Italian Government towards League of Nations as test case of their sincerity to respect rights of small countries. Agree that Ambassadors' Conference is not suitable body to conduct enquiry into circumstances so clearly envisaged by Covenant.[9]

Thus, briefly, it looked as though Cecil's desire for the Covenant to be upheld would be realized, and that Mussolini would go down in history as a ruler whose aggression had been prevented by the League of Nations – a circumstance which would have raised its prestige to a great height, and also rendered the Duce's hold on power in Italy precarious.

This was not to be. On 3 September 1923 Mussolini declared his refusal to accept the competence of the League, *inter alia* because the Greek government had not been officially recognized, and because the 'delimitation commission' of the Ambassador's Conference was well qualified to investigate the 'crime'. The next day Mussolini announced that if the League of Nations were to act, Italy would leave the League, and Della Torretta informed the Foreign Office of this officially. Kennard reported to Curzon that Mussolini had already 'gone so far in opposing submission to the League that if he now acquiesces his prestige here, which is always his main consideration, will be greatly affected', in which view he was entirely correct.

During the afternoon of 4 September Kennard saw Mussolini again, and off his own bat made a suggestion to him which was to alter Curzon's stance. Kennard suggested to the Duce that although the League might consider the dispute to be fully within its competence, it might also decide to leave action to the Conference of Ambassadors. Mussolini, in an amiable mood, replied that 'this formula might prove acceptable'. The Foreign Office reaction was anger with Kennard, and Sir William Tyrell, acting head of the Foreign Office, was on the point of sending him a cautionary telegram not to continue to exceed his instructions. Curzon, however, after taking advice from Graham, who was in London (and minuting that British Ambassadors always seem to be shooting or on holiday when there is a crisis), decided to follow Kennard's lead.

In Geneva, Cecil claimed that he was constantly hampered because as soon as he got members of the Council to agree what was to be said, Paris phoned instructions to Albert Hanotaux, the French representative, 'not to do anything to which Italy objects': France was out to foment trouble between Italy and Britain.[10] Curzon was determined to foster the Anglo-French Entente, and the French attitude persuaded him to turn his back on Cecil; he feared that unless Britain co-operated with France over the Corfu crisis there would be a wide rift in the Entente, so he plumped for a solution involving the Conference of Ambassadors, on the lines proposed by Kennard to Mussolini. The French government also preferred this solution. Cecil, to his distress, had to climb down, and the Council of the League of Nations requested the Conference of Ambassadors to appoint neutral representatives to a Committee of Enquiry, and to separate the issue of reparations to Italy for the murder of Tellini and his colleagues from the occupation of Corfu, now nominally in the hands of the League.

Curzon put the onus of ejecting Italy from Corfu on Poincaré, threatening the French Premier that if the problem of Corfu were to come before the League Assembly, Britain would support the Covenant, which would result in sanctions against Italy. The affair was cleverly manipulated by Curzon and the French, and in the end the League played no part in the settlement of the dispute. The upshot was that the Conference of Ambassadors persuaded Greece to pay Italy an indemnity of 50 million lire, and Mussolini promised to evacuate Corfu by 27 September.

In order to uphold the League's credibility, Cecil, with strong support from the smaller nations at Geneva, still hankered after a Declaration of the League's competence to adjudicate over the Italian aggression at Corfu. This angered Mussolini, who threatened not to evacuate Corfu if the issue was taken further, and expressed anger against both Cecil and Curzon.

Curzon was incensed by Mussolini's bluster, minuting on 16 September: 'I really am not at all disposed to yield to the threats of this man who, having agreed to evacuate, announces his intention on the flimsiest of pleas to break his word and re-occupy.' Harold Nicolson, then a First Secretary, minuted:

> Although we must discount the exuberant petulance of Mussolini's language, yet it is evident that he is determined in the end to secure the triumph of 'might is right'. To him this phrase is no vapid or ecstatic formula, but a firm political conviction. We must cope with it as such. We were able, by diverting the dispute from Geneva to Paris, to evade the embarrassing question, 'Will HMG uphold the Covenant or not?'. . . We must face the fact that Mussolini will defy everything except force . . . unless we are prepared to go the whole length it would be better to retreat at once and to allow Mussolini to secure a triumph which may well be galling but can hardly be permanent . . . if we are not prepared to defy Mussolini we should instruct Lord R. Cecil to use every endeavour to prevent this matter being raised at the Assembly in any form, and endeavour in the last resort to pacify Mussolini by confining the League's action to a mere reference, without debate, to the Hague Assembly.

Britain climbed down. A Committee of Jurists was set up by the Council of the League to determine whether incidents like Corfu came within the competence of the League, but their report was ambivalent, and was approved by Italy. It left what Robert Dell, the *Manchester Guardian*'s diplomatic correspondent, described as 'a dangerous latitude' for members of the League to evade the terms of the Covenant. Mussolini had done grave damage to the League, and secured a notable diplomatic victory over Britain, setting an unfortunate precedent for his behaviour in 1935.[11]

Smarting under their ignominious defeat by Mussolini over Corfu, Curzon and the Foreign Office were not now, as they had been in July, in a mood to give in to Italy over the other controversial items on the agenda — the Dodecanese islands and the former German territory of Jubaland, adjoining Italian Somaliland and now under British control.

In October a speech by Mussolini attacking the League further antagonized the Foreign Office. Cecil wrote from Geneva:

> It really amounts to a declaration by the Prime Minister, who is also the dictator of a great power, that he was quite ready to tear up the Covenant and go to war without notice . . . I really think that this Government [Britain's] must lose no opportunity of upholding the sanctity of treaties or not only the League, or Europe, will be lost.

Francesco Coppola, one of the Italian delegates to Geneva, had early in October written articles highly critical of the League. The Ambassador in Rome, Graham, commented that 'Italy, deprived of the fruits of her great victory, regarded the League as an international instrument for her own repression', but Cecil's reaction was: 'It is little short of an outrage that one of the delegates should publicly advocate the destruction of the League from within by Italian efforts.' Sir Eyre Crowe, Head of the Foreign Office, tried to cool Cecil down by pointing out to him that it was inadvisable to raise these matters in Rome while the Duce was having friendly talks with Graham.[12]

Mussolini was anxious to separate the two issues of Jubaland and the Dodecanese. He wanted to claim that as a result of his diplomacy the Allies were giving Jubaland to Italy as a reward for her part in the victory over Germany: Curzon insisted that Jubaland would only be ceded as part of a general settlement with Italy in which Mussolini made large concessions over his claims for the Dodecanese islands.

As has been seen, under the secret Treaty of London in 1915 Italy had been promised some of the Dodecanese islands and additional colonial territory in Africa, in return for joining the Allied side. The Dodecanese issue had become complicated when Turkey emerged from her short war with Greece as, according to Curzon, 'a quasi victorious power', not a vanquished one. The abortive Treaty of Sèvres of 1920 had merely left the problem in the air, with Italy committed to make undefined withdrawals.

On 10 October 1923 Curzon saw Della Torretta, and agreed with him that the Corfu incident belonged to the past; he recorded that he had however insisted, 'as he had done a score of times', that Jubaland could only be ceded by Britain to Italy as part of a general settlement which included the Dodecanese.[13]

A Foreign Office memorandum by Harold Nicolson admitted that

Italy had complete rights, on paper, both to compensation in Africa and to the Dodecanese:

> We thus designed to use the question of Jubaland as a lever to force the Italians to an agreement over the Dodecanese, refusing to cede the territory promised until the Dodecanese could be settled. The result of this policy was a deadlock, and relations between Great Britain and Italy were unquestionably affected.

The Baldwin government was defeated in the General Election of 10 December 1923. No party gained an overall majority, but it was virtually certain that the Conservatives would have to leave office. Curzon nevertheless continued to work as hard as ever at the Foreign Office. He saw Della Torretta again, on 16 December, and reiterated Britain's position that Jubaland would not be conceded unless there was agreement over the Dodecanese; he privately christened Della Torretta 'Grabski' because of his persistent requests for extra territory adjoining Italian Somaliland.[14]

On 12 January Graham reported that Contarini had explained to him Mussolini's feeling that from the point of view of internal politics it was 'absolutely necessary to show that he had obtained something more than had been considered insufficient by preceding Italian Governments'; this had no effect on Curzon, who saw Della Torretta again on 21 January. It was now known that Ramsay MacDonald would be forming a Labour government; as he left the Foreign Office for the last time, making way for his successor, Curzon noted the Italian Ambassador's proposals:

> . . . as to Jubaland, we were to surrender the maximum of what we had ever offered for no return at all . . .
>
> Had I continued in office I could not have concluded an agreement in any such terms . . . Signor Mussolini's passionate desire to represent every situation as a triumph for his own diplomacy over other powers makes me more than doubtful.
>
> . . . We must not act unfairly to the Greeks . . . and we must on no account allow Signor Mussolini first to dupe us and then to bully nor squeeze them. The one effective card that Italy can play is, of course, the annexation of the whole of these islands [Dodecanese]. But if she proceeds to that extreme, I hope we shall recede from the Jubaland offer except for the minimum.

Ramsay MacDonald formed Britain's first Labour Government on 23 January 1924. As his own Foreign Secretary, he was more conciliatory to Mussolini than Curzon. At first he continued Curzon's policy of insisting on linking the settlement of Jubaland to satisfactory Italian negotiations with Greece over sharing out the Dodecanese islands. However, Graham reported in a private telegram to the Prime

Minister on 6 March 1924 that Mussolini was inclined to give up all hopes of an enlarged Jubaland, and instead annex all the Dodecanese; he suggested that a private letter from the Prime Minister to Mussolini offering to hand over Jubaland to Italy would give great pleasure to the Duce, if it emphasized there was no connection between Jubaland and the Dodecanese.

Graham's suggestion was ill-received in the Foreign Office; MacDonald, however, recorded that while he could not pretend his predecessors had been completely wrong in connecting Jubaland with the Dodecanese, he had no desire to score a diplomatic triumph off Mussolini, and was ready to agree a formula which would save his face. Accordingly, on 1 April MacDonald wrote personally to the Duce saying that he would like to settle Jubaland and the Dodecanese 'concurrently', without making the settlement of the one depend on the other, and that he was 'anxious immediately to execute the promises which we have made to you in regard to Jubaland'.[15]

This resulted in the conclusion in June 1924 of the Jubaland Treaty, by which all the territory in question was ceded to Italy, even though Mussolini was showing no haste in his negotiations with the Greeks. The Jubaland discussions were conducted by Raffaele Guariglia for the Italians and Harold Nicolson for the British. Mussolini got, not the minimum desired by Curzon, but the maximum; he made much of his diplomatic triumph in the Italian press.

Ramsay MacDonald's government fell in October 1924, and Baldwin became Prime Minister again. He did not reappoint Curzon as Foreign Secretary – largely, it is alleged, because he had made an enemy of Mussolini, and of too many others in Europe. So we do not know how Curzon would have reacted to this reversal of his policy. Instead, Austen Chamberlain became Foreign Secretary. Much to Mussolini's impatience, it still remained for the Jubaland Treaty to be ratified by the British Parliament; but Chamberlain assured Della Torretta on 14 November 1924 that 'there is no difference between us and our predecessors over Jubaland', and sent a message to Mussolini that he wanted to visit him in Italy, where he had spent 'many happy holidays'.[16]

Mussolini had found MacDonald 'soft' in 1924. Eleven years later, when the more important Stresa Conference was held in April 1935, MacDonald was again Prime Minister; the Duce expected him to be as accommodating over Abyssinia as he had been over Jubaland.

On 30 July 1923, four weeks before the Corfu incident, Abyssinia had applied for admission to the League of Nations. Thus this vexed question, which was to have disastrous consequences for Italy and Europe, was on the agenda concurrently with the Corfu crisis. According to Foreign Office minutes, the French prompted Abyssinia to apply for membership in an effort to damage British and Italian interests in Africa. An explanation of French motivation is to be found in a letter dated 23 September 1923 from the War Office to the Foreign Office, stating that the Army Council considered 'the following military objects' might underlie France's efforts to obtain Abyssinia's entry to the League of Nations:

> a. The unrestricted sale of arms and ammunition to Abyssinia by France.
> b. An increase of French influence over North African nations and tribes generally by supporting them in this application.
> c. An attempt to damage our influence in Abyssinia.

> The Army Council consider that (a) would be an inevitable sequel to Abyssinian entry into the League; that (b) is a logical deduction from the established French policy *vis-à-vis* the North African race; and that as regards (c) the French would welcome, in accordance with this policy, this or any other chance of weakening our position in North Africa by the establishment of a preponderating French influence on the borders of the Sudan and Kenya Colony.

There is also other evidence that in 1923 the French wanted to clip British and Italian wings in East Africa.[17]

Mussolini was opposed: on 6 August he cabled to the Italian legations in Geneva and Addis Ababa that he was 'absolutely opposed (*assolutamente contrario*) to the admission of Ethiopia to the League of Nations'. He followed this up on 10 August with telegrams to Paris and London:

> There is no doubt that it is in our interests to oppose the Abyssinian request but we must proceed with great caution in our opposition to prevent understandable offence being taken whether we are successful or unsuccessful.

On 25 August Della Torretta sent Mussolini a revealing telegram:

> I have spoken to Tyrell [Sir William Tyrell, of the Foreign Office] about the request of Ethiopia to be admitted to the League of Nations. Tyrell told me that the British Government had not discussed this question. From my talk I am sure that the British Government does not want Ethiopia admitted but has no intention of opposing it openly. I deduce that the British representatives at Geneva will follow the majority line. If the Assembly is in favour of admission Great Britain will agree but their representative will try and make admission subject to certain guarantees about slavery (and also the traffic in slaves, which could easily be stopped) which the Abyssinian Government will dislike and will not

accept. In my opinion the British Government will neither now nor in the future take a hard line, but I believe they will try at Geneva to make admission practically impossible. Tyrell has confirmed to me that from information received in the Foreign Office from Addis Ababa the request by Ras Tafari [Haile Selassie] is due to a push from the French Legation there.[18]

On 3 September Lord Robert Cecil in Geneva was instructed by letter from Curzon that the Italian representative to the League had been ordered by Mussolini not to oppose openly the admission of Abyssinia, but to keep in close touch with his British colleague with a view to imposing such conditions on Abyssinia as to make admission practically impossible; if, however, the British representative raised no opposition, the Italians were ordered to go to 'even greater lengths' in supporting admission. Another Foreign Office telegram invited Cecil's views.[19]

The author has been unable to trace how it was that on 3 September Curzon was able to tell Cecil categorically that the Italian representative at Geneva had been instructed to oppose Abyssinian entry if Britain would co-operate; the information must have been sent by Mussolini himself, through the Italian Embassy in London.

In his reminiscences Cecil recorded how difficult he found it to get on with Curzon, and this personality clash was partially responsible for the disastrous admission of Abyssinia to the League of Nations. When Cecil joined the government in May 1923 as Lord Privy Seal with responsibility for League of Nations matters, he was promised a room in the Foreign Office by the Prime Minister, Stanley Baldwin. Curzon 'peremptorily' refused, on the grounds that there could not be two Cabinet Ministers in the Foreign Office simultaneously, ignoring the fact that in the past Grey and Baldwin had managed it perfectly well. According to Cecil, there was 'continual friction and difficulty'. Curzon had little faith in the League and did not make a single trip to Geneva; he and Cecil were poles apart over its role.[20]

On 8 September Cecil telegraphed to the Foreign Office that he had had 'some conversation' with the Italian representative, and that he (Lord Robert) would personally regret the exclusion of Abyssinia from the League; he ignored the opposition of Curzon and the Foreign Office, which was based both on the slavery practised in the Abyssinian empire and on their blatant arms traffic. An Abyssinian Department minute on Cecil's communication by Geoffrey Warner, endorsed by Curzon, reads:

. . . Conditions in the country are so bad that Abyssinia ought not to be admitted . . . the prestige of the League will suffer. What will be said in

America and the anti-League press there? . . . We have a strong case for *résistance à l'outrance*, and the Italians will back us up when they see we are firm. We know them to be secretly opposed to admission.

Francis Russell, the head of the British Legation in Abyssinia, was even more emphatic:

I trust the League of Nations realise the admission of Abyssinia will be a blow to the cause of progress here. Success of application will be regarded by its promoters as a compliment to their abstention from culture. I hope . . . British delegate will urge rejection of application.

In another despatch Russell referred not only to slavery and the arms traffic, but to the defective administration of justice in respect of foreigners.[21]

Meanwhile the Foreign Office had become worried by the tone of Cecil's messages, and wondered if he had received their instructions of 3 September; although he gave his own views in favour of Abyssinia's admission, he made no reference to communicating with the Italian delegate to ensure that Abyssinia was excluded, while other reports made it clear that the Abyssinian application was making rapid progress through the committees. Accordingly, a telegram was sent on 8 September asking Cecil whether he had received the instructions of 3 September; he replied that he had not, and duplicates were sent on 10 September. On 11 September, Cecil found the 3 September instructions (together with a further memorandum instructing him to raise a recent case of bad faith by the French government in allowing an unauthorized consignment of rifles to pass through Djibuti): he had received these instructions, and then put them in an envelope containing other material of 'a less urgent nature'. He was unmethodical, and an idealist, convinced that the League of Nations would preserve the peace of the world; in his dream world he was confident that once Abyssinia joined, the evils of slavery would automatically be stamped out because of the beneficial influence of the League. Curzon, in contrast, was a pragmatist.

By the time the British delegation in Geneva attempted to act on Curzon's instructions of 3 September it was too late, in the words of the Foreign Office, 'to chill the misplaced sentimentality' which had been generated in the sub-committees. On 19 September Edward Wood MP, Under-Secretary for the Colonies (later Lord Halifax), spoke at length against the application, but the sub-committee had already decided to recommend approval, provided declarations about slavery and the arms traffic were signed by Abyssinia. Wood explained how Britain suffered through the uncontrolled importation of arms by Abyssinia but, the Foreign Office commented, 'Unfortunately he did not take the opportunity of referring to the recent irregular consignment from Jibuti in regard to which instructions had been given on 11 September.'

In the sub-committees the Abyssinian delegation stated that their government intended to suppress the slave trade 'in so far as it still existed', and claimed the so-called slaves of Abyssinia were merely 'serfs of a comparatively enviable type' who could appeal to a court if they were maltreated: this was entirely tendentious.

Charles Tufton, of the British delegation in Geneva, reported that 'the whole brunt of showing that Abyssinia is not fit has been thrown upon us' – a result of Cecil ignoring London's orders to co-operate with the Italians. The Foreign Office told Cecil, prophetically but in vain, that should Abyssinia be admitted 'we should be liable with the whole League in respect of her territorial integrity'. On 15 September Cecil telegraphed to Curzon:

> Admission of Abyssinia is, I think, unlikely to be turned down, and it is unlikely whether postponement for another year can be achieved . . . I presume you would not wish British vote to be cast against admission in a minority without Italy and France . . . no support for British views has been forthcoming from Italian delegate, and it is quite evident that he has had instructions not to go against his French colleague.

Curzon replied on 17 September:

> I personally entertain no doubt that Abyssinia is quite unfit to be admitted and that her admission will neither redound to future credit of League nor promote the interests of Britain. Only in last week fresh official evidence has reached us as to rampant slave raiding in southern and south western parts of country and to complete anarchy in those depopulated areas. No such conditions exist in Iraq [Cecil had argued that by refusing admission to Abyssinia Britain might damage the case for admission of Iraq, which Britain favoured], and to throw shelter of League over them would, in my opinion, be contrary to principles for which League exists. If the answer be made that admission will bring about a curtailment of these shocking abuses the reply is obvious, that this can only be done at the cost of an interference which would be calamitous.
>
> At the same time I realise you are in a better position to judge the temper of Assembly than I am, and if they are activated by what seems to me a misplaced sentimentality, and if no one agrees with me, I would not carry my opposition to the point of standing out alone, for in that case, we should incur the entire odium without doing any good. If, on the other hand, Italy will side with us I should be inclined to maintain our opposition . . . if Abyssinia is admitted there will be no future ground for excluding anybody.[22]

Mussolini, with his customary unpredictability, had changed his mind, and was now ready to condone the admission of Abyssinia; on 21 September he informed Antonio Salandra, former Italian Prime Minister and now head of the Italian delegation in Geneva, that he (Mussolini) had as Prime Minister telegraphed instructions to his legation in Addis Ababa to inform Prince Ras Tafari, the Abyssinian Regent (later known as Haile Selassie) that he could count on the support of Italy, that there had never been any intention 'on our part to frustrate the action of the Ethiopian delegation', and that he had instructed his delegation to brush away all suspicions of Italy's hostility.[23]

In the debate in the Assembly the Australian delegate, Sir Joseph Cook, made a telling point when he emphasized the anomaly that would result if a slave-owning state were placed in a position, as a League member, to cross-question countries like Australia as to whether they had been sufficiently zealous in suppressing slavery in mandated territories committed to their charge. Unfortunately the members of the Sixth Committee (also the Slavery Committee) – Britain, France, Italy, Romania, Finland, Latvia and Persia – gave no support to the British or the Australians, and on 20 September recommended Abyssinia's admission to the Assembly.

On 18 September the Abyssinian Regent complained of Britain's attitude in a personal letter to Baldwin, the Prime Minister. The Foreign Office discovered that the letter had been composed in the French Legation at Addis Ababa; Baldwin did not reply.

On 13 October 1923, after an enthusiastic speech in support by the Italian delegate, the League Assembly – including Britain – voted unanimously for Abyssinia to be admitted. Alec Cadogan minuted a trenchant criticism of Cecil's behaviour:

> Unless more effective control over the proceedings of the British delegation by the Foreign Office can be established, it is to be feared that similar incidents may occur in the future.

In the middle of December Russell reported a raid by Abyssinian tribesmen into Kenya which resulted in the carrying off of 19,000 cattle and 50,000 sheep and goats. On this Curzon minuted: 'A deplorable situation; these are the people whom our representative, contrary to clear instructions, admitted to the League of Nations.'[24]

In 1923 Britain would have produced an unanswerable case against Abyssinia being admitted to the League of Nations. If Cecil had not bungled, but had carried out Curzon's wishes, Mussolini would have authorized co-operation in committee with Britain, and Abyssinia would have been excluded. Curzon's allusion to 'misplaced sentimentality' was a justified criticism of Cecil; Cecil, an autocratic aristocrat, son of a former Prime Minister, burning with zeal for the League, despised Curzon for not sharing his romantic enthusiasm.

The French had been successful in a cynical manoeuvre which reflected no credit on them, and the Italians fell into their trap. Her support for Abyssinia's admission had horrific consequences for Italy, but in these early days of power Mussolini had little grasp of the complex Abyssinian problem. The Abyssinians were xenophobic and opposed to development or progress as understood in the western world. Their only motive for reform was fear of invasion by a foreign power. In the event, they interpreted membership of the League as meaning that there was no reason why they should introduce reforms, because they were no longer in danger of coercion; and if they were subjected to coercion, they could appeal to the League, which under the Covenant would support them.

Much of the so-called Abyssinian Empire was not legally a state. In 1891 Anglo-Italian protocols had assigned almost all the eastern part of this area of north-east Africa to Italy, apart from French Somaliland. After their defeat in the Battle of Aduwa during the first Italian–Abyssinian war the Italian government was not, in 1906, enthusiastic for the acquisition of colonies, and a large but ill-defined area (excluding the coastal strips of Italian Eritrea and Somaliland) was allocated to Abyssinia by a French–Italian–British agreement; the ruler of Abyssinia then conquered and occupied all the tribal territories up to the coastal strip, but formal frontiers were never drawn. The ruling Amharas were settled on the land at the expense of the existing inhabitants and each Amharic family was allocated one or more families of the conquered tribes in servitude. If the serfs escaped, they were subject to barbarous penalties.

The total population of the so-called Abyssinian Empire was between five and ten million, but the ruling Amharas under Emperor Menelik occupied less than one third of the territory – in the central nucleus surrounding the capital, Addis Ababa – and were less than one third of the total population. In 1935 about two-thirds of the population consisted of the conquered tribes, who differed from the Amharas in almost every respect. The Amharas were Christian, and spoke a common language; the conquered tribes were pagan or Moslem, and spoke seventy different languages. The economic and social system depended on slavery, which was supported and practised even by the Church. Abyssinia was not only a source of slaves for the Arab market, but also a link in a slave-trade route connecting the Sudan with the Red Sea.

Abyssinia continually attacked her neighbours across her ill-defined borders – not only Kenya and the Sudan, but also Italian Eritrea and Somaliland. To protect their colonies, both Britain and Italy needed to keep troops on their frontiers.

After admission to the League of Nations, the Abyssinian government refused to put an end to slavery. Lady Simon, wife of Sir John Simon (later Foreign Secretary) and Chairman of the Anti-Slavery Society, was right when she claimed, amid considerable publicity, that nothing short of a crusade would ever free Abyssinia from the disgrace of the slave trade, and that not only were the peasant agricultural labourers bound to the land as serfs, but a flourishing export trade in slaves from Africa to Arabia and Iraq continued unabated.

The proper course for the League in 1923 would have been to create a mandate for Abyssinia, and either divide it between Great Britain, France and Italy, on the basis of the 1906 Agreement, or give the whole mandate to Italy, as part of the spoils due to her as a victor of the First World War under the Treaty of London. Such a mandate would have been in the best interests of the inhabitants of the area. However, no one at the time foresaw the immense importance this seemingly unimportant country was destined to assume. Italian diplomats calculated that Abyssinia was on the point of disintegration, and that it was merely a matter of time before she was handed over to Italy.

It is an irony of fate that such disastrous consequences should have flowed from what was an almost farcical misunderstanding between the Foreign Secretary and Lord Robert Cecil. Once Abyssinia was a member of the League, Italy could not annex her territory without calling down on her own head the wrath of other members.

Matters were exacerbated by an unfortunate postscript in December 1925, one which has been overlooked by most British historians. By this time Austen Chamberlain, Curzon's successor as Foreign Secretary, had struck up a strong personal friendship with Mussolini, and the two agreed in the autumn of 1925 after meeting at Livorno that in return for Italian support over the disputed sovereignty of Mosul – an oil-rich territory on the boundaries of Turkey and British-mandated Iraq – Britain would give Italy concessions in Abyssinia. Sir Robert Graham was instructed to negotiate an agreement with the Italian government, which was finalized on 20 December 1925.

The waters of Lake T'ana Hāyk' (a large lake 6,000 feet above sea level, south of Gondar) in western Abyssinia, close to the Sudan frontier, form the main reservoir for the Blue Nile and are important for irrigation in Sudan and Egypt, both of which were under British protection. Britain had long sought permission from Addis Ababa to construct a barrage at Lake T'ana to create an artificial reservoir. In

November 1919 the Italian government had offered co-operation over the barrage project in exchange for British support of Italy's request for permission from the Abyssinian government for Italian construction of a railway linking Italian Somaliland with Italian Eritrea. The British government would not entertain the suggestion in 1919, but by the autumn of 1925 relations between Italy and Britain were so favourable that on 14 December 1925 Graham was in a position to write to Mussolini requesting Italian support for the barrage proposal and to promise in return

> . . . to support the Italian Government in obtaining from the Abyssinian Government a concession to construct and run a railway from the frontier of Eritrea to the frontier of Italian Somaliland, and for identical instructions to be sent to the British and Italian representatives in Addis Ababa to concert common action with the Abyssinian Government to obtain the concessions desired by Britain and Italy over Lake Tsana [*sic*] and the railway.
>
> In the event of His Majesty's Government with the valued assistance of the Italian Government obtaining from the Abyssinian Government the desired concession on Lake Tsana they are also prepared to recognize an exclusive Italian economic influence in the west of Abyssinia and the whole of the territory to be crossed by above-mentioned railway. They would further promise to support with the Abyssinian Government all Italian demands for economic concessions in the above zone.

In Mussolini's reply, dated 20 December 1925, the Duce wrote that his government took note

> . . . that in the event of His Britannic Majesty's Government, with the effective support of the Italian Government, obtaining from the Abyssinian Government the concessions asked for on Lake Tsana they will recognize the exclusive character of the Italian economic influence in the west of Abyssinia and in the whole of the territory to be crossed by the above-mentioned railway, and will also support with the Ethiopian Government all Italian demands for economic concessions in the above zone.[25]

Western Abyssinia comprised the central nucleus of the Abyssinian state, such as it was, and allowing exclusive Italian economic influence there and in the area to be crossed by the proposed railway meant in effect abandoning the zone to Italy: a cavalier way to treat a newly admitted member of the League of Nations, since because of constant tribal insurrection Mussolini could not hope to build his railway without asserting military control over the area through which it passed. Mussolini, with reason, looked on this agreement as giving him a free hand in Abyssinia, as far as the British were concerned.

Mussolini and Chamberlain met at Rapallo on 28 December, a few days after the agreement was signed – a meeting Mussolini had requested on 21 December, through Graham, and travelled from Milan especially to keep. There is no written record of their talk, but on 2 January 1926 Graham told Chamberlain that Mussolini 'was delighted with the meeting and conversation'. However, in reply to a Parliamentary Question on the subject on 17 February 1926 Chamberlain was cagey, saying that 'It was not in the public interest for him to state what had been discussed in informal conversation with Mussolini at dinner at Rapallo', and adding, inaccurately, that 'no new obligations were undertaken or suggested on either side'.[26]

The agreement was ill-received in Addis Ababa, and Ras Tafari appealed to the League of Nations, denouncing it as an attempted plot against the sovereignty and independence of Ethiopia and demanding that the League discuss it. This forced Chamberlain to disclose the existence of the agreement to Parliament on 16 April; he stated on 5 July that the agreement had been 'misconstrued'.

The Italian reaction was that Abyssinia had been pushed into making the protest by France, the 'real villains', alarmed that their monopoly of the Abyssinian railways was being threatened by Italy. In the House of Commons on 2 August 1926, Chamberlain was attacked by the Opposition for making the agreement; he was unapologetic, emphasizing that the notes did not reserve 'any part of Abyssinia to Italian economic influence'. This was specious.

As the Abyssinian government would permit neither the barrage nor the railway, and France supported neither, the matter dropped from view until 1935 when, a few days before his invasion of Abyssinia, Mussolini declared, with some accuracy, that 'England only recently regarded Abyssinian independence as an absurdity. In 1925 Sir Ronald Graham and I signed an Agreement which practically cut Abyssinia to pieces.' The Italian historian, Gaetano Salvemini, a bitter opponent of Mussolini, writes: 'What Sir Austen was actually doing in December 1925 was pledging the British Foreign Office not to interfere with Mussolini even if he landed himself in a war with Ethiopia, on condition that British "special interests" in the Tana region remained unchallenged.' It is hard to dispute this judgement.[27]

This background to the Abyssinian War of 1935 is not widely known. Indisputably the Graham–Mussolini agreement of December 1925, coupled with the admission of Abyssinia to the League of Nations in 1923, were important factors in bringing about the Abyssinian War of 1935, which in turn contributed to the causes of the Second World War.

CHAPTER 4

The Matteotti Murder and Dictatorship

Mussolini was forty when he became Prime Minister – the youngest in the history of unified Italy. Out of his cabinet of fourteen, only five ministers were Fascists, together with nine under-secretaries. Mussolini himself took over the Home Office and Foreign Ministry. None of the former prime ministers were in his Cabinet; General Diaz, the hero of the final Italian victory in the First World War, became Minister of War, but had previously had no political affiliation.

In private Mussolini was polite and well-mannered, without much sense of humour but revealing glimpses of peasant wit. In public he was an actor who knew every trick of the demagogue orator, but off the platform he was natural, and charmed almost everyone he met. The Italian civil servants and diplomats with whom he now came in contact for the first time were pleasantly surprised to find him easy to work with, and he would chat amiably with doormen and messengers. His great weakness was his superficiality. In his previous life, devoted to daily journalism, his day's labours had come to an end as the paper went to press – and he applied the same principle to government. As Denis Mack Smith has noted, he was the master of 'Government by press statement'.

As we have seen, Sir Ronald Graham, the British Ambassador, met Mussolini on 1 November 1922. After a 'long conversation' he reported that he was 'agreeably surprised and favourably impressed'. Mussolini drew Graham's attention to the 'discipline' of the Fascists, and said he hoped to impose the same discipline on the whole country. According to Ivone Kirkpatrick, then Second Secretary at the Rome Embassy, Graham had expected to meet a hot-head and came away with the feeling that Mussolini 'was a man with whom one could do business'.

According to Graham, Mussolini was serious and earnest and seemed sincere and friendly, with no hint of the hostile references to Britain he had lately been giving vent to in the press. Graham reported that when a mutual friend asked Mussolini whether his recent journalistic denunciations of Britain's refusal to back Italy's territorial ambitions might prove embarrassing now that he was Prime Minister, the reply was statesmanlike: 'There are things one says when one has no responsibility but forgets as soon as possible when one has.'

As Graham explained to Curzon:

> I confess that I went to visit Signor Mussolini with a certain degree of prejudice . . . Apart from his attacks on Great Britain in the press he has during the recent demonstrations at Naples and elsewhere, in which he was the principal figure, adopted an unnecessary degree of pose and mannerism which can only be described as Napoleonic. He has stalked about with his hand across his breast and thrust in the lapel of his coat; his gaze was fixed; he never smiled and appeared wrapt in fierce gloom.

On the Sunday following his accession to power Lina Waterfield, the Italian correspondent of the *Observer*, wrote of Mussolini that '. . . he rules successfully more because he inspires fear than love; [he] teaches a particular brand of patriotism which enlivens national vanity.' She has left an interesting account of him in his early days as Italy's ruler:

> . . . the lift door opened and out of the darkness a short sturdy man advanced, very slowly, towards me, making curious grimaces with his head slightly lowered; the whites of his dark eyes showed while his eyebrows met in a fierce frown and his lips seemed to pout in anger.
> Did he mean to impress and frighten me? I think he did, but he only succeeded in making me want to laugh and I nearly choked in trying to suppress it. Of course he saw my amusement, and with the swiftness of a good actor he dropped his bravado and changed his expression to one of friendly welcome as he shook hands with me . . . He spoke chiefly of the Socialist leaders, on whom he poured utter contempt as being spineless and incapable of leadership.[1]

The right-wing *Spectator* foresaw menace, noting in their edition of 14 November 1922:

> The dangers are grave . . . Less than two years ago the Fascisti combined together in order to help to make the law prevail over anarchy. They have ended up by over-riding all law and asserting they are the State.
> The Fascisti soon descended to conduct which was as much outside the law as that which they professed themselves to be punishing. Hotheaded youths, not to mention soldiers and sailors of mature years, who were curiously enough not less hot-headed, flocked to the banners of Fascismo . . . Signor Giolitti encouraged the new movement perhaps because like Signor Nitti he felt too weak to oppose it. The Fascisti more and more abused the encouragement they received. They terrorized the

Press. They beat magistrates who gave decisions against them. They required officials who were obnoxious to them to resign under threat of death. Their numbers grew. Today there is a Fascist army of 40,000 men. When Signor Bonomi succeeded Signor Giolitti the situation was already out of hand . . . Newspapers which speak against it are suppressed in the name of Fascism . . . The attempt to stop the class warfare of the Bolsheviks has become a class warfare by the Fascists.

James Rennell Rodd, British Ambassador in Italy from 1908 to 1919 (later Lord Rennell of Rodd), disagreed; in a letter to the *Spectator* he wrote:

The impotence of existing institutions demanded a drastic remedy . . . they have usurped the authority which no one else in the country seemed able or disposed to execute, and they have proceeded to direct action with the ever-increasing support of their countrymen . . . they have already in the last two years accomplished much useful work. Their organization includes every class – the noble, the intellectual, the bourgeois, the peasant and the working man. [They have] remarkable organizing ability and a powerful central direction which has secured absolute loyalty. They stand for patriotism, for a sound and healthy national life, for the stimulation of efficiency, for economy and the reduction of an inflated bureaucracy.

Rennell's additional comment that he was favourably impressed by Mussolini 'adopting a frock coat and silk hat on assuming office' must have detracted somewhat from the force of his letter.

In the same issue Lord Sydenham, an influential right-wing peer and a regular contributor, added his own fulsome praise of Fascism to Rennell's, and on 20 January 1923 the Editor of the *Spectator*, St Loe Strachey, commented:

Fascism draws its support from all political parties except the Communists, official Socialists, and the Roman Catholic population. We pin our faith on Signor Mussolini's sense of responsibility.

A fortnight later his verdict was:

He said he could save the nation and he did. If he succeeds [in overcoming his economic difficulties] then Mussolini must go down in history as one of the greatest administrators the world has ever seen.

The right in Britain saw Fascism as a bulwark against the spread of Russian Communism in Europe.

At first the left-wing press in Britain did not appreciate the threat Fascism posed to Italian trade unions and the Socialist Party. Within a week of Mussolini coming to power, the *New Statesman*, organ of the Labour Party and the Asquithian Liberals, published a report written by their Italian correspondent, J. C. Bailey:

The *coup d'état* of last week which placed Mussolini in control of the engine of state was carried through peacefully enough thanks to the immense popular backing he commands and to the good sense of King Vittorio Emmanuel [*sic*] . . . The revolution contemplated by Mussolini is a political and social reconstruction on essentially democratic lines. Having eliminated the irreconcilable element of Marxism and in the process of doing so kindled up and down the country a great fire of patriotic feeling, his idea is to unite and co-ordinate all classes in the service of their country.

On 10th March 1923 the same author wrote that Signor Mussolini was giving proof every day of 'his good sense in command'.

Mussolini's first speech to the Italian Parliament, on 16 November 1922, was well received. He said, 'I could have transformed this grey hall into an armed camp for blackshirts, a bivouac for corpses. I could have nailed up the doors of Parliament' – bombast, but a confirmation of his intention to govern, if not as chairman of a committee, at least like an American President. By 275 votes (including those of the former prime ministers Giolitti, Bonomi and Salandra) to 90, he was granted full powers for a year, to carry out what he claimed were 'essential reforms'. Here was a cover of legality for a slide into dictatorship – and the lesson was not lost on Hitler.

Giolitti wrote at the time that the new government had 'the strength of will so rare in Italy', and thought 'it is certain that they have dragged Italy out of the ditch in which they were rotting', while Nitti said:

The Fascist experiment must be allowed to proceed undisturbed; no opposition should come from our side. I cannot join them but I do not want to oppose them. If the experiment does not succeed no one will be able to say that the failure was due to us or that we created difficulties. If it does succeed we must return to normality or to the Constitution, which is my main aim, and the Fascists will have done us a great service.[2]

On 31 October 1923 *The Times*, reviewing Mussolini's first year in office, wrote:

Italy has never been so united as she is today . . . Fascismo has abolished the game of parliamentary chess; it has also simplified the taxation system and reduced the deficit to manageable proportions; it has vastly improved the public services, particularly the railways; it has reduced a superfluously large bureaucracy without any very bad results in the way of hardships or unemployment; it has pursued a vigorous and fairly successful colonial policy. All this represents hard and useful work, but the chief boons it has conferred upon Italy are national security and national self respect . . . Fascismo has had a great deal of courage, very considerable wisdom and immense luck . . . it has deserved the sincere birthday greetings of the world.

On 27 January 1924 the Fiume crisis was resolved by negotiation and the Pact of Rome was signed between Mussolini and the Yugoslavs. Under this treaty Yugoslavia recognized Italy's full sovereignty over both the city and port of Fiume, a new frontier was defined, and one important harbour basin was leased to Yugoslavia at a nominal rent for fifty years. This amounted to a considerable sacrifice by Yugoslavia and was enthusiastically received in Italy. Mussolini was delighted, and the King awarded him the Collar of the Annunziata – the highest Italian decoration.

Flushed by his diplomatic success Mussolini decided to hold a General Election under his new electoral law, with 6 April 1924 as polling day; parliament was dissolved on 25 January. To make sure of victory, Mussolini persuaded national and local figures from the liberals and other parties to add their names to the Fascist list. He secured the former prime ministers Salandra and Orlando; Giolitti refused, while declaring that this did not signify hostility to the government. Benedetto Croce, the most influential liberal of his day, campaigned openly for the Fascists. Salandra, Orlando and Croce later bitterly regretted their part in this election.

While an overwhelming majority of faithful Fascists dominated the list, the accession of well-known politicians from other parties was important to Mussolini because it created confidence in his regime and helped to persuade Italian bankers and industrialists to contribute large sums towards his election fighting fund – a mistake German industrialists were to repeat with Hitler.

The Conservative British press, like the Conservative Party itself, now expressed enthusiasm for Mussolini. Typical was a *Times* article of 14 February 1924 explaining the new electoral law:

> Mussolini cannot endure parliamentary routine, which takes time available for real work . . . One is glad Fascism will win because it [Fascism] is the only coherent party and it is a complete fallacy to regard it as a capitalist party. Its opponents are intellectuals and bourgeois.

Mussolini himself gave undertakings that the election campaign should be conducted without violence, and the historian Renzo De Felice has produced evidence that he did his best to keep it orderly. However, the Duce could not control his more militant Fascists. In Genoa, Milan, Turin, Udine, Savona, Urbino and Rome, opposition MPs and leaders were physically attacked. One Socialist candidate, Antonio Puccini, was murdered, and unruly Fascists attacked priests, prominent Catholic laymen and Catholic clubs. There is also evidence of intimidation of voters at the polling stations, and of tampering with the counts. Deplorably typical of Fascism as this outrageous conduct was, it had little effect on the overall result; in fact, the violence proved counter-productive as it alienated sensible voters, and in those areas where there was most violence the Fascist list fared less well.[3]

In 1924 Giacomo Matteotti was 38. Well-to-do, he had been a Socialist Deputy (MP) since 1919. He was always an outspoken opponent of Fascism, and his savage attacks in Parliament on the excesses of the Blackshirt militia in the north made him feared by the party. On 30 May 1924, six days after convocation of the new parliament following the General Election, there was a debate about the conduct of the election. Matteotti had not been expecting this issue to arise and spoke *ex tempore*, declaring that in certain constituencies the results had been affected by Fascist violence against opposition parties. He claimed there had been orgies of violence in some constituencies, and demanded that the results should be treated as 'invalid', pending enquiries. Fascist MPs interrupted continuously and there were brawls in the Chamber itself, so that a speech which should have taken half an hour lasted three times that.

The next day Mussolini's paper *Il Popolo* denounced Matteotti's speech as a 'monstrous provocation'; rumours circulated that Matteotti had prepared another speech which would expose financial scandals and corruption among Fascist leaders, especially on the part of Mussolini's brother Arnaldo. On 4 June, following a scene between the two men in the Chamber, Mussolini shouted to Matteotti: 'You should receive a charge of lead in the back.' *Impero*, a Fascist paper, wrote that the Fascist giant was about to deal its opponents 'a terrible blow', with execution squads in every piazza. The stage was set for a tragedy.

On 11 June came the news that Matteotti had disappeared, and rumours grew apace that he had been abducted by the Fascists. In fact, it later transpired that on 10 June Matteotti had been killed by Fascist thugs: as he came out of his house he was seized by kidnappers, who then stabbed him to death in a motor car.

In 1947 the Matteotti case was reopened in the Rome criminal courts. According to the evidence of Carlo Silvestri, a *Corriere della Sera* journalist and the most important witness, Matteotti's murder was committed by extreme Fascists in order to create an irrevocable breach between Mussolini and the Socialists. He claimed that Mussolini's overtures to Socialists, with the object of bringing them into his government, were much resented by militant Fascists, and maintained that Mussolini would never have given the order to kill Matteotti, because Matteotti was secretary of the Socialist Party and Mussolini at the time was seriously considering asking leading members of it to become ministers in his government.

The Matteotti murder nearly toppled Mussolini. It is unlikely that he personally gave the order to kill Matteotti, because his sophisticated political sense must have told him that such barbarity would recoil upon him. However, Mussolini had already exhibited an unsavoury taste for organizing assaults on his political opponents, and continually encouraged violence over the years; there can be no denying his moral responsibility.

It was immediately evident that the crime was a political disaster for both Mussolini and the Fascists. There was a sudden swing of public opinion against the Duce. In place of admiration for his success, the prevailing feeling was one of disillusion and hostility, together with indignation against both a specific ghastly political crime, and the continual violence of the Fascists.

Deputizing for Graham, Kennard had an interview with Mussolini on 29 September 1924; Mussolini told him that he could not for a moment tolerate the government being associated with the crime, which was not a premeditated assassination — it had not been intended to kill Matteotti, but merely to play a practical joke on him. As reported by Kennard,

> The abductors merely wished to take the Socialist deputy to a hut on the Lago di Vico, some thirty miles from Rome, and lock him up there for a short time. He had however struggled and insulted his captors, who had placed a cloth over his face and, as he was in weak health, had smothered him.

A fortnight later (8 October) Sir Ronald Graham returned from a long leave in England, saw Mussolini, and reported that he had rarely seen him in better spirits, or more genial and friendly. The Duce, telling Graham not to quote it, gave him a similar account of the murder:

> Until quite recently the enquiry had been all at sea as the accused refused to give any evidence at all. But a few days ago Dumini, the principal culprit involved, had at last made up his mind to speak. This Dumini, a young man of 27, had an English mother and his parents were rich.
>
> It was a hot day and a coat was wrapped round Matteotti's head and held there for about ten minutes. Matteotti was found to be dead, partly from suffocation and partly from cerebral congestion, for he was a delicate man, and it would be proved.

Mussolini said that as the whole affair was one of personal vendetta – 'a bestial crime carried out by one man with a few accomplices' – the government would be 'completely exonerated and all the fantastic stories which had appeared in the opposition press about the Fascists plotting to suppress a political opponent would disappear into thin air.'

In a despatch written on 29 August 1924, after his own return to Rome, Howard Kennard had noted the change in atmosphere during his two months' leave. In the second week of June 1924 Matteotti had only just disappeared,

> . . . and the fortunes of Fascismo still stood apparently as high as ever. The pro-Fascist press was extolling the doings of Signor Mussolini both at home and abroad with fulsome praise. The continual Fascist demonstrations were still hailed with enthusiasm and little sign of the approaching storm was visible. On my return I found the majority of the press sharply criticising the Government. Even making full allowance for the mercurial temperament of this people, who pull down idols as fast as they set them up, it was at first difficult to realize that so great a change would have taken place in a few weeks. Foul as the Matteotti murder was, it hardly seemed to justify so great a revulsion of feeling . . .
>
> While there is a general impression that he [Mussolini] personally may have weathered the storm, it is to be feared that this is not so much due to the blind confidence which was formerly felt in his leadership but rather to the apprehension that should he fall the pendulum might swing from the extreme right to the extreme left . . . Signor Mussolini must walk very warily during the next few months, as a single false step might prove his undoing . . . There is of course the danger that he might attempt to improve his position by some theatrical coup . . . such as the occupation of Corfu, but fortunately there seems little opportunity for his doing so for the present moment . . . There is one relatively bright spot in the present gloom and that is the economic situation which is, comparatively speaking, good. Unemployment figures continue to improve.

Kennard thought the anti-Fascist tide was swelling, and reported the general opinion to be that Mussolini's days were numbered. More alarming was the report two days later by Kennard, of 'a somewhat ludicrous panic' in Rome due to alarmist rumours that the Fascisti were contemplating a '*seconda ondata* [second *coup d'état*] or a massacre of the leaders of the Opposition and forcible reassertion of Fascist performance'; there was genuine fear, he noted, in Opposition circles.[4]

The Matteotti crime shocked public opinion in Britain. Only a few days previously, Matteotti had been well-received when he addressed a Labour Party meeting in London. The *Daily News*, the *Manchester Guardian* and the *Daily Herald* condemned the crime, and prophesied that it must, 'as it should', lead to the downfall of Fascism. The right-wing papers were non-committal; on 5 July 1924, after King Victor Emmanuel had made a call for unity, *The Times* commented:

> It is because of the murder of Matteotti by the extreme and the unreasonable section of the Fascists that the popularity of Fascism has for the time

being waned as suddenly as it emerged . . . For ourselves, we hope that Signor Mussolini, who is unquestionably a great administrator and a great political foreman of the works, will not lose his hold on the people. The whole business is a curious example of how easily power demoralises . . . when they think it unlimited.

The *Daily Mail* rallied to Mussolini, and *The Times* commented on 2 August:

Fascism will stay in power in the immediate future, [first] because there is no practical alternative given the weakness and disunity of the opposition; second, the country is more prosperous and therefore contented than for many years.

In January 1924 the *Spectator* had taken the strange course of publishing a letter from Mussolini to the British people, to enable them 'to understand the meaning of Fascism and the new inspiration of Italy'. At the time, the *Spectator* boasted that for ninety-seven years since the Risorgimento it had been 'Italianissimo', and expressed pride that the Italian Prime Minister, who was not usually available to foreign correspondents, should have sent his message through their channels. Their Rome correspondent, Amethe MacEwen, wrote:

The leader of Italian public opinion, the pilot who weathered the storm and took that mighty and beautiful ship of state 'The Italia' triumphantly into harbour during a tempest so fierce and full of dread and peril, seems to think that people here do not understand his hopes and aims. We can assure him this is not so. As ever the hearts of the English are with Italy.

As if this were not cloying enough, the editor, St Loe Strachey, a moulder of Conservative opinion, endorsed Mussolini even further by writing that the coming of Fascism to power was

. . . one of the most notable events in the social and political history of the modern world.

The most marvellous thing about the Fascist counter-revolution is that it represents a reaction to the violent breaking-up of the morale of the nation which was almost instantaneous . . . Italy found in Mussolini the Chatham of Labour.

The great impulse . . . [was] . . . 'We will not have the country divided. We have got together and we will keep together . . .' It shall show mankind that a national state cannot be overthrown by the anarchists within it, and that the forces of unity are stronger than those of disunity.

Strachey here demonstrates the right-wing British reaction to Mussolini in early 1924, despite the record of Fascist brutality. The *Spectator's* reaction to Matteotti's murder was muted; they recalled Matteotti's recent visit to London, and wrote that Mussolini's government had been greatly shaken:

> Obviously Mussolini will have to purge the administration to retain confidence . . . He is pulled one way by the extremists and the other way by the dissidents in his party.
>
> However, we cannot think that the friends of Italy will hope for the immediate fall of Fascism. It is almost certain that anarchy will return.

In early 1924 the *New Statesman* took a hostile line against Fascism, after an assault by Fascists on Professor Gaetano Salvemini of Florence University. The magazine had published an article by him on 'Fascismo and the Coming Election', attacking Mussolini's policy. Although it was couched in terms which would be regarded as fair criticism in Britain, the *New Statesman* had been warned that if Salvemini put his name to the article he might be murdered by Mussolini's agents. After its publication, a band of armed Fascists took the Professor to their Florence headquarters; they insulted him and beat him, and then pursued him and his son home with sticks. He was only saved by passing soldiers. Salvemini was told by the Florence Fascists that he would only escape further molestation if he refrained from breathing any word of criticism of Fascism. Wisely, he departed to Switzerland.

On 12 April 1924 the *New Statesman* commented that 'The Fascists are in their methods as barbarous as the Bolsheviks. For the moment at any rate foreigners cannot regard Italy as a civilised country.' The magazine did not allege that Mussolini was personally responsible for the Salvemini assault, but it felt that he could 'not avoid responsibility for it'; it feared 'armed ruffianism' would destroy Mussolini, and hoped that after his steam-roller majority in Parliament he would 'turn his dictatorship of violence into a moral dictatorship'.

After the murder, the *New Statesman* commented that:

> Mussolini's position seems to have been more severely injured by the Matteotti crime and its reverberations than even his enemies had ventured to hope, and it is not impossible that in the near future he may be forced to resign.
>
> Of Signor Mussolini's full responsibility for the murder . . . there can be no doubt. He may realize that his moral authority is all that he needs and that he can rule Italy without force or daggers, and if having realized that he proceeds to abandon his irregular forces and to punish crime as it should be punished irrespective of the political views of the criminals; and if at the same time he stamps out the financial corruption which has become so marked a feature of his regime . . . then he may regain the respect of the world and earn the reputation of a great patriot statesman

. . . Certainly Signor Mussolini is a patriot; certainly he is strong; certainly he has worked wonders in the political reorganization of post-war Italy; and certainly he has justly earned the confidence of his fellow countrymen.

At this time the *New Statesman*, like the *Daily Herald*, had been banned in Italy.

The Liberal weekly journal *The Economist* was more antagonistic to Mussolini after the Matteotti murder than *The Times* or the *Spectator*. On 5 July 1924, after outlining how the most important Italian opposition journals had had their 'mouths stopped', that many clubs and cafés had been closed and many suspected revolutionaries arrested, *The Economist* pointed out that Mussolini 'stands near the edge of the precipice, and if we are asked whether we want Mussolini down we say quite frankly "Yes".' However, by 15 November 1924 *The Economist* was noting that 'a constitutional regime seems in a fair way to being restored'.

In December 1924 the King could have dismissed Mussolini, and indeed several times, in private, threatened to do so. He would not act, however, without a clear parliamentary vote against Mussolini. And at the end of 1924 Mussolini, after a period of dithering, and considering a coalition, decided to trust to his gambler's luck, and plump for a dictatorship.

His decision was triggered by the publication in *Il Mondo* on 27 December by the disloyal Cesare Rossi (head of the Duce's press office, and suspected of being involved in the murder) of a memorandum accusing Mussolini of being responsible for Matteotti's murder; the memorandum was republished in the *Corriere della Sera* on 27 and 28 December. Simultaneously, a group of Fascist Party leaders told Mussolini that he could no longer sit on the fence, and that the Fascists would only stay loyal to him if he initiated strong government. Mussolini yielded, and prepared to counter-attack. He gave orders for anti-Fascist newspapers to be banned, and prepared the Fascist militia for drastic action.

On 2 January 1925 the Rome correspondent of *The Times* reported that Mussolini 'was finished'; on 3 January that it was 'confidently expected' that Mussolini would announce the resignation of his government; that his ultimate resignation was inevitable, 'but not today'; and that a Giolitti–Amendola government of the left would arrest and imprison Mussolini, with disastrous results for the peace of the country. But he could not have been more wrong.

Encouraged by Margherita Sarfatti, in parliament on 3 January, Mussolini boldly outlined his change of course.

In his speech he said:

> I here declare before this chamber and before the whole Italian people
> that I alone assume the political, moral and historical responsibility for all
> that has happened . . . If Fascism has a criminal association I am the head
> of that association . . . If all the acts of violence have been the result of a
> certain political, historical and moral climate, well then mine is the
> responsibility.

He challenged his opponents to impeach him. This was mere
rhetoric; he did not intend that they should do so, and when a censure
motion was tabled, immediately proposed an adjournment. He was
acutely nervous before his speech, but the weakness of the Opposition's reaction made him confident that he could successfully bid for a
dictatorship. This day sounded the death-knell of civil liberties in Italy.

Immediately the Fascist militia went into action. Ninety-five politically suspect clubs were suppressed, and a hundred branches of the
anti-Fascist 'Free Italy Association'. House searches were made, and
there were many arrests of anti-Fascists. The prefects were ordered to
take strong action against any signs of anti-Fascism; the press laws were
rigorously applied to ban newspapers carrying anti-Fascist articles,
and a number of journalists were arrested. As he tightened his grip on
dictatorship, Mussolini summed up his policy: 'We want to make the
nation Fascist (*fascistizzare la nazione*).' The Opposition papers were
censored: *La Stampa* and *Corriere della Sera* carried no political
comment on the next days.

The British press was ambivalent regarding Mussolini's coup. The
left wanted him out; the right was muted. On 6 January the *Daily
News* declared forthrightly against him, describing his speech as that of
a desperate man 'throwing off all constitutional pretences'.

> The mentality of a man like Signor Mussolini leaves us in no astonish-
> ment at anything he may say or do. How far and how long he will be able
> to impose his will upon an angry and disillusioned people will depend
> upon how far and how long he can retain the disciplined allegiance of the
> armed forces at his command. But Italy is not Russia; and if he seeks to
> carry out his threats to the last audacity it is quite possible that a popular
> *coup de main* will sweep away Mussolini and Mussolinism for ever.

The *Daily News* also reported that in Brussels the Executive
Committee of the Socialist International had passed a Resolution
expressing indignation at recent events and sympathy with the Italian
proletariat. On 20 January they wrote that 'political chaos [in Italy]
was complete'.

The *New Statesman* stated on 10 January 1925 that 'If we are asked
whether we want Mussolini out we say quite frankly "YES". Fascism

has behaved barbarously with its castor oil and revolvers and Mussolini has for long been surrounded by shady characters.' The article deplored the closing of clubs, cafés and ex-servicemen's institutes, as well as the arrests and the house searches, and declared that the continuation of Fascist domination was not in the best interests of either Italy or the rest of the world.*

Three months earlier (24 October 1924) the *New Statesman* had declared that Fascism was recovering its strength after the Matteotti murder, and that Mussolini still had 'the support of the vast masses of middle and professional classes throughout Italy', although they felt it was the man and not the creed which was accepted, and that the Matteotti affair had broken the reputations of many of Mussolini's colleagues, while revelations of Fascist dishonesty 'had their effect'. They criticized the violent denunciations of Mussolini on the part of Communists in other countries, especially France, which had drawn from Salandra, the liberal leader, a declaration of renewed loyalty to 'Il Duce'. They also felt that the murder of the prominent Fascist Casalini had contributed to Mussolini's recovery in popularity.

On 6 January *The Times* reported Mussolini as saying in his speech that he had been 'accused of forming a Cheka' (Russian secret police), and as claiming that the occupation of Corfu had been beneficial to Italy. They noted that while some sections of the Italian press had proclaimed his speech as another personal 'victory' for Mussolini, the *Corriere della Sera* and *La Stampa* had carried no political comment on it, and the *Lavoro* of Genoa had ceased publication. In spite of this, *The Times* leader declared,

> Mussolini appears to have grasped the situation with his usual sagacity. It remains to be seen whether a great modern state can long be ruled, even when that system brings such significant benefits as Fascism, with the tyrannical but efficient rule of Signor Mussolini.

The *Spectator* now back-pedalled on its enthusiasm for Mussolini's regime, writing on 3 January that the Rossi memorandum published on 27 December 'inculpates Mussolini in many of the worst deeds of violence which have disgraced the Fascist regime . . . he is revealed (if Rossi's document is correct) as one of the most violent and utterly lawless of the Fascists.' They described it as 'ominous' that he had suppressed the Opposition newspapers; a week later they noted that 'force is now in the ascendancy. The Saviour of Italy has returned to his orig-

---

* They also quoted a story about Curzon which was going round the clubs: Asked what he was doing at the Zoo, the Foreign Secretary replied, 'I am watching the lions, to practise the appropriate expression to wear at my forthcoming meeting with Signor Mussolini.'

inal method, and in a country which has once tasted constitutionalism this cannot last.'

The *Manchester Guardian* headline of 5 January was 'Mussolini attacks. All pretence of pacification abandoned', and their Rome correspondent wrote: 'The day has been one of pronounced success for Mussolini . . . The only thing to be hoped for now is that the return of the current of reaction may not bring with it grave violence on both sides.' In their leader on that day the *Manchester Guardian* summed up:

> Most of us have willingly assumed that, although the murders of Matteotti and other opponents of Fascism were committed in the interests of the Fascist party, they were done without his [Mussolini's] connivance and against his wishes. Signor Rossi, who is himself under arrest for complicity in the murder of Matteotti, has now made statements which if true incriminate Signor Mussolini himself. In any constitutionally governed country a Minister lying under such a charge would not rest until he had cleared his character before a court of law. Signor Mussolini does nothing of the sort. He tries to hush up the charge by suppressing newspapers in which it is published. He defies the Chamber which he has packed to impeach him if it dares; in fact, anyone who wants to go the way of Matteotti is welcome to get up and propose such an impeachment.

The *Daily News* leader on 10 January was also sharply critical:

> Why is the prospect of his fall anticipated without regret almost everywhere and with unconcealed satisfaction by men of liberal mind and sympathies all over the world . . . he set up a tyranny . . . There will be no quiet return to 'normality' for Italy after its doses of castor oil.★ It is easy for any violent fool given the power to close clubs and arrest alleged revolutionaries and burn the offices of opponents, and even to condone their murder.

By this time the *Daily Herald*'s Rome correspondent had been expelled from Italy. He took up residence in Lugano, on the Swiss border, from where he was able to provide accurate reports of the political situation such as would have caused the expulsion of British journalists living in Rome. His remarkable report of 8 January 1925 gave details of Mussolini's interview with a delegation of extreme Fascists headed by Roberto Farinacci, and alleged that Farinacci had threatened Mussolini with the same fate as Matteotti, saying that in the face of such determination Mussolini 'gave way and without the least warning proclaimed in his now famous speech his decision to finish with the Opposition within 48 hours.'

Mussolini's speech of 3 January 1925 marked the beginning of dicta-

---

★ Fascist thugs forced their victims to drink large quantities of castor oil.

torial Fascist rule. By a succession of Enabling Acts, Mussolini now governed by decree. He had little in the way of a long-term programme but made decisions *ad hoc* – censoring the press, taking into central government hands the conduct of both the judiciary and provincial government – creating a totalitarian state by one measure after another.

Mussolini became responsible, no longer to parliament, but only to the King, who never questioned his decisions; the Grand Council of Fascism became part of the Constitution in December 1928, while the local Fascist parties became, in effect, organs of the State, as a type of militia, with the duty of enforcing obedience. The Fascists were no longer a political party – the term 'party' now became as much a misnomer for the Fascists as it was for the Communists of Russia or for the Nazis of Germany after Hitler became Chancellor. Political parties compete for the right to govern: once the Fascist Party possessed this, it had no rivals and existed only to carry out the dictates of the Head of State. The Constitution of 1932, produced to celebrate the tenth anniversary of the March on Rome, enshrined the position thus in its first article: 'The national Fascist Party is a civil militia at the orders of the Duce at the service of the Fascist State.'

Italian trade unions were officially suppressed, on the orders of Mussolini, following a meeting between Confindustria (The Employers' Association) and the Confederation of Fascist Syndical Corporations on 2 October 1925 under the chairmanship of Roberto Farinacci, Chairman of the Fascist Party, at the Palazzo Vidoni, the Fascist headquarters.

Agreement was reached to the assertion by Fascism of full and sole control over organized labour. Factory councils were made illegal; Chambers of Labour were occupied by the police; strikes and lockouts became illegal; and all wage contracts were given the full force of law, with provision for compulsory arbitration. The Palazzo Vidoni agreement signed by employers and worker representatives marked the death of Italian trade unionism under Fascism.

In 1926 a confederation of employers and workers was formed covering all industry, the armed forces, and civil and local government employees. All workers and employers were enrolled in organizations controlled by the Secretary of the Fascist Party. This was the main institutional basis of Mussolini's Corporate State, by which he brought under his control all the nation's means of production and at the same time fixed wages and prices. In some ways it proved successful, and right-wing statesmen and social theorists in other countries described it in glowing terms as 'the Italian experience'.[5]

Italian trade unionists had strong ties with their British counterparts, and this fierce attack on trade unionism was much resented in

Britain, as were Fascist attacks on the Italian Socialist co-operatives which British Socialists admired. In a long article in the *Observer* and a report to the Embassy in Rome, Lina Waterfield gave an account of atrocities in Molinella near Bologna, where the Fascists disrupted a long-established, thriving Socialist agricultural co-operative group with 7,000 farming members, causing much hardship. The British Embassy commented to London that her report threw 'a lurid light on the seamy side of Fascism', but when Lena urged that Sir Charles Trevelyan, Minister of Education, should raise the matter in Parliament, Sir Ronald Graham advised caution, for fear that Mussolini would expel her from Italy. However, Lena subsequently had a friendly interview with Mussolini who, after hearing her complaint, promised to curb Fascist excesses at Molinella.[6]

On 27 July 1925 Graham wrote:

> Government and Opposition leaders have practically no dealings with each other.
>
> Foreign pressmen are naturally influenced against the Fascist Government, not only by the disrespect Signor Mussolini has shown against the sacrosanct rights of the press but also owing to the fact that they naturally come into closer contact with journalists of the Opposition newspapers than with the very mediocre contributors to the Fascist press. On the other hand, I admit that it is difficult for this Embassy not to fall under a certain degree of official and social influence in the opposite direction. Any suspicion of undue sympathy with the Opposition would have destroyed my usefulness here to British interests with a Government which has lasted for nearly three years and does not seem to be menaced by any immediate fall, and with a statesman who is, I believe, more satisfactory to deal with and more friendly disposed towards Great Britain than any of his immediate predecessors . . .
>
> It may be said that the country acquiesces in the present regime because it is relatively prosperous and is at least able to do its work without over-much disturbance, because any conditions are better than those of 1919 to 1922, because it is sick of politics, and also because it is in no way convinced that the fall of Mussolini and the advancement of the Opposition would result in an improved situation. To sum up, Signor Mussolini seems more firmly in the saddle than ever.

A Special Tribunal was created in 1926 to adjudicate on crimes against the State (by which was meant attacks on the Fascist Party). Culprits had their goods sequestrated and were sentenced to imprisonment, or to confinement with comparative freedom on islands or other such isolated places. Forty-two sentences of death were passed during the Special Tribunal's seventeen years of existence (many of those sentenced were granted clemency), and 4,600 were condemned to imprisonment or confinement. The Tribunal also dealt with pederasty, the Mafia, and so on. It was unacceptably undemocratic, but not an expression of ferocious dictatorship.

From his Embassy in Rome Sir Ronald Graham saw the evolution of the Fascist state through rose-coloured spectacles, writing in a despatch to Austen Chamberlain of 28 July 1926:

> Things are being attempted here today with confidence, energy, and already some measure of success that were never thought of before or never undertaken with any heart owing to the inevitable pre-supposition of failure. There are dragons still in the way, old weaknesses and old scandals that persist, but I do not believe it possible for any experienced and unprejudiced observer to deny that there is a new spirit working strongly in this country, a new faith and determination.

Graham also wrote glowingly of the suppression of trade unions, describing Mussolini's attempt to solve the industrial problem as his 'pet child', about which he had shown a boyish enthusiasm during a recent conversation, declaring his conviction that 'he had put an end once and for all to industrial disputes in Italy' because when capital and labour met at a round table under the presence of a Government nominee they 'would invariably reach agreement'. When Graham suggested to him that if labour were represented by leaders like the British Mr Cook (Secretary of the Miners' Union, who enjoyed in his day a reputation similar to that of Arthur Scargill), friendly solutions would not be so easy, Mussolini replied that if there were a labour leader in Italy like Mr Cook 'he would have long since been taking an enforced rest cure on some remote island in the Adriatic'.

Graham appears to have had little idea of the red-hot anger of British trade unionists at the suppression of their Italian brethren. At all events, Austen Chamberlain conveyed to Graham his 'high appreciation of the very able and interesting summary'.[7]

The next year, in a despatch dated 15 July 1927, Graham shaded down his golden view of the advantages of corporatism over free trade union wage bargaining:

> I learn that in various concerns the employers have met their workmen for a friendly discussion and have suggested that wages should be reduced, but in every case the employees have refused to consider the problem or to contemplate any reduction either in wages or in increased cost of living (*caro vivere*) bonus. In some cases they offered to work an extra hour, but as most industries are already on short time and more stock is being produced than can be disposed of, this was not helpful.

On 9 July 1927 twelve representatives of the federated organizations, selected by their colleagues, had called upon the Duce to express their views. Graham learnt that their reception by Mussolini had been extremely unsympathetic, the Duce having accused them of being unreasonable and grasping and wanting to bring down the value of the lira (he had revalued it, with unfortunate consequences); Graham noted that the deputation had left 'in a depressed and somewhat irritated frame of mind'. However, his verdict was that Mussolini was a nice man who was great enough 'to make a sudden and radical change of policy' if devaluation of the lira became necessary.[8]

In public, Austen Chamberlain was fulsome about Mussolini, describing him as a 'strong man of singular charm . . . and not a little tenderness and loneliness of heart . . . I am confident that he is a patriot and a sincere man; I trust his word when given and I think we might easily go far before finding an Italian with whom it would be so easy for the British Government to work.'

Winston Churchill, who had become Baldwin's Chancellor of the Exchequer in 1924, was equally enthusiastic for Mussolini. In January 1926, against the advice of his Treasury officials, Churchill as we shall see negotiated a generous settlement of Italy's war debts to Britain, and during a visit to Genoa in 1927 he described the atmosphere of Fascism, writing to his wife, 'This country gives the impression of discipline, order, goodwill and smiling faces.' He went on to Rome, where he told journalists he could not help being charmed by the Italian dictator:

> Anyone could see that he thought of nothing but the lasting good . . . of the Italian people . . . it was quite absurd to suggest that the Italian Government does not stand upon a popular basis or that it is not upheld by the active and practical assent of the great masses . . . if I had been an Italian I am sure I would have been wholeheartedly with you from the start . . . your movement has rendered service to the whole world.

Such praise from the Chancellor of the Exchequer aroused a furore in Labour circles. In 1933 Churchill praised Mussolini as the 'Roman genius', describing him as 'the greatest lawgiver amongst living men'.[9]

While Mussolini basked in the admiration of British Conservatives, the British Trade Union Movement writhed in rage. Their indignation surfaced when in early November 1925 it became likely that Mussolini would visit London again for the formal signing of the Locarno agreements. Many unions tabled resolutions declaring that Mussolini was not a fit and proper person to be received as an honoured guest, and urging that if he came he should be boycotted by 'leaders of the Trade Union and Co-operative movements and by the leaders of the Labour Party'.

John Bromley, secretary of the rail drivers' union ASLEF, told the *Daily Herald* on 17 November 1925:

Railwaymen generally are both good trade unionists and co-operators, and they have naturally with dismay and indignation seen the suppression of trade unions and co-operative societies under the Mussolini regime. Although our union as such has not considered the question, it would not surprise me at all to find some of the stronger trade union footplate men refusing to work a train through if they knew the oppressor was on it.[10]

Sensitive to this criticism, Mussolini decided not to come to London in person for the signing of the Locarno Treaty.

CHAPTER 5

Locarno, the Briand Plan and the Austro-German Customs Union

NEGOTIATIONS FOR THE Locarno Pact to guarantee the post-1919 frontiers between Germany, France and Belgium began in January 1925 with a German Memorandum issued by Dr Gustav Stresemann, the German Minister for Foreign Affairs. During his previous short period as Chancellor, from August to November 1923, Stresemann had already taken the initiative by calling off passive resistance to the French occupation of the Ruhr and lifting the ban on reparations deliveries. Although he was Chancellor for only a few months he remained Foreign Minister until his death in 1929, and he was intent on negotiating a settlement with France, Britain and Italy. His policy, which inspired a much improved relationship between Germany and France, was to allay hostility and produce European pacification. He was never reconciled to Germany's loss of territory in the east under the terms of the Treaty of Versailles, but steadfastly dismissed any idea of using force to recover it.

Stresemann's Memorandum of January 1925 proposed that Britain, France, Germany and Italy should enter 'into a solemn obligation for a lengthy period not to go to war'. A Pact was suggested, under which the four states would bind themselves reciprocally to observe the inviolability of the present territorial status on the Rhine, 'and, jointly and individually, [to] the fulfilment of the obligation to demilitarize the Rhineland which Germany had undertaken in Articles 42 and 43 of the Treaty of Versailles.' Proposals were also put forward for the removal of British and French troops of occupation from the Rhineland, and Germany indicated her readiness to abandon claims to Alsace and Lorraine.

On 12 March Sir Ronald Graham spoke to Salvatore Contarini, Secretary General to the Italian Foreign Office; Contarini said that Italy would support Britain if Chamberlain wanted to go ahead, but that the idea of an Anglo-French-Belgian Pact 'was particularly distasteful to the Italian Government. They would dislike being omitted from such a combination but would be equally reluctant to join it . . . to reject it without consideration would be a grave mistake.'

However, on 3 April Graham reported from Rome that Italy would agree to a Guarantee Pact (to include Belgium); in an interview with Austen Chamberlain, Della Toretta, the Italian Ambassador in London, also confirmed his government's favourable view.[1]

By 25 March Viscount d'Abernon, the British Ambassador in Berlin, was able to report that the German government was ready to discuss modifications of the proposal to achieve agreement. It was now suggested that as part of the Pact, Germany should become a member of the League of Nations.

On 17 April 1925 Aristide Briand replaced Édouard Herriot as French Foreign Minister, and French hostility to the proposed Pact disappeared. Briand was one of the most remarkable men in modern French history; he was Prime Minister on twelve occasions, and Foreign Minister for seven years between 1925 and 1932. He and Austen Chamberlain were firm friends. Briand was from Nantes, unlike Poincaré, whose part of France had been occupied by the Germans in both 1870 and 1914; this was a factor in his greater sympathy with the Germans.

Conversations between Briand and Chamberlain in London produced agreement over draft terms for the Pact, and these, couched in conciliatory language, were sent to the Germans in reply to their Note. The main difficulty was the nature of the action to be taken in the event of German remilitarization of the Rhineland in breach of Articles 42 and 43 of the Treaty of Versailles. Stresemann's reaction was favourable, and arrangements were made for a meeting of the five parties in Locarno on 5 October.

The Rome Embassy reported to London that Mussolini accepted the proposed terms 'without reserve'. At first Mussolini had been somewhat disturbed by the absence of any guarantee affecting the Italian frontier on the Brenner Pass, but eventually concluded that the Pact 'while not affording Italy any special guarantee, will be to her general interest and advantage'.

The behaviour of the Italian delegation was impeccable when the talks began at Locarno between Germany, France, Britain, Belgium and Italy. After initial rumblings over the return to Germany of some of her colonies, the Italian representative Scialoja declared that Italy would definitely adhere to the Pact. This chapter of happy Anglo-Italian relations owed much to the Chamberlain–Mussolini friendship, without which, as Sir Ronald Graham surmised, Mussolini might well have gone off in a different direction. At Mussolini's request

Italian newspapers emphasized the value of Chamberlain's contribution, and contrasted Italy's position at Locarno with that which she had occupied at Paris immediately after the war.

On 29 September Mussolini had been violently attacked in the *Daily News*, who accused him *inter alia* of wanting to negotiate a triple alliance with Germany and Russia as a counter-stroke to Locarno (there may well have been something in this). The Italian Embassy had complained to the Foreign Office, and Austen Chamberlain had replied:

> Please tell Mussolini that I deplore this attack but that I cannot control the newspapers of our own Party, still less those of the Opposition. Mussolini can however give a triumphant refutation of these silly attacks in the most dignified and unanswerable form by attending personally the Conference, fixed at Locarno especially to suit his convenience, and assisting us in the negotiations by his authority and experience.

Mussolini replied that he would do his best to take part, but asserted that his plans could not be affected by 'journalistic fables'.[2]

The *Daily News* story was headlined 'Mussolini's Wild Dream: Ally of Soviet':

> Benito Mussolini, acclaimed by legend as the man who saved Italy from Bolshevism, has made proposals to Moscow for an alliance with Soviet Russia.
>
> More than that, he has sought – so far without success – to gain the adhesion of Germany to the projected Treaty so as to constitute a new Triple Alliance directed mainly against France but also against Great Britain. Although Italy is to be represented at the coming Security Conference [Locarno] her Dictator Premier has used his most strenuous efforts to dissuade Germany from entering the Pact.

The truth is obscure. Mussolini was always unpredictable: he may have entertained such thoughts and even discussed them.

Indeed, Sir Ronald Graham had already reported, in July 1923, that one direction in which Italy might eventually proceed was towards Russia:

> . . . there were signs already of this trend, and a friendly association of interests with Russia might help towards the fruition of other ambitions, not solely commercial. Nor is an eventual reversion towards Germany to be excluded if France continues in her present negative attitude towards Italy and Italian interests . . . It would be rash to assume that Italy is inevitably yoked to the car of the Western Powers.
>
> Signor Mussolini is determined that Italy's signature shall be essential to European contracts. My conclusion is that Italy must inevitably gravitate towards the Power or group of Powers ready to assist her in the expansion towards which she must eventually be driven by irresistible force.

On this despatch Harold Nicolson minuted: 'The bother of asking Italy to dinner is that when they arrive they are apt to order their own wine and when it comes to pay the bill it is discovered that they have selected the most expensive.'[3]

According to Austen Chamberlain, Briand was not sorry that Mussolini had not come personally to the Locarno deliberations; he said that Briand felt the view from the terrace more than compensated for the absence of the Prime Minister of Italy. But suddenly, on 14 October, when agreement had been reached among the delegates, Mussolini informed Sir Ronald Graham that he would after all go to Locarno. He wanted Austen Chamberlain to know, reported Graham, that he was going there 'almost entirely to see you because he knew you wished him to come'.

When Chamberlain and Mussolini met in Locarno on 15 October, Mussolini was most cordial, reiterating Graham's message that he had only come from a desire to meet Chamberlain. Mussolini told Chamberlain he had not raised the question of the Brenner frontier lest Germany raise the question whether Germany and Austria should be united, thus inviting 'the danger which he wished to avoid'. Chamberlain recorded that nothing of great consequence passed between them, yet the interview was valuable because it confirmed their cordial personal relations, which had proved so useful in settling Anglo-Italian differences. At the final session, at which the Treaties were initialled, Mussolini said, 'I believe that when the Treaties become, as they must, a living reality, a new era must open in the history of the world.'

While the Locarno Conference was in progress and before his own descent upon it, Mussolini told Graham in Rome that Germany's pose as a defenceless lamb amongst wolves was absurd while she possessed an excellent and well-equipped army of at least 400,000 men, probably the most powerful military power in Europe next to France. Mussolini expressed his intention to draw Stresemann's attention to this in a friendly way at Locarno, if the opportunity arose.[4]

By the terms of the Locarno Treaty, Britain actually weakened her obligation to come to the help of France if Germany menaced her, becoming liable only in the case of a flagrant violation of the Treaty of Versailles (including remilitarization of the Rhineland) on Germany's western frontiers.

Austen Chamberlain's attitude was that 'every measure of alleviation should be granted to the German government, and everything possible done to mark that Britain's future relations with Germany were on a wholly new footing.'[5] The great difference between Versailles and Locarno was that in the negotiations at Locarno

Germany was treated as an equal, not a defeated, power. The agreement guaranteed Germany's western frontiers in return for a pledge to keep the Rhineland demilitarized, and it was agreed that Germany should become a member of the League of Nations.

Locarno was a Treaty of Mutual Guarantee, with the obligations of France to Germany the same as the obligations of Germany to France, while the obligations of the guaranteeing powers (Italy and Great Britain) were the same to Germany as to France and Belgium. In the event of a future Franco-German conflict, Great Britain and Italy undertook to throw all their weight, both material and moral, on whichever side was considered to be innocent of aggression; it also assured a (supposedly) disarmed Germany against any abuse of strength by a fully-armed France and her allies. The weakness of Locarno was that it left the frontiers of Poland, Czechoslovakia and Austria unguaranteed against rupture by Germany. With Stresemann in power Germany presented no threat in these areas; but Hitler and the Nazis ranted against the terms of Locarno, claiming that the treaty maintained the hated frontiers laid down at Versailles. Its reception in Germany was cold.

Locarno marked a triumph for Austen Chamberlain who, throwing himself whole-heartedly into the struggle for agreement, had been able to use his close personal friendships with Briand and Stresemann and his cordial relations with Mussolini to good advantage.

The Locarno agreements were initialled at a moving ceremony on 16 October, and the actual signing of the Treaty was scheduled for 1 December 1925, in London.

Denis Mack Smith has written that Locarno was 'one of those many pieces of paper' which Mussolini signed for little other reason than to avoid being left out on his own, and that Mussolini was 'glad to sign almost any Treaty because Treaties always made news and so gave him a sense of importance'. This is a harsh judgement; Mussolini genuinely believed, as did the other Powers, that Locarno improved the chances of a lasting peace in Europe.[6]

Two unfortunate incidents marred Mussolini's visit to Locarno. The head of the Belgian delegation, Émile Vandervelde, a moderate Socialist who had known and disliked Mussolini during the latter's early Socialist days, refused to shake hands with him; and journalists rebuffed him. Chamberlain noted Vandervelde's discourtesy 'with deep regret', and asked Graham to communicate this regret to Mussolini. As to the journalists, when Mussolini gave a press conference in his hotel, all but two of the foreign correspondents boycotted the meeting, as a protest against news censorship in Italy. The assembled journalists refused to walk from the foyer of the hotel to the room reserved for the Press Conference. When Mussolini returned to the foyer he angrily asked a London journalist if he were a Communist. 'No,' replied the journalist. 'Then I am mistaken,' said the Duce; whereupon a Dutch journalist said, 'That often happens to you.'

Austen Chamberlain's friendship was, in Ivone Kirkpatrick's words, 'balm to Mussolini's egotistical soul', and Anglo-Italian relations 'remained for many years unclouded by any difference'; this was evidenced by Britain's approval of the Treaty of Tirana, an Italo-Albanian Pact signed on 27 November 1926 by which what amounted to an Italian protectorate was established in Albania, much to the exasperation of the French and Yugoslavs.

Mussolini intended to come to London for the formal signing of the Locarno Treaty but, as we have seen, hostile articles appeared in the *Daily News*, *Daily Herald* and *Manchester Guardian*; the Italian Embassy in London warned him of the danger of Labour Party and Trade Union demonstrations against him, and he decided to send Scialoja instead.[7]

After Locarno Austen Chamberlain, worn out by his endeavours, spent a long holiday over Christmas at Rapallo in Italy, where he was visited by Mussolini. Chamberlain recorded most friendly talks with the Duce, and his singular charm.[8]

Inspired by Mussolini, the Italian press unanimously expressed the 'greatest satisfaction' at the result of the Locarno Conference, and the opinion that it gave hopes of a period of genuine peace.

On 17 September 1926 the high point of Franco-German postwar co-operation and friendship was reached at Thoiry in the French Jura, near Geneva, when, in secret, with only an interpreter present, Briand and Stresemann met at a small hotel and, cheered by good food and wine, reached important agreements in a friendly manner. Austen Chamberlain approved of the meeting and had in advance given Briand *carte blanche* to agree the best possible solutions.

Briand and Stresemann agreed that German war guilt should be wiped out; Germany should have colonial mandates; the Saar should be returned to Germany without a plebiscite; and the Rhineland should be evacuated within a year. Germany would repurchase the Saar mines for around 300 million gold marks, and buy back the industrial districts of Eupen and Malmédy from Belgium. At this time the economies of Belgium and France were in difficulty, and would be greatly strengthened by the large payments which Germany, with a basically strong economy, could for the foreseeable future afford.

At a press conference in Geneva on 23 September Stresemann, with Chamberlain at his side, recited his achievements at Thoiry. The agreements reached with Briand received wide publicity, and were held to herald a new dawn in Europe. Stresemann stressed the point that as a result of the Locarno Treaty and his meeting with Briand, Germany would receive a colonial mandate and the occupation of the Rhineland would be terminated. Austen Chamberlain was delighted with the outcome, but feared that the two statesmen 'dreamed dreams and saw visions that will not be easily realized'. (Though he could not know it, the economic blizzard soon to blow across the world was to make nonsense of the financial implications of Thoiry; once the Depression began, Germany could not afford to make the promised payments to France and Germany.)

After his visit to Geneva in September 1926 to be present when the League of Nations made Germany a member, Chamberlain went for a Mediterranean cruise. Mussolini went to Livorno on 30 September especially to meet him, and insisted that Chamberlain should inspect an Italian destroyer so that he might be given a 19-gun salute. Chamberlain spent five hours with Mussolini, later describing their talk as 'frank and cordial'. Mussolini approved of the outcome of Thoiry, but appeared to be anxious lest meetings of such a private and confidential nature between France and Germany be carried too far, thus weakening the Locarno Treaty, which he saw as the basis of European policy. Chamberlain expressed agreement, but reassured him that neither Briand nor Stresemann would depart from the terms of Locarno. Mussolini spoke with regret of recent misunderstandings over Albania; they finally agreed on the importance of 'maintaining complete harmony', and jointly promised to communicate fully and frankly with one another.

Chamberlain recorded after Thoiry that he had had 'very satisfactory conversations' with both Mussolini and Briand, and that they all three wanted to develop the policy of Locarno as the best security for peace and progress.[9] Mussolini recorded that Chamberlain had shown Fascist sympathies, and that Lady Chamberlain had worn a Fascist badge. Passing through Paris on his way home, Chamberlain called to see Briand, to kill rumours that his meeting with Mussolini had had any sinister significance.

In a private letter of 14 October to Lord Crewe, the British Ambassador in Paris, Austen Chamberlain informed him that he had spoken to Rosso, the Italian Chargé d'Affaires in London, in pursuance of a suggestion by Briand about the necessity of 'moderation in the language of the Italian press and indeed in Mussolini's own utterances'. The Italian account states that Chamberlain told Rosso Briand had complained that certain newspaper reports and speeches in Italy were felt in France to be wounding and irritating, damaging relations between the two countries, though Briand had always tried to suppress his resentment. Chamberlain must have felt sure of his friendship with Mussolini to embark on criticism of the sensitive Duce.

Chamberlain informed Briand that in his talk with Mussolini at Livorno the Thoiry meeting was considered a natural development of the politics of reconciliation and collaboration, of which the basis had been formulated at Locarno, and that Mussolini had agreed with him that, as such, Thoiry must be looked on 'with sympathy by all the Locarno signatories'. Chamberlain clearly felt he had encouraged Mussolini to be friendly towards France, and Briand told Chamberlain that he held Mussolini 'in great esteem and had sincere sympathy with him'; Chamberlain must have worked hard to elicit this expression of approval from Briand.[10]

Both Sir Austen and Lady Chamberlain seem to have succumbed to Mussolini's charm. In a memorandum dated 20 October 1926 prepared for the Imperial Conference in London, Chamberlain wrote:

> The fortunes of Italy are directed by a very remarkable man ... he became the founder of a new political system and the creator of a new Italy. It is not my business to approve or to blame his creed or his actions in the sphere of internal politics. He is the Government and it is my business to get on with him, but this I will permit myself to say – that no one can form a fair judgement of his course who had not taken some pains to inform himself as to the conditions of political corruption, social anarchy, industrial strife, and national degeneracy from which he sought to save the country. If there be acts of his which excite severe criticism, no candid observer will deny that alike at home and abroad he has given a new life and a new standing to Italy.

Chamberlain told the Conference that relations between London and Rome were most cordial; Mussolini was a man of his word, and

> we have settled without any serious difficulty two or three questions which in other hands might have given rise to a serious crisis ... For my part I frankly confess that I hold it as a misfortune for the peace of the world that the expectations which Italy had been encouraged to entertain when she entered the war were not more fully satisfied than they were.

He went on to suggest that the Fascist regime had restored the international prestige of Italy, seriously undermined by a series of feeble post-war governments: 'Mussolini is a man of shrewd sense and I am confident that he does not mean to embark on a policy of aggression which the resources of his country would be unable to sustain.' According to Chamberlain, Albania was the danger spot: Italy felt she could not afford to see the Albanian coast fall into other hands.

At this time Chamberlain also instructed his Foreign Office officials to be as accommodating as possible to Mussolini; on 7 October 1926 he wrote:

> Italy wants above all things now to be treated as a great power on a footing of equality with France, Germany and ourselves . . . what she asks is more a moral satisfaction than material concessions. Let us keep this constantly in mind. Mussolini said to Sir W. Tyrell, 'You treat me like a gentleman and the others don't' . . . let us rather seek opportunities for consultation, for confidence, and the like. Fine manners (if not fine words) will butter more parsnips in Italy than anywhere else; and it is essential that we should keep Italy, a growing power, in sympathy with our policy and co-opera-tion with us.[11]

Italy's entry into the First World War on the Allied side in 1915 had resulted in her borrowing extensively from both Britain and, later, the United States. At the beginning of 1925 she owed £576 million to Britain, and £415 million to the US. Mussolini recruited a leading Fascist industrialist, Alberto Pirelli, to help his Finance Minister, Count Volpi, conduct negotiations over the repayment of these loans in London and Washington.

Negotiations in Washington went smoothly. Mussolini's popularity in the US was considerable, helped by numerous articles by him (ghosted by Margherita Sarfatti) published in the Hearst press which convinced much American public opinion that his dictatorship was benign. In November 1925 Count Volpi and his team reached agree-ment with President Coolidge and his advisors on terms highly favourable to Italy.

London was another matter. In February 1925 there was tension between Britain and Italy over Albania, whose government wanted to establish a *gendarmerie* trained by a Colonel Stirling and other British officers; Albania had also given a concession to the Anglo-Persian Oil Company over a large part of their territory: Mussolini complained bitterly to Britain. In March 1925 Miles Lampson of the Italian Department of the Foreign Office wrote to Sir Otto Niemeyer at the Treasury, expressing the opinion that there was no reason why Britain should display 'any undue leniency to her [Italy] over the war debts', and that Italy could not come to Britain and expect huge financial sacrifices while simultaneously blocking Britain over perfectly *bona fide* British interests in the Anglo-Persian Oil Company's concession in Albania.

Austen Chamberlain handled the matter tactfully; the British officers were withdrawn, and the Italians were awarded a concession for oil exploration outside the area being exploited by the Anglo-Persian Oil Company. To Chamberlain Mussolini stressed the suscept-ibilities of Italian opinion over Albania, and the difficulties this created for his government, but assured the British Foreign Secretary that he desired to treat the matter 'as between friends and to prevent it affecting our friendship'.[12]

In June 1925 the British government issued a Note to the nations to whom she had lent money during the war, asking them to submit definite proposals for the cash settlement of their debts.

A cynical letter of 5 January 1925 from Sir Frederick Leith Ross of the Treasury to Miles Lampson spoke of the business-like attitude Count Volpi had adopted in America, but complained of 'many and painful experiences of the attitude of the Italian experts to confuse matters by inventing arguments of the purest chicanery'. The Treasury, he explained, had accordingly prepared in considerable detail a study of Italy's national wealth and capacity to pay, which indicated that current production in Italy was immensely greater than it had been pre-war, whereas in Britain it was substantially less. Leith Ross expressed the hope that Volpi would get down to business and not waste time in what would probably be acrimonious theoretical discussion of the comparative importance of the sacrifices made by Italy and Great Britain during the war.

Sir Ronald Graham in Rome wrote to Chamberlain explaining the concern of the Italians that, whereas the American debt had been generously settled in the light of political factors, Britain had given the impression that the settlement of the Italian debt 'must remain a purely business transaction'. This caused Graham misgivings, and he felt that if the principle were to be applied too drastically it would produce 'a difficult situation'.

Foreign Office officials in London were not in favour of generous terms for Italy. Miles Lampson's view has already been noted. John Troutbeck of the Italian Department minuted on 14 January: 'The question boils down to this: how much are we prepared to pay for Italian goodwill? It seems to me that it is really a matter of very little consequence – certainly not worth the sacrifice of material gain.' However, Lampson pointed out that, Foreign Office opinion notwithstanding, the Foreign Secretary himself was well disposed towards the Italians, and wanted a settlement.

The Treasury study of Italy's ability to pay perturbed Graham, who asked the Foreign Office to keep an eye on the negotiations because failure might have 'a grave effect on Anglo-Italian relations and they should remember the way in which the Italians have in practically all important questions agreed with and supported us.'

Sir William Tyrell forwarded Graham's communication to Winston Churchill, then Chancellor of the Exchequer, pointing out how anxious Chamberlain was to agree a settlement – especially because of 'the happy personal relations which he has established with Mussolini and which have already yielded a good harvest in the case of Locarno.'[13]

In December 1925, after arrangements had been made for the Volpi team to go to London, Mussolini told Graham that although he knew the British government to be well-disposed he was disturbed by his own unpopularity 'in labour and radical circles', and wondered whether influence from this quarter would 'render less favourable' the terms which might otherwise be conceded by Britain. Graham assured him there was no foundation at all for 'any such misgiving', because members of the British government would never allow themselves to be persuaded by such considerations, Winston Churchill least of all.

After Treasury negotiations with Volpi and his team had reached tentative agreement, Churchill told the Cabinet on 19 January 1926 that he favoured a generous settlement. Austen Chamberlain (holidaying in Italy, it may be recalled) sent a message that he wanted such a settlement from a political point of view. The Cabinet then approved an agreement under which Italy would make repayments at a flat rate of £4 million a year. It was also agreed that the sums paid by Italy would be reviewed if the United Kingdom received more in reparations from the defeated nations than she paid out to the United States to service her own war debts.

The settlement was extremely generous, far more so than Treasury officials had recommended. According to a sharp note from Leith Ross to the Foreign Office, British taxpayers were paying £30 million a year to service the Italian debt, while the total war debt burden in Britain represented £52 per head, against only £18.5 in Italy. Backed by Austen Chamberlain, Churchill had over-ruled his officials, and Mussolini was overjoyed.

The agreement was signed on 28 January 1926. In an accompanying statement Churchill justified his action on the ground that Britain's relationship with Italy both during and since the war had been one of unbroken friendship and cordial co-operation. He continued:

> At the time of the proposed entry into the war [1915] considerable offers were made to Italy which carried with them, subject to conditions which have not been fulfilled, the principle of the virtual cancellation of the overwhelming bulk of the obligation . . . We have felt bound to consider this as a factor which must be borne in mind . . . I must pay my tribute to the loyal and manly attitude which the Italians have adopted . . . the effort they are making does them credit.
>
> Italy is a country which is prepared to face the realities of post-war reconstruction . . . It possesses a Government under the commanding

leadership of Signor Mussolini which does not shrink from the logical consequences of economic facts, and which has the courage to impose the financial remedies required to stabilise the national recovery.

This was fulsome praise. Churchill, both by words and deeds, was expressing his admiration for Mussolini's 'commanding leadership'. January 1926 marked a high spot in Anglo–Italian relations. Mussolini was delighted with the agreement, seeing it as a tribute to his standing in Britain. He instructed his brother Arnaldo to write an article expressing his approval, which was reported in *The Times* on 29 January 1926:

> Every problem has now been solved, and the ground is absolutely clear for the closest collaboration between the two countries, and the fulfilment of the obligations as guarantors and arbiters of European peace undertaken at Locarno. The agreement of London confirms the power of the Fascist regime and the respect it enjoys in Europe.

Under Mussolini's guidance, press comment in Italy gave the enthusiastic impression that Britain had dealt with a difficult problem in a most friendly and generous way. There were frequent references to British sacrifices, and much emphasis was given to the political importance of the agreement, which showed, it was suggested, how the two countries were bound together by friendship and common interest. Churchill's flattering reference to Mussolini was especially well–received: Mussolini sent a handwritten note (in French) to Graham, saying that Fascist opinion had been particularly touched by Churchill's sympathetic phrases. The Italian Ambassador called on Austen Chamberlain at the Foreign Office; Chamberlain reiterated the great importance of close and continuous co–operation, doubly so because of Britain and Italy's 'common position' as guarantors of Locarno. Rumours circulated in Britain that some sort of secret polit- ical understanding had been reached between Britain and Italy in connection with the debt agreement, and on 10 February 1926 Austen Chamberlain thought it necessary to emphasize to the Cabinet that there had been no mention of war debt repayment when he and Mussolini met at Rapallo at Christmas time.

Mussolini, convinced that Churchill was responsible for Britain's generous settlement, wanted him to receive the ancient Italian order of St Maurice and St Lazarus as a mark of gratitude. Austen Chamberlain was in favour, but it was found to breach the British protocol that ministers could not, in peace-time, accept foreign orders. Mussolini's gesture stands, however, as evidence of his warm friendship with Churchill at this time.[14]

The Conservatives, defeated in the General Election of May 1929, were succeeded by a second Labour government, under Ramsay MacDonald; but it was another hung Parliament and Labour were dependent, as in 1924, on Liberal support. Arthur Henderson became Foreign Secretary in place of Austen Chamberlain, with Hugh Dalton as Under-Secretary. Henderson, a veteran of the Labour movement, was prejudiced against Mussolini because of the suppression of Italian trade unions and co-operatives and the imprisonment of Italian Socialists like Pietro Nenni, who had many friends in the British Labour movement. MacDonald's government lasted until October 1931, and during this period there was not the same close alignment of British and Italian foreign policy as during Austen Chamberlain's tenure of the Foreign Office.

At the League of Nations in Geneva on 5 September 1929 Aristide Briand, then French Premier and Foreign Minister, launched a gallant plan for a Federal Europe which envisaged a customs union and free trade throughout Europe. The plan was welcomed by Willie Graham, President of the Board of Trade in Macdonald's government, but his was a lone voice in the Cabinet; the Foreign Secretary, Arthur Henderson, and the Chancellor of the Exchequer, Jim Thomas, rejected the plan out-of-hand.

Briand's detailed proposals were essentially a blue-print for the Common Market subsequently achieved by the Treaty of Rome in 1957; had they been taken up, perhaps they would have united Europe a quarter of a century earlier, and prevented the Nazis coming to power in Germany.

Mussolini's opinion of the Briand Plan was initially not unfavourable, but with the replacement of Austen Chamberlain by a Labour Foreign Secretary he had become, in the British Ambassador's word, 'uncertain' of Britain's attitude to Italian claims, and fearful that France might attempt to dominate Europe. At the time, too, he was toying with the possibility of a dramatic *rapprochement* with Germany and the creation of a German-Austro-Italian economic community. Mussolini therefore instructed Dino Grandi, his Foreign Minister, to reject Briand's plan. One British Foreign Office comment was that so rapid a decision to reject 'augured very badly not only for these proposals but also for any attempt to improve Franco-Italian relations', and it was suggested that Mussolini and Grandi might be persuaded to water down a blank refusal if the British government made it clear that they considered the Briand proposals 'worthy of very sympathetic consideration'.

Another opinion minuted was that 'the Italian attitude kills the scheme from the start'. However, MacDonald's Cabinet had also decided to kill the Plan, and in the face of this it withered on the vine. Mussolini's final argument against the Briand Plan was that he wanted a special economic position for Italy in Austria and Hungary, and was afraid the Plan would tip the balance in favour of France in those countries. However, he was careful not to say so directly, and no more blame attaches to Mussolini than to Britain for the failure of this promising plan.[15]

By early 1931 the world depression was hitting Austria and Germany hard and both governments displayed enthusiasm for an Austro-German Customs Union. Such a Union would, technically, represent a breach of the Treaty of Versailles, and as such was violently opposed by Dr Beneš, President of Czechoslovakia. Briand himself saw merits in it, but French public opinion generally was fiercely hostile, on the grounds that it marked the first step towards an *Anschluss* which would enhance Germany's military strength. Again, only Willie Graham in the MacDonald Cabinet was in favour; on 6 May 1931 the Foreign Secretary, Arthur Henderson, told the Cabinet that 'means must be found for removing this proposal from the domain of international politics'. He wanted to replace 'this dangerous proposal' with some 'progressive scheme for the economic union of Europe'; this did not make sense in light of Henderson's recent blank refusal to endorse the possible Briand Plan.[16]

At first Mussolini favoured an Austro-German Customs Union, thinking it could lead to a wide-scale revision of the Versailles Treaty which might benefit Italy, and that, contented by the Customs Union, Germany would not hanker after a political union with Austria. However, a study (by his Foreign Minister Dino Grandi and Raffaele Guariglia of the Italian Foreign Office) of the technical implications convinced Mussolini that it would have serious disadvantageous economic consequences for Italy, and inclined him too to the view that it might prove the first step towards an *Anschluss*. Furthermore, Mussolini wanted Austria under Italian influence. At this time he was still aligning his policy with Britain's, and at Geneva the Italians argued against the Customs Union. Its failure was to have dire consequences for both the German and Austrian economies, and the resulting economic distress contributed to the rapid rise of the Nazis to power in Germany.[17]

Sir Oswald Mosley, a prominent minister in MacDonald's 1929 government, left the Labour Party and in 1931 started a British Fascist

Party. With Harold Nicolson, now retired from the Foreign Office, he went to Rome, where he became friendly with Mussolini. Mosley's policy, based on the Fascist idea of a corporate state, proposed to organize the industrial and commercial life of Britain into a network of twenty-four 'corporations', each including employers, workers, ministers and civil servants. Mussolini, flattered by this imitation, decided to subsidize Mosley's party. At first it seemed that Mosley might have some chance of electoral success, but the violence at his meetings and his anti-Semitism, combined with the coming to power of Hitler in Germany, caused the collapse of his movement.

Dino Grandi, now Italian Ambassador in London, at first favoured the subsidy, but as Mosley's star began to fade he wrote to Mussolini on 1 March 1935:

> You are spending a great deal of money in England. At any rate until a few months ago you were giving Mosley about 3,500,000 [lire, per annum: worth about £60,000] . . . All this money, believe me dear Duce, even on the best supposition simply goes down the drain. At the present time we should concentrate our efforts in a different direction. With a tenth of what you give Mosley, that is, with a monthly allowance to the Embassy of 35,000 lire, I could produce a result ten times better.

Mussolini cut off the subsidy. He had taken great pains to keep the contribution secret, anxious lest it should interfere with the good diplomatic relations he was enjoying with Britain at the time. Mosley always denied the existence of this Italian subsidy, but his denials are somewhat implausible in light of the fact that his party suffered a financial crisis in 1935.[18]

CHAPTER 6

War Debts, Disarmament, and the Four-Power Pact

THE LONG-AWAITED League of Nations Disarmament Conference began in Geneva on 2 February 1932, with American participation. The political climate was unfavourable. The Japanese were bombing Manchuria, while the economic depression triggered off by the Wall Street crash of eighteen months before was at its height in Europe. The democratic parties in the Weimar Republic were being hard-pressed by the Nazis, who made themselves popular by claims that they would conquer unemployment, refuse to pay any more war reparations, and demand equality of rights for German rearmament, together with territorial revisions of the Treaty of Versailles. The Nazi vote had leapt in September 1930 from 2.6 to 18 per cent, and in the presidential election of April 1932 Hitler secured 37 per cent of the poll, against Hindenburg's 49.6 per cent. Hitler was knocking on the doors of power.

The moderate and able Heinrich Brüning was still Chancellor of Germany when the Conference opened, and acted as his own Foreign Minister. To counter Hitler's growing popularity he took an aggressive line, and attempted to wrest from the Conference a form of words which for internal propaganda purposes could be construed as a triumph for Germany, particularly over arms parity.

As early as 1925 the Council of the League of Nations had established a commission to prepare for a Disarmament Conference, but little useful preparatory work had been accomplished, and it soon became clear that no effective agreement on reductions or limitations of national armies could be enforced except by an efficient system of international control, involving rights of inspection and the provision of sanctions against any offending power.

Under the terms of the Treaty of Versailles the Allied Military Commission had been given wide powers to prevent illegal German rearmament. These included entering factories without notice, since in theory German arms manufacture was limited to a few specially-licensed firms. A new League of Nations supra-national authority with similar powers would considerably diminish national authority, and Mussolini was not prepared to accept such supervision; nor were Britain, Germany, the United States or Japan. The French, however, as a result of their appalling experiences in the Franco-Prussian War and the First World War, were ready to agree to some loss of sovereignty in their desperate desire to avoid further such conflict. Their alarm was heightened by the British refusal, at Locarno and afterwards, to guarantee automatic armed help in the event of an attack by Germany; they were prepared to accept any measure which might tend to dispel their fears of German rearmament.

One of Mussolini's main interests at the Conference was to secure Italian parity with French naval power; he also wanted a revision of the terms of the Treaty of Versailles, hoping that in the course of it Italy would receive Albania and a slice of Yugoslavia. In pursuit of these aims, he was prepared to back Germany's stance.

The abject state of the German economy at this time made Brüning anxious for relief from the burden of reparations payments. On 7 January 1932 he announced Germany's inability to pay any more reparations 'either now or in the future if the economic life of the world is to be revived', and at the Reparations Conference which began at Lausanne on 16 June it seemed as though this problem, which was bedevilling Germany's relations with the rest of Europe, might be resolved. In Britain, the Prime Minister Ramsay MacDonald, Sir John Simon the Foreign Secretary, and Neville Chamberlain, Chancellor of the Exchequer, had agreed after consultation with Treasury officials that further reparations payments should be wiped from the slate. Simon wrote in a memorandum for the Cabinet that at Lausanne a resolution ought to be passed to the effect that 'It is in the interests of the world that there should be an all-round cancellation of reparations and the war debts owed by European powers to one another should similarly be discharged.' The Cabinet agreed.[1]

Unfortunately, shortly before the Lausanne Conference opened President Hindenburg had insisted on the dismissal of Brüning (because of his proposals to tax landowners); thus Germany, on the eve of this important Conference, lost the services of her leading statesman, one who enjoyed the confidence of the other European powers. Brüning was succeeded by the ultra right-wing Franz von Papen, who had little support in parliament.

Ramsay MacDonald at first headed the British delegation to Lausanne, but Neville Chamberlain took over when he fell ill. The Italian industrialist Alberto Pirelli headed the Italian delegation, and on Mussolini's instructions argued, like Britain, for a 'clean slate' policy. The Belgians took the same line, but Édouard Herriot, the French Premier, was intransigent. Eventually Neville Chamberlain deferred to the French proposal that Germany should pay 3 milliard marks in final settlement of her debts – the minimum the French would agree to. Von Papen offered to pay 2 milliard, in exchange for German parity of arms and cancellation of the 'war guilt' clause of the Treaty of Versailles. It was inept diplomacy to attempt to wring such concessions from a conference convened solely to deal with reparations, properly the province of the Disarmament Conference sitting simultaneously in Geneva, and revealed von Papen's incompetence. In the event, Chamberlain bullied von Papen into agreeing to pay 2.6 milliard, and the settlement signed on 9 July 1932 made no allusion to parity of arms or German war guilt.[2]

It was a settlement which proved disastrous for the democratic parties in Germany, providing Hitler and the Nazis with excellent propaganda. Goering declared that when the Nazis came to power they would not pay a penny, the Nazi press indulged in violent abuse of von Papen, and the settlement was widely condemned. In his memoirs von Papen wrote: 'When MacDonald made his report to the House of Commons he received an ovation . . . Herriot in his turn received a great welcome from the French chamber . . . But when I returned to Germany I was received with a shower of bad eggs and rotten apples.'[3]

Mussolini was in no way to blame for this gratuitous boost to the popularity of the Nazis; he wanted a 'clean slate policy'. It was Neville Chamberlain who had given in to the French, and in so doing had driven another nail into the coffin of German democracy – his failure to stand up for Germany at this time was in sharp contrast to the way he was later to lean over backwards to appease Hitler.[4] And had the French been persuaded to be more forthcoming – as the Italians were – in the early days of both the Disarmament Conference and the Reparations Conference, when Brüning was still in power, the rise of the Nazis to power might have been halted.

The Nazis made startling gains in the German General Election of July 1932; they were now the largest single party in the Reichstag, with 230 seats out of 608. Hindenburg refused to give the Chancellorship to Hitler, but von Papen's position was now very weak, and he was no more successful at the Disarmament Conference than Brüning had been. On 22 July, on von Papen's instructions, Nadolny, head of the German delegation, declared that Germany could not continue to participate unless the principle of her equality of armament was recognized by the other powers. He claimed that Germany did not intend to rearm, but sought only cessation of the discrimination against her. On 14 September 1932, von Papen and the rest of the German delegation withdrew from the Conference, which was then suspended for three months.

On 15 September 1932, in an effort to resolve the deadlock at Geneva, Britain addressed a guarded Note to Germany and France, suggesting that while equality of status for Germany would probably be granted before the end of the Conference, it was premature to force it to the front at this stage; the hope was expressed for a conclusion calling for no distinction of status, and subjecting every member's armaments to control by the same process. Mussolini approved the British document, while emphasizing that the only way over the deadlock was to accept Germany's 'academic claim to equality in principle', and that in his view a failure of the Disarmament Conference would be 'disastrous'. In Geneva on 25 September Sir John Simon and Pompeo Aloisi, head of the Italian delegation, agreed that Italy and Britain were prepared to admit Germany's claim to equality of status. In thus allying himself with Britain, Mussolini was taking a statesman-like view of the German claim for equality in the light of the importance of preventing the Nazis coming to power, as well as pursuing his own aims. Again, it was the French who were causing difficulties.

In mid November, following further German elections, von Papen resigned and was replaced as Chancellor early in December by Kurt von Schleicher – a dangerous individual with links to the Nazis.

The Disarmament Conference reconvened in Geneva on 4 December 1932 and on 11 December, after a series of meetings, Germany was granted equality of rights with other nations, a move strongly supported by Mussolini; only with considerable difficulty had the French objections been over-ruled. On the signing of this so-called Geneva Protocol, the German government declared that Germany would return to the Conference when it was resumed on 2 February. But it was too late: on 28 January 1933 von Schleicher's government fell, and on the 30th Hindenburg, quite constitutionally, called Hitler to the Chancellorship.[5]

In his memoirs, von Papen complained that the 11 December communiqué came a few days too late to save his government. That might be so – but its existence was already precarious, without the same prospect of a long period in power that the Brüning government would have enjoyed had they had a diplomatic success at Geneva.[6]

Mussolini, who consistently favoured both German parity of arms and the 'clean slate' policy, can in no way be blamed for the failure of the Disarmament Conference to provide any relief to the hard-pressed German democratic parties in their battle to keep the Nazis out of power. The responsibility lies with the French.

A delegation from Hitler's government took part in the reconvened Disarmament Conference, but it soon became clear to the British government from the reports of their Ambassador in Berlin that the Nazis were organizing rearmament on a massive scale and had no intention of agreeing to limitations. Anthony Eden, then an Under-Secretary at the Foreign Office, told the Cabinet Disarmament Committee on 2 March 1933 that 'the Conference was tottering to failure': because of the rigid instructions given to his diplomats by Hitler, 'it was no longer normal diplomacy at Geneva'.

Mussolini shared Eden's pessimistic view. Sir Ronald Graham reported on 2 March that the Duce considered the Polish corridor★ to be 'one of the most dangerous and pressing questions to be got out of the way' and he suggested that Danzig and a strip of coastline not wider than 10 or 15 kilometres should be surrendered to Germany; perhaps Mussolini thought this would divert Hitler's attention from Austria to the east. In pursuit of these aims he made an innovative proposal for a Four-Power Pact, between Germany, France, Italy and Britain, to keep the peace in Europe.

Downcast by the poor reception of the British plan for disarmament at Geneva, Ramsay MacDonald was delighted to receive an invitation in March 1933 to discuss Mussolini's ideas in Rome. He had every expectation of a warm reception, after his generous treatment of Italy in 1924 over Jubaland. Mussolini sent a luxurious *wagon-lit* to convey MacDonald's party from the Disarmament Conference at Geneva to Genoa, from where a seaplane piloted by Italo Balbo, his Minister of Air, took them to Rome's port of Ostia. In Rome, Mussolini spared nothing in his welcome, even giving an evening party at the Palazzo Venezia to which the whole staff of the Embassy was invited, together with the most important British clerics and other residents in Rome.

Mussolini had spent the previous weekend drafting his proposed Four-Power Pact, believing it to be a major contribution to European peace. His draft specified revision of the Versailles Treaty within the framework of the League of Nations, including a rider that should the Disarmament Conference lead to only 'partial' results, German 'equality of rights' should nevertheless be put into practice; it also contained clauses about colonial changes. MacDonald and Simon flattered Mussolini, but they disliked the references to colonies, were displeased with Mussolini's contention that the Polish corridor was 'one of the greatest mistakes of Versailles', and disliked

---

★ By the Treaty of Versailles, Germany had been granted a corridor through Polish territory to link Danzig and East Prussia with Germany.

his conviction that Germany was determined to join up the two halves of Prussia.

In discussions which followed, Hitler welcomed the Pact initially; to Graham, Simon expressed the view that Mussolini's own feelings were very friendly to Britain, and that he had influence over Hitler, 'who seemed by agreeing to the Pact to have reverted to Stresemann's policy'. Simon could not have been more wrong. As the French amended Mussolini's draft provisions, to Germany's disadvantage, Hitler blew cold, much to Simon's disappointment.[7]

The French so emasculated the Pact that the 'revision' and 'colonial' clauses from which Mussolini had hoped to benefit were eradicated; the final version bore little relation to Mussolini's original. He achieved no more than a promise by Germany that she would 'consult' with France, Italy and Britain and pursue within the framework of the League a policy of effective co-operation. Nevertheless, he ordered the Italian newspapers to claim that the Pact made Italy the arbiter of the destinies of Europe, and that because his plan guaranteed peace for ten years it had been hailed with more applause than any other Treaty. He was gratified when Dino Grandi, now Ambassador in London, wrote on 22 June 1933 of a meeting with Lloyd George, who had sent expressions of 'sincere admiration' for the Pact and said:

> 'Either the world decides to follow Mussolini or the world is doomed. Only your leader has clear vision . . . Does it not seem strange to you that an old Liberal like me can think and talk like this about someone who was the executioner of Liberalism?'

The Pact was initialled at the Palazzo Venezia on 6 June 1933 by Mussolini and the Ambassadors of Great Britain, France and Germany. Despite Mussolini's jubilation, it made no difference to Hitler's plans for aggrandizement. He had acceded to it without enthusiasm, observing to Werner von Blomberg, his Minister of Defence, that it committed him to nothing and was therefore to a certain extent not unhelpful since it showed Germany's general willingness to be co-operative (which had to be his attitude while Germany remained weak) without tying his hands.[8]

Germany continued to participate in the Disarmament Conference until October 1933. No headway was made. The German service chiefs were placed in an invidious situation, having at Geneva to pretend to be genuinely seeking limitations on arms while at home, on Hitler's instructions, they were re-equipping the German forces as quickly as possible. On 14 October the farce played itself out.

Germany left the Conference, and also the League of Nations. In his diary that evening Eden wrote that the Conference was becoming a sham, and that he would not care to have Simon's conscience about the earlier part of the previous year, when Brüning was still in power: 'We missed the bus then.'

Mussolini was furious with the Germans. Sir Ronald Graham reported that he had never seen the Duce 'show more annoyance and disgust' than when he talked to him about the German withdrawal. Mussolini said that by their precipitate and ill-judged action the Germans had 'broken three windows at once' – those of the Conference, the League of Nations, and the Four-Power Pact, and that 'They now expected him to pick up the pieces, but he refused to do anything of the kind.'

Mussolini went on to tell Graham how von Papen had suggested to the Italian Ambassador in Berlin that now was the moment to bring the Four-Power Pact into operation. Still intensely proud of his creation, Mussolini was offended by this, informing Graham that having designed his pact within the ambit of the League of Nations he entirely disagreed that it could come into operation now that Germany had left the League, and that he refused to take any initiative whatever. As reported by Graham, Mussolini had added that

> . . . in a purely altruistic spirit and in the hope of furthering international friendship he had stretched every point to Germany and the only thanks he got were a series of German actions calculated to injure Italian interests and susceptibilities. He had told Signor Suvich [Mussolioni's Under-Secretary for Foreign Affairs] to warn the German Ambassador here that he had better keep out of his [Signor Mussolini's] way as His Excellency felt he could hardly refrain from being discourteous to Herr Hassell if they met.[9]

These were strong words, but the Duce knew Graham well and liked and trusted him; they clearly represented Mussolini's feelings about Hitler, and Germany, at the time.

CHAPTER 7

Mussolini and Austria: 1934

ON THE FIRST page of *Mein Kampf* Hitler had written that Austria must be annexed to Germany, and when he came to power in 1933 this was his first target in foreign policy. As Chancellor, Hitler immediately initiated a 'cold war' against the Austrian government. He imposed a thousand–mark fine on German tourists going there, among other hostile measures designed to cripple the Austrian economy; at the same time, the Nazi propaganda machine directed vicious attacks at Austrian political leaders in order to undermine them. Austrian Nazis were given secret instructions from Berlin to initiate terror campaigns involving bomb attacks on various Austrian institutions.

When in 1918, at the end of the First World War, the vast Austro-Hungarian Habsburg Empire which had held the Danubian countries together for two centuries ceased to exist, it was replaced by a number of small, weak, nationalistic and uneconomic states. Austria became a small republic of six and a half million (more than two million in Vienna) and poor economic prospects. She had no access to the sea, no sources of fuel and raw materials for her industries. Her markets for industrial products were gone with her Empire, and she was surrounded by unfriendly states. Salvation lay either in economic union with Germany, or in the formation of a Confederation of the new Danubian states. Neither materialized, and although the late 1920s saw a brief economic revival, this was wiped out by the world economic crisis of 1930. By 1931 the problems of the Austrian economy were endemic. Countries formerly part of the Austro-Hungarian Empire imposed high import duties on Austrian goods – ironically, since the Austrian industries had originally been developed to produce manufactured goods for those predominantly agricultural regions. Even before Hitler came to power, the Nazis had been causing trouble in Austria. Engelbert Dollfuss had become head of an Austrian coalition government in May 1932, and in March 1933, prompted by Nazi-inspired unrest, he suspended parliamentary government and ruled by decree with the consent of the President, Wilhelm Miklas. German

Nazi activists were expelled and the Austrian Nazi Party was declared illegal, but it continued to operate and foment trouble underground.

The three Austrian political groupings were bitterly opposed to one another. On the left were the Social Democrats (ranging from Socialists to Marxists), who governed Vienna and controlled a powerful private army known as the *Schutzbund* (Defence League); on the right was the Nazi Party, which grew increasingly belligerent after Hitler became Chancellor in Germany; and in the centre were the Christian Socialists, the ruling party. The Christian Socialists controlled a paramilitary formation known as the *Heimwehr* under the wealthy, aristocratic Prince Starhemberg, who had a horror of Nazism and was a ruthlessly patriotic opponent of *Anschluss*, and was also a close friend of Mussolini, who in return had a great admiration for him. Outside Socialist-dominated Vienna the remainder of the country had a substantial anti-Socialist majority.

British support for Dollfuss was lukewarm. On 3 April 1933 the British Ambassador in Berlin, Sir Eric Phipps, wrote: 'Italy will presumably continue to support Dr Dollfuss and the Starhemberg *Heimwehr* in their fight on two fronts against Socialists and National Socialists [Nazis] alike, and so I think will France, and so I hope will HMG in a spirit of benevolent neutrality.' A statement in the House of Commons by Anthony Eden, now Under-Secretary for Foreign Affairs, on 2 June 1933 gave little indication that Britain was on Austria's side against Germany, although in London in June and July 1933 at the World Monetary and Economic Conference Sir Robert Vansittart, the Permanent Under-Secretary at the Foreign Office, gave Dollfuss the impression that Britain would back him in his struggle against Hitler (Dollfuss had made a strong appeal for British help, and left believing that he would receive stronger support than he did); and in August the Foreign Office was considering the acceleration of authorization of an increase in the size of the Austrian army in excess of the Versailles limit. There is, however, no indication in the Foreign Office files that keeping Austria independent of Germany was a priority; the Foreign Secretary, Sir John Simon, expressed minimal interest in Austria, and on 24 October 1933 Britain even urged moderation on Dollfuss in his battle against Nazi infiltration.[1]

On 19 August 1933 Dollfuss went to Riccione, in north Italy, to meet Mussolini. They became firm friends. Dollfuss explained to Mussolini that considerable numbers of Austrian Nazis, encamped just across the German frontier, had been formed into a legion to attack whenever Hitler gave the order. In pursuance of his own plan to save Austria from Hitler by making Austria and Hungary a pro-Italian Fascist bloc, Mussolini agreed to a large financial subsidy plus rifles and machine-guns for the *Heimwehr*. He also promised Dollfuss economic aid. In return Dollfuss agreed that 5,000 Italian troops could cross the frontier into the Kufstein area of Austria if Hitler attempted a coup. The Austrian Chancellor was immensely relieved by these promises from the Italian dictator, which boosted his morale at a time when the French and British were cool towards him from dislike of his unconstitutional methods of government.

When Sir John Simon saw Mussolini in Rome on 3 January 1934, Mussolini emphasized that Italy had no desire to see Germany become unduly strong, and pointed out that German and Italian policy did not follow the same line; although there were superficial resemblances between Nazism and Fascism, Italian policy over Austria was wholly opposed to Germany's. He was of the opinion that if it had not been for his (Mussolini's) strong support of Dollfuss, the Nazis would already have become established in Austria and brought about virtual unity between Germany and Austria.[2]

In January 1934 Dollfuss announced that Austria was to protest to the League about German interference in her internal affairs. His government had compiled a dossier of complaints which they proposed to bring before the League, and Britain, France and Italy were asked for their comments.

Simultaneously, France proposed to complain to the League about, and ask for an investigation into, illegal German rearmament. Failing this, the French hoped at least to provoke a discussion at Geneva of the facts contained in their dossier on German rearmament. The British were hesitant about supporting the French complaint. A memorandum on the French intentions stated: 'Once the legal remedies had been exhausted and Germany still remained recalcitrant HMG would have to discuss with France the question of joint coercive action against Germany. This might lead to an awkward situation.'

In February Dollfuss asked Britain for full support of his appeal to the League. Simon did not want to support Austria because the British government still nourished high hopes of Germany at the Disarmament Conference, and feared support for Austria's complaint would antagonize Hitler. Here was appeasement.

At a long and significant meeting of the Cabinet Committee on Foreign Affairs held on 9 February 1934, Simon told his colleagues the Austrian situation was 'serious' and of 'some embarrassment', but expressed uncertainty whether the production of the dossier before her appeal to Geneva had actually been made was in Austria's best interests; he noted a wide feeling among all shades of public opinion that Britain ought to do all she could to help Austria.

Vansittart suggested that the Italian government were playing a 'double game': having at first encouraged Austria to make the appeal, they were now putting pressure on her not to go to the League. Instead, Mussolini wanted to install a Fascist regime in Austria, which regime might reverse the decision to appeal to the League; Italy wanted to rid Vienna of the Socialists, and was trying to secure a free hand in Austria. Vansittart's view was that unless the appeal was made to the League now, Dollfuss 'would inevitably be lost'; he wanted both Italy and France to be told that, having seen her dossier, Britain felt Austria should appeal to the League. Three days later Suvich told Sir Eric Drummond (later Earl of Perth), who had succeeded Sir Ronald Graham as Ambassador in Rome, of Italy's fears lest the Council might not take strong action on the Austrian dossier, or might make any decision to support Dollfuss conditional on a pledge that Dollfuss would not act against his political opponents; Suvich further expressed the opinion that Dollfuss ought to take strong action now against the Socialists.

Vansittart had correctly read Mussolini's intentions. Eden, supporting Vansittart, maintained that the sooner Austria's appeal was made, the better; Vansittart reiterated his concern that 'we must avoid being let in for any extremely tricky negotiations with Italy and other countries as a substitute for an appeal to the League', and expressed a fear of discouraging Dollfuss, who was expecting British advice as to whether he should appeal to the League. The Prime Minister, Ramsay MacDonald, backed Simon, but the Committee decided to instruct Britain's ambassadors to take the line that there were two sides to the case, and that it would therefore not be right for HMG to make any comment beforehand. Accordingly, Sir John Simon informed the Austrian Ambassador that Britain could not pronounce a view on the dossier before it had been considered by the Council of the League of Nations.

With Mussolini guiding Austria and no positive lead from Britain, events took an ugly turn. Despite a warning from Britain on 12 February 1934 that if Dollfuss struck at the Socialists and established a Fascist or quasi-Fascist regime 'there would be in Britain and probably in France a very marked cooling in the unanimity of the support given to Austria by the press and public opinion, and further attempts by the British Government to assist Dollfuss might be rendered increasingly difficult', in the first weeks of February Dollfuss finally dissolved all political parties (including the Socialists) except his own. This brought into the open the deadly rivalry between the Socialists' *Schutzbund* and Dollfuss's *Heimwehr*, and Austria was at the mercy of these private armies. When the *Heimwehr* tried to disarm the *Schutzbund* in Linz and Vienna, a rebellion broke out. Dollfuss ordered the *Heimwehr* to put down the rebellion, but the *Schutzbund* barricaded themselves inside the giant council house blocks on the outskirts of Vienna; many Socialists fought from their own flats. The fighting lasted for four days and then, fearful of a Nazi coup if he did not assert his authority, Dollfuss ordered the shelling of the workers' housing complex, which resulted in heavy casualties on both sides, and promised a free pardon to all rebels who surrendered. Suppression of the Socialists had been Mussolini's aim, but the dissident Socialists proved to be fruitful recruiting material for the Nazis, and the operation was in the long run self-defeating. Dollfuss had aligned himself with Fascist Italy – but in the face of Britain's cold attitude he had no other friend to whom to turn. On 17 February the British, French and Italian governments issued a declaration emphasizing their joint interest in the preservation of Austrian independence, but the Austrian complaint to the League was dropped.[3]

Mussolini, concerned at the vulnerability of the Dollfuss government and British indifference to the fate of Austria, invited Dollfuss and Julius Gömbös, the Hungarian Prime Minister, to Rome on 14 March. Mussolini's plan was to negotiate a number of agreements which would prevent Hitler's expansion to the east, and to keep both Austria and Hungary under his influence; he believed France and Britain would be co-operative with his design because of the danger of Hitler seizing Austria.

On 17 March 1934 a series of agreements which became known as the Rome Protocols were signed between Italy, Austria and Hungary, providing for military combination in case of need, for lower import duties between the three countries, and for economic aid from Italy. (In contrast, Britain's move to Imperial Preference and the Import Duties Act of 1932 were hindering the access of Austrian products to British markets.)

Grandi reassured Sir John Simon that Italy did not have the slightest desire to interfere with the independence of either Austria or Hungary; rather, their independence as 'strong buffer states' was a prime object of Italian policy. Germany had not expected Mussolini to show so much determination, the outcome of which had materially obstructed and discouraged Hitler's hopes of spreading Nazism across the Austro-German frontier.[4]

In 1934 Mussolini was far more highly regarded than Hitler in Britain and the United States. Accolades bestowed on him by Conservative public figures in the 1920s and early 1930s led him to believe he was the great statesman of the era, and he deeply resented suggestions that there were resemblances between him and Hitler. He would go no further than to agree that Nazism, like Fascism, was authoritarian, collectivist, anti-parliamentary, anti-democratic and anti-liberal; he dismissed the Nazi idea of a master-race as 'arrant nonsense', and at the time despised anti-Semitism.

It is alleged that German diplomats encouraged Hitler to arrange a meeting with Mussolini in the hope that the Italian dictator would influence him towards moderation. Whether this is true or not, on 14 June 1934 the two men met for the first time, in Venice. Mussolini had not been looking forward to the meeting, and in the event found Hitler even less attractive than he had expected; on his first sight of Hitler at Venice airport the Duce took exception to his ill-brushed hair and watery eyes, and murmured, 'I do not like the look of him.' Mussolini was wearing a well-cut Fascist uniform complete with boots, spurs and a dagger, while Hitler, having been wrongly advised not to wear uniform, was at a disadvantage in civilian clothes, with a yellow mackintosh.

Although it is not difficult to piece together how the talks went, there is no official record. His German was faulty, but Mussolini refused an interpreter. After their first discussions, Mussolini announced in his own circle that Hitler was 'quite mad', and amused Suvich by exclaiming, 'What a clown this Hitler is.' Hitler antagonized Mussolini by monopolizing the conversation, during which he proclaimed the superiority of the Nordic races and condemned the Mediterranean people (including the Italians) for having Negro blood in their veins. There was no meeting of minds, but instead a violent dispute over Austria, in which Hitler fruitlessly demanded the admission of Nazis to Dollfuss's government. The talks achieved nothing; afterwards, Suvich told Drummond that Mussolini had found it impossible to pin Hitler down to anything 'concrete' during four hours of conversation.

In a speech from a balcony in the Piazza San Marco Mussolini declared, to Hitler's indignation, that he and Hitler had agreed to preserve an independent Austria as a buffer between their two countries, and that if necessary Italy would defend Austria by force. This was received by the crowd with great enthusiasm as an angry Hitler listened to an interpreter inside. Hitler's line afterwards was that Mussolini had acquiesced in increased Nazi influence in Austria so long as Germany made no move to annex the country, but this was not the case. Mussolini left Venice after two days of meetings with an intense dislike of Hitler's personality, and remarked that talking to Hitler was like having a conversation with a record-player.[5]

Mussolini's declarations that he would defend Austrian independence had little effect on Hitler's plans. German documents disclose details of a plan to capture the entire Austrian Cabinet after a

Nazi raid on the Chancellery on 25 July 1934, together with seizure of the Vienna radio station and a simultaneous propaganda campaign designed to produce a popular Nazi uprising; the plan included the assignment of a special commando force to arrest the Austrian President Wilhelm Miklas and coerce him into legitimizing a Nazi regime. According to General Adam, Commander of Military District VII in Munich, Hitler told him at 9 a.m. on 25 July that 'the Austrian Government will be thrown out today. Rintelen [General von Rintelen, a leading Austrian Nazi] will be Chancellor.' Adam was instructed to arm thousands of Austrian Nazi legionaries and facilitate their crossing of the frontier between Germany and Austria.

Dollfuss had accepted an invitation to spend a holiday with Mussolini at Riccione with his family. His wife and children went on ahead, arriving there on 25 July. That morning in Vienna a convoy of trucks carrying 150 armed Nazis disguised in Austrian army uniforms drew up at the Chancellery in the Ballhausplatz; they rushed the guards, and mortally wounded Dollfuss. Simultaneously, other parties of armed Nazis tried to take over centres of government in Vienna and other big towns. In the fighting which followed over a hundred people were killed and more than two hundred severely wounded.

Starhemberg was in Venice on the morning of 25 July. When he was informed of the attempted coup he at once telephoned an order to Vienna for the *Heimwehr* to call out their men and put down the Nazis – without the help of the regular army, in which he feared there were too many Nazi sympathizers. Mussolini sent a military plane to fly Starhemberg from Venice to Vienna where President Miklas authorized him as Vice Chancellor to put down the Nazi rising and to head the government temporarily. Mussolini was enraged by the murder of Dollfuss. Sir Oswald Mosley, who saw him a few days after the murder, believed Mussolini, in his anger, to be contemplating war on Germany.

Mussolini supported Starhemberg to the hilt; he moved Italian troops to the Austrian frontier in accordance with the agreement made with Dollfuss, and sent a telegram to Starhemberg promising military aid. Italian intervention was not required, however, because Starhemberg was quickly able to put down the revolt and restore order. The Italian press roundly condemned the rising, and pointed to the moral responsibility of the Nazis. Ulrich von Hassell, the German Ambassador in Rome, protested vigorously to the Italian Foreign Office about the anti-Hitler tone of the Italian press, and especially about the impudent cartoons insulting Hitler; his protest was ignored.[6]

Like so many bullies when their opponents stand up to them, Hitler climbed down abjectly. Feeling the unexpected strength of the Austrian resistance and Mussolini's support for Austria to be a personal humiliation, he temporarily abandoned his policy of political interference in Austria; not only was the Nazi propaganda campaign halted, but the murders and bomb attacks ceased. On 1 August Hitler stated that he intended 'to wind up the National Socialist Party in Austria and disband the Austrian Legion', merely retaining a charitable organization for the care of Austrian refugees 'under the impeccable cover of the Red Cross'. On 13 August Hitler ordered all aggressive wireless and press programmes to cease, and despite the fact that many of the Austrian Nazis who died on 25 July had done so shouting 'Heil Hitler', he ordered the exclusion from the leadership of the Austrian Nazi Party of all persons compromised by having been leaders of the fight, declaring that 'such persons must not be rewarded for their services by being given important posts in the Reich.'[7]

From the ignominious failure of the Nazi revolt in Austria — Hitler's first attempt at the sort of State take-over at which he was to be so successful later — Mussolini emerges as the clear winner in the first round of the struggle to prevent Hitler becoming master of Europe. But it was Hitler's only pre-war foreign policy defeat after his accession to power in January 1933, and he was to lose no more rounds until 1942.

Sir John Simon sent a personal message congratulating Mussolini on his policy over the Austrian crisis. In it he recognized the right of Austria to demand that there should be no interference in her affairs from any quarter, and said that 'Britain could not interfere in internal affairs in Austria'. In the autumn of 1934 Mussolini suggested to France and Britain a three-power guarantee of Austrian independence; the British, wishing to avoid continental commitments, demurred. The outcome was a meek joint declaration by France, Britain and Italy reaffirming the declaration of 17 February 1934 regarding the independence of Austria.

Austria would have fallen to Hitler in 1934 had it not been for Mussolini. The combination of Italian and Austrian firmness proved that determined opposition to Hitler could prevent Nazi aggression, and Mussolini had set a fine example to Britain and France. Tragically, Britain ignored his success and failed to accept the lesson of the Austrian crisis — that, despite all his defects, Mussolini's continued co-operation was essential if Hitler was to be kept in check.

CHAPTER 8

The Stresa Front

THE LEAGUE OF NATIONS Disarmament Conference finally ended at Geneva in May 1935 in complete breakdown, caused by Nazi intransigence and unconcealed, rapid, German rearmament – which the British government, to the consternation of both Mussolini and the French, continued to condone. France and Britain became estranged when Britain refused to support France in arraigning Germany before the League of Nations for illegal rearmament under the terms of the Treaty of Versailles. Then on 2 May 1935 France, seeking an alternative policy to defend herself against a German military attack, signed a Franco-Soviet pact of mutual assistance, despite strong British opposition to such a course. Mussolini, who hated Soviet Russia, was much displeased.

Meanwhile, on 4 March 1935 the annual British Defence White Paper had drawn attention to German rearmament, stating that 'it might produce a situation where peace will be in peril', and that the British government, having given up hopes of world agreement on disarmament, intended to start rearming.

Hitler had reacted aggressively to this White Paper. On 9 March Goering had announced the existence of the underground German Air Force, and on 16 March Hitler introduced conscription with the aim of creating an army of thirty-six divisions, amounting in peacetime to 500,000 men. The Treaty of Versailles had been torn up.

Mussolini reacted sharply, delivering fruitless strongly-worded notes of protest to Berlin. He then, still very conscious of Hitler's blatant and illegal rearmament and of his ambition to annex Austria as revealed by the attempted coup of the previous year, consulted with Sir Eric Drummond, the British Ambassador in Rome, and suggested that France and Britain should hold a three-power conference with Italy at Stresa to discuss further steps to bring Hitler to heel.

On 8 April 1935 the British Cabinet, in negative mood, considered Mussolini's initiative. They agreed that Britain must avoid a complete breach with Germany, and decided to take no strong action. The

Cabinet Minutes reveal that they 'declined' to agree to any undertaking at Stresa

> . . . that we would be prepared to take forcible action anywhere. Germany
> was in a volcanic mood and not inclined to yield to threats. We ought not
> to agree to such a proposition unless we were prepared to take action any-
> where (e.g., in the event of trouble in Memel).* There was general agree-
> ment that we ought not to accept further commitments . . .[1]

The same cowardly attitude was displayed at the meeting at Stresa
between 11 and 14 April 1935.

The British were in a delicate position, because they had already
told Hitler they were 'proposing to discuss naval questions with
Germany'. Sir Robert Vansittart later mentioned this to the French
and Italians at Stresa, but gave no indication of the enormity of the
breach of the Treaty of Versailles which Britain had in mind. Baldwin's
telegram to Simon at the end of the Stresa Conference shows the
British dilemma:

> We understand it was not possible to mention to French and Italian
> Governments at Stresa proposed informal exchange of views in London
> between British and German Governments (re Naval Pact) and we do not
> know if it is intended to do so at Geneva . . . It is evident that announce-
> ments of naval programme outside Treaty limits on eve of London discus-
> sions would greatly complicate the situation . . . [because] we should,
> whilst theoretically reserving the [Versailles] Treaty position, be discussing
> with a Germany which had already broken the Treaty.

In his reply to Baldwin, Simon noted that 'we were pledged to discussions on a naval agreement with a Germany which had already torn
up the Treaty by her air and land rearmament.'[2]

Had they known of these proposed Naval discussions with
Germany, the French would probably have broken off the Stresa
Conference – in which case they and the Italians, ignoring Britain,
might well have taken a firmer stand against German rearmament.

The Stresa Conference has been neglected by historians. The two
important issues on the agenda were Hitler's designs on Austria, and
how the League of Nations could prevent illegal German rearmament. On both issues the British delegates dragged their feet, although
France had already protested to the League regarding illegal German

---

* Memel, the largest port in Lithuania and with a predominantly German population, had
been taken away from Germany in 1923; Hitler was agitating for its return, and seized it in
March 1939. It is now again in Lithuania, and known as Klaipėda

conscription and the creation of an air force in defiance of the terms of the Treaty of Versailles.

The British delegation was headed by Ramsay MacDonald, the Prime Minister, and Sir John Simon; the French, by their Premier, Flandin, and Laval, the Foreign Minister; Mussolini, again acting as his own Foreign Minister, brought his Under-Secretary, Fulvio Suvich.

Mussolini bluntly informed the Conference that the situation in Austria was 'not good', mainly because the present government had neither the prestige nor the strength of the Dollfuss administration; he declared that the youth of Austria was in favour of an *Anschluss*, that if conscription was introduced 'the majority of the army would be Nazi', and that while an *Anschluss* would not be a direct threat to Italy, Germany in Vienna meant Germany on the Bosphorus and the revival of the Berlin–Baghdad drive.

In this he was undoubtedly correct: once Hitler was in possession of Austria, his road to the east was open. Mussolini said that the conference 'must do something for Austria', who were awaiting the outcome 'with anxiety'. With Laval's enthusiastic support he proposed a Central European Pact under which the defeated powers of the First World War (Austria, Hungary, Bulgaria and Romania) would be freed from the arms limitations imposed by Versailles and allowed to combine to create a strong military alignment.

Laval complained that Britain 'had no intention of taking any part in the effective defence of Austria'. Simon could not deny this, and replied that Britain would 'support' such a Pact but 'could not contract into it', claiming that it might cause misunderstanding if Britain were to support a declaration about Austria in the same way as France and Italy. MacDonald declared that Britain 'blessed and approved' the independence and integrity of Austria without further committing herself, insisting that he would not be shifted into more positive support for Austrian independence. A statement was issued at the conclusion of the Conference to the effect that 'The Three Powers recognized that the integrity and independence of Austria would continue to inspire their common policy.' Had it not been for British caution, the statement would have been far more strongly worded.

The second important item was illegal German rearmament, and the forthcoming appeal by France to the League to take action against Germany for her repudiation of her obligation not to impose conscription or to rearm. The French circulated a paper written by their representative in Cologne, which must have left the delegates in no doubt that Hitler intended in the near future to remilitarize the Rhineland, either by agreement or by unilateral action. This led the Three Powers at Stresa to reaffirm their obligations under the Treaty of Locarno and declare their intention, 'should the need arise, faithfully to fulfil them'.[3]

At Stresa the three victorious powers of the Great War committed themselves for the last time to hold Germany down and prevent her rearming, and the 'high tide' of resistance to Germany was reached when a British–French–Italian resolution condemning the German rearmament and conscription in breach of the Treaty of Versailles was passed by the Council of the League of Nations at Geneva on 17 April, two days after the Stresa Conference had ended. Condemnation of Germany was unanimous (with only Denmark abstaining), and a Committee of thirteen – which included Russia – was set up to consider how sanctions against Germany could be applied.

In spite of British lukewarmness, Stresa had set up a solid three-power front against Hitler. Phipps, the British Ambassador in Berlin, reporting on the German reaction to the Geneva resolution, wrote:

> . . . it might have far-reaching consequences in Germany, and would probably put an end to Germany's return to the League . . . German public opinion is so hostile to the League that it will support Herr Hitler unreservedly in any action which he may choose . . . Moderate opinion in military and official circles is unanimous in regarding the League's attitude as the acme of hypocrisy . . . Hitler may now press on with rearmament at an increased pace.

In the Foreign Office, R. F. Wigram of the Central Department added a resolute Minute to Phipps's telegram on 17 April:

> We must stand firm now. As to the League I don't know that we want Germany back while she is trying to blackmail us about colonies and no doubt other things. Perhaps Hitler will 'associate further negotiations on disarmament with other European questions', but there too we must not be blackmailed. The possibility of a further expansion of the Air Force is not surprising. It is inevitable as long as Germany is not convinced that the other powers cannot expand quicker than she.

Unfortunately, Wigram's strong line did not appeal to either Simon or Eden. In a telegram to Baldwin, Simon revealed his antipathy to the Geneva resolution:

> It became in fact clear at an early stage in the Stresa negotiations that no such solidarity could in fact have been achieved except on condition of collaboration at Geneva on French reference. It should be added that I succeeded in considerably altering terms of the resolution agreed at Geneva.

Anyone reading the small print of the British documents must be left with the clear impression that Mussolini was ready to use Italian armed strength to restrain Hitler, while Britain was not. The Oxford historian R.B. McCallum has written that 'Italy with her military force and strong and virile Government held the balance of power in Europe'. The three participants at the Stresa Conference had ample strength to prevent further German rearmament, but all chance of this was dissipated by Britain's reluctance to act.[4]

On 25 and 26 March 1935 Eden (Under-Secretary at the Foreign Office) and his chief, Sir John Simon, had talked to Hitler in Berlin. However, there was a sinister development. Simon had previously told Hitler that the British government 'earnestly desired' an agreement with Germany over limits on naval power, and on 16 March Hitler had told the British Ambassador in Berlin that he would be content with 35 per cent of the strength of the Royal Navy. In Berlin on 26 March Simon indicated to Hitler that this figure was probably too high.

By a Foreign Office quirk of the time, all issues of naval disarmament were dealt with by the American Department — not the Central Department, where the German problem was understood. Unlike the American Department, the Central Department, and especially Wigram, were against any naval agreement. Although the Department recorded the opinion that the proposed agreement was 'gratuitously providing the German Government with just the kind of opportunity they so much relished to drive a wedge between Britain and her closest friends', these warnings were disregarded by their colleagues and by the Foreign Secretary.

Eden initially reported to the Cabinet (although later he did not stick to his guns) that 'there was no basis for agreement with Germany in view of her demands on land and sea'. The Cabinet ignored the fact that to make a bilateral naval agreement with Germany divorced from general disarmament, and to permit her – the vanquished power – 35 per cent of British naval strength, was a clear breach of Part 5 of the Treaty of Versailles; and that to do so in the absence of consultation with the other powers was a breach of the Treaty of Locarno. Simon and the Cabinet yielded to Admiralty arguments that the Royal Navy were acutely short of ships, too short to police, at the same time, the Far East, the Mediterranean, and German coastal waters.

Following Simon's visit to Berlin, Anglo-German talks began in London on 4 June 1935. Ribbentrop, the chief German delegate, declared in his opening speech that he would end the talks forthwith unless Britain conceded at the outset the principle of the 35 per cent ratio which Hitler had demanded from Simon in Berlin in March. At first the British delegation asserted that they must give other governments an opportunity to express their views before a final agreement could be reached, but in face of Ribbentrop's intransigence this was dropped; the Cabinet Committee responsible was told by Simon and his advisors that 'it would be a mistake to withhold acceptance merely on the ground that other powers might feel some temporary annoyance at our action', and warned that 'if we now refuse to agree the offer for the purpose of the discussions Herr Hitler will withdraw the offer and Germany will seek to build up to a higher level than 35 per cent'.

On 7 June 1935 the Conservative Stanley Baldwin succeeded Ramsay MacDonald as Prime Minister and formed a new National Government in which Sir John Simon moved to the Home Office and Sir Samuel Hoare took his place as Foreign Secretary. Only two days before, on 5 June, following a lunch at 10 Downing Street for the British and German delegates to the talks, the Prime Minister (MacDonald) had called a short, informal discussion in the Cabinet Room with the Ministers responsible, at which it was quickly agreed that Simon should be authorized to accept Ribbentrop's take-it-or-leave-it demands for a 35 per cent ratio.

Simon subsequently confirmed to the Germans Britain's agreement 'to a permanent relationship between the two fleets in the proportion of 35 per cent for the German fleet and 100 per cent for the British', noting that it was 'extremely important that we should officially inform the other Governments before anything at all appeared in the press'. Simon's signature appears on an *aide-mémoire* of the agreement dated 6 June 1935 – his last day as Foreign Secretary; Sir Samuel Hoare brought it to the House of Commons a few days later.

The Germans were cock-a-hoop. They never had the slightest intention of abiding by the agreement, but the 35 per cent gave them a cloak behind which they could build as fast as they liked. The Anglo-German Naval Agreement signed on 18 June 1935 also allowed Germany the right to submarine tonnage equal to the total possessed by the British Commonwealth. Over submarines Ribbentrop told one lie after another. British secret service reports about the building of illegal German submarines must have been conveniently ignored. In the cross-examination of Admirals Raeder and Dönitz during the Nuremberg Trials after the war it emerged that both the Weimar Republic and the Nazis had built submarines and warships in breach of Versailles. Churchill later correctly assessed the Anglo-German Naval Agreement: 'What had in fact been done was to authorize Germany to build to her utmost capacity for five to six years to come.'

The news of the Agreement was immediately sent to all the London ambassadors of other countries. The French reaction was to deplore it as 'an unauthorized revision of Versailles', and 'a serious

blow to the common front of Stresa six weeks before which had prejudiced the prospect of reaching an acceptable solution of the armament problem as a whole'.[5]

It was reported from Rome that Mussolini had nearly gone
through the roof of the Palazzo Chigi when he heard about the
Anglo-German Agreement. He could hardly believe that, after con-
curring with him about the need to guarantee independence for
Austria and the need to stop German rearmament, the British could
so soon after Stresa have made such a volte-face; he felt the British
government were so frightened of Hitler that they had lost faith in the
League of Nations' ability to prevent war. Beyond doubt this episode
encouraged him to believe that Britain would not invoke the League
to prevent his Abyssinian adventure.

Unknown to Britain, the Duce had sent a memorandum to
Marshal Badoglio, Commander of the Italian Army, on 30th
December 1934:

*Memorandum by Mussolini for Marshal Badoglio, Chief of the General Staff;
Directive and Plan of Action to Solve the Abyssinian Question.*

The problem of Italian-Abyssinian relations has very recently shifted from
a diplomatic plane to one which can be solved by force only. The Negus
[the Amharic title for the Supreme Ruler, or Emperor] has aimed at
centralising the Imperial authority and reducing to a nominal level,
through continuous violence, intrigue and bribery, the power of the
Rases [chieftains] living in the peripheral areas. A long period will be
needed before Abyssinia can be described as a state in the European sense
of the word . . .

Abyssinia is equipped with really modern arms, the number of which is
beginning to be considerable . . . Time is working against us. The longer
we delay the solution of this problem, the more difficult the task will be
and the greater the sacrifices . . . I decide on this war, the object of which is
nothing more or less than the complete destruction of the Abyssinian
army and the total conquest of Abyssinia. In no other way can we build
the Empire . . .

For our arms to achieve a rapid and decisive victory, we must deploy on
a vast scale the mechanised forces, which are now at our disposal, and
which the Abyssinians either do not possess at all or do so only in an
insufficient degree, but which they will possess within a few years . . . The
speedier our action the less likely will be the danger of diplomatic
complications. In the Japanese fashion there will be no need whatever
officially for a declaration of war and in any case we must always emphasize the purely defensive character of operations. No one in Europe
would raise any difficulties provided the prosecution of operations
resulted rapidly in an accomplished fact. It would suffice to declare to
England and France that their interests would be recognized . . .[6]

Mussolini believed it when he said that 'No one in Europe would raise any difficulties', overlooking the delicate matter of Abyssinia's membership of the League of Nations. It did not occur to him that Britain, who had taken a generous line over Corfu, would refuse to acquiesce in his conquest of Abyssinia on the grounds that he was breaching the Covenant of the League. After all, she had condoned Japanese aggression in Manchuria in September 1931, when the Japanese occupied the Chinese town of Mukden, and from then on waged what was in everything but name a war against China. The Chinese had appealed to the Council of the League, but instead of citing Japan as an aggressor and imposing sanctions against her, in January 1932 the Council had appointed a Commission to report on what had happened. The Commission, under the chairmanship of Lord Lytton, reported that a large area of what was indisputably Chinese territory had been forcibly seized by the armed forces of Japan. The Assembly of the League met on 6 December 1932 to consider the Lytton Report, but Simon surprisingly whitewashed the Japanese, and the League capitulated, greatly damaging its standing. The Duce could not bring himself to believe that Britain would take a less friendly attitude to Italy over Abyssinia than she had to Japan over Manchuria.

The Foreign Office archives reveal that for the preceding ten years Britain had consistently taken the line that Italy ought to be allowed to colonize Abyssinia and be the dominating power in that area, and that the only British interest was in the headwaters of the Nile. This is clear from a long secret report from Sir John Maffey, Permanent Under-Secretary at the Colonial Office, who in March 1935 was appointed chairman of a committee of top civil servants asked to report whether British interests would be damaged if Italy took over Abyssinia. His report, ready in June 1935, stated that 'No vital British interest is concerned in Ethiopia except the head waters in Lake Tsana [*sic*] and the Nile basin.' Although a spy in the British Embassy in Rome immediately sent the report to Mussolini, it added little to what had been known to the Italians beforehand. In February 1936 the Prime Minister, questioned about the Maffey Report in the House of Commons, stated that it had not been completed; Mussolini then immediately published it almost in full in *Il Giornale d'Italia*, much to Baldwin's embarrassment.

The Abyssinian crisis had begun in December 1934 on the badly defined border between Italian Somaliland and Abyssinia at Wal Wal, when Italian troops fought Haile Selassie's for possession of the wells there. The Italians demanded compensation from the Abyssinian government; the Abyssinians invoked the arbitration procedure pro-

vided by her 1928 treaty of friendship with Italy. When the Italians
rejected this, Abyssinia applied to the League of Nations. No friendly
solution of the dispute could be found; the Abyssinians tried in vain to
get it put on the agenda for the session of the League of Nations following the Stresa Conference on 18 April 1935, but France shied
away from this because of the importance of presenting a solid front,
with Italy, on the more vital question of German rearmament.

Mussolini had begun to fear lest, as part of Britain's appeasement of
Hitler and her search for a 'general' settlement with Germany, African
colonies would be offered to Hitler; and Abyssinia was a likely candidate. He believed that as one of the victors Italy should at Versailles
have been given a colonial mandate over her, similar to the French
mandate in Morocco and the British mandate in Egypt, and that the
Ethiopian part of Abyssinia – to which Haile Selassie had little legal
claim – was ideal for economic exploitation by Italy. Abyssinia was
landlocked, her only exit to the sea through French Somaliland: one
attraction for Mussolini was that acquiring the Abyssinian Empire
would link the existing colonies of Italian Somaliland and Italian
Eritrea.

Between 4 and 7 January 1935 Pierre Laval, French Foreign
Minister (and soon to be Premier), had held talks with Mussolini in
Rome, resulting in the Rome Accords, which marked a much-to-be-
welcomed improvement in Franco-Italian relations. The agreement
included secret military clauses with promises of mutual support, the
terms of which were not revealed to the British. France ceded territory, mostly desert, adjoining the Italian colonies of Cyrenaica (Libya)
and Eritrea, and offered the Duce two thousand shares in the
Djibuti–Addis Ababa Railway. In return Mussolini relinquished
Italian claims in Tunisia, where there were nearly as many Italians as
French. Laval ceded to Italy all French economic interests in
Abyssinia, and in private conversation promised Mussolini a 'free
hand' in Abyssinia. There is controversy over what Laval intended by
this, but Mussolini's subsequent conduct makes it clear he considered
Laval to mean that he would condone a military operation. Without
this, Mussolini's bargain would have been an extremely poor one. No
record of the conversation can be found in the French archives; it
is possible that Laval was deliberately ambiguous, or he may have
thought that Mussolini did not seriously intend a military operation.
Nevertheless, on 23 January 1935 the Duce ordered preparations for
war against Abyssinia, and in February a military build-up began in
the Italian colonies of Eritrea and Somali.[7]

The Rome Accords included provision for consultation between
France and Italy if Austrian independence was threatened, and if

Germany rearmed in contravention of her Versailles obligations. The meeting between Laval and Mussolini was followed by military talks between General Badoglio and General Gamelin to concert plans against Germany if she broke the Treaty of Locarno; 2,000 French war veterans paraded in Rome, and a French naval squadron visited Naples. De Felice produces convincing evidence that Laval promised Mussolini a 'free hand' for military operations in Abyssinia, in return for an Italian guarantee to come to the help of France in the event of war with Germany. He considers this Mussolini's greatest diplomatic triumph.

A Franco-British conference was held in London in February 1935, at which Britain approved the published agreement; but the British were told nothing of the secret clauses, the 'free hand' mentioned by Laval, nor the undertaking to approve Italian military designs on Abyssinia. Later, in Geneva, Laval emphasized to Anthony Eden that France had only given Mussolini a 'free hand' in Abyssinia in economic matters, and claimed to have warned Mussolini against the use of military force: he was not speaking the truth.

On 25 December 1935 Mussolini wrote to Laval that he had understood him to have several times mentioned a 'free hand' during the conversation of 6 January, and claimed that it was the belief that he (Mussolini) had obtained Laval's compliance and sympathy that had set him off on his path; Laval's reply was that he had never given his consent to a war. Mussolini was later to tell Eden that, while there was no written record of Laval's compliance, since Italy had yielded to France the future of 100,000 Italians in Tunis and received in return 'half a dozen palm trees in one place and a strip of desert which did not even contain a sheep in another', it was plain that France must have disinterested herself in Abyssinia.[8]

On 30 January 1935 Leonardo Vitetti, Counsellor at the Italian Embassy in London, went to the Foreign Office to give Geoffrey Thompson, Head of the Abyssinian Department, an outline of the Laval–Mussolini Rome Accord; Vitetti said that Italy was anxious to come to some similar agreement with Britain. In addition Dino Grandi, the Italian Ambassador, had told Sir John Simon on 29 January that France had renounced any interest in Abyssinia she might have under the tripartite agreement of 1906, except over the railway. Following this, Vitetti saw Thompson again and provided details which should have alerted the Foreign Secretary to the imminent crisis, but the only action taken was to appoint the Maffey Committee, as we have seen, to report on the situation, about which the Foreign Office already knew the pertinent details.[9]

Believing that France had given him a 'free hand' in Abyssinia,

Mussolini felt he had reason to hope that he would be able to make a similar bargain with Britain, and his later complaints about Britain's failure to respond to his overtures have some justification. It has never been properly explained why Abyssinia was not put on the official agenda at Stresa. Sir John Simon was well known to be hostile to Haile Selassie's regime, through his support for his wife's activities with the Anti-Slavery Society. In a speech in London on 9 May 1933, Lady Simon, referring to the 'five million slaves in Abyssinia', had declared that '. . . these human chattels are marched down to the coast, never to see their families again'. After her speech, Sir John Simon announced that he had left the House of Commons early in order to be present, because 'Both my wife and I have this subject deeply at heart.' Probably Simon did not want Abyssinia on the Stresa agenda. After Stresa, Ramsay MacDonald wrote to Vansittart that he could not understand why

> . . . Mussolini had not said a word about Abyssinia at Stresa, and that it had never come to my ears that the delegates had mentioned it. [Junior officials on both sides had mentioned it in private conversation.] Mussolini had privately mentioned various things to me that had not come before the official conference. I could not understand why he never whispered Abyssinia in my ear.[10]

MacDonald was well past his best by 1935; it is alleged that at Stresa Mussolini called him 'an old dotard', and that on one occasion the interpreter found it impossible to make sense of what the British Prime Minister said. However, Simon was at the peak of his powers, and bears a heavy responsibility for misleading Mussolini about the 'likely' British attitude to an Italian invasion of Abyssinia. The historian E.H. Carr has said of the meeting at Stresa that 'Their silence in face of undisguised Italian preparations for war was interpreted by Signor Mussolini to mean that Great Britain like France was content to regard his [Mussolini's] African venture with a benevolent eye.'[11]

Mussolini had taken pains to let the British know of his plans. On 16 February 1935 the Italian diplomat Marchese Theodoli, President of the League of Nations Mandates Commission, had told Drummond, the British Ambassador in Rome, that Italy was planning a military conquest of Ethiopia, and later in conversation with Drummond Mussolini said that 'if the League took action contrary to Italian interests he would know what conclusions to draw', adding that until a *modus vivendi* was reached he would continue to send troops, to a total of half a million.

Simon had previously telegraphed to Drummond on 16 January that

We must make last attempt to prevent matter going before the Council of the League. The Italian attitude as you forecast it may provoke a lamentable crisis at Geneva in which the blame would not be put on Ethiopia . . . This appears to be the last contribution that we can make to assist in bringing about the amicable settlement which Italy desires; and if Signor Mussolini rejects it there will be nothing further that I personally, or this country individually, can do to avert a crisis which may be disastrous for the League.[12]

Simon brought up Abyssinia in Cabinet on 27 February 1935; he said 'the situation had deteriorated', and that he felt it necessary to put on record to Mussolini, in the friendliest manner, 'our misgivings'. After that the Cabinet, surprisingly, did not discuss Abyssinia again for four months, despite increasing evidence of Mussolini's build-up for war. Significantly, on 9 March Vitetti, the Counsellor at the Italian Embassy, told Ronald Campbell of the Foreign Office that since their agreement with France on 7 January, Italy 'now felt able to embark upon a more imprudent [the word used by Campbell in his report] policy than had previously been possible'. Campbell's minute was that 'this is most unpleasant'.[13]

According to Geoffrey Thompson at the Abyssinian Department, Simon had said to him in Geneva in January 1935, 'You realize, don't you, that the Italians intend to take Abyssinia?' A minute by Thompson dated 17 March notes that the Italian Foreign Office had let it be known that they considered Stresa to be an opportunity for informal talks (on Abyssinia) 'between Italian, French and British statesmen which should not be missed'.

Mussolini took to Stresa his Abyssinian experts, Vitetti and Giovanni Guarneschelli; Simon took Thompson; and Thompson had four cordial talks with the Italians. Guarneschelli told him that the Duce regarded a settlement of the Abyssinian question as urgent, and that he did not consider it could be settled as Britain wanted, by the Conciliation Committee of the League. Abyssinia, according to the Italians, was a fourteenth-century state with a continuing tradition of slavery and cruelty, and had failed to develop her resources; whereas Italy was denied the opportunity for constructive work in her colonies because they consisted only of arid stretches of coastline.

Thompson warned the Italians of the dangers of a 'forward' military policy in Abyssinia, the consequences of which would be impossible to foresee. The Italians countered by expanding on Italy's need for more colonies – especially as Germany now wanted overseas possessions in Africa. Thompson evaded this point, but when Guarneschelli suggested that Britain should aid Italy in her Abyssinian adventure, he told the Italians it was useless to expect it. He had however no authority to warn the Italians that Britain would treat an attack on Ethiopia as a breach of the Covenant of the League of Nations, with its attendant consequences; nor were the Cabinet in a mood to do so. It was agreed that the Italians and French would exchange views in Geneva with Gaston Jèze, the French legal adviser to Haile Selassie.

In his hotel bedroom, Thompson wrote four long memoranda explaining his deep concern at the danger of an Italian attack on Ethiopia with the resultant menace to the League and to the collective security of its members. He was invited to breakfast by Simon on 14 April to discuss his concerns, but after five minutes Simon's private secretary came in and interrupted the *tête-à-tête*. Simon did not refer to Abyssinia again, and immediately after breakfast announced that it was time to go to the island on the lake for the main conference. Thompson described his meeting with Simon as 'a sad anti-climax'.[14]

When Ramsay MacDonald held a press conference in Stresa at the end of the talks, he said nothing about Abyssinia, and when Alexander Werth, the diplomatic corespondent of the *Manchester Guardian*, asked the Prime Minister whether Abyssinia had been discussed, MacDonald replied, 'My friend, your question is irrelevant.' This was widely reported, and Mussolini interpreted it as another nod to go ahead with his invasion. Gladwyn Jebb (later Lord Gladwyn), then at the British Embassy in Rome, recorded in his memoirs the amazement there that Abyssinia had not been discussed at Stresa, and his opinion that Mussolini had been 'tipped the wink' to go ahead. Perhaps the best comment comes from Sir Eric Phipps, who after the war wrote to Lord Hankey, Secretary to the Cabinet:

> How could MacDonald, Simon and Vansittart have gaily omitted even to mention Abyssinia? . . . All the Ethiopian imbroglio sprung from that hideous error. Naturally Mussolini thought he could go safely ahead despite what Drummond and Grandi may have told him.[15]

Mussolini must have realized that to attack Abyssinia would put at risk the coalition of France, Britain and Italy, pledged at Stresa jointly to prevent German rearmament and aggression, yet it was with reason that he had convinced himself Anglo-French opposition to an Abyssinian adventure would be confined to diplomatic gestures.

Margherita Sarfatti begged Mussolini to abandon his 'dangerous adventure', pointing out that there were opportunities for greater projects in Italy:

> You have enough already to colonise in Apulia, in Sicily and in Calabria. There's positive work to do here. If you go into Ethiopia you will fall into the hands of the Germans and then you will be lost. If we have to pay for the Empire with the ruin of Europe we will pay too high a price.

Mussolini would not listen to her. It was too late; her sexual attraction for him was waning (she was in her mid fifties), and with it her power to influence him.[16]

On 21 May 1935 Drummond and Mussolini talked in Rome. Mussolini alarmed Drummond by stating that while he did not want to quit or damage the League, if it became hostile to Italy and supported Abyssinia, he would leave. Drummond probed to discover whether the Duce would be satisfied with an Italian mandate or protectorate over Abyssinia, such as Britain had in Egypt. The Duce suggested that Abyssinia should come under Italian influence, as Morocco was under French and Egypt under British. He cited the example of Egypt in particular: it was a more or less independent country, with a King, but would not be allowed to do anything to endanger the Suez Canal or any vital British interest while Britain had there a High Commissioner and provided the head of the Army, the Chief of Police, and various other advisers. Vansittart minuted on Drummond's despatch reporting this conversation:

> There is one ray of hope in this: the analogy of Egypt with her 'King and political independence'. We ought to bear this in mind and explore it further. It is probably the least that the League (and the peace of Europe) will get away with. We ought to think of this seriously and in advance.

Here was a possible solution which might both satisfy Mussolini and keep the Stresa Front united, a means of allowing Italian penetration of Abyssinia to proceed without infringing the Covenant of the League of Nations. Unfortunately, Vansittart quickly changed his mind; three weeks later, on 12 June, he minuted:

> I also at one time had played with the Egyptian analogy. I have now abandoned it. If therefore we cannot satisfy Italy at Abyssinia's expense we are as before confronted with the choice of satisfying her at our own (plus some eventual Abyssinian frontier rectification) or letting things drift on their present disastrous course.

On 8 June Vansittart had minuted the Foreign Secretary suggesting, not an Italian mandate in Abyssinia, but the sacrifice of part of British Somalia to Mussolini:

> Italy will have to be bought off – let us use and face ugly words – in some form or other, or Abyssinia will eventually perish. That might in itself matter less if it did not mean that the League would also perish (and that Italy would simultaneously perform another volte-face, into the arms of Germany) . . . we cannot trade Abyssinia. The price that would now satisfy Italy would be too high for Abyssinia even to contemplate . . . either there has got to be a disastrous explosion – that will wreck the

League and very possibly His Majesty's Government – or else *we* have got to pay the price . . . with British Somaliland . . . Personally I opt unhesitatingly for the latter . . . We are grossly over-landed (and British Somaliland is a real debit).

This sensible suggestion might have resolved the dispute; unfortunately, it did not appeal to Eden. He wanted to stick by the Covenant of the League of Nations, and agreed emphatically with a minute dated 3 June by Owen O'Malley of the Italian Department: 'We must stick to League principles and stand the racket and the sooner this is made plain to Mussolini the better.'

Another constructive suggestion came from Ronald Campbell, who minuted on 12 June that Mussolini's colonial ambitions might be satisfied through 'an international conference which would redistribute colonies as part of a readjustment of the colonial mandatory settlements made after the 1914–1918 war.' This escape route did not appeal to Vansittart, who minuted: 'I don't think we can follow this. In any case it would be too indefinite to produce any effect on Signor Mussolini.'

Simon set out the dilemma in a Cabinet Paper dated 15 May:

We now have the clearest indication from the Italian Government that they contemplate military operations on an extended scale against Abyssinia as soon as climatic conditions permit and Italian preparations are complete . . . it is probable that the advance will take place in October . . . The choices facing the British Government are unpalatable. If they support against Italy a practical application of League principles their action is bound greatly to compromise Anglo-Italian relations and perhaps even to break the close association at present existing between France, Italy and the United Kingdom. On the other hand if the UK acquiesce His Majesty's Government will undoubtedly lay themselves open to grave public criticism.[17]

Simon concluded that substantial Italian forces would be locked up in north-east Africa at a time when Germany was rearming, and that Italian co-operation in Europe was more precious than Abyssinia's sovereignty. He advised the Cabinet that Britain and France should recommend Abyssinia

. . . to follow a policy more in accordance with modern conditions by recognizing Italy's claim to taking fuller part in increasing the trade between Abyssinia and the outside world and in assisting the development of the economic resources of the Abyssinian Empire.[18]

When Sir Samuel Hoare became Foreign Secretary in place of Sir John Simon on 7 June 1935, Vansittart immediately briefed him about the Abyssinian crisis, warning him that:

Italy might take military action against Abyssinia at the end of June at which point Italy will leave the League and thereby throw herself into the arms of Germany. The League and the Stresa Front will therefore be simultaneously broken and all our past policy shattered and our national future will be in clear danger.

These were strong words; at the same time, Vansittart made the constructive suggestion that Britain should give Mussolini a 'definite and concrete inducement' by ceding to Abyssinia the port of Zeila in British Somaliland, asking Abyssinia in return to cede part of the Ogaden to Italy.

Hoare put Abyssinia on the Cabinet agenda on 19 June 1935, but was unable to persuade the Cabinet to agree outright to Vansittart's suggestion, despite the fact that, as he told them, there was 'no sign of Mussolini's enthusiasm waning', while the French showed every sign of siding with Italy rather than the League, and there was every prospect of

> ... our being placed in an most inconvenient dilemma ... either we should have to make a futile protest to the League which would irritate Mussolini and perhaps drive him into the arms of Germany or we should make no protest and give the appearance of pusillanimity.

The Cabinet ruled that 'there should be no question of concluding any agreement involving the cession of British territory except as part of a complete settlement which had ruled out every prospect of war, and that every precaution should be taken to avoid facilitating the slave trade.'[19]

Hoare finally said he was not prepared at that time to propose to Mussolini that Britain should cede a part of British Somaliland; however, he asked permission from the Cabinet to allow Eden (who now had a place in the cabinet as Lord Privy Seal and Minister for League of Nations Affairs) to visit Rome to propose to Mussolini some sort of settlement on that basis; a proposed European air and naval agreement would provide ample cover for such a visit. Some members of the Cabinet suggested that it must be made clear that this was a 'sequel to long negotiations', otherwise Britain might be confronted with an early demand by Germany for colonies.

Drummond was instructed to see Mussolini and find out if he would be pacified by the cession of territory in the Ogaden and economic concessions in favour of Italy. At first Drummond thought the proposition was worth trying, but after talking to Suvich about it he changed his mind. The message from London had been leaked to Mussolini by the spy in the British Embassy, and the Duce had told Suvich he would not agree.[20]

It will be recalled that Eden was the most enthusiastic supporter of the League in the Cabinet, and that he had not favoured any transfer of territory from British Somaliland. He saw Mussolini on 24 June: Mussolini rejected the Ogaden–Zeila proposal out of hand, on the grounds that it would shift much of Abyssinia's trade towards Zeila and away from Italian Eritrea and Italian Somaliland. He explained to Eden that although he foresaw a crisis with both the League and Britain, he was determined to go ahead and annex Abyssinia. With considerable frankness, he warned Eden that there would either be a peaceful solution, with outright cession of the territories surrounding Abyssinia to Italy together with Italian control over Addis Ababa and the central nucleus – or there would be a war 'which would wipe Ethiopia off the map'. Eden replied that 'the difficulty of the situation was Abyssinia being, through no fault of England, a member of the League of Nations'.

The Duce then told Eden that Laval had promised him 'a free hand'. When Eden interjected that Laval had only given Italy a free hand in economic matters, a row was sparked off. Mussolini flung himself back in his chair in incredulous surprise. He later showed Eden on his maps the parts of Abyssinia where he insisted on direct dominion, and those where he would allow Haile Selassie nominal sovereignty, subject to Italian control. Eden did not refer again to the Zeila proposals.

Mussolini and Eden had in fact had a violent quarrel, rumours of which spread swiftly through the embassies and seminaries of Rome. A second meeting on the following day was even less successful. Eden had been lunching with Count Ciano, Mussolini's son-in-law, and was very late. (There is no doubt that the unpunctuality was Eden's own fault: he was enjoying the luncheon party, and reluctant to talk again with Mussolini.) The upshot of the meetings was that Eden became convinced – correctly – that Mussolini was determined to pursue his colonial war with Abyssinia, and impervious to British and League opinion. The Italian press, instructed by Mussolini, was openly contemptuous of Eden and his mission.[21]

According to the Italian diplomatic historian Mario Toscano, 'The dictator was said to have used violent language, and after this visit Eden was the symbol of blind opposition to Italy's legitimate place in the sun in Africa.' Samuel Hoare has recorded that Eden and Mussolini did not conceal their dislike of one another.[22]

From this time onwards, as will be seen, Eden's dislike of Mussolini almost amounted to a personal vendetta against him. Professor Camillo Pellizzi of London University – an Italian – told Tower of the *Manchester Guardian* that the generally held view in the Italian Foreign

Office was that Eden felt personally insulted by Mussolini's remarks and his subsequent behaviour at a luncheon, and that as a result 'he had adopted an almost vindictive approach to Italy'. Tower passed on Pellizi's remarks to the Foreign Office; Eden's minute on his report read:

> Pure balderdash. There was nothing in my reception at which I could have been offended, even were I an Italian and therefore susceptible to such feelings at the dinner table. Mussolini was definitely cordial through-out – our final interview was, of course gloomy – it had to be – but sad rather than bad, and there was no personal feeling whatever.

The use of the words 'even were I an Italian' indicates that Eden had indeed taken offence.

In the Foreign Office Vansittart, opposing Eden, argued with great vigour that nothing should be done to compromise the anti-Hitler front embodied in the Stresa agreement, and that to alienate Mussolini 'over so relatively petty a matter as Abyssinia, where there were no direct British interests, would be lunacy'.[23] Vansittart pressed his views upon Hoare with fervour; against them, Eden argued that it was vital for Britain to honour her obligations under the Covenant of the League of Nations. Eden's was a minority voice in the Cabinet, where the predominant view was that in the face of the current Nazi menace, nothing should be done which would involve Britain in a crisis with Italy.

Then came a bombshell which caused the government to put Vansittart's plan to appease Mussolini into reverse, to the delight of Eden and with immense detriment to the prospects of peace in Europe: this was the outcome of the 'Peace Ballot', announced on 27 June 1935.

During the early part of 1935 the League of Nations Union orga-nized a 'Peace Ballot' to ventilate popular feeling in Britain towards the League of Nations and its aims. It became a crusade in support of the League. Half a million people acted as canvassers; memories of the First World War were still vivid, and with Hitler raising the threat of another war, emotions were easily aroused. Debate over how much power the League of Nations should have to prevent the outbreak of another world war was sustained over eight months, and 11½ million people filled in the ballot forms. Ten million answered 'Yes' to the question whether, if one nation violated the covenant by attacking another member-state, the other states 'should combine to compel it to stop'; however, three million more voted in favour of the use of 'economic and non-military measures' than did so for 'if necessary, military measures'.

Although Lord Cecil (Lord Robert, now Viscount, Cecil), one of the leaders of the League of Nations Union, did not announce the final result until 27 June, the organizers skilfully contrived to make the progress of the ballot into a propaganda drive, which came to its climax in the last few weeks when the spotlight was on Mussolini's threat to attack a fellow member of the League. Thus, the announcement of the final figures triggered a political crisis.

In the House of Commons Winston Churchill and Austen Chamberlain argued with passion that sanctions must be taken against Italy if Mussolini violated the Covenant of the League by attacking Abyssinia; however, most Conservative MPs were more cautious. Strong support for Mussolini was voiced in the right-wing monthlies *English Review* and *Saturday Review*, while the *Daily Mail*, *Morning Post* and *Daily Telegraph* were also pro-Mussolini. The League of Nations Union organized their members to send letters demanding sanctions to every MP. The Labour front bench, Lloyd George, nearly all the Labour and Liberal MPs, and the *Manchester Guardian* and *Daily News*, supported the line taken by Eden and the League of Nations Union, that sanctions must be the inevitable corollary of an Italian attack on Abyssinia.[24]

Several English Catholic writers were pro-Italian, among them Hilaire Belloc, Christopher Hollis (whose book *Italy in Africa*, published in 1941, justified Mussolini), and Hollis's friend and fellow-convert, Evelyn Waugh. They saw Mussolini not only as the protector of Catholicism against the Nazis, but as the only effective barrier against Hitler's threatened annexation of Catholic Austria. Waugh wrote in the *Evening Standard*:

> Abyssinia is still a barbarous country . . . it is capriciously and violently governed and its own Government machinery is not sufficient to cope with its own lawless elements. It is entertaining to find a country where the noblemen feast on raw beef, but less amusing when they enslave and castrate the villagers of neighbouring countries. The Emperor Menelik succeeded to a small hill kingdom and made himself master of a vast population differing absolutely from himself and his own people in race, religion and history. It was taken bloodily and is held, so far as it is held at all, by force of arms . . . the Italians have as much right to govern; in the matter of practical policies it is certain that their Government would be for the benefit of the Ethiopian Empire and for the rest of Africa.

Such views were held only by a minority. Waugh was subsequently the *Daily Mail*'s correspondent in Abyssinia, from where he reported on the war with a strong pro-Mussolini bias; he was later glowingly appreciative of Italian colonial achievements.

Despite his domination of French foreign policy, Laval had to take into account the French League of Nations lobby, which like their British counterpart looked on the League as the best guarantee against German military aggression, On 8 August 1935 Charles Corbin, the French Ambassador in London, saw Vansittart and made it clear that France would not back Britain in demanding sanctions in the event of an Italian attack on Abyssinia, except in return for a firm assurance that Britain would support sanctions against Germany if that country violated the Covenant by attacking Austria or resorted to force anywhere in Europe. The Cabinet refused to give such assurances in terms which were satisfactory to France.[25]

During August the crisis deepened. Mussolini had an army of 800,000 on the Abyssinian borders, and his intention to invade was clear. On 22 August Hoare told the Cabinet that there would be a wave of public opinion unfavourable to the government if Britain failed to stand by the League and support sanctions against Italy in the event of an invasion. The Cabinet reluctantly agreed, with the reservation that 'we must keep in touch with the French and avoid trying to force nations to go further than they wished'. As Robert Rhodes James (Eden's official biographer) comments, 'When Ministers contemplated the possibility of the League imposing economic sanctions on Italy if she invaded Abyssinia, they became as apprehensive as Laval.' On the other hand, a General Election was due, and the Peace Ballot had made plain the strength of British public support for the League.

There was a sharp contrast between the government's public attitude over Abyssinia, the private views of individuals in the government, and the actual policies pursued. On 10 September and with the British voters in mind, Hoare addressed the League of Nations in Geneva. He gave ringing support to the Covenant, and stated that Britain would 'back the League in steady and collective resistance to all acts of unprovoked aggression'. The speech was accompanied by the despatch of a strong British naval force to the Mediterranean, which caused the French acute uneasiness; they feared they would lose the promise of Italian military support against Hitler. However, the government's public enthusiasm for the League was combined with contradictory attempts to appease Mussolini. This tug-of-war was the result of the irreconcilable split within the Cabinet. Hoare's Geneva speech in support of the League was, according to Eden in his memoirs, only a 'bluff', intended to force Mussolini into surrender.

Indeed, on 2 September Hoare had partially undone in advance what he was to say at Geneva, by sending a personal message to Mussolini to the effect that there had been no discussion within the League on closing the Suez Canal to Italy or taking military sanctions against her. Laval told the head of the Italian delegation in Geneva, Baron Aloisi, the same thing.[26]

On 18 September the League's Committee of Five (France, Britain, Spain, Poland and Turkey), set up in May to try to devise a compromise between Italy and Abyssinia, recommended in their report a system of League supervision and control of Abyssinian territories which would have amounted to a mandate for Italy. Mussolini was informed privately that their intention was that Italy should have the lion's share of control. Abyssinia appeared to be ready to agree, and the Italian diplomats at Geneva were conciliatory. Briefly, Mussolini was on the brink of acceptance. The report of the Committee of Five stated that: 'The representatives of France . . . and Britain are prepared to recognize a special Italian interest in the economic development of Ethiopia. Consequently these Governments will look with favour on the conclusion of economic agreements between Italy and Ethiopia.'

In despatches to Rome on 18 and 19 September Aloisi implored Mussolini to accept the proposals of the Committee of Five, pointing out that Britain would never agree to any solution which did not provide for the nominal continuation of the Abyssinian Empire, and that the advantage of the proposals was that they could be revised in five years' time, when Italy could make 'another leap forward', as the French had with their protectorate of Morocco after the Treaty of Algeciras in 1906. Aloisi also cited the advantages of reconciliation with the rest of the League 'in the deplorable circumstances of an *Anschluss* between Germany and Austria'. A meeting of his delegation and all the Italian politicians available in Geneva unanimously supported his entreaty to Mussolini to agree to the Committee of Five's solution 'in principle'.

Aloisi stressed to Mussolini the argument that once Italy had accepted in principle, pressure could be put on Britain and the other powers to allow Italy a working majority on the League institutions which would administer Abyssinia. Baron Astuto, one of the Italian delegation, telephoned a dedicated Fascist in the Italian Foreign Office in Rome and tried to convince him of the advantages to Italy of accepting the Committee of Five's proposals; the official's reply was: 'Yes, the frame is excellent, but there is no picture of the man inside' – implying that Mussolini would not derive enough personal glamour from such an agreement. Astuto responded: 'We are in Geneva to look after the interests of Italy, not to make collections of family pictures.' For this remark he was sacked.[27]

CHAPTER 9

Abyssinian War, and Sanctions

MUSSOLINI HESITATED ON the brink of invasion, wondering whether the Committee of Five of the League of Nations would allow him his way in Abyssinia; then on 3 October 1935 he ordered the bombing of Addis Ababa as his armies crossed the borders of Italian Eritrea and Italian Somaliland. Thus, five months after the creation of the Stresa Front, Europe was on the slippery slope leading to the Second World War; Mussolini was never trusted again. Fascist propaganda had convinced the Italian people that Italy had a right to an Empire in Africa, and Mussolini's appearance on the balcony at the Piazza Venezia to announce the invasion aroused genuine enthusiasm. Mussolini himself was longing for a military triumph to ensure his continued popularity, knowing he must give his people some dividend for the economic sacrifices they had made to create his armed forces.

On 10 October the League of Nations (with Hungary and Austria abstaining because of their special relationship with Italy) agreed to apply economic sanctions against Italy under Article XVI of the Covenant. Hitler was highly delighted, seeing in Mussolini's action an opportunity to change the balance of power in Europe. However, it was agreed in Geneva that a Committee of Eighteen should negotiate with Mussolini in the hope that an early settlement would make the imposition of sanctions unnecessary.

For a moment it seemed that the League had survived its most crucial test since its foundation, and might indeed fulfil the aspirations of those idealists who still believed that it could be an effective instrument in preventing war. But this was an illusion. There were no precedents for the use of sanctions as a deterrent, and improvising a mechanism for their implementation by many different countries, some of them unenthusiastic, was a lengthy process. Initially, consideration was given to closing the Suez Canal to Italy, and cutting off her oil supplies. Either would have halted Mussolini, but the necessary agreement was not forthcoming.

Laval told Eden that an agreement might be reached by giving

Mussolini a mandate for all Abyssinia except for those areas inhabited by the Amharic races – thus forfeiting to him three-quarters of Haile Selassie's Empire. Eden replied that the British government would not agree to reward an aggressor in this way; Hoare's reaction was less firm.

Eden pressed Laval to promise that France would support Britain over sanctions, expressing concern about the hostile attitude of the French press; it was, he felt, 'hard to believe the French would not stand shoulder to shoulder with us'. Laval replied that France must not be judged by her press, and that French opinion was much divided. Mendaciously, he promised to seek a mandate for economic sanctions.

On 24 September Hoare had asked Charles Corbin, the French Ambassador in London, whether Britain could count on military support from France if Italy attacked her in revenge for her stand over sanctions. Laval would not permit Corbin to reply until 8 October, when he informed Hoare that Laval would require '*consultation et accord*' before rendering assistance. Vansittart minuted that this was not an honest reply, his opinion being that Laval wanted 'a loophole for French inaction if we got into trouble'. On 7 October the French Foreign Minister Pierre Flandin had told Hugh Lloyd Thomas (British Minister in Paris) that the average Frenchman had no faith in the League, and that no French government would risk war to carry out obligations under the Covenant; Vansittart minuted: 'This is an exceedingly grave statement coming from the late French Prime Minister . . . he is probably speaking the truth.'[1]

In the ultra-nationalist *Echo de Paris* the French historian Louis Madelin expressed surprise that the British, who had been so passive over German rearmament, should work themselves into a rage over the far less dangerous problem of Ethiopia: 'What are one hundred thousand Italians threatening Ethiopia next to ten million soldiers who are being drilled between the Rhine and the Niemen, and to what end? To defend themselves? Who is threatening them?' An editorial in the same paper expressed anguish at the 'dreadful prospect' which was about to unfold. If the sanctions against the Italian aggressor now being talked about in Geneva were to have any practical effect they would have to be imposed by force, leading to war between Italy and Great Britain; and if the French refused to support the British against the Italians, the British would have a ready-made excuse for not lifting a finger to help the French in case of further trouble with Germany.

Leading French intellectuals and anti-Fascist writers such as André Malraux continued to register strong support for collective action by the League against Italy; but there was not the same enthusiasm for the

League in France as in Britain. Instead, there was widespread fear that only lukewarm French support for sanctions against Italy might provoke the British to let the French fend for themselves the next time Hitler made an aggressive move. Five months later, when Hitler remilitarized the Rhineland in defiance of the treaties of Versailles and Locarno, such fears were shown to be well-grounded, as will be seen.[2]

Laval then caused the British government concern by asking them to reduce the Royal Navy's fleet in the Mediterranean, on the grounds that its strength was unjustified; unless it was reduced, he reserved his right to refuse to come to the help of Britain if Mussolini made a wild attack on her, although he would honour France's obligation after reduction, when Mussolini could no longer 'make his specious claim' that British ships constituted a menace to Italy.

The strength of Britain's Mediterranean fleet had been increased following articles in the Italian press threatening attacks upon Suez, Gibraltar and Malta; according to Aloisi, Mussolini had privately informed the British that he would have taken the same action in their position, while publicly denouncing it as an intolerable threat. There was talk in Italy of sinking the British fleet in one surprise attack, of a suicide squad of pilots, and of a bomber capable of flying from Italy to London at such a height that it could not be detected.

Hoare reported the French attitude to the Cabinet on 16 October, stating that the French Admiralty had refused to discuss co-operation between the two fleets with the British Naval Attaché in Paris. The Cabinet, already lukewarm about sanctions, now had to consider the possibility of Britain having to take the lead at Geneva over their imposition without proper backing from France, and in some doubt as to whether France would come to Britain's aid if she were attacked by Mussolini.

At this Cabinet meeting Hoare and other members claimed that at Geneva Eden was 'giving the impression' of making all the proposals for sanctions while the French were constantly wrangling with Britain. The Cabinet accordingly authorized Hoare to send a message to Eden that they were extremely worried by Laval's stance, and asking him 'to go as slow as possible'. Eden was told to inform Laval that if Britain had felt confident of French naval co-operation, including the use of French ports, in the event of Italian aggression, she would have sent fewer reinforcements to the Mediterranean. The Cabinet recorded a concern that if Italy were to attack Britain in the Mediterranean, France might refuse co-operation on the basis that the Royal Navy had been 'provocative', and decided accordingly that until the French situation was cleared up, no further sanctions should be applied.[3]

The Foreign Office repeated a request to Paris for a 'plain and unequivocal assurance' of full support from France in the event of any attack by Italy. In return they emphasized that Britain had no intention of attacking Italy, except in the event of and in accordance with a League decision approved by France. If France would give the assurance requested, Britain was prepared to withdraw two battle cruisers from Gibraltar, provided Italy reduced her Libyan forces to approximate parity with the British garrison in Egypt. The Note warned of the grave consequences should France fail to make this assurance, to the imperilment of the Locarno Treaty: Britain might not honour the terms of the Locarno Treaty in the event of France being attacked by Germany, if France had been provocative to Germany in the same way as she alleged Britain was now being to Mussolini. This marked the lowest point in Anglo–French relations between the two wars. Laval's conduct justified this play on French fears that she might in similar circumstances be left to face a German attack without support from Britain, and the ploy worked. A satisfactory French reply was received on 18 October:

> In the concrete case . . . that is to say, a possible attack by Italy upon Great Britain by reason of the latter's collaboration in the international action undertaken by the League of Nations . . . French support of Great Britain is assured fully and in advance.

France further agreed that the Royal Navy could use the ports of Bizerta and Toulon in the event of an attack by Italy. The Cabinet decided that Laval should be asked to inform Mussolini that an Italian war with Britain meant war with France and, simultaneously, to resume naval staff talks. Laval then gave a categorical undertaking to co-operate, which he repeated to the Italian Ambassador in Paris. A nasty breakdown in Anglo–French relations had been averted. Then peace negotiations in Paris began to overshadow military considerations.[4]

Grandi wrote to Mussolini from London on 18 October 1935:

> I have had several talks with Ramsay MacDonald, now Lord President of the Council. He insists these must be kept secret because he tells me all the members of the Cabinet have promised Baldwin strict confidentiality.
>
> MacDonald no longer carries much weight in the Cabinet [he had been Prime Minister until June 1935] but he will stay as deputy Prime Minister and Lord President until the next General Election [14 November 1935]. He is strongly on our side.
>
> MacDonald is enraged against Eden and Vansittart; and more than anyone else against Baldwin, who with his policies is throwing away all the fruits harvested during the five years when MacDonald was Prime Minister, and has destroyed the Stresa Front, which MacDonald had hoped to bequeath as his political testament to his successor so that his

work would continue along realistic lines in the true interests of Britain. He [MacDonald] said:

'I went to Rome and accepted the Pact of Four because even today I am firmly convinced that this was the right path. If Mussolini and I had been listened to and followed, Europe would not find itself in its present condition. It is the Conservatives who are the demagogues, not me. For ten years they tried to make Mussolini believe that they were his friends, insisting that Fascism was the ally of a reactionary programme, and today they are throwing aside their mask . . . I will continue to fight in Cabinet against this unreasonable policy . . .'

In a letter to Sir Samuel Hoare, the Foreign Secretary, MacDonald told him that at Stresa Mussolini had confided that he had no confidence in France, and longed 'to keep up the old Anglo-Italian traditions'; he also informed Hoare of his [MacDonald's] own fears that, 'Although Mussolini is no mad dog, if he came to regard us as an enemy it would change the diplomacy of Europe, bringing in Germany as a deciding factor.'[5]

The Parliament elected in 1931 was nearing the end of its tenure, and on 18 October a General Election was called for 14 November. The Prime Minister was on the horns of a dilemma. He knew the Foreign Office were trying to negotiate a solution favourable to Mussolini with Laval in Paris and there was, he knew, strong opposition to sanctions within the Conservative Party. This erupted a few days before the Dissolution of Parliament on 19 October. A Conservative Parliamentary delegation of the Imperial Policy Group headed by Leo Amery (a former First Lord of the Admiralty and Secretary for the Colonies) and Lord Milne (Chief of the Imperial General Staff from 1926 to 1933), together with twenty MPs (including the young Alan Lennox Boyd, a rising star and former President of the Oxford Union) and several influential peers, had a meeting with Baldwin and Lord Stanhope, the Under-Secretary for Foreign Affairs.

Amery argued that British policy over the Italian–Abyssinian crisis was 'a complete and inexplicable reversal' of what it had been, in contrast to the spring of that year (an obvious reference to Stresa) when British foreign policy was 'on the verge of a happy fruition'. Amery claimed the government was being accused of following 'a peace ballot policy', and referred to a letter in *The Times* from a Colonel Gerogellerbet explaining why the Conservative Party should not follow it. Amery appealed to Baldwin to make a declaration now that the government would neither advocate, nor be a party to, sanctions that could lead to war.

Baldwin was in grave difficulties. Personally he agreed with the delegation, but he had already called a general election for which he had approved a manifesto seeking votes on the Peace Ballot policy, although a more honest course would have been to admit to the nation that the sanctions policy could be operated only if the French supported it. His reply revealed his indecision: he explained that there were 'obviously very great difficulties in saying in public' how far he would go.

At the next Cabinet meeting, on 23 October, Hoare informed his colleagues of the reply received from Laval on 18 October (which had been heavily leaked to the French press); he described it as satisfactory, although it still required Britain to reduce her naval forces in the Mediterranean; he also informed his colleagues that he had sent Maurice Peterson, head of the Abyssinian Department of the Foreign Office, to Paris to help the British Ambassador negotiate terms with Laval which would satisfy Mussolini.[6]

Before the Dissolution of Parliament, Hoare had emphasized in the House of Commons that Britain would support the League; but there would be no military measures – only economic sanctions – and no blocking of the Suez Canal; Baldwin too had reiterated the government's support for the League.

At this stage Mussolini was hoping for a quick end to the war through Anglo-French negotiations, writing to Vittorio Cerruti, his Ambassador in Paris, on 25 October that the British government wanted an agreement which would give 'a satisfactory recognition to Italian rights and interests', but that they must wait until after the General Election when Britain, able to be more flexible, would not rush into a failure which would give the world the impression that Italy had refused a fourth effort at conciliation. A week before, Alexis Léger, head of the French Foreign Office, had told Cerruti that Laval was angry over the British attitude to sanctions and would not support the closure of the Suez Canal, military sanctions, or a blockade; so that relations between France and Britain had become very strained.[7]

In flagrant disregard of the fact that Peterson had been sent as a secret envoy to negotiate a deal with Laval which must favour Italy at Abyssinian expense, Baldwin opened the Conservatives' election campaign with a broadcast endorsing the government's support for collective security through the League of Nations, at the same time pointing out the risks inherent in sanctions. The Conservatives maintained this line throughout the 1935 election, and government spokesmen emphasized their commitment to the Covenant of the League and their determination not to allow Italy to reap the rewards of aggression.

With his invasion not going completely according to plan,

Mussolini had suddenly become propitiatory. On 16 October he told Chambrun, the French Ambassador in Rome, that he was not opposed to a settlement, but wanted a mandate for Italy over the non-Amharic part of Abyssinia, together with strong Italian 'participation' in the Amharic central nucleus and a generous rectification of the frontiers in Ogaden and Danakil in Italy's favour. 'Participation' was interpreted in Paris to mean that 'instead of international help, the [economic] help would be Italian'; Peterson minuted, 'Signor Mussolini's latest ideas appear to me much more encouraging than anything we have before had' and Vansittart added, 'This seems to me a distinct step in advance . . . we should endeavour to give an encouraging tone to our communication.'[8]

Mussolini genuinely believed he could have the best of both worlds, maintaining the Stresa Front against Germany as well as conquering Abyssinia. He did not realize how difficult his aggression was for Britain to swallow in the aftermath of the Peace Ballot, with the majority of British public opinion rigidly opposed to Italy achieving her ambitions in Abyssinia. Even so the British government, anxious to propitiate Mussolini, held out an olive branch. On 17 October Drummond was instructed to tell Mussolini that the British government had no interest in the Italian–Abyssinian dispute beyond what was required by her obligations as a loyal member of the League, and that any statement or impression that they were seeking a quarrel with Italy 'can only have been spread by misinformed or ill-intentioned persons'. In discussing Drummond's instructions, some Foreign Office officials thought this soft line might harden Mussolini's terms for settling the conflict; Vansittart, however, strongly advised Hoare to send the telegram, because of his own worry lest an Anglo-Italian war be 'brought about by not only French lack of co-operation but [French] disloyalty and treachery in its dirtiest and blackest form'.

When Drummond gave Hoare's message to Mussolini the next day, the Duce replied that he was glad to receive it, but regretted that such a message was necessary; sanctions would constitute a state of siege for Italy, and make it more difficult for Italy to come to terms to end the war.[9] Drummond reported that while Mussolini was friendly, when he spoke about 'a state of siege his eyes popped and his mouth opened wide like a goldfish'. According to the Italian version of the conversation, Mussolini admitted that Italy had breached the Covenant, but considered this to be no justification for the punishing sanctions being discussed at Geneva, which could lead to war.

In Paris, Peterson and René de St Quentin of the French Foreign Office produced a draft plan which gave Italy a large slice of Abyssinian territory for 'exclusive economic development'. Peterson had been told to use as the text for his draft the Committee of Five's proposals nearly accepted by Mussolini on 18 September; but he went further. The draft provided for the British and French to suggest a settlement which involved a special regime for the non-Amharic territories, stated to be 'depressed by wars, slavery and famine so that the Central Abyssinian Government had been unable to administer them properly'. The draft pointed out that it would be difficult to get agreement at Geneva to an Italian mandate over Abyssinia, to which this amounted; instead, it was proposed that the area should be nominally under League supervision, with security exercised by a Foreign Legion under Italian command. Additionally, Italy would enjoy exclusive rights of economic development in the south, and sovereignty of the Danakil and Ogaden; all country south of the 8th parallel was to be ceded to Italy by Abyssinia; and the Abyssinian army was to be disbanded. In return, Abyssinia was to be compensated by a port at either Assab in Italian Eritrea, or Zeila in British Somaliland.[10]

From London Hoare sent a message to Laval that while he did not favour exclusive Italian control in Abyssinia, he was ready to concede to Italy 'an appropriate share in the personnel both of the Central Commission in the capital and of the administration of the provinces'; he agreed the proposed boundary changes. He preferred a *gendarmerie* to a Foreign Legion and expected Abyssinia to object to any port and corridor enclosed by Italian territory (which meant she would choose Zeila rather than Assab). Hoare wrote: 'To sum up, we feel the right and least complicated solution is by a simple exchange of territory, which on this basis clearly entails a large advantage to Italy.' In the end the main difference between Hoare and Laval lay in 'exclusive control by Italy' or 'a major share of the officials'.

On 29 October Drummond found Mussolini depressed and bitter, extremely pessimistic about avoiding war with Britain: 'if Italy was faced with the choice of being forced to yield, or war, she would definitely choose war even if it meant that the whole of Europe went up in a blaze . . . no Italian, and least of all himself, could contemplate that Adowa should revert to Abyssinia.' (Italian troops had just taken Adowa, which had been the scene of an ignominious Italian defeat in 1896.) Mussolini insisted that the proposals for a settlement which he [Mussolini] had made to Laval were 'very reasonable and in full accord with the spirit of the League'.[11]

While the British election campaign was in progress, Hoare and Eden went to Geneva, and on 1 November talked to Laval. Laval expressed disappointment at the British reply to the draft agreement, and told them he had heard that Mussolini was anxious to settle on the basis of the British giving Zeila to Abyssinia. Hoare told

Laval he favoured the Committee of Five's proposals for the central part of Abyssinia (which, as has been seen, meant virtual Italian control), and settlement otherwise by territorial concessions to Italy. Eden raised no demur at this plan, which would reward Mussolini for his aggression.

Hoare reminded Laval that he hoped Italy would, as a gesture, withdraw one of her divisions from Libya, where the Italian army posed a potential threat to the British in Egypt: the Laval-Mussolini bush telegraph was working well, and two days later the Metauro Division began to embark from Tripoli for Naples, in accordance with Mussolini's assurance to Laval. Hoare later told Baron Aloisi in Geneva that Britain was anxious to continue talks, asserting that prospects for an agreement were good. Italian press comment held that Laval was being prevented from coming to an agreement because the General Election was causing Britain to drag her feet.

At a meeting with Peterson in Hoare's room at the Foreign Office, Hoare informed him that, as soon as the election was out of the way, negotiations would continue with Laval for a simple exchange of territory and a plan of assistance for Abyssinia, effectively amounting to something near an Italian mandate.

On 14 November the Conservatives were returned with another overwhelming majority; Hoare and Eden continued in office. However, a thunder-cloud was now looming: the Canadian delegate to the League of Nations, Dr Riddell, had raised at Geneva the question of oil sanctions against Italy. In his alarm at the prospect Mussolini became belligerent, demonstrating all his inherent volatility and irresponsibility; he threatened to break his alliance with France and leave the League, hinting that he might bomb the French Riviera; he even moved troops to the French frontier. The Foreign Office feared that although relatively little separated Britain from agreement with Mussolini, war remained a possibility. Drummond's signals from Rome were very disquieting.

From Berlin, Phipps reported on 13 November that Germany was 'living in a state of war', and that military expansion would be followed by territorial expansion: Britain had 'no policy to stop them'. Abyssinia 'was not the only pebble on the beach . . . the present Ethiopian imbroglio [Phipps pointed out] is mere child's play compared with the German problem that will in the not very distant future confront His Majesty's Government.' Vansittart told Hoare, 'There is not a moment to lose.'[12]

Meanwhile, League officials began to plan oil sanctions. On 23 November Vansittart told Eden and Hoare that 'We must not have the oil sanction or the Duce will make war on us', and followed this by describing as 'suicidal' any idea of proceeding with oil sanctions unless Britain had 'full and concrete arrangements with the French' (for military support).

Baldwin's fears are betrayed in a letter to the Cabinet's Deputy Secretary, Tom Jones, who records him as writing that

> If Mussolini broke out there would be more killed in Valetta in one night than in all the Abyssinia campaign up to date, and until we got agreement with the French we would have to go single-handed fighting Italy for a month or so. French mobilisation would have led to riots. They are not ready in the air for mobilisation. Malta is the only harbour apart from those of the French where you can take ships with our wounded.[13]

Alarmed by the possibility of an Italian attack on Egypt from Libya, on 26 November the Cabinet despatched tanks and an infantry brigade with supporting troops to Egypt, and authorized the calling-up of some volunteers and reservists. Two days later the Chiefs of Staff reported grave shortages of anti-aircraft ammunition, and no hope whatever that any would become available within a reasonable period of time.[14]

On 21 November Hoare and Eden had instructed Peterson to go back to Paris to continue his quest for a compromise peace plan with Laval. Peterson was instructed not to engage in tripartite talks with Italian diplomats, but to confine himself to the French. Both Hoare and Eden were agreeable to an 'exchange' of territory, but Peterson was told to be cagey about the participation of Italian personnel in the League's plan for economic assistance. If pressed on this point, Peterson was to refer home for instructions.

On 25 November Peterson reported from Paris that the minimum terms which Laval expected Mussolini to accept were: outright cession to Italy of the whole of the Tigre, including Makale (now Mek'elē); frontier rectification of the Ogaden and Danakil, which 'would probably not, at least in the case of Ogaden, involve cession *in toto*'; creation of a very large special zone in southern Abyssinia bounded by the 8th parallel on the north and the 37th meridian on the west; this zone was to remain nominally under the 'Emperor's sovereignty', but 'Italy must be assured of complete control from the point of view of economic development and colonial settlement'. Peterson wrote that while in theory the area was only to be 'administered' by an Italian chartered company, this in fact amounted to cession to Italy. In return, the Emperor was to receive the port of Zeila in British Somaliland. It was a 'carve-up'. Peterson wrote that 'the present suggestion completely eliminated League control while making maintenance of Ethiopian sovereignty no more than a transparent fiction'. In the Foreign Office Patrick Scrivener, who had been in Addis Ababa from December 1933 to April 1935, minuted on Peterson's memorandum: 'One wonders whether in the light of Laval's evident intentions to be more Italian than Signor Mussolini, the continuation of these conversations will serve any *really* useful purpose.' The comment of Sir Lancelot Oliphant, a Foreign Office expert on the Middle East, was: 'It has all along been decided that we should try and hold the scales between Rome and Addis Ababa and not expose ourselves to a possible charge of tilting them in favour of Rome.' Vansittart, enthusiastic, minuted:

> . . . the terms are the best we can hope for; we should be very happy if the Italians accepted. We shall never get the Italians out of Adowa (the S[ecretary] of S[tate] has always been convinced of this too, I think) and we ought not to try . . . I would authorize Mr Peterson to go ahead at once . . . If we can convince the French I would be prepared to go to Rome next . . . we, I think, might use General Garibaldi [grandson of the Liberator] here.

Eden ignored the reservations expressed by Scrivener and Oliphant, minuting on 26 November 1935:

> I agree with Mr Peterson's (1) and (2) [cessation of Tigre and Makale plus Ogaden and Danakil to Italy] subject of course to the proviso we have always made and must always maintain, that a settlement must be acceptable to the three parties Italy, Abyssinia and the League. How large the area might be for the Italian chartered company would have to be a matter of bargaining. The Emperor could never agree to one third of his territory, or more, being so dealt with, and such a proposal would certainly have to be combined with non-Italian League control.

– evidence that in principle he was in agreement. Hoare minuted on 28 November: 'I agree. Let us proceed for the present on the lines of the last two minutes [Vansittart's and Eden's], which might satisfy Mussolini.'

Mussolini sent General Garibaldi to London as his personal emissary in an attempt to oil the wheels. Garibaldi told Vansittart on 28 November that Mussolini wanted a mandate for Italy over all the non-Amharic territory (exactly what Peterson had been told to suggest in Paris), and the cession of Zeila or Assab to Abyssinia in return; Mussolini also asked for a League of Nations mandate over the Amharic nucleus, the majority of League officials to be Italians. It was a promising approach.[15]

Mussolini's written proposals were circulated to the Cabinet, and at a subsequent meeting no objection to an Italian majority on the staff of any League of Nations team formed to administer the Amharic nucleus was recorded; it looked as though a solution might be within reach. Britain was prepared to concede almost as much as Mussolini wanted – but the government's difficulty was that the electorate would be shocked by such a volte-face hard on the heels of the Conservatives' election propaganda in favour of sanctions.[16]

Peterson reported from Paris on 30 November that he had agreed with the French that Adowa and Adigrat should be ceded to Italy and a large zone in the south put under Italian control, and that Laval was sounding Mussolini. A Foreign Office memorandum to the Cabinet set out the Peterson–St Quentin proposals, and the Cabinet agreed, with the proviso that the Tigre area should not be ceded formally to Italy for two or three years, and that in the interim its sovereignty should remain indeterminate under a League Commission (which clearly would be Italian-dominated). Eden in Cabinet concurred.[17]

A meeting about oil sanctions had been fixed for 29 November in Geneva. This panicked Vansittart, who sent an urgent note to Hoare saying that the paper on the oil embargo should not go to the Cabinet until he had discussed it with both the Foreign Secretary and Eden, and warning Hoare that 'we ought to walk very warily'. In several handwritten minutes he earnestly pressed that Britain should not proceed at Geneva with organizing oil sanctions 'because our mea-sures of defence and supplies of munitions are startlingly deficient', and that Britain should only take part in oil sanctions if France, Spain, Yugoslavia, Greece and Turkey would put in hand their military preparation

> so that the consequence, if any, will be shared . . . it must be clearly under-stood that we are neither the League's policeman nor its whipping boy . . . I beg you and Mr Eden to modify your oil paper to the Cabinet in this sense. We are getting very near the knuckle; we must have time and a big spurt at home immediately. To run the risk alone and unprepared would surely be unthinkable.

After seeing General Garibaldi, Vansittart wrote a further minute to the effect that the General had told him definitely that he feared Mussolini would go to war if 'oil goes on the list', and that 'he thinks Mussolini is in despair and has lost his head'. As a result of Vansittart's entreaties, Hoare agreed to the postponement of the scheduled meeting at Geneva.

On 18 November the Grand Fascist Council had met in Rome; Count Theodoli, President of the League of Nations Commission on Mandates, told Drummond that only three members, including Grandi, had taken a moderate stance on the subject of Abyssinia. All the others were extremists and, according to Theodoli, had announced that '. . . if Britain thinks she can compel us to submit by sanctions we would rather die fighting'; it was Theodoli's opinion that it would be a great mistake to assume that Mussolini and the Grand Council were bluffing. On this despatch Vansittart minuted, 'We are not in a position to call bluffs. We had better get on with peace-making (our own peace-making) as soon as possible . . . we are pushing on with Peterson's proposals.' He added that Grandi was an unsatisfactory channel, which was why he was using Garibaldi. Hoare agreed; he saw Garibaldi twice and assured the Italian he might tell Mussolini that Britain was ready for a serious negotiation. Garibaldi confirmed that Mussolini fully admitted the need for some kind of concession to the Emperor, and did not object to the cession to Abyssinia of an outlet to the sea at Zeila.[18]

The British Legation in the Vatican reported that the strong reaction of the Italian bishops against sanctions had strengthened Mussolini's hand, while the Pope had not checked the Cardinal of Milan's fervent anti-sanctions crusading. They also reported Pope Pius XI's confidential written opinion that it would be 'a truly meritorious action if the Great British people in a spirit of fraternal accord would realize by peaceful means the legal aspirations of the Italian people', and that although the Pope disapproved of Mussolini's methods, he was against unequivocal support of the League. On 21 November the British Legation sent the Foreign Office reports received from British Consuls in Italy which revealed widespread church support of Mussolini and dislike of 'iniquitous sanctions'. Hugh Montgomery, the Counsellor, concluded that while the Pope personally disapproved of the Abyssinian adventure, he abstained from discouraging the martial ardour of his bishops, feeling that nations must be allowed to espouse a national cause 'if they consistently feel able to do so'; he reported the Archbishop of Siena as claiming that 'our troops are fighting for civilisation', and the Archbishop of Brindisi as having described Haile Selassie as 'a half-savage king, a slave-owner and aggressor of the people'.

According to Drummond, the Italian nation 'in the face of sanctions was today united as it has never been before', while a well-known senator had said to one of the Embassy staff, 'You have achieved the miracle of uniting the whole of Italy behind Mussolini'; it was Drummond's opinion that unless Mussolini got the type of settlement he wanted, 'the Italian people under his direction will be prepared to fight until the last man'. In a letter to Vansittart Drummond reiterated that the threat of sanctions was bringing Mussolini near the end of his tether, to the point that he was 'determined to perish gloriously . . . by attacking us'. Vansittart insisted that

Hoare read this, noting gloomily, 'No one doubts that Italy is behind Signor Mussolini.'

Vansittart's alarm at the likelihood of war between Italy and Britain had its effect on Eden, once the keenest supporter of the imposition of oil sanctions: he now, on 29 November, told his Cabinet colleagues that the imposition of oil sanctions should be postponed until the result of the Hoare–Laval negotiations in Paris was known. A special meeting of the Cabinet was called for 2 December.[19]

In a paper circulated to this meeting Vansittart warned:

> We must be sure of our ground, i.e. Italy not making war on us, before we embark on oil sanctions . . . suicidal to press on with oil sanctions unless we come to a full and concrete agreement not only with the French, but with other military powers concerned

while Hoare noted:

> No AA guns available for defence of Alexandria . . . the only thing that could deflect an Italian attack would be to attack Italian bases in North Italy. We should require not only facilities for our own aircraft, but active co-operation (of French) air force in attack and defence.

Hoare told the Cabinet that an embargo on oil raised the risk of a 'mad dog' act by Mussolini. He had received a number of alarming reports that Mussolini would regard an oil embargo 'as rendering defeat inevitable', and it was feared he might use it as a pretext for attacking the British 'in the Mediterranean, although it was tantamount to suicide', while Imperial defence was weak as compared with an Italy 'mobilised for war'. Hoare pointed out that there was currently a barrage of peace moves on behalf of Italy, including those made by General Garibaldi in London and even by Grandi himself, who despite his previous gloom was now 'an enthusiast for peace negotiations'.

Hoare did not want to announce that Britain had abandoned the principle of an oil sanction; he favoured pressing on with Peterson's negotiations in Paris, so that when the League Committee met they might be told that peace talks were going on satisfactorily: 'For that reason we and the French were not asking for the immediate imposition of an [oil] embargo.' The Cabinet endorsed the Foreign Secretary's proposal that if peace talks showed a reasonable prospect of success, the oil sanction should be postponed. Hoare determined to go to Paris himself.

The Cabinet were given secret information indicating that 'the Italian threats of an active retaliation to an oil embargo had been implemented by actual preparations'. Duff Cooper, Secretary of State for

War, played down the shortage of anti-aircraft ammunition, claiming that 'clouds' would render AA guns of little value. Baldwin asked every member to give his view. The Cabinet Minutes do not identify the views expressed by particular individuals, but overall it was hoped the Foreign Secretary would take a generous view of the Italian attitude.

Eden was sufficiently impressed by Vansittart's alarming minutes about an imminent Italian attack to withdraw his demand for an immediate imposition of oil sanctions; he had previously had reservations about the correctness of Vansittart's views, as expressed by him in the following internal Foreign Office minute, quoted in his autobiography:

> . . . this danger [of an Italian attack] has always seemed to me very remote and I am quite unimpressed by the threats of such persons as Marchese Theodoli, who has clearly been instructed to frighten us as much as possible . . . In calculating the likelihood of a mad dog act the isolation of the Italian forces in East Africa should not be overlooked.
>
> Moreover Signor Mussolini has never struck me as the kind of person who would commit suicide. He has been ill-informed about our attitude in this dispute, and while he may well be exasperated, there is a considerable gap between that condition and insanity.

In summing up the Cabinet discussion of 2 December, Baldwin considered that there would be 'strong criticism of the Government unless it had done its utmost to avoid war', and that this criticism 'would be all the more bitter once the details of our defensive preparations became known'; it should be remembered that, whatever was done to try to ensure collective League action, Britain would almost certainly have to withstand the first shock of a hostile Italian reaction to the imposition of sanctions; finally, if anything went wrong with Mussolini, 'no one would be willing to tackle Hitler'.[20]

In his memoirs Hoare wrote of having made a mistake in not calling for a special Cabinet meeting to discuss the Paris negotiations, but his memory was at fault: the Cabinet meeting of 2 December discussed the peace plan at length.

Vansittart went first to Paris, where Hoare joined him on 7 December. The discussions which Peterson had held with St Quentin in October about possible peace terms had ended in near deadlock, but Peterson had been able to go back to Paris on 22 November expressing a more pliant British attitude. The talks then made rapid headway, with Britain ready to agree to any terms which stood a chance of being accepted both in Geneva and by Mussolini. Mussolini too was in an easier mood, and was in constant touch with Laval by telephone.

An alarmist message from Drummond on 6 December instilled a sense of urgency, however. He reported that after consultation with their French colleagues, his naval and air attachés in Rome considered it most probable that there existed a picked body of between one hundred and two hundred volunteer Italian pilots 'willing to take exceptional risks in air attacks upon British fleet'.

On 7 and 8 December, at Laval's request, Hoare agreed to surrender to Italy more territory in the Tigré, and to offer Abyssinia a port at Zeila; it was stipulated that Abyssinia should not be allowed to build a railway from Addis Ababa along the corridor carved out of British Somaliland to the port. Hoare also agreed to an economic monopoly for Italy, under League supervision, in a large zone in the south and south-west; and that Italy should keep Adowa and Adigrat. Laval telephoned to Mussolini, who replied that the proposals were acceptable. Vansittart congratulated Hoare on having stopped the Abyssinian war and re-established the Anglo-French front, and also on having brought Mussolini back to the Stresa Front. An agreement in French was typed out and initialled by both Hoare and Laval. The original agreement lies in the Public Record Office; it stipulates that the proposals must be referred to the League of Nations for approval or rejection, and that the terms must not be published before the League has considered them.[21]

Laval assured Hoare of French military support in the event of a 'mad dog' act by Mussolini, but Hoare afterwards recorded that the British Embassy in Paris 'doubted whether this could be forthcoming without a risk of internal disturbance'; he cited this as a reason for coming to an agreement. Under pressure from Laval, Hoare agreed that the terms should be sent immediately to Mussolini, but only later to the Emperor.

On 8 December Hoare sent an account of the talks to the Foreign Office, and Vansittart reported by telephone. Between them, they gave a full briefing, yet in his autobiography Eden claimed that he was 'astonished' when on the morning of 9 December Peterson stepped off the train from Paris and handed him that four-page document in French, initialled 'S.H./P.L.'[22]

In 1972, when the government archives for 1935 became available in the Public Record Office upon the shortening of the fifty-year rule to thirty years, R.A.C. Parker, the historian of Queen's College, Oxford, read all the documents referring to this agreement; he has written:

> After the Hoare–Laval Plan was condemned and abandoned, other members of the Cabinet began to treat it as a strange and personal aberration of Hoare's. In fact the Cabinet gave him a free hand, and after-

wards approved of what he had done. This is the only possible unbiased conclusion.

Eden's memory appears to have been much at fault when he was writing his memoirs, with such distortions of history as: 'We did not discuss any other possible peace terms either at Cabinet or between Ministers before the meeting with Laval'; he also recalls being astonished by the Peace Plan because he could not reconcile it with the instructions given to Peterson, writing that 'those terms went beyond anything which Peterson had earlier been authorised to accept when he left for Paris'. Eden cannot have had access to all the relevant documents when writing his memoirs. Unfortunately Eden's official biographer, Robert Rhodes James, writing twelve years after Parker, ignored Parker's research; he reiterates the Eden version, claiming that 'Hoare had no instructions to negotiate with Laval'; this has been shown to be incorrect.[23]

Before Hoare left Paris for Switzerland he wrote a letter to Baldwin strongly advocating acceptance of the proposals; and at the Cabinet meeting on 9 December Eden did not reveal to his colleagues any 'astonishment'. Instead, he asked for two amendments. The first was that Haile Selassie should be informed of the plan simultaneously with Mussolini; the other concerned a point of procedure in Geneva. He also stated his expectation that the question of an oil sanction would now be postponed, and demonstrated to his colleagues (with the help of maps) that all the territory Abyssinia was being asked to cede was non-Amharic, and the compensation to the Emperor involved in the outlet he was being given to the sea.

At this Cabinet meeting Eden supported the Hoare–Laval Plan in principle; he did however state his conviction that some features might prove 'distasteful' to some countries in the League; and gave it as his opinion that 'Laval wanted to interpret the proposals as generously as possible for Mussolini, and it was doubtful if French co-operation over sanctions could be relied upon once Mussolini had accepted but Haile Selassie refused'. The Cabinet agreed with Eden that the Emperor must be informed of the terms simultaneously with Mussolini (ignoring the fact that Mussolini already knew of them from Laval's telephone calls), and that the Emperor should be 'strongly pressed' to accept them.

Hoare, in Switzerland, was informed that the Cabinet had unanimously approved the proposals subject to their simultaneous transmission to Italy and Abyssinia. According to Hoare:

Eden while clearly not enthusiastic about the developments in Paris did not seem much worried. The only part of the scheme he disliked was the big economic area in the south. I told him to repudiate me on the extent of the area if he wished and that I fully agreed with the Cabinet decision to inform Abyssinia and Italy simultaneously.[24]

In Paris Laval told Vansittart that if Abyssinia refused the terms 'his colleagues' would not accept 'bringing into play' further sanctions, and the next day (10 December) Vansittart telephoned from Paris and told Eden that Laval would agree to send the text to Haile Selassie only on the understanding that should the Emperor refuse the terms, there would be no question of imposing an oil sanction. Eden reiterated the Cabinet's insistence that Laval send the terms immediately to Addis Ababa, adding that while 'It seems very unlikely that oil sanctions would now materialize unless Italy refused the proposals', the Cabinet members would not pledge themselves to oppose further sanctions under new conditions. Laval was disappointed; he wanted to be able to assure Mussolini of a British promise that sanctions were dead provided that Italy accepted the Hoare–Laval Plan. With a bad grace, Laval agreed that the proposals should go officially to Addis Ababa.[25]

On 10 December the Cabinet were told that Laval wanted an 'engagement' between Britain and France to the effect that if the peace proposals were refused by Abyssinia 'with a view to bringing an oil sanction into play', further sanctions against Italy need not be imposed. Peterson was summoned to this Cabinet meeting, where he told the members that Laval had taken 'soundings' in Italy and as a result was confident Mussolini would accept the terms; he added that Laval had in mind bringing Italy back 'to the Stresa Front'. Cabinet decided it could not give the 'engagement' asked for by Laval, but confirmed that if 'the anticipated refusal' by Abyssinia materialized there would be no question of the imposition of petrol sanctions. When Eden asked whether he were to 'support' the proposals at Geneva, Baldwin replied that 'this must be done'.

The Cabinet Minutes recorded that these 'were the best terms which could be obtained, from the Abyssinian point of view, from Italy', and noted that if Britain rejected the terms France would not go on with sanctions.[26]

The clause forbidding the building of a railway by Abyssinia through the corridor in British Somaliland to Zeila had been inserted at the behest of Laval, to prevent competition with the existing French line to Addis Ababa from Djibuti. In the 1906 Tripartite Treaty between Britain, France and Italy the British and Italians had committed themselves not to compete with this French line, and Laval, Peterson, Vansittart and Hoare agreed in Paris that it was reasonable to expect Abyssinia to join in this guarantee if she was given a port in British Somaliland. Peterson pointed out on 16 December that 'the world had suffered enough from superfluous railways in the last six years without setting up a duplicate system in East Africa'; he also disclosed that Haile Selassie personally had 'a substantial holding' in the Djibuti line and would doubtless be interested in higher profits. It remained open to Abyssinia to build a railway line to link Zeila to Djibuti and the French railway (the two ports were not far apart). Haile Selassie had presumably been aware of its monopoly when he acquired his shares in the French railway, and there is no reason to believe that he objected to this clause in the Hoare-Laval Plan.

Eden did not think the prohibition of a railway important. Indeed, during the Cabinet meeting of 18 December he reaffirmed the case against a competitive railway, quoting the terms of the 1906 Treaty and Haile Selassie's holding in the Djibuti line; he also considered that a second railway would be unlikely to succeed economically. *The Times*, however, published a leading article headed 'Corridor for Camels' which provoked the League of Nations lobby in Britain to frenzy. It was a brilliant headline, but a red herring, since the writer was apparently not briefed about the prohibition in the 1906 Tripartite Treaty, nor about Haile Selassie's shareholding. The article ran:

> Emperor to be informed at a convenient moment (probably when he had recovered from the shock of dismemberment) that he was forbidden to build a railway along the corridor. It was apparently to remain no more than a patch of scrub restricted to the sort of traffic which has entered Ethiopia from the days of King Solomon.[27]

French Foreign Office officials had immediately leaked full details of the Hoare–Laval Plan to French journalists, who published everything; their reports, repeated in London, produced an outcry. *The Times* declared on 14 December that 'It is proposed to hand over to Italy effective ownership and control of a good half of Abyssinian territory.' It became clear that British public opinion could only be persuaded to accept the proposals if they were convincingly defended by Baldwin and other members of the Cabinet; but this they never were, and in the absence of a strong lead from the government the Hoare–Laval Plan was hailed by a majority of the British public as an outrage, and an abandonment of election pledges. The Plan quickly died.

Opinion in France was less divided. The British Ambassador in Paris, Sir George Clerk, wrote that Laval was sure Mussolini would fight if the oil embargo were imposed (as Vansittart had been told on 10 December by the Italian Ambassador in Paris).[28] According to

Clerk, 'the sober and reasoned' reports of Drummond from Rome pointed to some desperate act of war by Italy if the oil embargo came into effect; he emphasized that French public opinion, unlike the British, was growing more and more opposed to the 'exercise of pressure on Italy' (that is, sanctions), while the French press was becoming 'poisonously anti-British'. He concluded by asserting that France was determined not to go to war with Italy, and that for Britain to try to force France into such a fight would risk a break with France, with disastrous consequences.[29]

The League of Nations Union organizers urged all their members to write to their MPs. Conservative MPs were inundated with complaints that they had won their votes in the General Election under false pretences. This in turn aroused a storm of protest from Conservative MPs to the party leaders which, in the words of Professor Toynbee, brought 'the Government to their knees'. On 14 December *The Economist* wrote:

> Conservative members were perplexed, confounded . . . for many of them a few weeks ago won their seats no doubt in all good faith – largely on the strength of assurance to the electors that the Government, if returned, would stand firmly for vindication of the League covenant in accordance with both the spirit and the letter of Sir Samuel Hoare's September speech at Geneva.

Seventy MPs who took the government whip put their names to a critical motion in the House of Commons. One junior minister, Geoffrey Shakespeare (a National Liberal), threatened to resign, and Harold Macmillan has recalled that 'MPs supporting the Government could not reconcile themselves to so rapid a change so soon after the election, with their election speeches still warm on their lips.'

In the United States, responsible newspapers condemned the proposals, in the words of the British Ambassador in Washington, 'unanimously, completely and unequivocally'. The plan was called 'an iniquitous bargain', one 'which must bankrupt the collective system and act as incitation to other ambitious states . . . It is a vindication of the Italian Government's aggression, and represents such terms as might have been exacted after victory', and 'an international disgrace'. It was accepted in the United States that this was the end of the oil embargo.

In a recent history of Ethiopia two modern scholars, A.H. Jones and Elizabeth Monro, have written:

> There were many good points in the Italian case against Abyssinia . . . Slavery, the wild conditions on the frontiers, the cruelty of many native customs, the lack of Imperial control over outlying provinces, the primi-

tive state of national development – all tended to be forgotten in the wave of world sympathy evoked by the tactics of the Italian Government.[30]

In a House of Commons debate on 5 December the Opposition had been insistent that the Italian dictator must not profit from his aggression, disregarding the possibility that such sabre-rattling might lead to war. The Conservatives were divided, however, and there was considerable support for the former Foreign Secretary and Mussolini's friend, Austen Chamberlain, who stressed that a solution acceptable to Italy and the League should not be held up by objections from Abyssinia,

> . . . a country which is not a client for whom I would have chosen to fight a test case. It is a slave-holding state; it is a slave-raiding state . . . I do not think that you can say to Abyssinia, 'We will continue indefinitely our pressure on Italy and go on heightening it until you agree . . .'; I think it must be 'until the League of Nations agree and a satisfactory solution is accepted by Italy'.

Hoare sat on the fence, explaining that France and Britain 'were working within the framework of the League' to find proposals that would be acceptable to Abyssinia, Italy and the League, but he failed to satisfy the Opposition that Mussolini would not benefit from his aggression.

On 11 December Drummond reported to London from Rome that he had seen the Duce, and

> Mussolini has not yet made up his mind what to do and feels very keenly his responsibility . . . I still think, although I cannot be certain, of course, that we shall secure his acceptance in principle if the question of oil embargo threat can be overcome. If Committee of 18 [responsible for sanctions] were to adjourn . . . he would, I believe, consider such an arrangement sufficiently satisfactory.

On the previous day the Foreign Office, with Eden's approval, had asked Sir Sydney Barton, Minister in Addis Ababa, to use his utmost influence to induce the Emperor to give favourable consideration to the proposals and on no account lightly to reject them. Barton replied that the Emperor and his advisers were 'bewildered'.[31]

Drummond was correct in his assessment that Mussolini was on the brink of accepting the Hoare–Laval proposals; indeed, he had already told Laval that they satisfied his aspirations. His acceptance would have meant the end of the Abyssinian war, and Italy would have happily rejoined the Stresa Front, leaving Hitler isolated.

The plan had a poor reception in Geneva. Some smaller nations believed that if Mussolini was rewarded for aggression, the League would lose its potential to save them from eventual attack by

Germany. In addition, Eden had changed his line, and was now hostile to the Plan. On 12 December he reported from Geneva: 'Impression which Paris proposals have made upon public opinion here is worse even than I had anticipated.'[32]

On 14 December Suvich sent a memorandum to the Duce pointing out the defects in the Hoare–Laval Plan – viz., it contained nothing about a railway to join Eritrea and Italian Somaliland, nor about disarming Abyssinia – but also that if it were rejected, the consequence would be an oil embargo and the impossibility of further negotiations if Italy left the League. On 15 December Mussolini told his Ambassador in Paris and Grandi in London that he could not accept the plan without modifications, but was prepared to negotiate. Laval replied that negotiations must take place in Geneva if the plan was to be modified, but expressed the hope that Italy would put herself on the right road by accepting the plan in principle; Vansittart's response was to tell Grandi that the British government had not expected such great opposition to the plan.[33]

Hoare had been unable to return to London from the Continent. Within minutes of putting on his skates on the ice rink at Zuoz, he had fallen and broken his nose in two places; his Swiss doctor told him he must not travel for fear of infection. Seldom had a Foreign Secretary been so urgently required at home; however, Baldwin told him not to interrupt his holiday, and Hoare was confined to bed in his hotel in Zuoz between 9 and 15 December while the furore over the Hoare–Laval Plan hit the world's press. He returned to London on 15 December, and his own doctor ordered him back to bed at his house in Cadogan Gardens.

Neville Chamberlain, Chancellor of the Exchequer, called on Hoare on 16 December. Hoare enthusiastically backed the terms he had obtained, saying that he wanted to make a vigorous defence of his Plan in the House of Commons, and insisting that it did not depart radically from the terms approved by the Cabinet. Chamberlain told him all was well, and agreed to be his spokesman at the Cabinet meeting on the next day. Unfortunately for Hoare, the Cabinet made a U-turn and decided that Eden should make it clear in Geneva that the British government no longer recommended acceptance if (as was now obvious) the terms did not have the approval of Abyssinia, Italy and the League. Nevertheless, the Cabinet decided to defend the negotiations in the Commons debate to be held on 19 December. Baldwin, Chamberlain and Eden went to Hoare's sick-room after the morning Cabinet meeting and assured him that 'We all stand together.' Hoare then dictated the speech he would make, as Foreign Secretary, in the debate on the 19th.[34]

However, the next morning the Cabinet, far from 'all' standing 'together', wanted to repudiate the Foreign Secretary, so scared were they by the mounting furore over the Hoare–Laval Plan. The majority insisted that Hoare must resign, and the Plan be killed. The Cabinet was in the most complete disarray of any Cabinet this century – although another Conservative Cabinet was to find itself in a similar predicament on 4 November 1956 when dithering over whether to cancel the attack on Port Said while the convoys were already at sea.

The record of the 18 December Cabinet meeting lies in the Public Record Office, but the key points were left blank in the circulated version and filled in later by Robin Hankey, Secretary to the Cabinet, in his own handwriting.

Baldwin was in a panic lest his government should fall, and stressed how worried he was about a sudden Italian attack on Britain, and his fear that Laval would refuse to come to Britain's aid.

Of the Cabinet Ministers, Halifax (Education), MacDonald (Lord President), Kingsley Wood (Health), Stanley (Labour), Thomas (Colonies), and Elliot (Agriculture) wanted Hoare to resign immediately and speak from the back benches in the next day's debate. Only Lord Zetland (India), in a woolly statement, backed the Foreign Secretary, while the previous Foreign Secretary, Simon (now Home Secretary), insisted the Plan must be repudiated.

Baldwin told the Cabinet he was not 'rattled', although he clearly was, but confessed that 'It was a worse situation in the House of Commons' than he had ever known. His final remark was that he had not made up his mind. He soon did: although he would have preferred him to recant and stay on as Foreign Secretary, he agreed that Hoare must go, so that the nation could be given the impression that he had not had a mandate from the Cabinet for his agreement with Laval. Chamberlain was given the distasteful task of seeing Hoare, who courageously refused to make any sort of recantation, and told Neville that resignation was his only course. At 6 p.m. Baldwin followed Chamberlain into the sick-room, and Hoare confirmed his resignation. He tore up the speech he would have made as Foreign Secretary, and prepared another to deliver from the back benches. Baldwin would have been far more honourable if he had himself resigned.[35]

In the debate on 19 December Baldwin perplexed the House of Commons by speaking of 'hidden truths', saying that it would be premature to disclose anything until the matter had been before the League and examined by both Italy and Abyssinia. His lips were not 'unsealed', but 'were the trouble over', he said, he could have made a case and guaranteed that not a single man would go into the lobby against him. Hoare's contribution from the back benches was dramatic. He said:

> From all sides I received reports that Italy would regard the oil embargo as an act involving war against her . . . If the Italians attacked us we should retaliate . . . with full success. What was in our mind was something very different: that an isolated attack of this kind launched upon another Power . . . without the full support of other Powers would, it seemed to me, almost inevitably lead to the dissolution of the League . . . We alone have taken military precautions . . . Not a ship, not a machine, not a man has been moved by any other member state.

Hoare finished by emphasizing how essential it was for a Foreign Secretary, more than any other minister, to have behind him the general approval of his fellow countrymen:

> I have not got that general approval behind me today. As soon as I realized that fact, without any prompting, without any suggestion from anyone, I asked the Prime Minister to accept my resignation.

With considerable generosity Hoare made no reference to the fact that the Cabinet had first approved the Plan and then recanted on the decision because of the public outcry; nor to the pressure put on him to resign by Baldwin and Eden. He may have had an eye on the likelihood of his swift return to the Cabinet; in the event, he did so six months later. Hoare became the scapegoat for the Cabinet's change of mind: the image of Eden as the knight in shining armour is founded on hypocrisy.[36]

In Rome, Mussolini had scheduled a meeting of the Fascist Grand Council for 19 December, at which he intended (as Grandi later confided to Leo Amery) to accept the Hoare–Laval Plan, at least as a basis for negotiations. However, Hoare's resignation made it pointless for Italy to agree the Plan since Britain clearly intended to renege; on 19 December Grandi told the Duce that the British government had decided to abandon the Hoare–Laval Plan; and Mussolini instead announced that he had rejected the Plan on 18 December.

The Laval government narrowly survived a vote on the Hoare–Laval Plan. On 22 December 1935 Laval wrote a personal letter to Mussolini in which he reminded the Duce that during their talk at the Palazzo Farnese on 7 January 1935 he had pointed out the dangers of Italian military aggression in Abyssinia, rebuked him for not accepting the Hoare–Laval proposals, and expressed the hope that Italy would not refuse any further opportunity of peace.

Mussolini replied on Christmas Day, indignantly repudiating Laval's suggestion that the 'free hand' offered at the Palazzo Farnese had applied only to economic affairs in Abyssinia, insisting that it also covered military operations. Affirming that the Hoare–Laval proposals had represented a satisfactory basis for discussions, he asserted that he had not refused them out of hand; instead, he had sought clarification in Paris and London; and the verdict of the Grand Council would have been favourable, had it not been for Hoare's resignation. Mussolini told Laval that he would be prepared to consider fresh proposals, and expressed the opinion that a French–Italian–United Kingdom front was essential for European peace.

This correspondence shows how near Mussolini was to accepting the Hoare–Laval proposals and returning to the Stresa Front; had Baldwin not accepted Hoare's resignation, the Abyssinian war would surely have been ended. One can, with hindsight, but wring one's hands. Laval's government was brought down in January 1936 by an economic crisis, and relations between Mussolini and France were never so amicable again.[37]

Hitler was greatly relieved; the prospect of an agreement to terminate the Abyssinian War had been unwelcome, as he knew that it would recreate the Stresa Front against him.

Hoare had been at the Foreign Office less than six months, but during that time had come to appreciate the menace posed by Hitler's rearmament, and the need to keep Mussolini's friendship as a counter to German aggression. Baldwin wanted Austen Chamberlain to succeed Hoare, but Chamberlain refused because of his health. Baldwin therefore chose Eden, who was to follow a policy of opposition to Mussolini and appeasement of Hitler.

What would have happened if the Cabinet had stood by Hoare? Mussolini would probably have accepted the Hoare–Laval Plan, and it is unlikely that outraged public opinion could have toppled the Conservative government. With his huge majority and his determination to cling to office, Baldwin would have been able to prevent a Dissolution, although a change of leadership would have been on the cards. Baldwin was immensely popular, and surely could have manipulated public opinion into accepting that, in spite of all the brave talk at Geneva, other countries were not prepared to risk war with Italy while they saw the real danger to peace coming from Germany; he could have deployed the argument that sanctions not involving oil would never halt Mussolini, and that oil sanctions would mean war.

As it was, Mussolini turned away from France and Britain and, reluctantly, towards Germany. Unfortunately, the crisis coincided with Margherita Sarfatti's fall from favour, and the lack of her sound advice was a grave loss to him.

Eden's attempts as Foreign Secretary to achieve the imposition of oil sanctions on Italy were frustrated by the United States: by 19

February 1936, US oil exports to Italy had increased threefold. Late in February the Cabinet reluctantly agreed to support an oil embargo at Eden's insistence, but because of French opposition it never came into effect.[38]

The whole episode of sanctions produced no concrete results, but served merely to antagonize Mussolini and drive a wedge between France and Britain. Mussolini went on to obliterate Abyssinia, and never resumed the terms of friendship with Britain which had endured from the time of his rise to power until Stresa, while Hitler profited enormously as Italy, France and Britain, victors of the First World War and guardians of the Treaty of Versailles, fell out.

CHAPTER 10

Mussolini Rejected by Eden: January–June 1936

MUSSOLINI WAS DISMAYED by Baldwin's appointment of the anti-Italian Eden to replace Hoare as Foreign Secretary. With the failure of the Hoare–Laval negotiations and the reluctance of the French to support the imposition of oil sanctions against Italy, Eden's options were limited; yet in spite of Hitler's rapid rearmament and his obvious intention to annex Austria, Eden did not seem to realize that Mussolini's help in restraining Germany was becoming increasingly important.

At first Eden would not admit that Abyssinia was lost, but still hoped to assert the authority of the League of Nations as an instrument to prevent war, ignoring the deadly danger to peace in Europe should Italy ally herself with Germany, having become alienated from Britain and France. Shortly after his appointment Eden, in conversation with Dino Grandi, formerly Italian Foreign Minister and now Ambassador in London, emphasized that there was no personal antipathy on his (Eden's) part, either to the Fascist regime or to Mussolini; Grandi told him that the reports of Eden's antipathy did not originate in Rome, but were a popular theme in French newspapers. Eleven days later (17 January) Eden talked to Grandi again. Grandi explored the British attitude to an oil embargo, and asked whether Britain would at Geneva propose an enquiry into the efficacy of such a embargo. Eden was evasive, but said that 'we' should not have any insuperable difficulty in agreeing to this; Grandi then asked whether he could report to Rome that Britain was not 'vehement' in support of an oil embargo. Eden ducked, claiming this was a matter solely for the League of Nations.

Grandi informed Eden that Germany did not conceal her desire for Italy to persist in the conflict in Abyssinia: Italian trade with Germany had increased since the imposition of sanctions, and now every consignment of German goods bore a notice in Italian urging the Italians to continue their fight, and assuring them of German support in a few months' time. Grandi claimed to find this profoundly disquieting; and to want the war settled as soon as possible, so that Italy could again play her part in Europe.[1]

The deeper Italy was engaged in Africa the less she could do to protect Austria from Hitler; but this argument did not weigh strongly with Eden when he talked to Laval in Geneva on 20 January 1936. (Laval was on the brink of resigning, and did so on 22 January.) When Eden urged the imposition of an oil embargo on Italy, Laval responded that Germany was rearming at a great pace, and that he expected Hitler soon to violate the Treaty of Locarno by sending troops into the demilitarized zone of the Rhineland. He was upset by Eden's refusal to give a definite assurance that Britain would stand by France if this occurred; nor would Eden agree that Mussolini must be handled carefully if he was to be used to help to subdue Hitler. Pierre Flandin's appointment as French Foreign Minister following Laval's resignation did not alter the divide between France and Britain; Eden refused suggestions from both for a fresh Anglo-French initiative to seek agreement with Mussolini to end the war.

With France opposed and Britain in favour, the question of the imposition of an oil embargo was referred by the League to an expert committee, which in February reported that it could only be effective if the United States could be persuaded to reduce her exports of oil to Italy. According to the British Ambassador in Washington, it was most unlikely that she would do so, as Congress preferred a stance of rigid neutrality; in fact, Italy was importing all the oil she required. On his return from Geneva Eden was dismayed to find Foreign Office minutes from Vansittart, Peterson, Sir George Mounsey, and his Under-Secretary Lord Stanhope, all expressing disapproval of an oil embargo and casting doubts on its efficacy. The MP Leo Amery, influential Conservative peers Lord Lloyd, Lord Mottistone and Lord Phillimore, together with the Labour peer Lord Ponsonby, were also opposed; they told Grandi so, and were personally thanked by Mussolini.

The American President F.D. Roosevelt sent Colonel (Bill) Donovan (later well-known for his OSS activities from Switzerland during the Second World War) to Europe as his special emissary, to try to find a solution. When Vansittart reported that Mussolini had told Donovan 'he did not see how a war could be avoided' if an oil embargo was pressed, Eden minuted crossly:

> I hope that nobody here is placing any credence on Colonel Donovan and his reports. They deserve no credence, of course, although they may be useful to Mussolini and Rothermere. I disagree with Sir George Mounsey's view that existing sanctions are failing.[2]

An oil embargo was discussed in Cabinet on 26 February 1936. Disregarding advice that the increasing supplies of oil to Italy from the US would nullify its effects, Eden urged the Cabinet to support an oil embargo even if it might not prove completely effective – 'about which evidence is inconclusive' – because 'it was bound to add to Italy's difficulties'. The Cabinet, surprisingly, considered the risk of an alliance between Italy and Germany to be small, while some ministers who had little confidence in the efficacy of an oil embargo supported it on the grounds that it was impossible, 'after all that had been said in the General Election and before and since', not to try it out, and that to repudiate an oil embargo 'after the statements that had been made in the debate on the Hoare–Laval peace proposals would be politically disastrous'. Although Lord Runciman (Board of Trade) and Eyres Monsell (Admiralty) registered dissent, the Cabinet, including Baldwin, authorized Eden to support an oil embargo at Geneva; but they wanted him to avoid taking the initiative.[3]

An oil embargo against Italy was as much an anathema to the government of the new French Premier, Albert Sarraut, as it had been to Laval's. The French insisted that efforts at peace talks must be tried before the oil embargo was considered at Geneva, as Flandin told Eden in Geneva on 2 March. In the ensuing heated argument, Flandin maintained that an extension of sanctions to include oil would lead not only to Mussolini leaving the League, but to war, and to a *rapprochement* between Germany and Italy; while an ineffective oil embargo accompanied by Italian victories in the field would make the League look ridiculous. Eden countered that the League would also look ridiculous if it did nothing; but he agreed that sanctions were not likely to stop the fighting before the end of the year, and expressed himself puzzled to know why, if the oil embargo was not going to be effective, Mussolini made so much fuss about it. Flandin was of the opinion that sanctions were inadmissible from the moral point of view, and united the Italian people behind Mussolini. After a long meeting the next day Eden and Flandin agreed there should be a further attempt at a negotiated settlement while the technicalities of implementing oil sanctions were under consideration.

In effect, Mussolini was being asked to open peace negotiations at the same time as he was being threatened with oil sanctions. Nothing could be calculated to anger the Italian dictator more; as Drummond pointed out, Mussolini was unlikely to negotiate while under threat of an aggravation of sanctions.

Grandi did his best to present Eden's behaviour at Geneva as more sympathetic to Italy than in fact it was; but Mussolini knew better, writing on 4 March 1936:

> Many believe because of his action (but not me) that Signor Eden has put a bit of water in his sanctionist wine. His attitude at Geneva has instead revealed Eden, as Italians already know, as a vehement enemy [*nemico acerissimo*] of Italy. I hope you will cherish no illusions about this.[4]

By now Mussolini had little interest in a negotiated settlement. His troops had been advancing triumphantly since January, and complete victory was within sight. A well-planned attack on 12 January 1936 by the new commander, Field Marshal Badoglio, was followed by a successful campaign which within four months had resulted in the flight of the Emperor and the Italian capture of Addis Ababa (on 5 May).

Meanwhile, taking a calculated risk, Hitler had decided to make the most of the collapse of the Stresa Front and of the Anglo-Italian differences to remilitarize the Rhineland, in defiance of the Treaty of Locarno and the Treaty of Versailles.

Eden, so resolute in opposing Italian aggression in Abyssinia, was less so over the Rhineland. Although the French had expressed alarm at the likelihood of a coup by Hitler, Eden did not share their misgivings, informing the Cabinet Foreign Policy Committee that:

> . . . it seems undesirable to adopt an attitude where we would either have to fight for the zone or abandon it in the face of a German reoccupation. It would be preferable for Great Britain and France to enter betimes into negotiations with German Government for the surrender on conditions of our rights in the zone while such a surrender has still got a bargaining value.

Eden's memorandum was approved by the Committee; it was appeasement of Germany at a moment when Italy was being threatened with more severe sanctions. Yet such complacency about Germany on the part of the Cabinet Committee was scarcely justified in view of the alarming reports from the Berlin Embassy which had been circulated to members. A typical extract reads:

> On every side giant military establishments are springing up . . . Enormous aerodromes either finished or under construction march, sometimes for miles, with the main road . . . military cars and lorries painted in camouflage colours mix with civilian traffic. In the air the ceaseless hum of aeroplanes bears witness to the expansion of the German air force . . . That military expansion will be followed by territorial expansion goes without saying.

Eden merely told the Committee that British rearmament should be hastened, and an effort made to achieve a *modus vivendi* with Germany.[5]

In a memorandum for the Cabinet dated 3 February, Vansittart had declared that the Versailles system had broken down, noting that until the Abyssinian crisis Hitler had repeatedly professed his desire for friendly relations with Great Britain and France; but as soon as the Abyssinian crisis arose, 'Hitler at once drew in his horns . . . we cannot make a stand for Abyssinia and connive at the spoilation of Lithuania, Czechoslovakia or Austria.' Vansittart wanted

> to try and come to terms with Germany before, as is otherwise eventually certain, she takes the law into her own hands. Hitler would have been far more likely to be reasonable and forthcoming in negotiation if faced by the Stresa unity. It is to the recent disintegration of this 'front' that we must in large measure attribute the sudden change of tone . . . we *are* committed to resist by sanctions the modification by force of the status quo; and sanctions in the case of Germany mean war, a land war.[6]

Eden, in an effort to appease Hitler, submitted a paper to the Cabinet Foreign Policy Committee on 2 March suggesting an air pact with Germany, negotiations for the remilitarization of the Rhineland, and recognition of the special interests of Germany in Central and Eastern Europe. He told Sir Eric Phipps, the British Ambassador in Berlin, that before long 'we shall be making a supreme effort to come to terms with Germany'. He was taking a softer line towards Hitler than towards Mussolini, but it proved a singularly unsuccessful ploy on Eden's part. On 7 March, without warning, German troops entered the Rhineland, to the delight of the population.[7]

Hitler had previously instructed his Ambassador in Rome, Ulrich von Hassell, to tell Mussolini that because of the Franco-Soviet Pact of May 1935, he had decided to renounce the terms of Locarno and send troops into the demilitarized zone of the Rhineland. Von Hassell had seen Mussolini on 22 February; Mussolini pronounced Stresa to be 'dead', and said that Italy would take no part in any action by France and Britain against Germany 'occasioned by an alleged breach by Germany of the Locarno Treaty'. He was now ready to condone remilitarization of the Rhineland – a far cry from his position at Stresa – in revenge against Britain's stand on sanctions. Perhaps, if the British Cabinet had known of this conversation between von Hassell and Mussolini, they would not have approved the oil embargo four days later.

Simultaneously with the entry of his troops into the Rhineland, Hitler declared Germany ready to rejoin the League of Nations and enter into twenty-five-year non-aggression pacts with Belgium,

Holland and France. His main excuse for the invasion was that the Franco–Russian agreement finally being ratified by the French parliament was an 'abrogation' of the terms of Locarno.

In Rome, at nine in the morning of 7 March 1936, von Hassell informed Mussolini that German troops had entered the defortified zone. Mussolini had already read the statement which accompanied the invasion: he told von Hassell that Germany had gone too far. Momentarily taken aback, von Hassell thought the Duce was expressing disapproval of the coup; however, Mussolini meant only that Hitler was being too accommodating to France and Britain. He particularly disliked Hitler's intention of returning to the League of Nations, as this would add renewed prestige to the League and diminish the effect of Italy's departure. On the main issue, Mussolini told von Hassell he sided decisively with Hitler, and confirmed he had no objection to the military move.

Von Hassell was anti-Nazi (he was executed after the 20 July 1944 plot to overthrow Hitler), yet like all Germans he resented the Treaty of Versailles. In his report to Berlin, von Hassell commented perceptively:

> The Palazzo Chigi [the Italian Foreign Office] welcomes everything that might strengthen Italy's shady connections with the League of Nations, which is apt to recreate something like Stresa. This school of thought has now got the upper hand, and France's hope of putting Italy more in her debt by means of a peaceful settlement of the Abyssinian conflict has been revived . . . We have provided this school of thought with a splendid alibi.

The 'splendid alibi' was a promise from Hitler, transmitted to Mussolini through von Hassell, that if Germany returned to the League she would always support Italy and oppose further sanctions. Von Hassell was well aware that Italian diplomats were anti-Nazi, and wanted to bring Italy back to the Stresa Front.

Three days later Mussolini emphasized to von Hassell that Italy would take no part in any sanctions against Germany which might be imposed over the breach of Locarno and Versailles (*sanzionati non sanzionano altri*). Nevertheless, Mussolini was in some doubt – which was to continue for the next four years – about whether he should stay in Hitler's camp, or repair Italy's friendship with France and Britain; on 12 March von Hassell reported that Mussolini was 'wavering', 'unwilling to decide whether his way is ultimately to lead back to Stresa or to co-operation with Germany; he would like to keep his options open.'[8]

The invasion of the Rhineland was the last opportunity to stop Hitler dead in his tracks, while the German army was still too weak to resist the French. We now know from the Nuremberg Trials and German archives that had the French invaded the Rhineland, the German troops would have withdrawn, although there might have been fighting. Unfortunately, the French had been relying on Italian support in the event of having to fight over the Rhineland, which at the time of Stresa would have been definitely forthcoming. Even in March 1936 some of the French Chiefs of Staff were still blithely hopeful: at a Chiefs of Staff conference on 8 March General Gamelin, Chief of the General Staff, said that France could 'only enter the Rhineland at the same time as the guarantor powers of Locarno [Britain and Italy]. British and Italian contingents must be with us'; and General Pujo (later a Vichy Cabinet Minister) thought 'the Italians might send us 100 bombers'; Gamelin considered that it would be 'most important that English and Italian troops should immediately be sent to France'. Before the imposition of sanctions Mussolini would have backed these now unrealistic hopes with both troops and military aircraft.[9]

The occupation of the Rhineland was enormously popular in Germany; failure here, following the débacle in Vienna in 1934, would have severely dented Hitler's credibility, and encouraged the anti-Nazis.

Eden went to Paris on 8 March for a meeting of the signatories of Locarno. Mussolini refused to send a delegate from Rome; instead, his Ambassador in Paris, Vittorio Cerruti, attended. He stated that, as a state subject to sanctions, Italy could not agree in advance to any action of a political, economic or military character. He could only listen and report. This was discouraging enough for the French, but even worse for them was Eden's assertion that Britain would not support the use of force, and that economic sanctions would be ineffective. Flandin insisted there must be no negotiations unless Germany withdrew from the Rhineland. The French Premier Sarraut and three members of his Cabinet were in favour of military action, but the majority of the French Cabinet would not agree in the absence of British and Italian military support. Flandin went to London with hope in his heart that Britain might yet back a French military move into the Rhineland; Belgium too was ready to attack if Britain would come in. But Flandin received an emphatic No from both Baldwin and Eden.

Eden insisted that Britain's obligations under the Treaty of Locarno were confined to economic and financial measures, with no commitment to military measures. Flandin's desire to use force was acutely embarrassing to the British Cabinet. Over the weekend Eden had consulted with Baldwin at Chequers, and they agreed not to support military action because it would be unpopular in Britain. Baldwin told Flandin categorically that he would not involve Britain in any measures which might lead to war, because 'Britain is in no state to go to war'. It has been reported that when Flandin found the British leaders were determined to repudiate their Locarno obligations, he burst into tears.

The failure of sanctions against Italy led to a lack of enthusiasm for the imposition of sanctions against Germany among all the member states of the League except France and Belgium. France, so hesitant in the case of Italy, was now militant for sanctions against Germany. Eden, who had been ready to risk war with Italy over sanctions, was strongly against their imposition. The British press, too, seemed unaware of the grave threat to peace posed by the military occupation of the Rhineland.[10]

On 9 March Eden told the Cabinet that:

> . . . force would not result only in letting loose another great war in Europe. They might succeed in crushing Germany with the aid of Russia, but it would perhaps only result in Germany going Bolshevik *and the French should be told military action was inappropriate as being out of proportion to what Germany has done, and the Council of Locarno powers should give Britain, France, Belgium and Italy a mandate to negotiate with Germany* an air pact, settlement in Eastern and Central Europe (it won't amount to much) on the basis of unilateral non-aggression pacts offered by Hitler, and Germany's unconditional return to the League . . . the essential thing will be to induce or cajole France to accept this mandate . . . The strength of our position lies in the fact that France is not in the mood for a military adventure. [My italics. R.L.]

What Eden meant by saying that 'settlement in Eastern and Central Europe' would 'not amount to much' is obscure; he was not being realistic. And what faith could be placed in non-aggression pacts with Hitler?

On 13 March a committee meeting of the Locarno powers in London was told by the French representative, Paul Boncour, that France wanted to impose economic and financial sanctions against Germany initially, and if necessary to follow them up with military action. Neville Chamberlain, Chancellor of the Exchequer, interposed with some heat, saying that the British people would not agree to sanctions against Germany, and that drastic measures were anyway out of the question because it was obvious that even if the German troops withdrew temporarily, they would soon be allowed back, following negotiations.

At a secret session on 17 March Flandin made a formal demand that the British government should impose sanctions against Germany, pointing out that Britain had repeatedly declared in the case of Italy that sanctions did not inevitably mean war. Eden declared this to be impossible, whereupon Flandin announced that in that case he would be compelled to declare that France felt morally obliged to discontinue sanctions against Italy. When Eden then claimed the German action was quite different from Italy's war against Abyssinia, Flandin stated that the occupation of the military zone was for the French 'an act of downright military aggression'.

Grandi, representing Italy, triumphantly reported Flandin's remarks to Mussolini, adding that in private, after the meeting, Flandin had confirmed to him that if the British refused sanctions against Germany, France would suspend sanctions against Italy; when Grandi suggested to Flandin that France would never break with Britain, Flandin had declared that he would never give in to 'English blackmail'.[11]

France did not officially withdraw sanctions against Italy, but from then on would not co-operate over them at Geneva; nevertheless, when the Sarraut government fell in early June and Léon Blum became Premier, he told Eden he did not want to lift the sanctions 'as his first act'.

On 20 March Alexis Léger, head of the French Foreign Office, told Cerruti, the Italian Ambassador in Paris, that if Britain did not impose sanctions against Germany, France would take it as an excuse to suspend sanctions against Italy; and if Britain objected to this action, the French government would blame the hostility of public opinion to the damage resulting from such sanctions. Cerruti had further similar talks in Paris, from which it became clear to Mussolini that sanctions must soon come to an end; on 28 March the Duce told the French Ambassador in Rome that he wanted to reconstruct the Stresa Front: 'It was inconceivable that had the Stresa Front remained intact Germany would have risked the action she had recently taken in the Rhineland.'[12]

According to a Foreign Office minute by Orme Sargent, it was a renewed offer by the League to mediate between Italy and Abyssinia that decided Hitler to precipitate his entry into the Rhineland; Hitler feared this offer might quickly lead to 'a reconciliation between Italy and Great Britain, and Italy and the League', and it was obviously in his interest to act while the quarrel between Italy and her Stresa partners was operating in Germany's favour. According to Sir Eric Phipps, senior German generals had objected to the Rhineland operations as being too risky, but Hitler had stifled their arguments by pointing out that the German Embassy in Rome had forecast Italy's defection from Locarno as a result of sanctions; according to Phipps, the German army felt they were being forced to run an unnecessary risk in order to provide an election platform for the Nazis, but would nevertheless fight to the bitter end if hostilities broke out.

As Abyssinian resistance to the Italian army collapsed, the Foreign Office pressed Eden for an early lifting of sanctions, on the grounds that Mussolini's antagonism to Britain was encouraging Hitler's aggression. During the Cabinet meeting of 19 March Eden asked his colleagues for their views about lifting sanctions; it was his view that 'they should not be raised merely in return for a truce, and that we must be assured of peace being in sight'; but there was mistrust of the sanctions policy in Cabinet. On 6 April Eden asked the Cabinet to consider closing the Suez Canal to Italian shipping. Baldwin emphatically refused to consider the suggestion because in his view it would involve war with Italy; Eden said he was still hoping that the Italians might be defeated by the rain in Abyssinia. Vansittart commented, 'It has got to rain very hard – and very quick – and very long.' On 10 April he minuted that 'nothing further could be done in the line of extended sanctions. The League is still too weak, too vacillating, and too divided. It would be unfair to give the Abyssinians encouragement.'[13]

Eden was still clinging to the vain hope that the League of Nations might yet undo Mussolini when on 28 April Haile Selassie's army was hopelessly defeated by the Italians. On 3 May the Emperor fled from Addis Ababa.

On 5 May, from the balcony of the Palazzo Venezia, Mussolini proclaimed before a delirious crowd the annexation of Abyssinia and the assumption by the King of Italy of the title of Emperor of Abyssinia. He considered this to be his moment of triumph; he had wiped out the shame of Italy's defeat at Adowa in 1896, and run great risks to acquire a new Empire for Italy. He said:

> I announce to the Italian people and to the world that the war is finished. I announce to the Italian people and to the world that peace is re-established . . . Ethiopia is Italian . . . the diverse races of the Lion of Judah have shown by the clearest signs that they wish to live tranquilly in the shadow of the Italian tricolor. We are ready to defend our resplendent victory with the same intrepid and incontestable determination as that with which we have won it.[14]

Mussolini was more popular with the Italian people than ever before, and dangerously over-confident. He had defeated not only Abyssinia but the League of Nations, with its fifty 'sanctionist states', led by Britain. But although the war might be over, sanctions were not lifted, and Eden still hoped to deprive Mussolini of the full fruits of his conquest.

Suggestions that sanctions might be lifted produced even more letters of protest to MPs than had the publication of the Hoare–Laval terms the previous December, and anti-Fascist feelings in Britain were an important factor in preventing the government from moving to restore the Anglo-Italian friendship. This was at a time when Mussolini, fearing the growing strength of Hitler, was having second thoughts about his attitude to the remilitarization of the Rhineland. Looking to repair his bridges with Britain, he ordered that press attacks on Britain should cease, and followed this with a barrage of conciliatory messages. He also instructed Grandi to use his personal influence with the new King, Edward VIII, to persuade the King to try to intervene with the Prime Minister in favour of Italy. (Both Mussolini and Grandi entirely over-estimated the King's influence with Baldwin, which was in effect nil.) On 28 April the King granted Grandi a secret audience which, according to Grandi's immensely long account, lasted six hours. To the Ambassador's outline of the gross errors the British had made by their hostility towards Italy during the Abyssinian war, the King replied that he completely shared Grandi's views. Grandi may have been wasting his time with the King, but he was having more success in pressurizing influential right-wing anti-sanctionist Conservatives such as Leo Amery and Lord Phillimore. On 1 May he was able to report jubilantly to Mussolini that he had seen Winston Churchill, and shown him a telegram from the Duce stating that the clash between England and Italy could only have one result – 'the supremacy of Berlin in Europe': Churchill had said that he was soon to make a speech advocating the abandonment of sanctions and bringing Italy back to the Stresa Front, and that it was time Britain accepted the triumphal victory of Italy in Africa. Churchill was as good as his word, and delivered a powerful speech demanding the end of sanctions. Mussolini cabled Grandi a personal message for Churchill: 'On your attitude and from your speech the future of Anglo-Italian relations depends, and on my part I desire them to be close and fruitful.' Leo Amery's comment on Churchill's speech was that 'It is amusing to see how far he [Churchill] has come round since he declared himself an out-and-out sanctioner in October.'[15]

Mussolini's efforts at conciliation peaked that month. On 5 May he promised Ward Price of the *Daily Mail* that he had no more colonial ambitions, and 'no hankering after Egypt'. At the end of the month he told the *Daily Telegraph*:

> Not only is an Anglo-Italian *rapprochement* desirable, but it is necessary; and for my part I will do everything which lies in my power to bring it about.

On 21 May Grandi and Vansittart talked at the Foreign Office. Grandi assured Vansittart that when he had spoken recently with Mussolini in Rome the Duce had been extremely anxious to create 'a chapter of collaboration' with England and France as soon as possible. Grandi earnestly hoped Mussolini would be neither rebuffed, nor kept waiting too long. Eden minuted on Vansittart's account of the conversation:

> There is a touch of blackmail about this, and we are not in a mood to be blackmailed by Italy. Some constructive contribution by her is also called for, and there is no evidence of it here. If Mussolini thinks he has only to beckon and we will open our arms, he is vastly mistaken.[16]

Eden clung to the vain hope of denying Mussolini the full fruits of his military victory through sanctions, and of showing the world that defiance of the Covenant of the League did not pay. When Phipps wrote from Berlin that it was 'fallacious' to believe that successful League action against Italy would have induced Hitler to change his policy, Eden minuted petulantly on 22 May:

> Sir E. Phipps does not appear to understand (and it is perhaps natural enough, for it is not his business to do so) the importance for this country and *for France* of a League success over the Abyssinian affair. British opinion will not take a part in Europe sans through the League, and if the League suffers, as it has done now, the cause of peace will suffer also. If France had been wise enough to see this, all our present troubles could have been avoided, and at least we could have been in better form and spirit to meet the German challenge if and when it comes. However, apparently the French Government took a different view and so does Sir E. Phipps.

Eden clearly blamed Hitler's military occupation of the Rhineland on the lack of success of sanctions against Italy. In this he was at logger-heads with his colleagues. His Under-Secretary Lord Stanhope minuted: 'I must agree with Sir E. Phipps that the most I thought a successful application of sanctions to Italy might have done to Germany would have been to make her pause.' And although the other Under-Secretary, Lord Cranborne, as usual agreed with Eden, others in the Foreign Office – Vansittart, Wigram and O'Malley – took Phipps' and Stanhope's contradictory line.

On another message from Phipps, of 27 May, which included the comment that 'If Anglo-Italian relations do not soon improve events will be playing into the hands of Herr Hitler', Eden wrote:

> This may be true but it is not we who have broken the Covenant, and the British public is not prepared to sit around the table on friendly terms with the aggressor for many a long day – nor can I blame them.

Cranborne again supported Eden; but to Eden's annoyance Vansittart, Wigram and Stanhope wrote minutes which advocated the lifting of sanctions.[17]

On 28 May, on Mussolini's orders, Grandi made another determined effort to repair Italy's bridges with Britain, indicating Mussolini's concern that he should not be forced into too close an association with Hitler. In conversation with Eden, Grandi said Mussolini wished for nothing so much as that 'bygones should be bygones', and a fresh start be made; he wanted a close *rapprochement* between Great Britain, France and Italy 'on a Locarno basis', with a view to a common approach to Germany. Grandi was emphatic that there was no question of a *rapprochement* between Italy and Germany; he said Mussolini had refused Hitler's advances, and did not want Austria to become Nazi. According to Grandi, Italy was now a 'satisfied power' and would have enough work in Abyssinia to keep her going for fifty years. Grandi insisted that Italy had no intention whatever of making difficulties for Britain in Egypt, Palestine, the Sudan, or anywhere else: Mussolini would be glad to contribute all he could to a *Paix Africaine*. It was a warm overture, but Eden replied frigidly that Britain had never been anti-Italian over the Abyssinian dispute; her actions had arisen because of her obligations under the Covenant of the League, but 'we did not regret it'. The report of this meeting, when circulated in Cabinet on 29 May, made a favourable impression, and Eden was asked to produce a memorandum as to the probable effects of continuing sanctions, and how long it would take for them to produce results.[18]

However in a long conversation with Grandi the same day, Austen Chamberlain informed the Ambassador that he thought Eden's policy was wrong, and that more than half the members of the House of Commons were anti-sanctionist. Grandi assured Chamberlain of the sincerity of Mussolini's friendly attitude to Britain, as displayed in his interviews with the British press in Rome, and later cabled Mussolini that the atmosphere in London was greatly improved. On 3 June Vansittart told Grandi that sanctions were about to be lifted, and that the Duce's friendly statements had had a good influence on the Cabinet.

In a speech on the evening of 10 June, Neville Chamberlain jumped the gun, declaring that the continuance of sanctions against Italy would be the 'very midsummer of madness' because it involved the risk of war. The statement aroused a storm, and Baldwin dissociated the government from it – pointlessly, given that the Cabinet was about to agree to lift sanctions. Eden was much put out. In a letter to his sister Chamberlain wrote, 'I did not consult Eden between ourselves because although I believed that he was entirely in favour of what I was going to say, I knew if I asked him he was bound to ask me not to say it.' However, to Eden Chamberlain wrote claiming he had been so occupied on the Treasury bench that, as Eden later recounted, 'he had not enough time to put his thoughts into a form which he could show me'. Already Chamberlain and Eden were out of step.[19]

Earlier on 10 June, Grandi had talked to Neville Chamberlain at Winston Churchill's house; Chamberlain told the Ambassador, 'Sanctions are dead. It is only a question of burying them. But sometimes a funeral is more complicated and takes longer than the death agony.' In reporting to Mussolini, Grandi was able to enclose press reports of Chamberlain's 'midsummer madness' speech later that day, eagerly pointing out how well it was received, and how the value of the pound and the Stock Exchange had gone up because of it.

The next day, 11 June, Eden circulated to the Cabinet the memorandum on sanctions requested on 29 May. Chamberlain's speech had forced him to moderate his attitude; he argued that it would be impossible to continue sanctions without the whole-hearted co-operation of France, which was unlikely to be forthcoming because France was dominated 'by the German dangers and by the heavy risk of German action under cover of a League war with Italy in the Mediterranean'. Eden thought that if Mussolini were to issue a soothing declaration about Italy's future policy, it would facilitate the lifting of sanctions. In Cabinet he stated that Grandi had given Vansittart very satisfactory assurances regarding a statement Italy was to make in Geneva about her future conduct, and the Cabinet agreed with Eden that Britain should take the initiative at the League over raising sanctions.[20]

On 17 June the Cabinet agreed to announce the end of sanctions against Italy. While supporting the decision, Eden advocated that Britain should not go so far as to recognize the Italian conquest of Abyssinia, because 'it would be bitterly unpopular at Geneva'. His lack of generosity in this matter was to prove costly, as will be seen. In the House of Commons on 18 June, after surveying the history of the Abyssinian crisis, he told the House that 'there is no longer any utility in continuing sanctions as a means of pressure upon Italy'.

In Geneva, following receipt of a conciliatory note from Italy, on 1 July the Assembly of the League of Nations debated the future of sanctions. Speaking there, Eden admitted the futility of continuing sanctions; but still he made no effort to propitiate Mussolini, going on to say that Britain would be prepared to advocate the continuance of sanctions, and even add to them, if they could 're-establish the position in Abyssinia'. Eden advocated, to Mussolini's annoyance, that the League should not 'in any way recognize the Italian conquest over

Abyssinia'; nor did Britain proffer any apology for having made the attempt to restrain Italy by the imposition of sanctions: 'However deeply, however sincerely we may deplore its outcome, we cannot regret – nor, I think, will history regret – that the attempt was made.'

Eden's antagonistic attitude was out of place at a time when British interests would have been best served by bringing Mussolini back to the Stresa Front. Instead, he was turning his back on all the overtures for a renewal of the former British–Italian friendship which Grandi in London and Ciano in Rome had been making on Mussolini's behalf. Even so, there was reason to suppose that Mussolini might be kept out of Hitler's camp. Then, on 18 July, the Spanish Civil War began; and Mussolini, encouraged by Hitler, embarked on a series of rash adventures there which were to estrange him from Britain and drive him step by step into a close alliance with Nazi Germany. Yet he continued, from time to time, to make overtures to Britain.

CHAPTER 11

The Spanish Civil War

BY 1929 THE right-wing Primo de Rivera, dictator of Spain for the previous six years, had lost most of his popular support; nor did he have the backing of either King Alfonso XIII, or the army. In January 1930 the King dismissed him. Though Mussolini considered that he had something in common with de Rivera, he did nothing to foster a Fascist regime in Spain, and took de Rivera's fall calmly, as he did the abdication of King Alfonso in April 1931 and the proclamation of a Republic. But he soon became hostile to the Republic, and aided and encouraged the anti-Republicans with subsidies, as he did Sir Oswald Mosley in Britain, and provided secret military training courses for terrorists. With the onset of the Abyssinian War in 1935 Mussolini temporarily lost interest in Spain, however, becoming more concerned with Italy's position in the western Mediterranean *vis-à-vis* France than with the aspirations of Spanish monarchists and neo-Fascist groups. Although Rome was certainly the centre of anti-Republican Spanish activity, some historians have exaggerated Mussolini's interference in the affairs of the Second Republic in Spain prior to the Civil War.

The left won the Spanish General Election of February 1936, and strikes, riots and disorders followed. On 17 July General Franco led a right-wing army mutiny in favour of the church in Spanish Morocco, and there were army risings in many places in Spain. By 20 July the rebellion had been successful in North Africa and in the conservative northern parts of Spain, while in the south the insurgents won control of Seville, Huelva, Granada and Cadiz; but the revolt failed in Barcelona and Madrid.

General Franco's plan to send 17,000 troops across the Straits from Africa into Spain was frustrated by the superiority of the government naval forces. Meanwhile the left-wing French government under Léon Blum complied with a request from the Republican government to send arms to quell the rebellion. Although they were not strictly Fascist, this decided Mussolini to aid Franco's rebels, lest Spain fall under French influence, or even turn Communist. At this stage Mussolini was more intent on exploiting Abyssinia as a colony than on installing a Fascist regime in Spain or expanding Italian influence in the western Mediterranean; he needed to concentrate his military forces on the pacification of Abyssinia.

Franco appealed to Italy for aeroplanes to protect his troop convoys from Africa to Spain, and Mussolini agreed to send twelve Savoia-Marchetti S-81 bombers secretly to Morocco. They set off from Sardinia on 29 July, but only nine arrived in Spanish Morocco; a petrol shortage caused by head-winds had caused three to make a forced landing in French Morocco. The next day newspapers all over the world headlined the fact that the Italian government was aiding the Spanish rebels. Sizeable rebel army contingents protected by Italian aeroplanes crossed into southern Spain from Morocco, but it quickly became clear that they would need more help if their march from Seville to Madrid was to succeed. The advance began on 3 August; four days later Italy sent fighter planes, tanks and machine guns, together with ammunition and bombs. From then on Mussolini found himself forced for the sake of Italian prestige to give ever-increasing military aid to Franco, on a slippery slope which led to massive commitments. Meanwhile the Blum government in Paris had cut down on French military aid to the Republican government in the face of intense internal opposition; but Russian help was forth-coming.

In Britain, the majority of the Conservative Party and the Cabinet sided with Franco in the dispute. Eden, the Foreign Secretary, differed. On 19 August he presented to the Foreign Policy Committee a memorandum hostile to Italy in which he pointed out that Mussolini might be tempted to take steps in the western Mediterranean (by seizing Majorca for use as an Italian base) calculated 'to upset the balance against us'; he urged that there was a strong case 'for making it publicly plain that this might prove the source of deep and enduring antagonism with ourselves.' Accordingly, he wanted a statement to be issued by either himself or the Prime Minister (Baldwin), that 'Any alteration in the status quo in the western Mediterranean must be a matter of the closest concern to His Majesty's Government.' His fear was that in the event of Italy becoming involved in a war with France, an Italian military presence in Majorca would threaten the route of the French African Army to Toulon and Marseilles.

The Chiefs of Staff pointed out that the establishment of an Italian military base in Spanish Morocco or on the south coast of Spain would prejudice the security of Gibraltar and British communications, whereas the occupation of Majorca or the other Spanish

Balearic islands 'would not vitally affect internal British strategic interests', while Sir Alec Cadogan, soon to be Permanent Under-Secretary at the Foreign Office, minuted that he was against any declaration at the moment; at the meeting of the Foreign Policy Committee on 19 August Eden therefore withdrew his suggestion.[1]

Eden told the Cabinet that Mussolini was intervening in Spain because he wanted to dominate the Mediterranean and looked on the Civil War not just as a struggle between Communism and Fascism but as a means of weakening British sea power in the western Mediterranean. This was a misreading of Mussolini's motives: at that time, he wanted only to resist any increase of French and Russian influence in Spain.

However, after receiving Grandi's specific assurance that Italy did not contemplate any deal with the insurgents for the cession of Ceuta (Spanish Morocco) or the Balearic Islands, Eden persuaded the Cabinet to send a private note to Rome expressing Britain's concern at the prospect of any alteration of the status quo in the Mediterranean; this was calculated to be less of a potential irritant to Mussolini than a public statement. Baldwin confided his concern over Eden's attitude to Italy at this time to Tom Jones, Secretary to the Cabinet, writing to him on 27 July, 'I told Eden yesterday that on no account, French or other, must he bring us to fight on the side of Russia.'[2]

Eden continued to regard Mussolini as a more imminent threat to peace than Hitler. He was inclined to try to meet Germany's more legitimate grievances under the Versailles Treaty; he did not view Hitler's proposals following the Rhineland coup of 7 March as entirely hypocritical, although Vansittart saw through them. Consequently, Eden was emollient towards Hitler while taking a hard line with Mussolini – a disastrous proceeding at a time when Mussolini genuinely wanted to mend his bridges with Britain and return to the Stresa Front rather than enter into an alliance with Nazi Germany.

Drummond wrote from Rome that 'few things would give Italian Government at the present moment greater pleasure than to return to really friendly relations with His Majesty's Government'. Unfortunately, with Eden as Foreign Secretary, this was to prove impossible. Mussolini had been acting as his own Foreign Minister, but in June 1936 he appointed his son-in-law, Galeazzo Ciano, Minister for Foreign Affairs; the Under-Secretary, Fulvio Suvich, went to Washington as Ambassador. At his first interview with Drummond, Ciano informed him that Italy was conscious of her strength and had no reason to fear the Germans – 'she could now more than hold her own against any single nation in Europe and the German bogey was laid'; Drummond agreed with him that this view of Italy was very widely held in Britain.

It seemed that Mussolini, satisfied by his conquest of Abyssinia, was ready to take the side of Britain and France against Germany. Yet, as so often, he showed no consistency: in October he sent Ciano to Germany where, amid great publicity, he signed an agreement for future collaboration between the two countries; in return Germany recognized the Italian Empire in Abyssinia. According to the account he subsequently gave Drummond, Ciano was, after his interview with the Führer, genuinely optimistic about a new Locarno agreement; he said that Hitler was frightened of the spread of Bolshevism. What he did not tell Drummond was that he had shown Hitler copies of a collection of British Cabinet documents, secretly purloined by Grandi in London, expressing the view that Hitler's aim was to destroy the peace settlement and by rearmament to establish Germany as the dominant power in Europe, and that it was therefore necessary to hasten and complete British rearmament. Hitler became very angry when he read them. In Milan on 1 November Mussolini made a significant speech in which he said that Ciano's visit to Germany had

> resulted in an understanding between our two countries over certain problems which had been particularly acute. This Rome–Berlin vertical line is not a diaphragm but rather an axis, around which may revolve all those European states with a will to collaboration and peace.

Although he used the word 'axis', the Italo–German relationship was at this time far from the close bond which later emerged.

In the same speech, Mussolini described the Mediterranean as

> . . . just one road, one of many roads, or rather a short-cut, for Great Britain, but for Italians it is life . . . Consequently there is only one solution: a sincere, mutual, rapid and complete agreement based on the recognition of interests.[3]

Four days later Eden made a direct reply in the House of Commons:

> For us the Mediterranean is not a short-cut but a main arterial road . . . In years gone by the interests of the two countries in the Mediterranean have been complementary rather than divergent. On the part of HMG there is every desire that these relations should be preserved. I repeat the assurances that we have no desire to threaten or indeed to attack any Italian interest in the Mediterranean . . . it should in our view be possible for each country to continue to maintain its vital interests in the Mediterranean not only without conflict with each other but even with mutual advantage.[4]

In the House of Lords, Halifax described British and Italian interests in the Mediterranean as being 'not divergent but complementary'.

Grandi saw Eden the next day and told him Mussolini would be disappointed by the speech, as he had hoped for 'something more'; the Duce also wanted the conquest of Abyssinia recognized 'without delay'; he would feel he had made an advance and suffered a rebuff; Grandi wanted Eden to send some message to Rome to make Mussolini happier, but Eden refused to yield over recognition of the Abyssinian conquest. Grandi told him that Italy felt Britain was considering 'revenge' and intended to take some action in Africa against Italy in support of British Imperial interests. In Rome, Ciano emphasized to Drummond that Mussolini had intended his speech in Milan to be very friendly to Britain. At this critical time, however, when Rome–Berlin co-operation was becoming more probable, Eden refused to extend the olive-branch. His antipathy to Mussolini is made clear by his minute of 5 November:

> Does anybody in the Foreign Office really believe that Italy's foreign policy will at any time be other than opportunist? We must be on our guard against increasing the dictator's prestige by our own excessive submissiveness. We will have no more approaches to Italy either official or unofficial until we know and have studied Italy's reactions to my speech.

In an interview with Ward Price of the *Daily Mail*, Mussolini spoke of the possibility of a 'gentlemen's agreement' with Britain and denied having any designs on the Balearic Islands, emphasizing that Anglo-Italian interests in the Mediterranean were complementary, not antagonistic; he gave it as his opinion that neither nation could afford the luxury of being hostile to the other in that sea. Grandi then saw Eden again and told him Mussolini wanted to carry the matter further; Eden indicated that he would favour an exchange of declarations, but not a pact; he was however adamant that no recognition of the situation in Abyssinia could be coupled with any such declaration. Despite this *caveat* Grandi appeared pleased, remarking that seven months of bad relations was not enough to destroy a traditional friendship.[5]

Although Grandi later told Eden there would be a general expectation in Italy that Britain would recognize Italy's conquest of Abyssinia, Mussolini agreed to leave it out of the discussions initially – an indication of his eagerness for a *rapprochement* with Britain, since *de jure* recognition of the new Italian Empire, particularly by Britain, was close to his heart.

On 2 December Drummond was authorized to begin talks; they lasted a month. Mussolini refused to allow France to be associated with any potential agreement, and Drummond reported that if Britain were to insist on the point, Mussolini would prefer to drop the negotiations. Eden found the Italian attitude exasperating, minuting on 10 December:

> The Italians are at their old game of getting something for nothing. They are apprehensive of our growing strength in the Mediterranean and would no doubt like to be greatly reassured. But what do we get in return? Anti-British propaganda in the Near East; a redoubling of activity in Majorca . . . An agreement that adds one more scrap of paper to the world and changes nothing is not worth so much effort.

On 16 December the Cabinet considered a strongly-worded memorandum from Eden drawing attention to the danger of Italian domination in the Balearic Islands and suggesting that Britain would be able to conduct her relations with Germany 'with very much greater advantage' if she stood firm in the Mediterranean. Eden received little support from his Cabinet colleagues, and two days later authorized Drummond to begin final negotiations for a declaration, provided the Italians agreed not to alter the national status of the territories in the Mediterranean area, 'particularly the territories of Spain'. Mussolini objected to this phrase as implying that Franco might be considering parting with some Spanish possession, which would be damaging to the General politically; another form of words was soon agreed between Drummond and Ciano. Although some members of the Cabinet, particularly Hoare, pressed for *de jure* recognition of the Italian conquest of Abyssinia, Eden would not agree. Despite this, negotiations in Rome went smoothly, showing Mussolini's anxiety for good relations with Britain, and agreement was reached on 1 January 1937.

On 2 January the Anglo–Italian Declaration (the so-called 'Gentlemen's Agreement') was signed and, with an exchange of Notes between the two governments, made public. Freedom of passage through the Mediterranean was declared to be a 'common vital interest', and it was affirmed that neither government would seek to modify the status quo of national sovereignty of territories in the Mediterranean area. In their Note it was stated that the Italian government had not engaged in any negotiations with General Franco about the status quo in the Mediterranean, nor would it do so in the future.[6]

The reference to Franco indicated a climb-down by Mussolini; had the Declaration also included *de jure* recognition by Britain of Italy's position in Abyssinia, Anglo–Italian relations would probably have been restored to what they had been at Stresa. The 'Gentlemen's Agreement' was only a half-way house, but it was greeted with satisfaction in the Foreign Office, Orme Sargent minuting: 'We have obtained all our requirements, and what is particularly satisfactory is the acceptance without alteration of our formula regarding Spain.' Vansittart noted that 'This is all most successful and gratifying. The Italians – and in particular Mussolini – have behaved very well and accommodatingly . . . we shall automatically loosen the Italo-German tie and so have a more reasonable or anyhow tamer Germany to deal with.' Eden was not unenthusiastic:

> It is particularly satisfactory that we should have obtained our formula regarding Spain. Let us bear in mind during our new relations with Italy that the latter has at least as much to gain from the better state of affairs as we. We shall lose nothing in Italian eyes by continuing *nous faire valoir* [*se faire valoir*: to make the most of oneself; to push oneself forward].

The signing of the agreement gave great satisfaction to the Italian public, who hailed it as a return to the friendship which had been so rudely shattered by the Abyssinian War.

The judgement of John Coverdale, the American historian, is valid:

> The fact that the 'Gentlemen's Agreement' eventually led nowhere, and that Italy finally entered the war at Germany's side, does not demonstrate that in 1936 she was more firmly committed to one line of policy than to the other. Fascist Italy was attracted to Nazi Germany by ideological considerations, by German willingness to support her claims to great-power status in the Mediterranean, and by the fact that as Germany's ally she could hope for tempting rewards in the colonial field from a successful war against England and France. On the other hand, were Germany to defeat France and Great Britain she would dominate the continent, and Italy would find herself reduced to the level of a German satellite. A balance of power within Europe was essential to Italy if she hoped to be able to exercise any influence. In the fall of 1936 Mussolini had as yet made no definite commitments. Italy still had not cast her lot definitely with Germany against England and was trying to follow a policy of friendship with both.[7]

Eden's coldness, however dampened Mussolini's enthusiasm for British friendship, and whatever his intentions may have been when he signed the 'Gentlemen's Agreement', the Duce quickly violated its spirit. Although Italy was a member of the Non-Intervention Committee set up to prevent military aid to either the Government of Spain or the insurgents, 3,000 Italian volunteers landed at Cadiz the day after the agreement was signed, and by the end of February Italian volunteers in Spain numbered 48,000. Radio Bari stepped up its anti-British propaganda to Egypt and North Africa (referred to by Eden in his minute of 10 December); the Italian press carried virulent anti-

British articles, some inspired by Mussolini, which gave the impression that British rearmament was directed solely against Italy. Sir Miles Lampson, Ambassador in Cairo, reported on 8 April 1937 that Italy's policy was to make as much anti-British propaganda in the Moslem world as possible, and said that Mussolini had no fear of 'an open conflict with Great Britain because Britain was not ready for a war and would not be so for at least three or four years'.[8]

In a note for the guidance of the Foreign Office dated 1 April 1937, Eden pointed out that Italy was equal to Germany as a potential aggressor, and that:

> We must not conceal from ourselves that Italy's hostility to us is at present real, and I believe vindictive. It is my own conviction that Signor Mussolini is speaking the truth when he says that he has not forgotten sanctions. In other words Italy's menace to us is limited only by her material weakness and not by her temper.[9]

The main stumbling-block to better relations continued to be Britain's refusal to recognize Italy's proclaimed Empire in Abyssinia, but with Eden's insistence that such recognition must be preceded by evidence of Italian goodwill, in the withdrawal of Italian troops from Spain and the cessation of anti-British propaganda, there was no progress. Though in Cabinet Neville Chamberlain and Samuel Hoare were disquieted by his attitude to Mussolini, Baldwin left foreign affairs entirely to Eden.

In his despatches from Rome, Drummond made strong pleas for *de jure* recognition. On 23 March he argued that Britain would get better terms from Mussolini 'if we accord *de jure* recognition at the earliest possible date and unconditionally'. Vansittart minuted in favour of *de jure* recognition right away, but Eden disagreed emphatically, saying that it must be refused at this time, as it was such an important diplomatic bargaining point.

Significantly, in his final despatch from Berlin before he was succeeded there as Ambassador by Nevile Henderson, Sir Eric Phipps wrote on 29 April 1937: 'The only way to keep the balance of power in Europe is to separate Mussolini from Hitler.' In a report of 4 May 1937 Drummond wrote that if Italian sovereignty in Abyssinia were still unrecognized after the League of Nations Council and Assembly meeting at the end of May, Mussolini was likely to conclude a complete alliance – political and military – with Germany; recognition would be very popular with the Italian people, to whom the Spanish adventure made no particular appeal. This should have been the red light. Lord Cranborne, Under-Secretary at the Foreign Office (later Lord Salisbury), minuted his agreement, as did Vansittart.

Two days later, Drummond wrote:

The vast majority of Italians consider that any offence Italy may have committed in attacking Abyssinia in violation of pledges . . . has been more than wiped out by the crime of sanctions, the attempt to reduce Italy by blockade . . . The Italians are irritated beyond measure by what they regard as the hypocrisy of the British contention that British rearmament makes for peace, with its corollary that Italian armaments make for war.

On 10 May Sir Alexander Cadogan sent Eden an important minute:

I have advocated the *de jure* recognition of the Italian conquest of Abyssinia – not lightheartedly nor without a sense of the enormous difficulties standing in the way (difficulties not made any easier by the Italians' own behaviour) – but because it does seem to me essential to remove this obstacle in the way of a real conciliation with Italy, both owing to our own anxieties in the Mediterranean region, and with a view to preventing the cleavage between the Dictator states and the rest of Europe becoming too irreparable and the hope of reuniting Europe too remote.

Vansittart minuted his agreement, but Eden disagreed, minuting: 'I have so long been promised that such and such action on our part would improve Anglo-Italian relations and so often been disappointed that I do not share those optimistic views of "de jure" recognition.'

On 11 June Drummond reiterated his request to Eden:

I had hoped that *de jure* recognition . . . would have given him [Mussolini] the psychological assurance that we accepted once and for all his Abyssinian conquest and consequently anti-British activities would considerably diminish.

As things stand I fear there is very little chance of his refusing to take such opportunities as events may offer of continuing to stir up trouble in the Arab world.

He added that Mussolini genuinely desired ten to twenty years of peace, in which to develop his Empire.

On 25 June Drummond wrote that Mussolini still believed that 'We intend some day to take our revenge on him for his Abyssinian adventure, and the best proof that we have no spirit of revenge would be [to give] *de jure* . . .'; he believed that Mussolini genuinely desired 'our friendship'.[10]

Neville Chamberlain had succeeded Stanley Baldwin as Prime Minister at the end of May 1937; unlike Baldwin, he took a strong interest in foreign affairs. He was also much more favourably inclined to Mussolini than was Eden, his Foreign Secretary, and was ready to concede *de jure* recognition in an effort to convert the 'Gentlemen's Agreement' into renewed and firm Anglo-Italian friendship. Here was an important change of attitude at the top, at a time when Anglo-Italian relations were still deteriorating.

Mussolini was adamant that the Crown Prince of Italy, Umberto, should not go to London in May 1937 for the coronation of King George VI, because Haile Selassie had also been invited; Umberto had been asked to stay at Buckingham Palace, and the King of Italy was furious with the Duce. This was followed in Britain by unwelcome press comments on an ignominious defeat of Italian troops at Guadalajara in Spain, and a sermon by the Dean of Winchester at a service for the victims of Italian rule in Abbyssinia in which the Dean called Mussolini, by inference, a madman. Relations worsened, to a point that the Chiefs of Staff and the Foreign Office became seriously worried about the danger of war with Italy.

The surest way for Britain to improve relations with Mussolini would have been to recognize the Italian conquest of Abyssinia, but this recognition Eden categorically refused to give, despite the fact that no matter how unreliable Mussolini might be, both Britain and France now needed his support to keep Hitler at bay.

Mussolini wrote significantly to Grandi on 3 June:

> I authorize you to confirm the contradiction that you have given [to the new Prime Minister, Chamberlain] about German–Italian relations. Nothing has occurred. There is only an improved atmosphere, in which it is understandable for obvious reasons that tomorrow something more could happen if the madmen of Geneva and London continue their hostile attitude to Italy and Fascism.

After receiving some encouragement on 19 June from Drummond in Rome about the British attitude, Ciano wrote to Grandi describing a reconciliation with Britain as 'not only possible but desirable', although the first step must be recognition of the Italian Empire in Abyssinia on terms which made it clear to the Abyssinians there would be no return to the past; once this was out of the way, there remained only the Spanish problem. As to this, Ciano felt the British now recognized that Italy had no ambitions in Spain, and that the war Italy was victoriously conducting was in British interests, since Britain did not want to see a Bolshevik regime installed there, or anywhere. Ciano authorized Grandi to indicate to the British government that Italy was ready to shake the hand Britain appeared to be tentatively offering, and that a suitable occasion might be the eve of his (Grandi's) departure from London for Rome, when he might obtain from Neville Chamberlain a message for the Duce which would break the ice. (This letter is missing from the official printed Italian documents, but is quoted from the Grandi archive by the historian Renzo de Felice.)

Since the end of the Abyssinian War, Grandi had been trying to revive Anglo-Italian friendship; in his diary he confessed to jumping the gun in his enthusiasm:

> Since June when Chamberlain came to Downing Street, I have believed that he was the only man with whom we could come to an understanding. I have felt that I must do everything in my power to establish a psychological understanding between the Duce and Chamberlain. I was sure that once there was created a feeling of sympathy and appreciation of good faith between Mussolini and Chamberlain it might be possible to come to a definite agreement between us and England . . . I felt this was the only battlefield on which to defeat Eden. Eden had a fixed idea that he must demonstrate the bad faith of Mussolini. I had to destroy this plan of Eden's by showing to Chamberlain that Mussolini could be trusted. In my reports to Rome I gave an over-optimistic picture of Chamberlain, making out that he was a friend and admirer of Mussolini – much more of a friend and admirer than he actually was. I, off my own bat, sent a message from Chamberlain to the Duce at the time of the Coronation. In fact, Chamberlain never gave me a message for the Duce. This is what happened. During a lunch at the Foreign Office for King George VI's Birthday, Eden introduced the new Prime Minister to all the Ambassadors. Chamberlain spoke a few words to each of them. This was enough for me to send a despatch to Rome in which I exaggerated greatly the tone of the few innocuous words of Chamberlain concerning his opinion of the Duce, which Chamberlain would not have dreamed of giving me.

Grandi continued his plotting. On 12 July he wrote to inform Ciano that Adrian Dingli, legal adviser in the Italian Embassy in London, was on his way to Rome. Dingli was in the confidence of Sir Joseph Ball, an intimate friend of Chamberlain and Head of the Research unit at Conservative Central Office: if Mussolini agreed, Dingli would on his return to London suggest to Ball an interview between the Prime Minister and Grandi, thus by-passing Eden who, Grandi commented, was anything but convinced of the Duce's trustworthiness.

At an interview with Eden on 21 July Grandi went even further, claiming to have a letter from Mussolini for the Prime Minister which he was to deliver at his own discretion. In it, according to Grandi, Mussolini emphasized his desire for permanent friendship with Britain, and a desire to discuss at any time 'any proposals to further the interests of the two countries'. No such letter existed. On his report of this conversation, Eden minuted to Vansittart: 'Mussolini has the mentality of a gangster . . . while reciprocating any advances we should be watchful in the extreme.'

Chamberlain saw Grandi, without Eden, on 27 July. Grandi did not give the Prime Minister a copy of his bogus letter, but read from four

1. Lord Curzon, Benito Mussolini and Raymond Poincaré at the Lausanne Conference, 1922, within a few weeks of Mussolini coming to power

2. King Victor Emmanuel III in London in 1924 visiting the Italian Royal Hospital

3. Mussolini and King Victor Emmanuel III, 1925

4. Mussolini (*left*) with Austen Chamberlain (*right*) at the Locarno Conference, 1925. They had become warm friends by this stage

5. Austen Chamberlain and Mussolini on the dictator's yacht, 1926

6. Lord Cecil, President of the League of Nations Union, speaking in London before the Disarmament Conference, 1932

7. Dino Grandi, the Italian ambassador, is greeted by London blackshirts as he arrives at the Italian Royal Hospital, May 1933

8. Sir John Simon, the Foreign Secretary (*left*), with the Prime Minister, Ramsay MacDonald, and Mussolini in Rome for the signing of the Four-Power Pact, 1933

9. Anthony Eden, Foreign Secretary, shaking hands with Pierre Laval, the French Foreign Minister, at Victoria Station, February 1935. They did not get on well

10. Sir Samuel Hoare at the height of the Abyssinian crisis,
August 1935

11. Lord Halifax, Lord Privy Seal (*right*), seeing off the German ambassador Joachim von Ribbentrop at Victoria Station, November 1937

12. Count Ciano and von Ribbentrop at the Munich Conference, 1938. They disliked each other. Both were later executed

13. Neville Chamberlain tries to make friends with Mussolini at the Munich
Conference, 1938

14. Ciano, Lord Halifax, Neville Chamberlain and Mussolini in Rome, January 193

15. Hitler gives Mussolini an enthusiastic welcome at the
Brenner Pass, 1940

16. A modern cartoon depicts Mussolini putting his heel on France after her defeat in 1940

pages of manuscript what he pretended was a translation, and so interspersed his own comments that Chamberlain was left in confusion about what precisely was in the letter. He told Grandi that *de jure* recognition would arouse very strong hostility from devoted adherents of the League of Nations in Britain, and could only be justified if it could be described as 'part of a great scheme of reconciliation which should remove suspicions and lead to restoration of confidence'; Britain would want to know why Italy was sending so many troops to Libya, and why she was conducting a wireless and press campaign against Britain. Grandi replied that Mussolini was now in personal control of the wireless and press, and that two divisions had been sent to Libya because Britain 'had frightened the Italians out of their wits' by spending millions on defence in the Mediterranean.

The interview was friendly. Grandi also told the Prime Minister that Mussolini was anxious to have conversations which would lead to a 'complete clarification of the situation', and when Chamberlain asked if the Duce would like a personal note in reply, he was assured that it would be acceptable.[11]

The same day, and without consulting Eden, Chamberlain wrote to Mussolini. Grandi's tactics had produced the result he wanted, but his was not the behaviour expected of an Ambassador. This is Chamberlain's letter:

Personal   *July 27, 1937*

Dear Signor Mussolini,

I have been having a long talk this morning with Count Grandi who brought me the message you were good enough to send me. No doubt he will report to you what I have said to him, but I should like to send you a personal note, and Count Grandi has encouraged me to write.

Although I have spent some of my happiest holidays in Italy it is now some years since I visited your country and so to my great regret I have never had the opportunity of meeting Your Excellency. But I have often heard my brother, Sir Austen, talk of you, and always with the highest regard. He used to say that you were 'a good man to do business with'.

Since I became Prime Minister, I have been distressed to find that the relations between Italy and Great Britain are still far from that old feeling of mutual confidence and affection which lasted for so many years. In spite of the bitterness which arose out of the Abyssinian affair I believe it possible for those old feelings to be restored, if we can only clear away some of the misunderstandings and unfounded suspicions which cloud our trust in one another.

I therefore welcome very heartily the message you have sent me and I wish to assure you that this Government is actuated only by the most friendly feelings towards Italy and will be ready at any time to enter upon conversations with a view to clarifying the whole situation and removing all causes of suspicion or misunderstanding. Believe me, etc.,

Chamberlain noted in his diary that 'I did not show my letter to the Foreign Secretary for I had the feeling he would object to it.' In his memoirs Eden commented that this behaviour on Chamberlain's part made a strong contrast to his own experience later as Winston Churchill's Foreign Secretary: 'complete confidence and candour between a Prime Minister and Foreign Secretary are indispensable', he said, but 'I made no difficulty about the incident at the time, thinking that there was no deliberate intent to bypass me as Foreign Secretary but that it was merely a slip by a Prime Minister new to foreign affairs.' Nevertheless, he was clearly put out by Chamberlain's failure to consult him, and objected to the tone of the letter. Writing to Vansittart to express the hope that no more letters would pass from Number 10 to Rome without him seeing them, Eden said:

> No doubt Mussolini wants recognition of Abyssinia, but so do we want the Italians out of Majorca, mechanised divisions out of Libya, explanation of the fortified islands in the Mediterranean and Red Sea, etc. It would be the height of folly to concede in fact what the Italians want in return for mere promises. By all means let us show ourselves ready to talk, but in no scrambling hurry to offer incense on the dictator's altar.

Ciano told Drummond that Mussolini was pleased with Chamberlain's letter and wanted conversations to start in Rome, to be looked on as a continuation of the December talks. Mussolini replied to Chamberlain:

> Count Grandi, the Italian Ambassador, has sent me your kind message and has informed me of the most interesting conversation he had with Your Excellency.
>
> I thank you wholeheartedly and I hasten to let you know that it is also my warmest wish to meet you personally and talk things over with Your Excellency.
>
> I remember with the greatest sympathy Sir Austen – the nobility of his mind, his broad and clear intelligence – and I cherish the recollection of the work we accomplished together in the interests of our two countries and of the political reconstruction of Europe.
>
> Count Grandi has already conveyed to Your Excellency my views on the present situation of Anglo-Italian relations and on their possible development.
>
> I wish to confirm that I share Your Excellency's opinion. I, too, believe it possible and sincerely wish to bring back the relations between our two countries on the basis of a cordial and far-reaching collaboration. The interests of Italy and Great Britain are not opposed either in the Mediterranean or elsewhere. On the contrary, through their peaceful co-

existence they may constitute a reason for increasing more actively the development of our relations.

If the atmosphere – as Your Excellency points out – is still shadowed somewhere by clouds of unfounded suspicions and misunderstandings, a thorough and frank clarification of our respective intentions shall certainly lead to the re-establishment of mutual confidence, which is the foundation of any international agreement.

To this end, I am glad to agree with Your Excellency's suggestion that conversations be entered upon, in the course of which will have to be examined, in a spirit of sincere collaboration, those questions which still wait for a solution, in order to ensure the understanding we desire to reestablish between our two countries.[12]

This was promising. In Rome Ciano told a journalist that he believed 'a great stride forward has been made', and after Grandi had seen the Prime Minister again on 2 August Drummond was instructed to tell Ciano that 'We hope to see discussions started towards the end of August or beginning of September.' Grandi later described this brief period of goodwill as 'a happy fortnight'; but it was clouded by Eden's continued obstinate refusal to recognize Italy's conquest of Abyssinia.

When Drummond wrote on 5 August that

the essential condition for any successful negotiations with the Italian Government for a general detente is recognition on our side of Italian sovereignty over Abyssinia. Unless we are prepared to grant such recognition conversations are bound to end in failure,

Chamberlain minuted to Vansittart, in Eden's absence on holiday:

We should give *de jure* recognition while it has some marketable value, but we must not offend the French or shock League friends at home. Italians will be quite satisfied if Abyssinia is declared no longer an independent state.

These dictators are men of moods. Catch them in the right mood and they will give you anything you ask for. But if the mood changes they shut up like an oyster. The moral of which is that we must make Musso feel that things are moving all the time.[13]

Lord Halifax, Lord Privy Seal with responsibility for foreign affairs, was left in charge of the Foreign Office during August while Eden enjoyed a country-house holiday near Southampton. Halifax took Chamberlain's side in the dispute, and disapproved of Eden's line. On 11 August Eden wrote to invite Halifax to stay for a few days, to 'walk through the pine trees by the sea shore or play tennis'; he added:

I am very reluctant to recognize *de jure* conquest of Abyssinia and really do not think I could bring myself to any kind of approval of what Italy has done, though I share your desire to be a realist. If it be true that she cannot 'make a job' of Abyssinia without *de jure* recognition from us, I find it all the more difficult to give it.[14]

Clearly, Chamberlain and Eden were poles apart; had Chamberlain steeled himself to sack Eden at this time, rather than later, it is probable that Mussolini would not have been driven to ally himself with Hitler.

During Eden's absence by the sea an important meeting was held in his room at the Foreign Office on 10 August, at which Drummond, recalled from Rome, emphasized that recognition of Italian sovereignty over Abyssinia was a *sine qua non* for the success of Anglo-Italian negotiations; so long as 'the idea prevailed that the Emperor might one day be restored, the Italians would have difficulty in maintaining law and order'; the Chamberlain–Mussolini letters, he said, had resulted in a strong expectation in Italy that the Abyssinian situation would be resolved. Drummond wanted the question of the position of Abyssinia put on the agenda of the League of Nations Assembly meeting due to take place in September.

Halifax and the officials present concluded that Britain should put the status of Abyssinia on the agenda in Geneva, and that talks should be started immediately with Ciano in Rome about *de jure* recognition as part of a general settlement with Italy; in return, Italy should be asked to reiterate the agreement made at Stresa that Austria must be kept independent, to reduce her garrison in Libya, to exchange military information, to cease anti-British propaganda on Radio Bari, and to reaffirm pledges about the status quo of Spanish territory.[15]

Halifax sent the office record of the meeting to Eden the next day with an accompanying letter: 'When we talk we shall liquidate the Abyssinian position. We must in some form grasp the Abyssinian nettle.' Eden replied: 'I disagree with the office note. It would be difficult to put all my objections on paper. I will put them to you when we meet . . . we should decline to be rushed into conversations.'

On receiving Eden's letter, Halifax wrote to Chamberlain:

> *Entre nous* Anthony is rather unhappy about the policy disclosed in that office discussion we sent you; and seemed inclined when he wrote to me on it to contemplate 'marking time' . . . I fancy what he jibs at is (1) our taking the initiative at Geneva and (2) the idea of *de jure* – which seems to connote some sort of approval – he is sceptical about getting anything out of the Italians. He dislikes and mistrusts their general make-up – and Spain with all the rather sinister shipping possibilities that these last few days have disclosed comes in to strengthen his instinctive recoil.

Halifax also told Vansittart that Eden's letter rather disquieted him: 'His attitude is dangerously divergent from the Prime Minister's . . .

onus is on me to say something to Anthony . . . Time is running out.'
Halifax must have been on the brink of telling Chamberlain that
Eden's attitude was so divergent that he must go. Chamberlain replied
to Halifax that he agreed with the 'Office' view expressed on 10
August.

On 16 August Halifax went to stay with Eden near Southampton.
He can have had little time to play tennis or walk in the pine woods by
the sea, as he was back in the Foreign Office the next morning. He was
convinced that further cold-shouldering by Britain would drive
Mussolini into an alliance with Hitler, but he could make no headway
with Eden. He had also failed to bring home to Eden the impossibility
of a situation in which the Prime Minister and the Foreign Secretary
held such diametrically opposed views on such a vital issue. So Eden
continued as Foreign Secretary, and recognition of the Italian conquest of Abyssinia was not put on the September agenda of the
Council of the League.

At a meeting of the Committee of Imperial Defence early in
September Eden urged that Italy should be treated as a potential
enemy against whom the CID should make certain preparations, thus
placing Italy in the same category as Germany, about whose rearmament alarming reports were continually being received. More sensibly,
Chamberlain argued that Germany was the greatest danger and
should take priority in Britain's defence preparations, while 'defence
preparations against Italy should be considered of secondary importance', since 'a unilateral war with Italy was unthinkable'.

Chamberlain was much disappointed and Eden almost justified
when, later in September, Mussolini's troops poured into Spain, and
Italy attacked British ships. Grandi commented:

> Relations between Italy and Britain put in peril by the Abyssinian war
> were further worsened and poisoned by the Spanish question. Abyssinia
> was a short but acute illness. Like all short illnesses it had a quick cure.
> Spain was a slow and progressive illness which in the end became chronic.
> It created a growing abyss between Italy and Great Britain and paved the
> path for the Anti-Comintern Pact and military co-operation between
> Hitler and Mussolini.

The news from Germany was even more alarming, however: on 1
September the new Ambassador in Berlin, Sir Nevile Henderson
(who had replaced Sir Eric Phipps), stated that by 1940 Germany
would have 146 divisions with adequately trained personnel, and that
she was already virtually unattackable; at the same time, Hitler had a
very low estimate of the present capacity of other nations to combine
against Germany. Yet Eden still gave the Italian threat priority.

Ominously, on 6 September Ciano told the British Chargé d'Affaires in Rome that if Britain was not going to grant *de jure* recognition, 'it was difficult to see what the proposed Anglo-Italian negotiations could deal with'.[16]

Chamberlain's hopes of an Anglo-Italian understanding were further dimmed by continued anti-British propaganda emanating from the Italians, and a bombastic statement by Mussolini praising Italian troops for their part in the capture of Santander in Spain, in co-operation with Franco's army. However, both these issues were dwarfed by the effrontery of Italian submarines and military aircraft in the seas around Spain, with their concerted attacks on ships carrying supplies to the Spanish Republican Government. One British, one French and one Greek merchant ship were bombed by aircraft which were either Italian, or belonging to the Spanish Nationalists. An 8,000-ton Spanish tanker was sunk by a submarine, and a Danish cargo ship was sunk by Italian aircraft off Barcelona. Attacks were made on a French merchant ship and a Panamanian tanker, and three Spanish freighters were sunk. Then two Russian ships were sunk off Cape Matapan, and on the night of 31 August/1 September the Italian submarine *Iride*, which was blockading the Spanish coast under the direct orders of the Admiralty in Rome, attacked a British destroyer; two days later, a British merchantman was sunk by a torpedo off Valencia.

This was little less than international piracy. Mussolini had ordered the naval blockade, but left the details to Ciano. Ciano realized it could not be continued without the gravest consequences, and ordered Admiral Cavagnari to suspend the attacks, even though Franco had sent word that the blockade would be decisive if it were continued throughout September.

In co-operation with the French, Eden called for an immediate conference at Nyon in Switzerland at which all the Mediterranean powers — not only France, Britain and Italy, but also Yugoslavia, Greece, Turkey, Egypt and the Black Sea powers Russia, Bulgaria and Romania — would examine the possibility of a Mediterranean Pact; France and Britain hoped agreement could be reached that submarines operating outside territorial waters should be sunk, and that no submarine should submerge outside clearly defined limits, so that any submarine detected in the open sea would be liable to be attacked. At first the Italian response was favourable, but an outspoken protest from Russia about the sinking of her two ships sent Mussolini into a rage, and he refused to allow Italian delegates to go to Nyon.

On 8 September, Chamberlain told a Cabinet meeting that he had hoped Britain would have been able to take the first steps towards recognizing Italian sovereignty over Abyssinia at the next meeting of the

League of Nations Assembly in Geneva, but that the whole situation had been changed

> . . . by the activities of the Italian submarines in the Mediterranean, and by Signor Mussolini's foolish boasting in connection with General Franco's capture of Santander. As a result the French Government were not now prepared to co-operate, and he [the Prime Minister] thought it was out of the question for us to proceed in the matter without France's co-operation.

While he knew Eden found it difficult to go quite as far as he would wish, Chamberlain said he hoped Britain would do everything possible to recover the better atmosphere of the summer. In general the Cabinet agreed with the Prime Minister. Eden stated that the British line with the Italians should be that Britain stood by everything Chamberlain had said to Grandi and to Mussolini in July, but that the events which had taken place in the interval had made the position very much more difficult, which was why Britain attached so much importance to achieving success at the Nyon Conference.

In a memorandum circulated to members of the Cabinet Eden, ignoring the threat Hitler posed to Austria, stressed the Spanish war iniquities of Mussolini, and that *de jure* recognition of her conquest of Abyssinia must await a general settlement with Italy. The Cabinet gave Eden discretion to choose the moment when he would raise *de jure*, and when the League Council met on 13 September, Britain did not take the initiative. The recommendation of the 10 August Foreign Office meeting was thus ignored, and the resultant delay was unfortunate: Mussolini met Hitler in Germany during the last week of September, and had he been sure of British friendship in advance, his attitude to Hitler would have been less co-operative.

In a letter to his sister Chamberlain expressed his anxiety about the Foreign Office attitude to Italy: '. . . they seem to me to have no imagination and no courage . . . I am terribly afraid lest we should let the Anglo-Italian situation slip back to where it was before I intervened.' In this Chamberlain was correct: the Spanish Civil War was a side issue, and Hitler's aggression made it essential that Italy should somehow be brought back to the Stresa Front; otherwise Austria would fall to Germany, and Hitler would then become unstoppable.[17]

The Nyon Conference met on 10 September; neither Italy nor Germany attended. On 14 September an agreement was signed which stipulated that the participating powers would destroy any submarine which attacked a merchant vessel not belonging to one or other party in the Spanish conflict; this would apply not only to submarines seen in the act of attacking, but also to any seen near an attacked ship in circumstances which gave valid ground for believing that the submarine was guilty of the attack. The Nyon powers agreed that none of their submarines would put to sea in the Mediterranean unless accompanied by a surface vessel. Britain would supply 35 destroyers, the French 38, to enforce the terms of the agreement. Full details were sent to Ciano, who said he must consult Mussolini; the agreement was signed without Italy.

Mussolini's vanity was hurt because Italy was only offered the Tyrrhenian Sea to patrol; he insisted that Italy should have absolute parity with the other powers, and by 30 September amicable arrangements had been made for Italy, in addition to the Tyrrhenian Sea, to patrol the Straits of Messina, the sea off Tobruk, the Adriatic and the Ionian Sea; the Italian Navy accepted all restrictions on the movements of submarines set out in the Nyon Agreement. This was encouraging. In his diary, Ciano interpreted Italy's part in the agreement as 'a fine victory, from suspected pirates to policemen of the Mediterranean'. After Nyon there were no more submarine attacks, and the Agreement represented a minor diplomatic triumph for Eden; however, it is unlikely that Italy had ever intended the submarine campaign to last indefinitely, since Mussolini could not have expected to continue to attack shipping off Spain without running the risk of a major international war. He certainly did not want this, and Ciano had suspended the attacks before the invitations to Nyon were issued.

After Nyon Chamberlain was more anxious than ever to resume negotiations with Mussolini. The problems remained the same: Mussolini's insistence on *de jure* recognition of Italy's sovereignty in Abyssinia, and Italy's involvement in the Spanish Civil War. Eden wrote on 16 September that there was no possibility of 'taking any fruitful initiative at the Assembly [in Geneva] in connection with Abyssinia' because of Mussolini's habit of breaking international obligations 'as exemplified by his Spanish policy and Italian submarine attacks off Spain'. He argued for tripartite talks with Italy, to include France, although Chamberlain wanted Ciano and Drummond (now Earl of Perth) bilaterally to hasten an Anglo-Italian settlement, as envisaged in his exchange of letters with Mussolini. The Foreign Office was divided. From Rome, Perth advocated the beginning of talks, as did the Counsellor, Edward Ingram, and Orme Sargent and Vansittart in London. Vansittart thought that to delay was to run unnecessary risks; but Cranborne and Eden remained adamant that *de jure* recognition must not be granted while Italian troops remained in Spain.[18]

Now let us take a look at German–Italian relations during those fatal months when Europe was sliding towards war.

In Naples, in May, Hitler had invited the Duce to visit him. Mussolini was initially reluctant to accept, since at the time his preference was for British friendship, but the succeeding weeks were black for Anglo-Italian understanding, with the British press violently hostile to Italian participation in the Spanish Civil War and the assassination in France, by Italian Fascists, of the anti-Fascist Rosselli brothers.* Between 8 May and 21 July Mussolini banned all British newspapers except the *Daily Mail*, the *Evening News* and the *Observer* from circulation in Italy, and recalled most of the Italian journalists in London.

In September 1937 Mussolini paid his visit to Hitler. During the course of it, the Führrer and the Duce had only one political talk, in which Hitler promised to continue to give military aid to Franco. It seems they did not discuss Austria, about which Mussolini must have had grave forebodings. Instead, it was Goering who assured Mussolini that no move concerning Austria would be made without a prior understanding with Italy; Mussolini wrote to King Victor Emmanuel of his impression that Germany had not given up the idea of *Anschluss*; but 'we must await events'. In Berlin, Mussolini proclaimed that 'German–Italian solidarity is a living and active solidarity'. The evidence for this was scanty, however, and Mussolini told the King that his visit was only a show-piece.

Baron Ernst von Weizsäcker, head of the German Foreign Office, told Ogilvie Forbes of the British Embassy on 1 October that there had not been 'a scrap of written agreement' during Mussolini's visit to Germany, and no mention made of Austria. Of the visit, Ogilvie Forbes wrote that 'There is no doubt that [it] was an enormous success', and that the Berliners had seen in Mussolini 'a bronzed, athletic and vivacious figure with a radiant and engaging smile'.[19]

This was all a far cry from 1934 when, after the murder of Dollfuss, in German eyes Italy had been Public Enemy Number One and the *Popolo d'Italia* had written of the Nazis, 'A national socialist is an assassin and a pederast', and as far from Stresa in 1935, when Italy had taken the lead in threatening Germany of the consequences of any adventure in Austria.

After the visit, however, Mussolini spoke bombastically of the creation of a Rome–Berlin axis, and on 6 November 1937 Italy joined the German–Japanese Anti-Comintern Pact against Russia. In his diary

---

* There is no doubt that the assassins were in the pay of the Italian secret service, but there is controversy as to whether Mussolini himself authorized the killing of the Roselli brothers. The Duce was very conscious of how the Matteoti murder had affected his popularity, and it is unlikely that he would have risked a repeat.

Ciano noted that the Pact might be anti-Comintern in theory 'but in fact was unmistakably anti-British'.[20]

But Mussolini was far from happy at the prospect of a close alliance with Germany. Uncomfortable with Hitler and worried about Austria, like Grandi he was nostalgic for the pre-Abyssinian War friendship with Britain.

On 6 November 1937 Grandi made his feelings about the Nazis clear when writing to Ciano about Ribbentrop's arrival as the new German Ambassador in London, still basking in Hitler's delight at the success of the negotiations for the Anglo-German Naval Agreement of 1935. It is unlikely that Grandi would have written in such terms if he had not been sure that Ciano shared similar feelings.

> I intend to give Ribbentrop plenty of rope with which to hang himself and to watch carefully how to bring him to heel.
>
> Ribbentrop's arrival in London, after six months without a German Ambassador and three months after his much-heralded appointment, was uproarious and lively. He was preceded by numerous motor-cars, a troop of public relations and press officers and other special aides who immediately began to beat the big drums; besides a son of fourteen years who Ribbentrop has sent to Westminster, with the result that all the British newspapers have published photos of the boy dressed in an Eton suit, with comments not at all favourable to a German Ambassador, in my view, such as: 'The German Ambassador wants to educate his son in the English tradition . . . The young Ribbentrop when he goes back to Germany will not know how to give the Nazi salute.' This in my view was Ribbentrop's first grave error.
>
> The second mistake made by Ribbentrop was to give press interviews as soon as he put his feet down on the platform at Victoria Station. He told the journalists he had come to London with the specific aim of achieving binding links of friendship between Germany and England, and that this task was not easy (first gaffe) and would need much time (second gaffe), but that Germany and England would in the end understand each other because they had a common enemy in Communism (third gaffe). These interviews naturally produced a lot of offence. For two days journalists have talked of little else. Many newspapers, not only those on the left, whose columns I sent to you, have been talking in phrases like 'impertinent', 'puts his foot in a false step', 'a bad beginning', and 'Ambassadors who do not know when to keep quiet are not Ambassadors', etc.
>
> At the beginning of his diplomatic mission one can only say that Ribbentrop has demonstrated the traditional German quality of being an elephant walking on plates.
>
> Neurath [German Foreign Minister, 1932–38] was right when he told you that it was easier to sell champagne to the English than to deal with them over policy.

There is only one point worth considering about Ribbentrop; that is Vansittart and the anti-German group of British die-hards denying the possibility of some sort of accord with Germany. Instead the majority of the English people and the majority of the Cabinet want an agreement with Germany that would for some time allay the nightmare of bomb attacks by the newly powerful Germany on London. Ribbentrop is like a fly driving a coach and horses through a complicated diplomatic game played between London and Berlin which depends mainly, if not entirely, on the way Hitler will receive advances from England, which appear always to be motivated by a desire for a purely temporary accommodation with Nazi Germany.[21]

During the late summer and autumn of 1937 Hitler had begun to whip up agitation in Germany over the treatment of the inhabitants of the Sudetenland, incorporated into Czechoslovakia at the break-up of the Habsburg Empire, where the Czech Government had not treated the many former German subjects well. In November he told his Foreign Office and War Office that the subjugation of Austria and Czechoslovakia would be his first step in acquiring more German territory in the East. Lord Halifax went to Germany to meet Hitler at the end of November 1937, and suggested to the Führer that alterations to the Versailles settlement might be possible; and that because 'Danzig, Austria and Czechoslovakia' were 'capable of causing serious trouble', Britain was not necessarily concerned to stand for the status quo but 'if reasonable settlements could be reached with the free assent and goodwill of those primarily concerned [Britain] certainly had no desire to block.' According to Hitler's interpreter, Paul Schmidt, Hitler told Halifax that 'a close union between Austria and the Reich was imperative, and had been desired by the Austrian people since 1919', to which Halifax replied that 'England' was ready to consider any solution provided 'that it be not based on force, and that applied to Austria'. Undoubtedly Hitler interpreted what Halifax said as implying that Britain would condone Germany's annexation of Austria.[22]

In reporting on his visit, Halifax told the Cabinet on 24 November that he had found in Germany 'friendliness and a desire for good relations'. The wool had been thrown over his eyes with a vengeance, because he said he had seen no signs that the Germans were planning any immediate adventure. Chamberlain wrote to his sister that Halifax's visit had been a great success, and had created 'an atmosphere in which it is possible to discuss with Germany the practical questions involved in an European settlement'; this was wishful thinking.

The archives show Vansittart to have been much worried by the words Halifax had used to Hitler, but the appeasement of Germany by the British Cabinet was given a fillip when the anti-German and pro-

Italian Vansittart was replaced as Head of the Foreign Office by Sir Alec Cadogan. Eden had found Vansittart not only diametrically opposed to his own views on Italy and Germany, but also bossy. When the French Premier Camille Chautemps and his Foreign Minister Yvon Delbos came to London at the end of November 1937 Eden, with Chamberlain's approval, made it clear to the French that Britain was lukewarm about resisting Hitler if he tried to annex the Sudetenland, while both Chamberlain and Eden agreed with the French that Germany's former colonies in Africa should be returned to her in the hope of achieving the longed-for general settlement with Hitler. In these talks, Eden showed himself as appeasement-minded as Chamberlain.[23]

On 2 December Eden asked Grandi to come to see him. Disregarding the mounting uneasiness about German plans, he told the Ambassador bluntly that Anglo-Italian conversations could not begin unless Italy ceased her anti-British and anti-French propaganda; otherwise, he said, the conversations would fail. Grandi told Eden that the one thing Italy wanted to achieve from the conversations was *de jure* recognition; Eden was unresponsive. When the conversation turned to Austria, the two noted with 'somewhat mournful recollection' that the last occasion on which the matter of Austria had formed the subject of a resolution was at Stresa. 'Mournful, yes indeed,' said Grandi. Eden indicated his frame of mind in a subsequent minute:

> I should like to improve our relations with Italy. At the same time I have noticed that approaches by us are apt to be regarded as weaknesses, and relations not bettered thereby, unless of course the Italians think we will give something, when they are polite until they have got it. This time we have nothing to give, since all agree we cannot recognize Abyssinia now. I have been in some difficulty to know what we can talk about.[24]

We 'all agree we cannot recognize Abyssinia now' was an overstatement: Chamberlain and other members of the Cabinet were ready to do so, and the Foreign Office were divided on the point; the worse the German menace, the stronger became the arguments in favour of recognition.

Grandi, enthusiastic for a British–Italian and much opposed to a German–Italian alliance, was so upset by Eden's cold attitude that he decided on another subterfuge. He knew that Chamberlain favoured granting *de jure* recognition and starting the Anglo-Italian talks; he must also have been aware that Mussolini desired British friendship.

On 11 December Mussolini announced that Italy would quit the League of Nations. This strengthened Grandi's resolve to approach Chamberlain behind Eden's back and convince him that Mussolini wanted a reconciliation with Britain to prevent Italy sliding into Hitler's arms. According to Grandi's diary:

> It was an almost insoluble problem to get in touch with Chamberlain unknown to Eden, who did not intend at any cost to allow my visit to Downing Street at the end of July to be repeated. I used Poliakoff of our London Embassy, and told him that I had a message for Chamberlain from Mussolini and I did not know how to deliver it. I asked Poliakoff if he could, through Lord Tyrell, a close friend of Chamberlain's, let Chamberlain know that I had this message but was unable to deliver it. Poliakoff went to Tyrell. Tyrell went to Chamberlain, and on the same day Poliakoff came back to the Embassy and informed me that at 5 in the afternoon Chamberlain would make a personal telephone call to the Embassy. At precisely 5 Chamberlain phoned, and asked if it was true that I had a message from Mussolini. I told him it was true, and read out over the phone the following bogus message invented by me, which contained three points:
>
> 1.   The Duce interpreted a recent speech by Chamberlain as meaning that Chamberlain retained his personal faith in Mussolini.
> 2.   The problem for the Non-Intervention Committee arose from the attitude of Russia and France and the attacks of the British press, but despite that Mussolini had decided to work for the adoption of the British Plan [for Non-Intervention Committee nations to police the waters around Spain, to prevent sinkings].
> 3.   Mussolini was keeping open his offer for a complete agreement with Britain either through or outside the [Non-Intervention] Committee.

Grandi claimed in his diary that Chamberlain expressed lively satisfaction at this 'message'; and that by means of its fabrication he was able to put Chamberlain into a state of mind favourable to the Duce, and encourage in the Duce a similar attitude to Chamberlain: a return, as Grandi describes it, to the position at the end of July when the exchange of letters between the two leaders took place. After this exercise Grandi kept in almost daily contact with Sir Joseph Ball, who had been authorized by Chamberlain to talk to him behind Eden's back.[25]

As we have seen, a proposal that the other European Powers should not involve themselves in the Spanish Civil War had resulted in the formation of a Non-Intervention Committee; this met in London under the chairmanship of Lord Plymouth, Under-Secretary at the Foreign Office. Twenty-six countries* attended the

---

*Albania, Austria, Belgium, Bulgaria, Czechoslovakia, Denmark, Estonia, Finland, France, Germany, Greece, Hungary, Ireland, Italy, Latvia, Lithuania, Luxembourg, Netherlands, Norway, Poland, Romania, Russia, Sweden, Turkey, United Kingdom and Yugoslavia.

inaugural meeting, but the main participants were Britain, Belgium, France, Germany, Italy and Portugal. In March 1937 the Committee had produced a scheme for the Spanish borders to be watched by international observers, all foreign troops to be withdrawn, observers to be stationed on ships trading with Spain, and the coast to be patrolled.

Nothing effective was done, however, and the existence of the Committee made little difference to the intervention of Germany and Italy on Franco's side in the war, or to Russia's on the Republican side; France paid some heed, marginally limiting her help to the Republicans. In Committee the diplomats fruitlessly exchanged charges and counter-charges. Grandi defended Italy's actions skilfully, and fabricated conciliatory instructions from Rome to impress Chamberlain; in fact, the sparse instructions which reached him from Ciano were the opposite of conciliatory.

As John Coverdale states, England did little or nothing in the Committee to oppose Mussolini's efforts in Spain. The best comment, however, is that of a British Foreign Office official, who wrote that the Non-Intervention Committee was 'generally admitted to be largely a piece of humbug, but an extremely useful piece of humbug. When humbug is an alternative to war it is impossible to put too high a value upon it.' During the entire course of its existence the Non-Intervention Committee never found sufficient evidence to convict Italy, Germany, France or Russia of violating the agreement not to intervene in Spain, although it was common knowledge that they were doing so regularly.[26]

Although Eden took a soft line with Germany, he would not give in to Italy over *de jure*. Italy's withdrawal from the League on 11 December 1937 only intensified his resistance, while it made Chamberlain even more positive that he must make a supreme effort for a reconciliation with Mussolini.

As evidence accumulated of Hitler's threat to Austrian independence, Chamberlain became increasingly concerned by Eden's intransigence over Italy. On 7 January 1938 he summoned Cadogan to discuss the opening of talks with Italy. Cadogan warned the Prime Minister against initiating talks with a personal letter to Mussolini and then leaving the difficulties 'and possibly the break' to Eden. On the same day Chamberlain wrote to Eden advocating the granting of *de jure* recognition provided the French agreed, and suggesting that he should write to Mussolini, associating Eden with himself in the letter to avoid any notion 'that we are not working together'.

Chamberlain drafted a letter to Mussolini for Eden's approval. Against the text touching on *de jure* Eden scribbled the words 'This will set half Europe against the conversations'. He then went to the south of France for a holiday. Much troubled by Chamberlain's attitude to Mussolini, from his holiday hotel in Grasse Eden sent the PM a long, rambling, handwritten letter dated 9 January, from which it is clear that he was more inclined to trust Hitler than Mussolini:

> There seems to be a certain difference between Italian and German positions in that an agreement with the latter might have a chance of a reasonable life, especially if Hitler's own position were engaged, whereas Mussolini is, I fear, a complete gangster. Moreover we mean to get something tangible for any colonial accession [by Germany] . . . What worries me much more is the effect that [*de jure*] recognition will have on our own moral position . . . There is no doubt that such a triumph is just what he [Mussolini] needs to rally his disgruntled fellow countrymen and maybe to reconcile them to a further expedition to Spain. At the moment the Abyssinian wine of victory is beginning to taste sour on the Italian palate . . . They [the US] have accorded no recognition yet, and we do not want to give offence in that direction.[27]

Eden added,

> . . . the big issues of this year are Anglo-American co-operation, the chances of effectively asserting white-race authority in the Far East, and relations with Germany. To all this Mussolini is really secondary and because he makes more noise we must not, to quieten him, take any step to cause discord amongst friends.

Eden's idea that 'we' should get something tangible from Hitler was flouting the facts, in view of Germany's military occupation of the Rhineland and obvious preparations for war. Hitler had in effect torn up the Treaty of Locarno, in spite of having given his solemn word that he would respect it, and was posing a grave threat to the peace of Europe. On the other hand, through Ciano and Grandi Mussolini was indicating that he wanted British friendship, and Eden was overlooking the facts of Italy's alignment of her foreign policy with Britain's between 1922 and 1935 (apart from the Corfu incident), and her prompt action to save Austria from the Nazis in 1934. Although both France and Russia were intervening heavily on the Republican side, Eden was unduly influenced by Italy's breach of the 'Gentlemen's Agreement' in sending troops to Spain, and could not see that in the face of the deadly threat of German aggression, Spain was a side-show outside the mainstream of European politics.

Unimpressed by Eden's letter, the Prime Minister replied:

> My plan is as you know to proceed both with Italy and Germany concurrently. I see nothing whatever that is inconsistent in this . . . You say you are worried about our moral position if we give Mussolini a triumph . . .

The one way in which we can maintain our moral position is to make recognition part of a general scheme for appeasement in the Mediterranean and Red Sea.[28]

In a letter of 12 January 1938 Cadogan advised Eden that it was of little use to worry unduly about Britain's recognition of Italy's position in Abyssinia, since it seemed likely that other members of the League would present the Duce with a series of such triumphs: 'the longer we leave it', said Cadogan, 'the more will be the defections from the League front on this question, and the more foolish we shall look.' Moreover, he thought the Italians had now made a definite advance, and that if no satisfactory basis for talks could be found, Mussolini would be confirmed in his suspicions of British intentions:

> The practical result is likely to be an accentuation of his nuisance value towards us in all its forms (propaganda, press campaign, subversive activities in Egypt and in the Arab world), the strengthening of the Rome–Berlin axis (possibly to the extent of a military alliance between Italy and Germany).
>   The situation created by such a hostile Italy in friendly relations with Japan and astride our Mediterranean communications will inevitably react on our freedom of action in the Far East.

Cadogan asked Eden whether the practical effect of Britain's failure to grant *de jure* recognition would not be

> . . . to solidify the Berlin–Rome Axis and increase the manifestation of its material strength and its capacity to affront and insult us with impunity . . . ? Moreover, is not Germany going to ask us a higher price for her friendship as long as we have a frankly hostile Italy on our flank, rather than a mere neutral Italy? . . . from the discussions I have had with the Prime Minister I am convinced that he is extremely anxious to reach an agreement with Mussolini, and that he attaches great importance to it.

Eden ignored this sensible advice.

Following the Anglo-French conversations with Chautemps and Delbos, an important Cabinet discussion on foreign affairs had taken place on 1 December; it was decided that, while a start should be made with conversations with Italy, following Halifax's visit to Germany talks with Germany would require 'a good deal of exploration' and should not be hurried. Yet without a change in Eden's attitude to *de jure* recognition, the Italian conversations were bound to fail. Guido Crolla, the Italian Chargé d'Affaires, told Eden on 23 December that unless *de jure* recognition was given his government would wonder 'whether they must consider a permanent state of bad relations with

Great Britain was the normal condition of affairs'. Crolla had brought a note from Rome stating that Italy wanted talks to begin in the spirit of Chamberlain's letter of 27 July. Eden received Crolla's overtures coldly.[29]

Ivy Chamberlain, widow of Austen Chamberlain, may have been responsible for Crolla's approach. She had been that winter in Rome, where she had been warmly received by Mussolini because of his friendship with her late husband, and wrote to Eden on 15 December giving details of a conversation she had had with Giuseppe Bastianini, the Italian Under-Secretary for Foreign Affairs.

> 'Lady C, may I talk frankly with you?' I said, 'Please, I would like to understand your point of view as to why there should be any misunderstanding between our two countries.' He replied, 'When Mr Chamberlain became PM and sent a message to *Il Duce* we were all so pleased and felt that here is someone, a brother of Sir Austen, who understood and sympathized with us, now we will forget all that has gone before and in September we will start our conversations, and we looked forward to that. But what happened? The conversations were postponed, and we have the feeling that and *believe* that the Prime Minister has opposition in his Cabinet – to be frank, we hear that Mr Eden and Mr Belisha are working against him, and the Labour Party are strong.' I denied all this hotly, and said that the PM had absolute confidence in his Cabinet and worked amicably with all his Ministers. 'Then *why* do we not have the conversations? We signed a "Gentlemen's Agreement" and when we signed we had *more* troops in Spain than we have now. *Il Duce* when he signs never goes back, he does not want anything of Spain – except to put down Bolshevism – he does not want Majorca or Minorca. Lady Chamberlain, for the safety of Europe, England and Italy must remain friends.' I replied that I was sure the Prime Minister wished for good relations between our countries and that he was working to that end.

Lady Chamberlain also told Eden that Mussolini had been very affable when they met; he had said, after speaking nostalgically of Austen, 'We believe Mr Chamberlain is friendly but Mr Eden is not', and that he wanted friendship with England as in the past, 'and having tried war did not want it again'. She added,

> I came away with the impression that he really wants an understanding and does not realize why the conversations have not commenced. I was with him over three-quarters of an hour and nothing could have been nicer. He seemed genuinely pleased to see me and talk of old times.

Eden minuted on 2 January that Lady Chamberlain's talk had been 'useful', although later he was to express strong disapproval of her intervention.

Lady Chamberlain also wrote privately to the Prime Minister, pointing out the dislike and distrust which Eden had aroused in Rome, and the general belief there that he did not want better relations. Neville Chamberlain's reply of 18 January was concealed from Eden; in it he praised her efforts, stating that he was going to try again to overcome 'difficulties', and that he expected to have Anglo-Italian conversations started well before the end of February.[30]

Mussolini was at this time extremely nervous about possible German aggression against Austria, and his conversation with Lady Chamberlain is prima-facie evidence that he was contemplating a return to the Stresa Front. At the same time, he desperately wanted Britain's *de jure* recognition of the Italian conquest of Abyssinia to set the seal on his victory, and for Britain to turn a blind eye to the armed help he was giving Franco. There would have been difficulties in persuading the British public to swallow either, but Chamberlain – still in his honeymoon period as Prime Minister, and widely regarded as the 'Apostle of Peace' – could have managed it, in which case the course of history would have been different.

Chamberlain considered that details of who was aiding which side in the Spanish Civil War were less important for the peace of Europe than the prevention of a German *Anschluss* in Austria, for which Britain urgently needed Mussolini's support; Eden, on the other hand, felt that no trust could be placed in Mussolini. One can find arguments to justify such a view, but surely in January 1938, with Austrian independence at stake, it was worth while making every effort to enlist Italian support.

Before his holiday on the Riviera Eden had written to assure Chamberlain that he would never 'resent any interest you take in Foreign Affairs', but this statement was soon overtaken by an irreconcilable quarrel. On 12 January, while Eden was still in France, President Roosevelt suggested to Chamberlain in a personal letter that he should call together the heads of all the diplomatic missions in Washington at the end of the month for talks to try to improve international relations. Chamberlain did not like the idea, and without consulting Eden replied to the President that it was not an opportune moment because Britain was 'about to start talks with Italy and Germany and this might cut across the efforts at quick results'. He further informed Roosevelt that in the forthcoming talks with Italy he (Chamberlain) was prepared 'to recognize *de jure* the Italian occupation of Abyssinia', provided that Italy gave evidence of her desire to restore friendly relations. Eden, called back from his holiday, was outraged by Chamberlain's reference to *de jure* recognition. The two met at Chequers; relations were strained, and Eden even mentioned resignation.* He reiterated to the Prime Minister that he 'would not have *de jure*', forcefully reminded Chamberlain that immediately after signing the 'Gentlemen's Agreement' Mussolini had sent 4,000 more volunteers to Spain, and stressed that conceding *de jure* recognition would shock public opinion in Britain; without consulting the Prime Minister, he sent a telegram to the Washington Embassy the next day saying that Chamberlain had not meant 'exactly' what he had said in his reply to Roosevelt.

Eden suggested to Chamberlain that they should at once call off the Italian conversations, for fear of offending the United States, and welcome Roosevelt's proposal for a diplomatic conference. The Prime Minister, very put out, said that the matter must be referred to the Cabinet's Foreign Policy Committee. The Committee decided that they wanted the Italian talks to go ahead, but compromised with Eden by agreeing that *de jure* recognition need only be granted as part of a general settlement.

For the benefit of the Prime Minister (and obviously at Eden's instigation) Lord Cranborne, Foreign Under-Secretary in the House of Commons, prepared a memorandum reiterating Eden's views: he advised that to enter into conversations with Italy on the basis of *de jure* recognition would be a policy error, and possibly a disastrous one, because it would annoy America. However, Sir Ronald Lindsay, the British Ambassador in Washington, contradicted this view, writing on 8 February:

> . . . I think it hardly necessary to worry much about the effects in America of *de jure*. No doubt in press and Congress we shall be to some extent jeered at for weakness and taunted for making friends with unrighteousness . . . It is more likely that our action would be regarded as an effort to pay the necessary price of peace. The whole issue has rather faded away into the background.

The Prime Minister seized on this as entitling 'us' to go ahead, and wanted Eden to summon Grandi at once to tell him that Britain would start conversations. Eden again demurred.[31]

Meanwhile, early in February Lady Chamberlain, in conversation with Ciano, emphasized the keen desire of her brother-in-law, the Prime Minister, for an early agreement with Mussolini. Ciano claimed not to believe what she was saying, which prompted Lady Chamberlain to show him Neville Chamberlain's letter of 18 January, regardless of the fact that it was intended for her eyes only, and that she had no permission from the Prime Minister to show it to anyone in

---

*It was impossible that he should have threatened resignation over the issue of Roosevelt's letter, as this was highly confidential.

Rome. The effect was electric ('magical', according to Chamberlain's diary). Ciano immediately said she must show it to Mussolini, and took her to the Palazzo Venezia. Mussolini asked her if he might see the letter, and Lady Chamberlain said she 'saw no objection'. After reading it Mussolini dictated five points which he wanted conveyed to the Prime Minister; they included the assertion that 'I will be very glad to reach an agreement with the Government of Neville Chamberlain because I would like to pay a tribute in memory of Sir Austen Chamberlain. As for the beginning of negotiations, I leave the date to Mr Chamberlain.' In his autobiography, Eden recorded that he was 'much annoyed' by this episode. Chamberlain was aware of Eden's reaction; in his diary he wrote:

> Unfortunately this episode seemed to produce in Anthony even further suspicion. If the Italians wanted talks there must be some catch in it, and we had better hang back.

Eden wrote on 8 February to Chamberlain complaining of Lady Chamberlain's unofficial diplomacy:

> Already Rome is giving out the impression that we are courting her, with the purpose no doubt of showing Berlin how worth courting she is . . . Mussolini is in an extremely uncomfortable position. He has commitments in Abyssinia and Spain, neither of which are turning out well. He now sees a Government in power in Berlin which, it is quite true, is comparatively enthusiastic for the Rome–Berlin axis, but which is also determined to pursue a more active foreign policy in central Europe, with Austria as the first item on its list of intended victims. In such a position we have nothing to gain by showing ourselves over-eager. If however the Italians feel we urgently need the conversations owing to our own anxieties, they will be all the less ready to co-operate effectively in liquidating the Spanish problem. The main plea of this letter is, therefore, to express the hope that you will ask Lady Chamberlain through the Embassy to be careful not to engage in any further conversations with Mussolini, for any continuation of them must inevitably confuse the situation, embarrass me, and I suspect Grandi also.

Grandi would not have been embarrassed; he welcomed anything that would make the start of friendly talks more likely.[32]

Unknown to Eden, Chamberlain and Grandi, communicating privately through Sir Joseph Ball as we have seen, were agreed that Anglo-Italian talks ought to start as soon as possible. As a result, Chamberlain fixed a meeting with Grandi and Eden at 10 Downing Street for the morning of 18 February. Eden shilly-shallied, saying he wanted first to talk privately with Grandi about a scheme for withdrawing Italian troops from Spain. But Chamberlain insisted that

Grandi should come to Downing Street. In a personal letter to the Prime Minister on 17 February, Eden wrote that the decisions that would be made the next day would 'entail momentous consequences'; his 'petition' was 'that whatever Grandi says to us tomorrow we should content ourselves with saying that we will carefully consider it and send for him again'.

Meanwhile Ivy Chamberlain, probably encouraged by the Prime Minister, continued to make use of her contacts in high places in Rome. On 17 February she lunched with Ciano, who asked her whether she had any further message from the Prime Minister: 'I said No. He then begged me to let you know time is everything. Today an agreement will be easy, but things are happening in Europe which will make it impossible tomorrow.' She added that she found Ciano completely changed, and intensely worried. She asked Perth to telegraph an account of this talk to the Prime Minister.[33]

Fortified by his sister-in-law's message, Chamberlain would have nothing to do with Eden's 'petition'. He was determined, Eden's objections notwithstanding, to make it clear to Grandi that he wanted conversations started immediately, while there was still time to save Austria.

On the morning of 18 February 1938 Grandi received a letter from Ciano urging him to use the interval before Austria fell to Hitler to try to accelerate the Anglo-Italian talks and reach some agreement, because 'tomorrow', when the *Anschluss* was a *fait accompli*, a powerful Germany with 70,000 troops would be on Italy's frontiers; and then it would be difficult to have discussions with England because it would seem to world opinion that Italy was 'going to Canossa' (eating humble pie) under German pressure, and there would be no alternative to a policy of immutable hostility to France and Britain.

According to Ciano, Mussolini wanted to keep his options open, and therefore hoped to reach agreement with Britain before Austria fell. Ciano noted in his diary on 18 February:

> The Duce was irritated with the Germans this morning over the way they have acted over Austria [see Chapter 12]. They ought to have warned us – but not a word. Should they intend to reach a real and proper *Anschluss* it would produce a situation completely different from that in which the Axis was created and the whole position would have to be re-examined.

According to the historian Renzo De Felice, Ciano's letter of 16 February to Grandi was an alarm signal, and an appeal to make friends with England, which Ciano could not have written without the approval of Mussolini. In his diary Grandi described the letter as a confession of the bankruptcy of the politics of the Rome–Berlin Axis, and a type of SOS to London: 'In Rome', he wrote, 'they are ready to betray Berlin for London.'[34]

At his Downing Street meeting with Chamberlain and Eden, Grandi vigorously denied that Mussolini had agreed with Hitler that Germany could take Austria: this was true. When Chamberlain asked whether all was lost in Austria, Grandi said it was only 'the end of the third of four acts'; but in Italy's view Germany was now at the Brenner Pass, and it was impossible for Italy to be left alone with two great potential enemies – Germany and Britain; the hopes of the 'Gentlemen's Agreement' of the year before had not been fulfilled, although there had been 'a happy fortnight' in July (1937) following the exchange of letters between Chamberlain and Mussolini. When Grandi was asked what effect the opening of conversations would have on the Italian attitude towards Austria, he answered that it would give his people 'more courage', but that Italy could not now exchange views with the other Stresa signatories about Austria. Grandi emphasized that it would be a mistake to hold up the conversations because of the Spanish question, and pressed for an announcement to be made that day that conversations had been opened.

An argument then ensued between Eden and Chamberlain, and Chamberlain adjourned the discussion until 3 p.m. After Grandi had gone, Cadogan recorded in his diary: 'PM and A had a "set-to". PM very violent – said this was the last chance of getting to terms with Italy . . . I am afraid there is a real rift and they will never work together.' Chamberlain told Eden privately that he had made up his mind to tell Grandi at 3 p.m. that he would open conversations, and that Perth must be recalled to London at once to begin preparatory work. To Eden's emphatic disagreement, Chamberlain angrily retorted: 'Anthony, you have thrown away chance after chance.' This was the end of the road for Eden.[35]

Grandi's report to Ciano the following day shows some embellishment. According to Grandi, Eden had said during the morning session that under present conditions the British government could not come to an agreement with Italy, above all to an agreement which recognized Italian sovereignty over Ethiopia; Chamberlain, however, told him (Grandi) that the Cabinet would take a definite decision the next day, and he would ask them to announce that Anglo-Italian conversations had been officially opened, the two countries being in agreement about the procedure for the withdrawal by both sides of volunteers from Spain. According to Grandi, after Chamberlain had said he was agreeable to recognizing Italian sovereignty in Ethiopia, Eden intervened saying there was no point in Anglo-Italian discussions unless the volunteers were effectively removed from Spain. Chamberlain then told Eden, in front of Grandi, that recent events in Europe (Hitler's demands on Austria) had changed the position, and then asked Grandi whether, if a statement were made that conversations as foreseen in the exchange of letters between himself and the Duce were officially opened, there would be a favourable atmosphere for a rapid conclusion of an agreement between the two countries. Grandi agreed there would be.

Grandi's report to Ciano continued:

> Yesterday's discussion is certainly one of the most strange and contradictory that I have ever experienced. Chamberlain and Eden were not a Prime Minister and Foreign Secretary discussing with an Ambassador a delicate international situation; they were, and showed it to me, disregarding convention, two enemies confronting each other like two cocks in a real fight . . . Eden had at the beginning tried to justify his miserable anti-Italian and anti-Fascist policies. Eden showed no reserve and unveiled in front of me, what I have always said, that he is an implacable enemy of Fascism and Italy. There is no doubt that the preceding contacts between me and Chamberlain through his trusted man Ball were precious. For the sake of history I inform Your Excellency that yesterday evening Chamberlain sent his man (we met in a banal taxi) to tell me that he saluted me warmly, and my statements were useful for him, and he confided that all would go well tomorrow.
>
> At this moment Germany and Austria are not the quarrel between Chamberlain and Eden; it is only Italy. Chamberlain wants to write the word 'Fine' to the Ethiopian chapter, to recognize the Italian Empire and conclude with the Italy of Mussolini a long-lasting treaty based on respect and mutual friendship. Eden wants to continue with his policy of rancour and vendetta . . .

A special Cabinet Meeting was called the next day, 19 February, at which Chamberlain put his case for the immediate opening of talks. Eden replied (according to Chamberlain's diary, 'ineffectively'), arguing that evidence of Italian faith and goodwill should be obtained before starting talks, and stating (without foundation) that his information was that Mussolini had agreed with Hitler not to oppose the *Anschluss* in return for Germany allowing him a free hand in the Mediterranean. Fourteen ministers supported the Prime Minister without qualification, four with some reservations. Eden said he could not accept their decision, and must resign. There was a gasp of horror; fruitless efforts were made to persuade him to reconsider his decision. The next day he resigned, to be succeeded by Halifax. Lord Cranborne also resigned.

In his diary, Ciano noted that he heard of 'Eden's fall at a party at the

Colonnas', where there was a general cheer at the news and the Prince of Piedmont insisted on drinking several toasts.[36]

In his resignation speech in the House of Commons Eden said he had not resigned on a question of principle, but 'on whether official conversations should be opened in Rome now'. He devoted much of his speech to Italy's intervention in the Spanish Civil War, and this lost him support because the majority of Conservative MPs wanted a Franco victory as a check to Communism. Eden did not mention his difference with the Prime Minister over the Roosevelt initiative, as this was being kept secret even from the Cabinet. However, he made a veiled reference to it, saying that the talks with Italy were not 'an isolated issue' in the dispute between him and the Prime Minister, and informing the House that 'within the last few weeks, upon one most important decision of foreign policy which did not concern Italy at all, the difference was fundamental'. Although it was not Eden's intention, this remark has led to the growth of the myth that Eden resigned because he was opposed to Chamberlain's appeasement of Hitler. Nothing could be further from the truth. As has been demonstrated, Eden considered Hitler more trustworthy than Mussolini, and was even more inclined to appease Germany than was the Prime Minister.

CHAPTER 12

The Easter Agreement: April, 1938

ON 10 MARCH 1938 Perth and Ciano held their first meeting in preparation for another Anglo-Italian agreement. Italy readily accepted a formula for a proportionate reduction in the number of her troops in Spain. Both Mussolini and the British government were hoping that their renewed friendship had come in time to save Austria from Hitler; additionally, Mussolini wanted to strengthen his hand in talks with Hitler, who was to visit Italy in May. The Duce ordered the cessation of anti-British propaganda on Radio Bari and in the Italian press.

Mussolini's priority was *de jure* recognition of the Italian conquest of Abyssinia, to secure his continued popularity with an Italian people dismayed by the expense and loss of lives in the Abyssinian campaign and in the Spanish Civil War. Chamberlain was willing to grant such recognition, but his Cabinet remained reluctant; the Cabinet's Foreign Policy Committee ruled that it should only be granted as an accompaniment to a 'general settlement', and what they envisaged by this would amount to an Italian climb-down in Spain, with almost complete withdrawal of Italian forces from the Civil War. Unfortunately for British–Italian relations, Republican resistance strengthened in Spain in April 1938, prolonging the war, and Italian involvement, and thus causing hopes of a fresh accord to founder.

The Cabinet Foreign Policy Committee would still not accept the threat to peace posed by Germany, even though despatches from Berlin made it clear that Hitler was rearming faster than ever and planning to seize not only Austria but part or all of Czechoslovakia. Instead of going all out to bring Mussolini back to the Stresa Front and restore the balance of power in Europe, Britain conceived the bizarre plan of buying Hitler off with the offer of a colony in Africa. The Führer rejected this with scorn; as Goering told Sir Nevile Henderson, the new British Ambassador in Berlin, 'If you offered us the whole of Africa we would not accept it as the price of Austria.'

205

Mussolini would doubtless have proved an unreliable and treacherous ally, and his claims on the French would have been difficult to satisfy, but faced with a rapidly deteriorating situation *vis-à-vis* Germany, Britain had no real option but to accept Mussolini's overtures of friendship and, as a corollary, formally recognize his Empire.

Perth was summoned from Rome for a meeting of the Cabinet Foreign Policy Committee on 1 March 1938; he warned that an Anglo-Italian agreement 'would have to be postponed for a very long time' if Italy's involvement in Spain must cease before it was signed. The Prime Minister said it would be a mistake to try to get an assurance from Mussolini about Austria, as he was most unlikely to do anything for 'us' which he was not prepared to do for Italy and himself.[1]

Events in Austria moved too fast for the Anglo-Italian talks. On 12 February Hitler had summoned Kurt Schuschnigg, the Austrian Chancellor, to Berchtesgaden, where he was bullied by Hitler and the German generals into signing an agreement which all but spelt the end of Austrian independence. During this interview Hitler said to Schuschnigg:

> With Mussolini I am in the clear; my ties of friendship are very close. England? England will not lift a finger for Austria . . . and France. Two years ago when we marched into the Rhineland with a handful of battalions I took a grave risk. If France had marched then we should have been compelled to withdraw. But now it is too late for France.[2]

Hitler ordered Schuschnigg to appoint the Nazi Arthur Seyss-Inquart as Minister of the Interior; imprisoned Austrian Nazis were released and began to run amok.

In desperation, on 9 March Schuschnigg announced a plebiscite to be held on the 12th, which was well received in Austria. The question was, 'Are you in favour of a free and German, an independent and social, a Christian and united Austria?' Schuschnigg had first consulted Mussolini, who warned him the plebiscite would be 'a bomb which would burst in his hands'. Alas, he was correct. The 'yes' votes would have won, constituting a setback for Hitler, who reacted with fury, sending Schuschnigg an ultimatum: he must cancel the plebiscite and resign forthwith, or German troops would attack. Schuschnigg attempted to reach Mussolini by phone, but was told he was unavailable. On 12 March, German troops crossed the frontier and reached Vienna. Schuschnigg resigned; and on 13 March Austria was declared a part of the German Reich.

Hitler had told Mussolini during the latter's visit to Germany that he would do nothing about Austria without prior consultation, and was apprehensive about the Italian reaction. While German tanks and infantry were advancing towards the Austrian frontier, he instructed Prince Philip of Hesse, married to Mafalda, daughter of the King of Italy, to take a long propitiatory letter to Mussolini. It was an anxious time for Hitler, as Germany was not strong enough to withstand any concerted military measures on the part of France, Britain *and* Italy. Late on the night of 10 March Hesse telephoned to Hitler that the Duce accepted the invasion in 'a friendly manner'. Hitler told Hesse to assure Mussolini that his forbearance would never be forgotten, and that if ever he should need help or be in danger, Hitler would 'stick to him' whatever might happen.

After hearing from Perth that Mussolini would do nothing to oppose Hitler, and had no intention of resuming the stance he had taken in 1934 when Dollfuss was assassinated, Halifax sent a message to Schuschnigg that Britain could not take the responsibility of advising 'any course of action which might expose Austria to dangers against which Britain was unable to guarantee any protection'.[3]

Mussolini was seriously perturbed by the fall of Austria, and as a result became more anxious to reach agreement with Britain. The *Anschluss* was unpopular with the Italian public, and the government received a flood of anonymous letters protesting against it. Not since the murder of Matteotti had any event so damaged Mussolini's popularity with the Italians as the way in which he 'sold out' over Austria. Obliged to explain his actions to the Italian parliament, he made a lame and unconvincing speech in which he claimed that Italy had not intervened to save the independence of Austria because she had not assumed any obligation to do so, either direct or indirect, written or verbal:

> The Austrians, I feel bound to state, have always had the understandable modesty not to ask for the use of force to defend the independence of Austria, for we should have answered that an independence which needed the help of foreign troops against the majority of the nation no longer deserves the name.

He assured the Chamber that Italy had nothing to fear from Germany.

Through the Italian Embassy in Berlin, Hitler promised Mussolini that the German army would stop at Innsbruck and not garrison the Brenner Pass leading to the South Tyrol – Austrian territory ceded to Italy after the First World War – but that promise was to be quickly ignored. The Italian port of Trieste was strangled by the loss of her traditional trade with Austria, and the bombastic guarantees of Austrian independence given by Mussolini following Dollfuss's assassination in 1934 and at Stresa in 1935 were made to look silly.[4]

Hitler's actions made Chamberlain very conscious of the danger to Czechoslovakia; in his diary on 20 March he wrote:

> The Austrian frontier is practically open; the great Skoda munition works are within easy bombing distance of the German aerodromes; the railways all pass through German territory. Russia is 100 miles away. Therefore we could not help Czechoslovakia – she would simply be a pretext for going to war with Germany. That we could not think of unless we had a reasonable prospect of being able to beat her to her knees in a reasonable time, and of that I see no sign. I have therefore abandoned any idea of giving guarantees to Czechoslovakia or the French in connection with her obligations to that country.

Chamberlain also wrote to his sister: 'It is tragic that this [the *Anschluss*] might have been prevented if I had had Halifax at the Foreign Office when I wrote my letter to Mussolini [in August 1937] . . . we must quietly and steadily pursue our conversations with Italy.'[5]

On 21 March the Cabinet Foreign Policy Committee met to consider a report from the Chiefs of Staff which emphasized Czechoslovakia's lack of fortifications on her Austrian frontier, and the sudden vulnerability of her munition factories. The report concluded: 'Neither France nor Britain could render any assistance to Czechoslovakia, and the only method of rendering even indirect assistance would be by staging offensive operations against Germany.' The Committee concluded that it was unlikely the French would mount an 'effective attack, and if Germany, Italy and Japan fought a war against us, the British Empire would be threatened by an immense aggregate of armed strength and would be faced with the gravest danger'. Cadogan's diary comments were, 'Thank goodness Cabinet firm on doing nothing about Czechoslovakia', and 'FPC unanimous that Czechoslovakia is not worth the bones of a single British Grenadier. And they are quite right too.'

Given the deadly danger to Czechoslovakia, it might have been expected that the Cabinet would ignore the Spanish Civil War and work wholeheartedly for agreement with Mussolini. The records of the Perth–Ciano talks in Rome show that Mussolini, although conscious that Nazism and Fascism had roots in common, was so angered by the *Anschluss* that he was ready to desert Hitler. The Duce wanted to keep open the option of British friendship; he was waiting to see whether this would better suit his aspirations than an alliance with Germany, but he remained passionately determined to secure British recognition of Italy's sovereignty in Abyssinia.[6]

The talks between Perth and Ciano went smoothly. Mussolini wanted to sign an agreement with the British before Hitler came to Rome in the first week of May. Perth stressed to Ciano that

Chamberlain was determined to bring the talks to a successful conclusion, but that if any agreement was to secure 'general and public approval' in Britain, it was essential that the Prime Minister should be able to present it as a big step towards the achievement of world peace. Ciano agreed that an Anglo-Italian agreement would be the greatest step towards peace in Europe which could be taken at that moment, and that the whole world would breathe more freely if the two countries could come to a settlement by which their ancient friendship could be restored.

Halifax pointed out to the Foreign Policy Committee that he was in a difficulty because, although the government had declared that they would not contemplate the negotiations 'unless the Agreement contained a settlement of the Spanish question', the precise meaning of that phrase had never been defined; and that it would not be fair to the Italians to expect them to withdraw their volunteers otherwise than *pari passu* with the French and Russians who were opposing Franco. Halifax himself did not want to delay the Anglo-Italian agreement pending a Spanish settlement.[7]

All that their colleagues would permit Chamberlain and Halifax to do was to put down a resolution for the League Council meeting at Geneva on 9 May that, since many members of the League had recognized Italian sovereignty over Abyssinia, the matter should now be for each member of the League to decide for herself. (Sixteen members of the League had already recognized *de jure* the Italian conquest of Abyssinia, and five of these – Belgium, Poland, Romania, Latvia and Ecuador – were represented on the Council.)[8] There was much fear within the Conservative Party that for Britain to grant *de jure* recognition without a settlement of 'the Spanish question' would be to provoke a revolt of public opinion such as had occurred over the Hoare–Laval proposals in 1935.

Mussolini, confident that the Spanish Civil War would soon end, was satisfied by the proposed British move at Geneva, and pressed for signature of the agreement by the middle of April. According to Perth, Ciano was 'delighted' at the British decision to table the resolution at the League of Nations, describing it as 'very good news'; but he firmly rejected a renewed suggestion by Perth that France should join in signing the agreement.

By 10 April what had become known as the Easter Agreement was in the bag. Ciano wrote in his diary: 'The Pact is good – complete, solid, harmonious. I believe it really will be able to serve as the foundation for the new friendship between Italy and Great Britain.' He could only have written like this if Mussolini also had been enthusiastic.

On 14 April Perth and Ciano went to the Palazzo Venezia for

Mussolini to sign the Agreement. According to Ciano, Mussolini greeted Perth 'with a trace of ill-humour', but Perth recorded that the Duce said he was very happy with the result, and thought the Agreement would not only have a most favourable effect on Anglo-Italian relations but also contribute to the 'peace of the world'. Perth explained that when the time came for Halifax to speak about the *de jure* resolution at Geneva, the Duce must expect to hear certain words about the Italians in Abyssinia which he would not like; these were included for internal British political reasons. Mussolini replied that he quite understood, and said he was only interested in practical results. He felt that 'it would be boorish to expect England to put on sackcloth and ashes', and suggested burning incense to the memory of Eden. Chamberlain sent a personal message of friendship which, according to Perth, Mussolini much appreciated.[9]

In the House of Commons Chamberlain described the vigour, vision and efficiency of the new Italy under the stimulus of 'Signor Mussolini', and declared that 'already the clouds of mistrust and suspicion have been cleared away'. Dislike of the Abyssinian War was so widespread, however, that fifty Conservative MPs abstained in the subsequent Division.

Leo Amery, a former Conservative Cabinet Minister who had high hopes of a post in Chamberlain's government, went to Rome on 20 April. He found Mussolini enthusiastically intending to keep the Agreement 'in the spirit as well as the letter', regarding it as 'a blessing not only for England and Italy but for all Europe'. Amery noted that the Italians as a whole were thoroughly bored by the prospect of Hitler's visit, and Mussolini most warmly concurred with Amery's regrets that Chamberlain had not pushed forward the Agreement six months earlier. Significantly, both agreed that Czechoslovakia could not survive.

Grandi told Amery that if only the Anglo-Italian talks had begun six months earlier, Austria might have been saved. After his return from Rome, Amery told Sir John Simon in a private conversation that Stresa 'was the high-water mark of our foreign policy since the war'; Simon wanted Amery to repeat the remark in a Commons speech.[10]

By the terms of the 'Easter Agreement', Britain agreed to recognize the Italian Empire in Abyssinia once there was a settlement of the Spanish question, while Italy disclaimed any designs on Spanish territories and reasserted pledges to maintain the *status quo* in the Mediterranean. Mussolini promised to reduce the Italian garrison in Libya, and it was agreed that Britain and Italy should exchange information about any substantial military movements in their colonies, territories and protectorates in the Mediterranean, the Red

Sea and North East Africa, while Italy pledged herself to cease anti-British propaganda in the Middle East. Britain was guaranteed rights to Lake T'ana water for Somaliland.

The drawback was that the Agreement was not to come into force until progress had been made with the withdrawal of Italian volunteers from Spain; and it did not become effective until 18 November, after Munich, by which time the mercurial Mussolini had a very different attitude to Britain.

Mussolini was in a dilemma as he awaited Hitler's visit to Rome in the first week of May 1938; in the wake of the *Anschluss*, he placed little trust in Hitler's pacific declarations. Evidence of this is his announcement that he would 'seal hermetically' Italy's Austrian frontiers (which were now German), and seal 'semi-hermetically' her frontier with Yugoslavia. The Foreign Office response to this information was a minute which deduced that 'A warning to Germany was at any rate at the back of his [Mussolini's] mind.' However, Mussolini had rejected out-of-hand a suggestion by France that Britain, France and Italy should examine the situation created by the *Anschluss* 'in the spirit of Stresa'.[11]

One problem for the Duce was the extreme unpopularity of Nazism inside Italy. At a meeting of the Fascist Grand Council the influential Italo Balbo and Giuseppe Bottai had expressed their disapproval of the *Anschluss* and their fears for the future of Trieste. The Italian public saw the *Anschluss* as the first real setback for Fascism; hostility to the Rome–Berlin axis mounted, fanned by memories of strongly anti-German sentiments during the 1914–1918 war, at a time when the anti-German tradition of the Risorgimento was still alive. The contrast between Mussolini's behaviour in 1934 over the assassination of Dollfuss and his complacency over the *Anschluss* was contradictory, and difficult to explain. In addition, Italian military involvement in Spain alongside Germany was unpopular, and gave rise to fears that Italy might slavishly be following Germany against her own interests. Mussolini considered following up the signing of the Easter Agreement with an approach to Paris.

Italy's attitude to Germany was thus clearly in the balance when Hitler arrived in Rome on 3 May 1938, accompanied by Ribbentrop, Goebbels, Hess and Himmler. Hitler was disgusted to find that he had to ride in a carriage with the King, not Mussolini, and the crowds on the drive from the station to the Quirinal Palace were distinctly cold towards the Germans. Hitler spent six nights at the Quirinal, and disliked the palace immensely. He described the King and his entourage as reactionary and anti-Fascist; Himmler said, 'This place smells of catacombs.' For his part, the King disliked Germans in general, and particularly Hitler, whom he found personally repugnant. He told his intimates that the Führer was a psycho-degenerate who took both stimulants and narcotics.

The Pope (Pius XI) was indignant about the visit, because of Nazi persecution of the Church in Germany and similar persecution in Austria during the seven weeks following the German occupation. He was bitterly anti-Hitler; told that Hitler was an art lover and wanted to see the Vatican Museum, he ordered it to be closed for the whole of the Führer's stay in Rome. Not only that, but he removed himself to the papal villa at Castel Gandolfo, and remained there until after Hitler had left. The day of Hitler's arrival, 3 May, was the Feast of the Holy Cross and Pius XI, amid considerable publicity, announced it to be wrong that on that day 'the banner of another cross [the swastika] should be raised in Rome'.

The King was not pleased to be obliged to entertain an ex-corporal who had assumed the birthright of the Hapsburgs in Austria and the Hohenzollerns in Germany. Hitler's table manners were bad, and he found himself in difficulties over the protocols of dining with royalty. As soon as the King had finished his first course at dinner, it was customary for the footmen to remove the plates from in front of all the guests; Hitler, who liked pasta and was making slow progress with a delicious dish, was annoyed when it was whisked away from under his nose. And the King refused to give the Fascist salute. Hitler was happy to leave Rome for Naples; but to his intense irritation he was obliged, at the Naples Opera, to wear a silk top hat, in which he knew he looked ridiculous.

Hitler's interpreter Paul Schmidt, a reliable witness, has left interesting evidence in his autobiography of Mussolini's reluctance to commit himself to Germany:

> Mussolini and Ciano were obviously trying to evade any serious political discussion – though Hitler, and more especially Ribbentrop, were constantly seeking it. The programme had been deliberately planned so that there was no time for serious talk, but even during the various social meetings, at which Hitler and Ribbentrop were always ready for discussions, Mussolini and Ciano showed quite clearly that they were not. This impression was confirmed beyond all doubt when we handed Ciano a draft treaty for an Italo-German alliance – for despite all the beautiful speeches we were still not formal allies. A few days later Ciano handed us an 'amended draft' of the treaty. It proved to be a completely meaningless paper whose emptiness amounted to a plain refusal. I inferred at the time . . . that the Italians had by no means got over their shock at the Austrian *Anschluss* and especially at Hitler's methods in carrying it out, and that their eyes were still turned westwards.

Ernst von Weizsäcker, head of the German Foreign Office, described Ciano's draft as more of a peace treaty with an enemy than an alliance with a friend; Ciano stipulated the formal guarantee of the common frontiers between Germany and Italy, and respect and safeguard for their mutual interest in the Danube Balkan sector.

An irritant for Mussolini was German propaganda among the Austrian inhabitants of the Alto Adige (South Tyrol) who, cheered by the German annexation of Austria, hoped Hitler would also liberate them from Italian rule. This had been inflamed by a speech Hitler made in the Reichstag on 14 March, in which he declared that 3½ million Germans were not yet free. This led to an official protest by Italy, the Italian press having interpreted the 3½ million to include German-speaking Italian subjects in the South Tyrol. Ciano was in favour of solving the problem diplomatically by an exchange of populations, but as Mussolini was dedicated to an Italianized Alto Adige talks on this issue got nowhere.

According to the historian Renzo De Felice, Hitler's visit was a 'non event'. He writes:

> The Duce, partly because of the *Anschluss*, partly under Ciano's influence, did not want to prejudice the good relations happily restored with London, and the favourable prospects for bettering those with Paris, and because of the difficulty of suggesting a minor agreement after he had been offered a full-scale Alliance, did not want to conclude with Hitler any binding official agreement . . . Hitler's visit did nothing to make the Italians more attracted to Germany.[12]

In the spring of 1938 Mussolini was becoming increasingly dismayed by the weakness of France and Britain *vis-à-vis* Germany, and by their acquiescence in both the remilitarization of the Rhineland and the *Anschluss* at a time when they were also taking a strong line against Italian intervention in the Spanish Civil War. He felt that Hitler was doing better than he was, and would become the dominant power in Europe. He was also worried by the way in which Republican successes were prolonging the Spanish Civil War, and blamed Franco for his flabby conduct of the war. He began to have doubts whether the Easter Agreement meant that Britain would prove as a firm a friend as he had hoped. Spies read and reported to him on documents in the British Embassy in Rome which caused him to wonder whether the British would ever take a firm line against Hitler, or whether they merely wanted peace at any price.

In June 1938 came the crunch. Mussolini had begun to worry that he might have made a mistake in rejecting the German offer of a military alliance. Britain was still refusing *de jure* recognition of Italian sovereignty in Abyssinia, the Spanish Civil War showed no signs of ending, and the British press was vehemently anti-Italian because Italian planes had bombed British merchant ships at Barcelona. Furthermore, Hitler had caused a crisis over Czechoslovakia,with threatening troop movements; the Nazis no longer talked of self-government for the Sudetenland, but of annexation by Germany. Britain was pressing the Czech Premier Beneš to make a generous offer of self-government to Henlein, the leader of the Sudeten Germans, and the European press was full of presentiments about an outbreak of war between Germany and Britain and France over Czechoslovakia.

More worried now by the worsening international situation and beginning, it would seem, to have doubts about the Rome–Berlin axis, Mussolini instructed Ciano to see Perth on 3 June in an attempt to clarify the position between Britain and Italy, which was obscured by the non-implementation of the Easter Agreement.* Ciano told Perth that the vital question was when the Agreement would become operative, and that Mussolini wanted this to be as soon as possible. He emphasized that Italy had faithfully performed her part of the agreement: she had withdrawn troops from Libya, ceased anti-British propaganda, and accepted the British plan for the proportionate withdrawal of troops from Spain. Mussolini hoped that, as a result, *de jure* recognition by Britain of his conquest of Abyssinia would follow 'comparatively soon', noting that there had been 'a rush of States to recognize' Italy's sovereignty. Because of British non-recognition, Ciano said, the Italian public were beginning to doubt British motives. 'Why, it was being said, does not Great Britain recognize, particularly since we have reached agreement on all points?'

Perth interrupted to say that the 'rush to recognize' was a result of the British action in Geneva. Ciano agreed, but felt that 'an agreement before marriage should not last too long'; he pointed out to Perth that it was being 'put about' that Britain was determined not to bring the Agreement into force until France and Italy had also reached agreement. Ciano begged Perth to put the matter before Halifax and ask for his and the Prime Minister's view. Perth told Ciano he knew Chamberlain wanted to put the Easter Agreement into operation, and was seeking some event which offered an excuse for claiming that the Spanish problem had been solved.

Halifax took thirteen days to reply. He consulted the Foreign Policy Committee on 16 June; they decided Mussolini should again be told

---

*Renzo De Felice believes that Mussolini was unhappy about Hitler's intentions, and produces evidence to support this conclusion.[13]

that there could be no question of recognizing Abyssinia until some settlement of the Spanish question had been reached. In his diary, (Oliver Harvey, Halifax's secretary, noted that Perth would not like such instructions, and that there was no chance of Mussolini accepting the position.) This proved to be a supremely important Foreign Policy Committee meeting. Chamberlain would have liked to make a gesture to Mussolini, but his colleagues were ultra-sensitive to political opinion in Britain, stirred up by the bombing of British ships by Italian planes. Moreover, prominent in the minds of the ministers was the knowledge that the Easter Agreement had not been popular, and the fact of the fifty Conservative abstentions in the vote following the Commons debate on it. Thus the opportunity to placate Mussolini was thrown away.[14]

On 17 June Halifax instructed Perth to acknowledge that Italy had faithfully fulfilled her side of the agreement with regard to Libya and the cessation of anti-British propaganda, and to state that the British government 'were as anxious as the Italian Government to see the Agreement enter into force as soon as possible'; the only obstacle was the Spanish question, a situation which had deteriorated so markedly, because of the recent bombing of towns and ships for which the Italian Air Force was held to be responsible, that British public opinion made it impossible to waive the Spanish 'pre-condition'. Halifax suggested three possible courses of action to Mussolini: both sides (that is to say, Russia and Italy) to withdraw their forces from Spain, which Halifax admitted would take time; unilateral Italian withdrawal from Spain; or an armistice between Franco and the Republicans.

But Halifax was dealing with a temperamental dictator wildly frustrated because *de jure* recognition of his new Empire was being withheld, in his opinion unreasonably, by the other great European Empire. In this context, Halifax's approach was a mistake.

Perth handed Ciano an *aide-mémoire* embodying the three British proposals, and a second *aide-mémoire* expressing concern over Italo-French tensions. Ciano told Perth there was no likelihood of Mussolini accepting the British proposals; but he would respond after he had consulted the Duce. In his diary Ciano noted that Halifax's proposals were 'not very fruitful from the point of view of Anglo-Italian friendship'.

Mussolini treated the British reply as a flat rejection of his plea for *de jure* recognition, and was not interested in the small print. On 1 July the Italian reply was given in writing; this reaffirmed that Italy had carried out her obligations under the Easter Agreement but asserted that Britain, despite the Geneva resolution on Abyssinia and Italy's acceptance of the British plan for withdrawal of her 'volunteers' from

Spain, had not fulfilled hers. Mussolini went on to point out that the physical withdrawal of Italian forces from Spain was impossible because the Russians would not do the same, and this was no fault of Italy's. When Mussolini wrote that Britain 'had not fulfilled hers', he was referring to *de jure* recognition. The Duce continued that the Italian government had therefore decided to wait, 'in the hope that an over-long and unnecessary delay would not diminish or annul the value of the 16 April Agreement, which not only in Italy and England but everywhere in the world had been greeted as an essential move towards peace'. The Note also claimed that 'the delay, which is not due to Italy, risks compromising the moral effects of the Agreement', and that Italo-French conversations could not take place until the Easter Agreement was implemented.*

According to Ciano, Perth was heart-broken, and said the majority of the British people were wrong in seeing dangers in the Easter Agreement, on which such great hopes had been based; Ciano said this was also the Duce's view. As Perth left, much dismayed, he said he feared the Agreement had reached 'a difficult stage'. Significantly, Ciano gave the German Ambassador in Rome, Hans Georg von Mackensen, a copy of the British Notes, the Italian reply, and his account of his talk with Perth; von Mackensen then expressed to Ciano his faith in the ever-increasing 'solidarity' of the Axis.[15]

In a despatch accompanying the Italian government's Note to London, Perth described Mussolini's contention that 'although the Italian Government had fully fulfilled the conditions of the Agreement the British Government had done nothing on its side' as 'most unfair'. He emphasized that he had pointed out to Ciano how Britain 'had taken the initiative at Geneva' which had led to 'the recognition of her Ethiopian conquest by such a large number of States', to which Ciano had responded that what Italy desired was *de jure* recognition by Britain. Perth complained that it was not appreciated in London how passionately Mussolini wanted British recognition, and that on this depended whether he favoured Britain or Germany.

Vansittart, himself usually Italophile, minuted: 'It seems to me that the whole tone of [Perth's] telegram is intolerable and needs a sharp reply.' Cadogan described it as 'a frightful telegram'. Halifax discussed his reply with both men; Cadogan noted that 'Van . . . wants to stiffen it up', but that he [Cadogan] had said it was 'important not to let Musso think we were excited'. Harvey noted in his diary that 'Van

---

*Talks with a view to a Franco-Italian agreement held between Ciano and Blondel, the French Chargé d'Affaires in Rome, had foundered in May.[16]

is now as violently anti-Mussolini as formerly he was pro.' Ingram minuted that Mussolini's Note must have been written on one of his bad days when 'he had got out of bed on the wrong side', and that he had had one of his fits of bad temper.

The instructions Halifax sent to Perth on 9 July closed the door on Mussolini. Perth was to tell the Italians that, although on the whole the British public had warmly welcomed the Easter Agreement, unless implementation was accompanied by the withdrawal of Italian volunteers from Spain, 'general and warm approval of bringing the Agreement into force would be impossible'. Halifax also insisted Mussolini must be told that the British government felt the action Britain had taken at Geneva was an adequate counterpart to the steps Italy had taken.[17]

Halifax made it plain he did not agree that implementation of the Easter Agreement should be dependent upon the conclusion of an agreement between France and Italy. However, he told Perth to state that if the Easter Agreement came into force at a time when relations between France and Italy were still strained, this could lessen both the effects of the Agreement in improving European relations and the cordiality and confidence between Britain and Italy which the Agreement had restored, because it would reinforce anxieties that Mussolini was trying to drive 'a wedge between England and France'. To use such language to Mussolini was fatal. He regarded all these words as no more than an excuse for Britain to withhold *de jure* recognition. The niceties of diplomatic exchanges meant nothing to him.

It is strange that neither the Foreign Office nor the Cabinet should have grasped the nettle and agreed that the only way to bring Mussolini back to the anti-Nazi camp was to recognize the conquest of Abyssinia immediately and implement the Agreement, because the Duce would never withdraw his troops from Spain unless the Russians did the same. To Mussolini, other issues were peripheral, and nothing less was going to induce him even to consider withdrawing any of his help to Franco.

Mussolini undoubtedly wanted to delay his negotiations with France indefinitely; he told the German Ambassador in Rome that France must not approach Rome via London because that would be to do so by way of 'the servants' staircase'. He was indeed hoping to drive a wedge between France and England, and there is evidence that he hoped for a new Pact of Four in which he would be the brake on Hitler, and Britain the brake on France. He also disliked the fact that France sheltered the more active Italian anti-Fascists, and was filled with rancour at the attitude of the French press, which he blamed for depriving him of a bloodless triumph in Abyssinia in 1935 at the time of the Hoare–Laval proposals. But this was mere childishness: the logical corollary of an Anglo-Italian accord was an Italo-French agreement.[18]

In his diary on 12 July Ciano noted that 'The Duce too is dissatisfied with the British reply.' This was an understatement. Ciano told Perth that Mussolini no longer considered himself bound to conform to the Easter Agreement, and that all the good progress made in Anglo-Italian relations since the departure of Eden had been undone. There was now little prospect of bringing the Easter Agreement into operation. Indeed Mussolini, indignant at the British attitude, now took an important step towards the Nazis with the publication on 14 July of his anti-Semitic policy ordaining oppressive measures against Italian Jews.

Hitler had urged Mussolini to take steps against the Jews during the Duce's trip to Germany in September 1937 and again during his own visit to Italy in May 1938. For the first fifteen years of Fascism Jews had been fairly treated in Italy, and it appeared that anti-Semitism was anathema to Mussolini. However, following his visit to Germany, anti-Semitic articles began to appear in the Italian press in the autumn of 1937. Ciano was probably reflecting Mussolini's views when he noted in his diary for 3 December 1937 that he did not believe 'we ought to unleash an anti-Semitic campaign in Italy. The problem does not exist here. There are not many Jews, and with some exceptions there is no harm in them.' Giovanni Preziosi, an unfrocked priest and friend of Mussolini, violently anti-Semitic, edited the small-circulation anti-Semitic review *La Vita Italiana*; on 29 December 1937 he asked Ciano for his support in organizing an anti-Semitic campaign. Ciano abruptly refused – obviously with Mussolini's approval. Nevertheless, the policy published on 14 July 1938 initiated real persecution of the Jews in Italy, a very black mark against the Duce. Hitler had suggested to Mussolini that Italian anti-Semitism would make him popular in the Arab world, and in view of the importance to Italy of Libya and Tunisia, this may have been a factor.[19]

Now, however, Hitler's plans for aggression in Czechoslovakia had begun to dominate the European scene. One might have expected the danger these posed to have brought home to the British Cabinet the over-riding priority of urgently coming to terms with Mussolini – especially as it was he who was making the overtures. It did not.

CHAPTER 13

Munich: 1938

DURING THE SUMMER of 1938 Mussolini, suffering from a stomach ulcer, was in a state of tension because of the long drawn-out Spanish Civil War. Only with difficulty could he maintain his outward appearance of confidence and calm. The continued British refusal to grant *de jure* recognition of Italy's conquest of Abyssinia became like a red rag to a bull to him. He was also greatly worried by Hitler's intentions in Czechoslovakia. He had tried to persuade Britain to return to terms of cordial friendship with Italy; without it, he saw no way of keeping Hitler from increasing Germany's influence in Yugoslavia and eastern Europe, which he regarded as Italy's sphere of interest. Yet he still hoped for German support in his claims against France on Djibuti and Tunisia (see Chapter 14).

Ominously, on 27 June Ribbentrop had dropped hints to Bernardo Attolico, the Italian Ambassador in Berlin, that Germany intended to seize at least part of Czechoslovakia, and renewed the offer of an Italo-German military alliance, one which would not be operative if a war should erupt over Germany's use of force in Czechoslovakia. Mussolini's reply was not, as previously, a downright 'No', but 'Not yet'. Ciano noted in his diary: 'The situation has changed since the beginning of May. Relations with Great Britain have not developed as we might have hoped. The offer assumes a new value. Mussolini is in favour.' Mussolini told Ciano, 'We shall have to explain to the Germans that I shall make the alliance when it ceases to be unpopular.' But Mussolini was still courting Britain, and was far from ready to throw in his lot wholeheartedly with Hitler.[1]

In May 1938 there had been a short-lived crisis over Czechoslovakia: two Sudeten Germans had been killed by Czech frontier guards, and the Czechs mobilized in the face of German threats and troop movements – which turned out to be part of a Nazi plan of provocation and intimidation. Ciano told Perth that Italy was 'entirely neutral' about Czechoslovakia: purloined documents from the British Embassy in Rome indicated to Mussolini that Britain was planning to do nothing to save Czechoslovakia, and further impressed him with a sense of Britain's weakness *vis-à-vis* Germany.

On 11 July Rudolf Hess arrived in Rome with a renewed offer of a military alliance with Germany. Ciano replied that the Duce wanted to see how relations with London developed; on the same day came the negative British reply to the Italian Note of 1 July. Ciano commented in his diary: 'Nothing to be done. Our point of view is not accepted [by the British]; for the settlement of the Spanish affair they demand effective evacuation. There is no alternative but to wait. With all the dangers waiting involves.'

Mussolini now veered towards Germany and away from Britain. Ciano's diary entry for 20 August notes that in the event of a flare-up over Czechoslovakia 'there is no alternative for us but to fall in beside Germany immediately with all our resources. The Duce is decided on action.' The next day's entry is that if the British were to allow the Easter Agreement to lapse, 'our path is clear for a military alliance with Germany', but also expresses the hope that if 15,000 men were withdrawn from Spain the Easter Agreement could be implemented, 'which would extricate us from an unpleasant impasse'. However, neither Mussolini nor Ciano contemplated going to war with Britain and France on Hitler's behalf over Czechoslovakia.[2]

In order to appease Hitler Chamberlain was trying to undermine the French guarantees to Czechoslovakia. Halifax told the French that, whereas Britain would always come to the assistance of France if she were the victim of unprovoked aggression by Germany, she would not automatically take military action with France to preserve Czechoslovakia from German aggression, because 'France and England, even with such assistance as might be expected from Russia, would not be in a position to prevent Germany over-running Czechoslovakia. The only result would be an European war, the outcome of which would be at least doubtful.'[3]

Worried that the French might become involved in war with Germany, Chamberlain conceived the plan of sending Lord Runciman, a former Cabinet Minister, to mediate between the Czechs and Germans over German demands for 'autonomy for the Sudeten Germans within a sovereign Czech state'. On 26 July Chamberlain misled the House of Commons, saying that Runciman was going at the request of the Czech Premier Beneš, but in fact neither the French nor the Czechs were consulted in advance, and they agreed only reluctantly. Robert Dell, the distinguished foreign correspondent of the *Manchester Guardian*, wrote in the *New Statesman*: 'Hitler has scored again, thanks to his faithful friend Neville Chamberlain. Lord Runciman has been sent to Prague to try and persuade the Czechs to commit national suicide.' Runciman interpreted his role as being to pressurize Beneš into kow-towing to Hitler's demands.

Mussolini, now alarmed lest Hitler should precipitate a European war, had made no military plans whatsoever, and despite what Ciano said in his diary, had no intention of going to war; he found himself in a humiliating position through his ignorance of Hitler's intentions. At Nuremberg on 12 September the Führer made a speech full of hysterical abuse of Beneš, and revealed his design of taking over the Sudetenland by force if it was not ceded to him: this brought Germany to the brink of war with France, who was set to honour her guarantee to Czechoslovakia. The day after Hitler's Nuremberg speech Ciano recorded that the Duce considered the situation very serious 'but thinks that Beneš will accept the ultimatum. Swallowing pills is what democracies are made for.' In an effort to play the role of a world statesman, Mussolini then published an open letter to Runciman supporting Hitler and urging Runciman to propose to Beneš a plebiscite, not only for the Sudeten Germans but for all the nationalities in Czechoslovakia, which he described as 'a weak and artificially created state':

> You have the opportunity, Signor Runciman, to do something historic. This is not the time to compromise. Beneš has lost his battle. You, Signor Runciman, must suggest to Beneš a plebiscite, not only for the Sudetens but for every nationality that asks for it. Beneš will refuse the plebiscite . . . and then you must let him know that Britain will think six times before going to war. If Hitler claimed he wanted to annex 3½ million Czechs, Europe would be right to be perturbed. But Hitler is not thinking of that. My letter is to let you know if Hitler was offered 3½ million Czechs he would refuse harshly but resolutely such a gift. The Führer worries only about 3½ million Germans. No one can contest his right . . .
>
> Courage, Signor Runciman. Suggest the plebiscite. It is a magnificent and delicate task. There are zones where the plebiscite will result purely and simply in the return of people to their brothers; vice versa, there are other zones which are terribly fragmented and a neat division is impossible. Here you should put into action a regime of cantonalisation or something like that . . .
>
> Fix the zones for the plebiscite, the dates, the methods and means of control, which should be international, as happened with satisfactory results in the Saar plebiscite.[4]

Meanwhile, the British government had received reliable information that Hitler intended to march against Czechoslovakia, and that this move was opposed by the German generals. Halifax and Chamberlain had strong evidence from secret sources that Hitler would be overthrown by his generals if he made the attempt; this was prima-facie evidence of Hitler's weakness inside Germany, which was largely ignored by the British. They did, however, decide to warn Hitler that to attack Czechoslovakia meant war. Sir Nevile Henderson, the British Ambassador in Berlin, was (prior to Hitler's Nuremberg speech) instructed to pass on to the Führer a solemn warning that 'Britain could not stand aside' if France was drawn into war over Czechoslovakia: almost incredibly, Henderson refused to give this warning because, he said, 'It will drive Hitler straight off the deep end'.

On 14 September Chamberlain revealed a secret plan, 'Plan Z', to the Cabinet: he was to fly to Germany to reason with Hitler. Mean while Runciman had written to advise Chamberlain that he thought it was essential self-determination should be given to the Sudetenland soon. On 15 September Chamberlain flew to Berchtesgaden in a desperate attempt to make Hitler see reason and avoid war.

When Mussolini heard of Chamberlain's plan, he told Filippo Anfuso, a senior diplomat in the Italian Foreign Office:

> As soon as Hitler sees this old man he will know he has won the game. Chamberlain has no idea that to present himself to Hitler in the guise of a bourgeois pacifist and British politician is like giving a wild beast the taste of blood. It is not that Hitler hates him, but it is a shame to make him think that anything will deflect Hitler when he has such an opportunity.

Mussolini added that he thought Czechoslovakia would only be a beginning: 'Not only will Hitler not stop, but he wants to tear up Versailles piece by piece, nation by nation . . . Better with them than with us.' (He was referring here to Trieste and the former Austrian parts of northern Italy which had been given to Italy after the first World War).[5]

Mussolini told Ciano that there would be no war, but that he saw Chamberlain's action as 'the liquidation of English prestige'. He followed his open letter to Runciman with a forthright speech at Trieste in which he again demanded a Sudetenland plebiscite; he also pledged his support for Germany if hostilities broke out – empty words, as Italy had still made no preparations for war. France called up three-quarters of a million reservists, and Britain mobilized the Fleet. Mussolini, thinking he ought to be a key figure in the negotiations, was offended that he was not consulted by either Britain or Germany over the Czech crisis. As soon as Grandi heard of Chamberlain's plan he decided to take the initiative, and via the private channel of Dingli and Ball sent a message to the Prime Minister that Mussolini must not be left out, or put in the position of only knowing what was going on from what the Germans told him.

Halifax, however, talking to Grandi on 19 September, made it clear that he looked on Italy as being one hundred per cent 'on the other side', and that he considered it useless for Britain to think Mussolini might be any help. Grandi insisted that the Duce did not want war and would do everything he could to prevent it, and that in view of the 'delicate' state of Italo-German relations it was impossible for Mussolini to take any initiative unless Chamberlain kept in contact with him.[6]

Chamberlain received a rude shock at Berchtesgaden when Hitler, refusing to discuss any general settlement of German claims, instead demanded an immediate solution of the Sudetenland problem. The Führer said he would only continue the conversations if Chamberlain agreed 'as a matter of principle' that the Sudetenland should be ceded to Germany, and made it clear that yielding to this demand was not the price of peace: it was only the price of continuing to negotiate. Chamberlain had no authority from the Cabinet to make such a commitment, and told Hitler that while he personally had no objection, he must consult the French government and his own colleagues.

The French Premier Daladier and his Foreign Minister, Georges Bonnet, came to London on 18 September and after tense discussion agreed to some cession of Czech territory, provided Britain would join France in a guarantee of the revised Czech frontier against unprovoked aggression. The Cabinet gave Chamberlain authority to negotiate again with Hitler, on the basis of Runciman's recommendations for boundary divisions. Meeting Hitler for a second time, at Godesberg on the Rhine on 22 September 1938, Chamberlain received a further shock. Hitler now raised his demands, and stated that because of the unstable situation in Czechoslovakia the problem must be settled definitely by 1 October at the latest, and the Czech army must be withdrawn behind the 'language frontier' – which meant handing over the powerful Czech fortifications to the Germans. Chamberlain withdrew, to consider what to do. He saw Hitler again on the evening of the 23rd, when the Führer gave him an infamous document, the 'Godesberg Ultimatum', which demanded that the evacuation of Czech troops from German-speaking areas should begin in two days' time (26 September), and be completed by 28 September.

Back in London, Chamberlain was disconcerted to find that, influenced by secret intelligence about the German generals' plot to overthrow Hitler and by firmer public opinion, Halifax wanted Britain to take a strong stand, and the Cabinet forbade further appeasement. Both Czechoslovakia and France rejected the Godesberg Ultimatum, and in a Foreign Office press statement Halifax announced that a German attack on Czechoslovakia would produce the immediate result of France coming to her assistance, and that 'Great Britain will certainly stand by France'.

This was the high point of Franco-British resistance. At last there was an unequivocal commitment by Britain to support France if war broke out. It looked as if Hitler would be stopped in his tracks: he could not fight Britain, France, Russia (also committed to intervene) and Czechoslovakia simultaneously; and if he had called off his campaign for the Sudetenland after so much bombast, the anti-Nazis would have gone into action, and it is likely the generals' plot to topple him would have succeeded.[7]

Meanwhile Mussolini had been living in a dream world, confident that France and Britain would cave in to Hitler over Czechoslovakia. Suddenly, on 26 September he was faced with the prospect of a Germany at war with France and Britain. Impulsively he told Ciano he would order mobilization; but he did nothing, and Italy was the one country which took no precautionary measures at this time. The German military attaché in Paris complained that the Italians were doing nothing to pin down French troops on their frontier, and that Mussolini seemed to be abandoning his ally in a critical hour: it was clear that he had no intention of intervening on Germany's side if war broke out.

In London, the pro-British Grandi was appalled. He invited Sir Ronald Graham, the former British Ambassador in Rome, to lunch on 26 September; they agreed that Mussolini alone could save the situation, and Grandi implored Graham to see Halifax and, using all the authority of his former position, try to persuade the Foreign Secretary that Chamberlain should make a direct appeal to Mussolini to intervene with Hitler. Graham did not succeed in obtaining an interview with Lord Halifax, but he made his plea in writing; Halifax sent it on to Chamberlain, and Cadogan confirmed to Graham that both the Prime Minister and the Foreign Secretary were considering it.[8]

Chamberlain had pressurized Beneš to agree to an immediate limited German occupation outside the Czech frontier fortifications and then to allow a German–Czech–British Boundary Commission to establish quickly the other areas to be handed over to the Germans. Chamberlain warned the Czechs:

> The only alternative to this plan . . . would be an invasion and a dismemberment of Czechoslovakia by forcible means and, though that might result in a conflict entailing incalculable loss of life, there is no possibility that at the end of the conflict, whatever the result, Czechoslovakia could be restored to her frontiers of today.

Hitler in his turn sent a cunning message to Chamberlain during the night of 27/28 September. Schmidt, who translated it into English, got the feeling that Hitler was 'shrinking back from the fatal step'; whether this is so will never be known. Hitler wrote that the final arrangements would be dependent not on a unilateral German decision but on a free vote, and that the immediate occupation by German contingents he had demanded represented no more than a 'security measure'; he went on:

> . . . that Czechoslovakia should lose a part of her fortifications is naturally an unavoidable consequence . . . The Government in Prague is only using a proposal for the occupation by German troops in order, by distorting the meaning and object of my proposal, to mobilize those forces in other countries, in particular in England and France, from which they hope to receive unreserved support for their aim, and thus to achieve the possibility of a general conflagration. I leave it to your judgement whether in view of these facts you consider you should continue your effort.

During the morning of 28 September Grandi had telephoned to Rome that only a miracle could avert a catastrophe; according to him, the miracle occurred when Chamberlain sent a telegram to the Duce which gave Mussolini a diplomatic triumph.[9]

Chamberlain wrote to Hitler at 11.30 p.m. on 28 September; he said that after reading the Führer's letter he was certain Hitler could get 'all essentials without war and without delay', and that he (Chamberlain) was ready to go to Berlin to discuss the transfer with him (Hitler) and representatives of the Czech government, together with representatives of France and Italy ('if you desire'):

> However much you distrust Prague's Government's intentions you cannot doubt power of British and French Governments to see that promises are carried out fairly and fully and forthwith . . . I cannot believe that you will take responsibility of starting a world war which may end civilization for the sake of a few days' delay.

At the same time Chamberlain telegraphed to Mussolini:

> I have today addressed last appeal to Herr Hitler to abstain from force to settle Sudeten problem which I feel sure can be settled by a short discussion and will give him the essential territory, population and protection for both Sudetens and Czechs during transfer. I have offered myself to go at once to Berlin to discuss arrangements with German and Czech representatives and, if the Chancellor desires, representatives also of Italy and France.
>
> I trust Your Excellency will inform German Chancellor that you are willing to be represented and urge him to agree to my proposal which will keep all our peoples out of war. I have already guaranteed that Czech

promises shall be carried out and feel confident complete agreement can be reached in a week.

Halifax had acted on Grandi's suggestion, as Graham had urged, and during the night of 27/28 September had told Perth to express to the Duce the hope that he would use his influence with Hitler to persuade him to accept a peaceful settlement. Perth saw Ciano early during the morning of 28 September, and Ciano went immediately to see Mussolini, who said that he hoped Hitler would postpone action for twenty-four hours to allow him (Mussolini) time 'to re-examine the situation and to put forward new proposals for a peaceful settlement'.

When Perth got back to the British Embassy he found Chamberlain's message to Mussolini, which had been telephoned from London; he rushed back to see Ciano again. Ciano said he would give the Duce this new message immediately, and Perth waited at the Palazzo Chigi while Ciano made a second trip to Mussolini at the Palazzo Venezia. After talking to him, Ciano returned:

> Good news; very, very good news. Hitler has agreed at Signor Mussolini's request to postpone the German mobilization for twenty-four hours, and I am also authorized to tell you that Signor Mussolini will support, and will recommend to Herr Hitler the acceptance of, the proposals for a conference between the four powers and ask to be represented at it.

In his subsequent despatch to Halifax, Perth pointed out that had Britain not pursued the policy of conciliation and friendship towards Italy which had culminated in the Anglo-Italian agreement of the previous April, it was more than doubtful that Mussolini would have acted as mediator. 'Had he not done so, could war have been averted?' As the Easter Agreement had not yet been put into operation, Perth was wide of the mark.[10]

On reading Chamberlain's message, Mussolini had telephoned his Ambassador (Attolico) in Berlin and told him to ask for an immediate interview with Hitler because the British government had asked him

> . . . to mediate in the Sudeten question. The point of difference is very small. Tell the Chancellor that I and Fascist Italy stand behind him. He must decide. But tell him I favour the suggestion, and beg him to refrain from mobilization.

At the time of this call Hitler was talking to the French Ambassador, André François-Poncet, who was suggesting that large chunks of Czechoslovakia should be handed over to Germany. The interview was interrupted, and Attolico delivered his urgent message. Hitler replied: 'Tell the Duce that I accept his proposal.' It was noon – two hours before Hitler's ultimatum to the Czechs ran out. Mussolini and

Hitler talked on the telephone and Hitler issued invitations to Britain, France and Italy to meet him the next day in Munich. Ominously, no invitation was issued to Czechoslovakia, although Chamberlain had specified her inclusion in his message to Hitler. Russia was also ignored.

Chamberlain had made a gloomy broadcast on the evening of 27 September, and on the afternoon of 28 September, while he was giving the House of Commons an account of the Czech crisis in which he informed the House, misleadingly, that the letter he had received from Hitler that morning contained 'reassuring statements', he was brought a message that Hitler had invited him to Munich. The House dissolved in wild applause and hysterical relief that war had been averted; the cost was not counted.

Grandi was at Heston Airport to see Chamberlain off the next morning (29 September); if Grandi is to be believed, Lord Halifax went up to him and, in the presence of his parliamentary colleagues, said 'Here is the wise man who was right.' When Chamberlain arrived at the airport, Halifax took Grandi to greet him; Chamberlain shook Grandi warmly by the hand, saying, 'Thank you very much. In a few hours I will be seeing your chief and I am sure that good will result from our meeting.'

When Grandi got back to his Embassy, Ball asked to see him and, according to Grandi's account, with his eyes full of tears put his arm around the Ambassador's neck, saying, 'The Prime Minister has asked me to tell you that you were right, and he is glad he has followed your advice to approach Mussolini directly. We owe world peace to Mussolini.' In the afternoon Halifax sent for Grandi and told him, smiling, 'You were right. Your advice was sound. It is thanks to providence that we followed your advice at the last moment.'[11]

In Berlin, meanwhile, the German Foreign Office had at once given Attolico a draft of the terms which Hitler wanted accepted at Munich; these he telephoned immediately to Rome, so that Mussolini would be able to produce them at Munich as his own formula for mediation.

On the morning of 29 September Hitler and Mussolini met at the frontier station of Kufstein. In the Führer's train on the way to Munich Hitler told Mussolini he intended to 'liquidate Czechoslovakia as she now is', because as things stood she immobilized forty of his divisions and tied his hands with France; without her fortifications, which would be lost to her as a result of the return of the Sudetenland to Germany, ten divisions would be enough to immobilize her. The Führer had with him a number of maps, and Mussolini found to his surprise that they were maps showing the Dutch, Belgian and French frontiers, not Czechoslovakia's. Furthermore, instead of talking any more about Czechoslovakia, Hitler described his plans to attack in the West. Mussolini listened without comment; he was alarmed by his ally's aggressive attitude. Finally he asked, 'What are your demands on Czechoslovakia?' – although he already knew them, from the notes sent to Rome from Berlin. Ribbentrop, who had accompanied the Führer, described them as 'minimum demands', and said that 'if France and England can induce Beneš to accept what the Führer has been demanding for so many months the Government of the Reich is not opposed to reaching an agreement.'[12] Mussolini was determined the Conference should be a success, and that there should be no war; his desire was to be acclaimed as a peace-maker.

Daladier, Chamberlain, Hitler and Mussolini assembled at the Brown House in Munich; neither Russia nor Czechoslovakia was represented. After lunch, they set to work to carve up Czechoslovakia. It was a disorderly conference with no chairman, no agenda and no agreed procedure. The senior British civil servant present, Sir Horace Wilson, made a caustic note: 'Organization was very imperfect, and there appeared to be no arrangement for the taking of notes. A Secretary General had been appointed but he took no part in the chaos which ruled for the last five hours.'

Mussolini was cock-a-hoop. Unlike Hitler he was something of a linguist, with good German and French, and even a few words of English. Mussolini, all smiles, with relish assumed the principal role, making suggestions to the other three leaders. He was determined the Conference should establish his reputation as a great European mediator and peace-maker. He strutted around with his chin stuck out, talking affably and enjoying being the king-pin. He produced his version of the proposals which had been previously agreed with the Germans. Paul Schmidt, Hitler's interpreter, had no difficulty translating them back into German because the day before, in the German Foreign Office, he had translated them into Italian. Mussolini was convincing: he successfully gave the impression that they were his own proposals. To Chamberlain's relief, Daladier soon announced his acceptance of them as a basis for discussion.

The atmosphere of goodwill was temporarily shattered when Chamberlain asked, quite reasonably, that the Czechs should be compensated for the buildings and other property which would pass to Germany when they occupied the Sudetenland territory. Hitler became angry and refused to discuss the matter, asserting that there could be no question of indemnification because everything had been paid for by taxes levied on the Sudeten population. The suggestion was dropped, and harmony was restored. It was notable that Hitler was more friendly towards Daladier than Chamberlain, whose reasonable attempt to bargain prompted the Führer to remark later:

> Daladier is a lawyer [this was incorrect] who understands the details and consequences. With him one can negotiate clearly and satisfactorily. But this Chamberlain is like a haggling shopkeeper who wrangles over every village and small detail; he is worse than the Czechs himself. What has he lost in Bohemia? Nothing at all! . . . [He is] an insignificant man whose dearest wish is to go fishing on a weekend. I know no weekend, and I don't fish.

Although Mussolini's draft proposals were at once accepted in principle by the British and French, according to Wilson there followed long delays due to 'inefficient organization and lack of control'. During the course of the evening, Daladier and Chamberlain refused an invitation to dine with Hitler, on the plea that they had to consult with their colleagues; they certainly did not want to be photographed eating happily with the dictators to whom they had sold the pass. Mussolini and Hitler dined alone in triumph, celebrating their rout of France and Britain.

Chamberlain had suggested, weakly supported by Daladier, that Czech representatives should at least be available for consultation, but Hitler would not tolerate Czechs in his presence. However, the Czech Minister in Berlin and a colleague from the Foreign Office in Prague were permitted to 'make themselves available', and were immured in an adjoining room – not only a piece of appalling rudeness, but a humiliating example of an abject bowing to Hitler's whim on the part of Daladier and Chamberlain. At 10 p.m. Horace Wilson handed the Czechs a map with the areas for immediate German occupation marked on it, and told them it had British approval. When the Czechs demurred they were told, 'If you do not accept, you will have to settle your affairs with Germany direct.'[13]

Various minor amendments to Mussolini's German-inspired proposals were subsequently agreed, including clauses about ceding certain areas to Poland and Hungary. The final draft included the following points:

1. Evacuation to begin on 1st October.
2. The powers England, France and Italy agree that the evacuation of the territory shall be completed by 10th October without any existing installations having been destroyed, and the Czech Government will be held responsible for carrying out the evacuation without damage as aforesaid.
3. The conditions governing the evacuation shall be laid down in detail by an international committee in which Germany, England, France, Italy and Czechoslovakia are represented.

4.   Doubtful territories will be occupied by international forces until the plebiscite. Under terms of the Memorandum the conditions of the Saar plebiscite shall be considered as the basis of the plebiscite. The final determination of the frontiers will be carried out by an international committee.

5.   The occupation by stages of the predominantly German territory by German forces will begin on 1 October.

It was not until two in the morning that the agreement was ready for signature, and it had already been a long day. According to Ivone Kirkpatrick (later Permanent Under-Secretary at the Foreign Office), who was present,

> . . . as the day wore on and night began to fall more people invaded the Conference room and it began to assume the appearance of a waiting room at Waterloo Station on a bank holiday . . . In this hurly burly Mussolini showed to the best advantage. He was the only one of the four who was not wholly dependent on the interpreter, and he enjoyed the deference which was demonstratively paid to him by the Führer.[14]

After the agreement had been officially signed Chamberlain agreed to see the Czech delegates. It was now half-past two in the morning and, tired out, he yawned without ceasing during the conversation. He told the Czechs they must without fail send a representative to Berlin by 5 p.m. that day for the first meeting of the International Commission which was to fix details of the evacuation of the zone to be occupied. According to one of the delegates, Jan Masaryck, 'It was a sentence without right of appeal and without possibility of modification.'

Mussolini, having engineered the dismemberment of Czecho-slovakia, did not bother to talk to her representatives. Nor did Hitler. The shabby treatment of the Czechs at Munich must have troubled Chamberlain: he was careful to tell the Cabinet on 3 October that he had suggested the Czechs should take part 'but it had been presented to him that the matter was too urgent to permit of the delay [since the Czechs could not arrive until the afternoon] because Mussolini had to be back in Rome for a reception'. But this was a lame excuse for a shameful incident. The Czechs, betrayed without notice by their ally France, could do nothing except consent reluctantly to the Munich formula.[15]

Almost certainly Mussolini's eleventh-hour intervention prevented the outbreak of a European war at the end of September 1938. Was this in the interests of Hitler's opponents? The evidence to the contrary is conclusive and irrefutable, while the view that the year Chamberlain bought at Munich was well-spent because it enabled French and British military strength to catch up with Germany's is unsustainable.

At the Nuremberg Trials General Alfred Jodl, Hitler's Chief of Operations of the Armed Forces High Command during the Second World War, gave evidence that in 1938 war was 'out of the question for Germany because there were only five fighting German divisions on the western fortifications, which were nothing but a large construction site, to hold out against 100 French divisions. This was militarily impossible.' Jodl explained to the court that in 1938 the German army had only one properly equipped plus two further skeleton Panzer divisions, and perhaps twenty-eight other divisions, whereas a year later there were seventy-three. In his evidence at Nuremberg, General Keitel (Chief of Armed Forces High Command) admitted that during the 1938 crisis 'We were extraordinarily happy that it had not come to a military operation because our means of attack against the frontier fortifications of Czechoslovakia were insufficient and the Czechs could have deployed an equal number of divisions to us.'

General Wilhelm Adam, who commanded the German army on the French frontier, has stated in his memoirs that the troops under his command in September 1938 were completely inadequate to withstand a French invasion, and that in his view any thought of a war then with France and Britain was 'sheer lunacy'; he has also highlighted the poor state at that time of the partly-constructed Siegfried Line.

From the record of talks at Geneva between Russia's Foreign Commissar Litvinov and Earl de la Warr (Lord Privy Seal) and Rab Butler (then Under-Secretary at the Foreign Office) there is irrefutable evidence of Russia's readiness to support Czechoslovakia militarily, and both in Geneva and in a subsequent press conference in Russia, Litvinov made clear Russia's intention to fight to save Czechoslovakia. Had the French attacked in force in the west, they would have quickly overcome German resistance on the Siegfried Line, and should within a short time have occupied much of the Ruhr, forcing Hitler to withdraw a considerable number of divisions from the east; thus the opportunity for Germany to over-run Czechoslovakia quickly would have been lost, and Russia would have had time to come to her aid.[16]

There is no reason to doubt the evidence of the German generals. Not only did the Munich settlement thwart the plans of the anti-Nazi generals to topple Hitler, but an excellent opportunity for the French, British and Russians to inflict a military defeat on Germany was lost. If Hitler's armies had been overcome, he would inevitably have been overthrown. (A detailed account of the conspiracy is given in the author's book *Ghosts of Peace* (1987).)

Churchill's claim in his memoirs that 'The year's breathing space said to be gained at Munich left Britain in a much worse position compared to Hitler and Germany than they had been at the Munich crisis', and that the alteration during that year in the relative strength of the French and German armies was 'disastrous', is correct. Furthermore, in the intervening twelve months the Czech Skoda factory produced as much as the total output of British armament factories – but instead of arms for the Allied cause, these were now arms for Germany.[17]

The French were undoubtedly nervous and irresolute at the prospect of war with Germany, but on 4 September 1938 all leave for the army had been stopped and reservists and men on leave were sent to the Maginot Line. Frightened at the prospect of having to fight alone, France needed a strong lead from Britain, and this she did not get.

Thus, Mussolini's intervention at Chamberlain's request was a disaster. If Chamberlain had abided by the Cabinet's decision of 27 September to stand firm – as he told his colleagues he would – Hitler's bluff would have been called. A year later Russia was on Germany's side and Hitler's armed forces were much stronger compared to the British and French.

Overnight Mussolini had gained a great European reputation for wisdom and moderation. He revelled in it, enjoying his moment of triumph, even letting Chamberlain know (through Lord Perth) that any favourable reference the British Prime Minister might make in London about his action 'both before and during the Munich Conference' would be much appreciated. (Perth added, 'Mussolini is apparently in a highly sensitive condition.')[18] Chamberlain complied: in the House of Commons on 3 October he described Mussolini's contribution to the Munich settlement as 'certainly notable and perhaps decisive . . . Europe and the world have reason to be grateful to the head of the Italian Government.' Ciano told Perth the Duce was 'very satisfied' – further evidence of his inordinate vanity.

Mussolini and Ciano left Munich the morning after the Conference, to be met as soon as they crossed the Italian frontier with lively and spontaneous demonstrations of popularity; the Duce was hailed as the Angel of Peace. According to Anfuso, who travelled with him, Mussolini's reception at Verona station was ecstatic; at the intermediate stations between Verona and Bologna peasants fell to their knees as the train passed, while at Bologna he was treated like a saint. Anfuso concluded that Italians much preferred olive branches to declarations about Italian military strength. The peak of the Duce's triumphal journey was at Florence, where the King was waiting to offer his personal congratulations. This was Mussolini's Indian summer. But it was short; never again was he to taste such success. From the balcony of the Palazzo Venezia in Rome he told a cheering crowd: 'You have witnessed stirring times. At Munich we have worked for peace with justice. Is this the wish of the Italian people?' Yet privately he was worried by these demonstrations of the fervent desire of the Italians to avoid war. How could he stir a pacifist nation with the warlike gestures he so loved?

At Munich Mussolini had had several 'extremely cordial conversations' with Chamberlain. He had told the Prime Minister that he was about to withdraw about ten thousand troops from Spain, half the Italian strength there. According to Mussolini, Chamberlain seemed pleased with this information; a suggestion that Chamberlain and Mussolini should have a private conference the next day was abandoned, however, because of Mussolini's fear that it would antagonize Hitler.

Instead, in Rome, Ciano sent for Lord Perth on 3 October. He told him 12,000 Italian soldiers were to be brought home from Spain, the Italian object of preventing Communism there having been achieved, and proposed that the Easter Agreement of five and a half months earlier should be put into force immediately. Ciano raised a spark of hope regarding the inclusion of France in the *rapprochement* by hinting that once the Agreement came into force negotiations between France and Italy might be held, with the suggestion that a general European *entente* would follow. If the Easter Agreement did not come into force, Ciano said ominously to Perth, the Italian government would be forced 'to take certain action which up to now they had definitely refused'.[19]

Following Munich, Mussolini was having qualms about German domination in Eastern Europe, and the threat she posed to Italian aspirations in Yugoslavia; and he still baulked at the definitive military alliance suggested by Germany in May. It is obvious that the 'certain action' Ciano referred to at his meeting with Perth was a full-scale German–Italian military alliance, and the death of the Easter Agreement and probable withdrawal of Italian Ambassadors from all countries which did not recognize the Italian conquest of Abyssinia.

The next day Perth wrote to Halifax that Britain and Italy had come 'to the parting of the ways'. If Britain put the Easter Agreement into force and recognized the Italian Empire, Mussolini would work for a European *detente* and general pacification; if she did not, however, he would

... conclude a definite military alliance with Germany, even though this is against his innermost wish and would be unpopular in the country ...

He feels while Prime Minister has come back from Munich with a signed Agreement with Herr Hitler for consultation with Germany he, in spite of his active intervention in support of the Prime Minister's proposals, has been left out in the cold, and that the bad boy has secured an award while the good one goes empty away.

On 5 October Halifax told Perth that he and the Prime Minister favoured early action; but it would have to be brought before Parliament, and Mussolini should be under no illusion about the difficulties there would be with public opinion.

Before his meeting with Lord Perth on 3 October, Ciano had outlined his plan for the interview in his diary: 'I shall bluntly ask him the question: "Are you now willing to implement the Pact of 16 April?" If they are, so much the better. If not, we must each play our own game.'[20]

After some dilly-dallying, the British government agreed to ratify the Easter Agreement and give Mussolini the longed-for recognition of his Abyssinian conquest. Chamberlain remained apprehensive of public opinion, however, and wanted assurances from the Italian government that there would be no more bombing of British ships, while Perth told London it was 'useless to expect Italian co-operation for any further measures connected with the cessation of the Spanish war'. On 26 October the Cabinet agreed to bring the Easter Agreement into operation. Mussolini and Ciano were 'pleased', according to Perth, and a protocol implementing the 16 April Agreement was jointly signed on 16 November. Mussolini had made no real concession over Spain, and the only consequence of the six months' delay had been to push him further towards an alliance with Hitler.[21]

When Perth in Rome confirmed the British decision to implement the Easter Agreement, Ciano noted in his diary that 'We must keep both doors open'; he mentioned this to the Duce, and 'he seemed to agree'. De Felice claims that at this stage Mussolini wanted to keep the balance of power in Europe, using the London–Rome relations as a 'hinge and pivot'; and that he did not want to distance himself from Berlin, but to keep his options open. Denis Mack Smith, however, considers that he was already committed inalienably to an alliance with Hitler. The evidence shows Mussolini to have been wavering, even thinking of mending his bridges with France, and still hoping to be the instigator of a four-power conference of Britain, France, Italy and Germany (without Russia) which would stabilize Europe, and also perhaps induce France to make concessions to Italy.[22]

On 31 October Halifax suggested to Perth that he and the Prime Minister should go to Italy. The suggestion clearly originated in London, although at Munich Mussolini had voiced a hope that Chamberlain might visit him in Rome. At all events, Mussolini welcomed the idea and the visit was fixed for the second week in January 1939. In a Foreign Office minute Ingram observed that 'the object of the visit is more to resume personal contact with Mussolini and to make a gesture of courtesy and goodwill than to stage an Anglo-Italian Conference . . . a round table conference would be anathema to Mussolini.' Any idea of a fixed agenda was excluded.

On the Duce's instructions, the Italian newspapers expressed enthusiasm for Chamberlain, and the omens appeared good for a resumption of Mussolini's friendship with Britain; the Duce was even more apprehensive of Hitler's intentions after the offhand way in which the Führer, refusing to be bound by the proposal for an International Commission to be set up at Munich, had instead simply grabbed further parts of Czechoslovakia.

Clouds appeared, however, almost as soon as the visit had been agreed upon. On 30 November the French Ambassador, François-Poncet, having been asked to attend a session of the Italian parliament to hear an important speech by Ciano, was treated to an obviously pre-arranged demonstration of hostility to France on the part of the deputies.

This was followed by a bizarre incident which nearly shipwrecked the proposed visit altogether. The *Popolo d'Italia* of 8 December carried a satirical article (written by Mussolini, and well up to the present-day standards of *Private Eye* and *Le Canard Enchainé*) describing an imaginary conversation at the London house of a British MP between Haile Selassie and Éduard Beneš (who had resigned as President of Czechoslovakia in October) which focused on the mistakes which had led to their loss of power. It spotlighted the bad faith of the British and the French, who had encouraged them to battle against Italy and Germany and then betrayed and abandoned them. The article finished with the MP telling the two former leaders they were 'the first victims of a terrible war which will be fought between two ideologies – democracy and totalitarianism; a battle has been lost but the struggle is not yet over', and forecasting that there would be two further victims, Juan Negrin (Spanish Prime Minister 1938–March 1939), and Chiang Kai-Shek (President of the Chinese Nationalist Republic).

The Foreign Office found the article 'amusing', seeing the emphasis of the sarcasm over Czechoslovakia as directed against France, not 'us'; and they liked the idea put forward in the article that if Haile

Selassie were to appeal for charity to Mussolini, it might be forth-coming. Perth sent London a translation of the full text of the article, and the Foreign Office minuted that no action was required. However, the Prime Minister and his Downing Street advisors took it more seriously, coming as it did after the hostile Italian parliamentary demonstration against the French.

Cadogan was instructed to draft a letter to Perth asking him to let the Italians know that unless the atmosphere improved the Prime Minister might find it too embarrassing to visit Rome, since the *Popolo d'Italia* article had been given publicity in *The Times* and *Daily Telegraph*, and also in the French press. Cadogan minuted that he was all for 'leaving it alone, as Signor Mussolini cannot be taught manners as we know them'. He wrote to Perth that the Prime Minister was anticipating considerable difficulty about his visit to Rome; as he pointed out,

> . . . Recent anti-French outbursts in Italy have resulted in further crit-icism here . . . Matters have been made worse by Signor Mussolini's recent article in *Popolo d'Italia*. That rather outrageous product is not unprecedented, and in ordinary times it might have been overlooked, but coming as it does only four or five weeks before Mussolini was to be the host of the Prime Minister it does not augur well for the spirit in which the conversations will be conducted . . . If things get worse it will proba-bly be impossible for him to go.

Perth replied that he was not at all anxious about the atmosphere in Rome, but if the visits were cancelled it would be disastrous for Anglo-Italian relations, and

> . . . I should regard the future outlook with something like despair. It could not but strengthen the extreme supporters of the Axis and the Anti-Comintern pact. Signor Mussolini would, I fear, regard the cancella-tion of the visit as a personal insult, and this is a thing he never forgets or forgives.

Perth saw Ciano, who took his complaints 'in good part', including the protest about Mussolini's article, and promised to keep the atmos-phere 'as good as possible pending the Prime Minister's visit'. The visit went ahead.[23]

Perth prepared for Chamberlain a lengthy assessment which described the unpopularity in Italy of the Rome–Berlin axis, the per-sonal popularity of Chamberlain, who with Mussolini was held to have averted war at the time of Munich, and the unpopularity of the Italian adventure in Spain; he also emphasized Mussolini's own popularity, and said that Italy would follow him in whatever he did. Perth pointed out that Italian claims against France were the major issue, and that Italy's foreign policy would always be based on blatant self-interest.

Gladwyn Jebb, Sir Alec Cadogan's Private Secretary, had sent Cadogan a memorandum suggesting that Mussolini's bargaining position was now much stronger than at Easter 1938, and that only by really tempting offers could he be persuaded to rejoin the British side. Jebb proposed offering Italy the two Somalilands (French and British), the southern half of Tunisia, a large loan, and a seat on the board of the Suez Canal. Cadogan disagreed: he thought a considerable section of public opinion in Britain would be shocked at such 'rewards' to Mussolini so soon after the Abyssinian War. However, alarm about Hitler's intentions was widespread, and in such a desperate situation Chamberlain might have been able to convince the nation that Mussolini must be propitiated. 'Pertinax', the influential anonymous columnist on the French *Le Temps*, also advocated cession of the Somalilands to Italy.

It was decided that the British would not discuss Italo-French relations with Mussolini. Chamberlain said his intention was to hold a 'heart to heart talk' with the Duce; but as he came without gifts in his hand – not even the prospect of an Italian seat on the Suez Canal Board – his conversations with Mussolini were doomed to be unproductive. Oliver Harvey, Lord Halifax's Private Secretary, observed in his diary that the only justification for the visit was to strengthen the likelihood that the Italians would betray the Germans in the event of war, and that Halifax had decided to give 'nothing for nothing'.[24]

Chamberlain and Halifax arrived in Rome on the morning of 11 January. Unknown to the British, the week before Mussolini had definitely decided to agree to a tripartite pact with Germany and Japan, and Ciano had accepted an invitation to go to Berlin on 28 January to sign the agreement.

Mussolini and Ciano met the British Prime Minister and Foreign Secretary at the station. Grandi and Perth were there, as were 1,500 members of the British colony in Rome. The whole city was covered with British and Italian flags, and large crowds applauded rapturously along the streets. The first talks began at the Palazzo Venezia that afternoon; the noise made by those outside the windows chanting 'Duce' and 'Chamberlain' was such that it made conversation difficult, and the crowd had to be dispersed by the police. Chamberlain was delighted with his reception.

After the Duce and the Prime Minister had affirmed their attachment to the Easter Agreement, Chamberlain put it to Mussolini that Hitler had made it quite impossible for conversations to be carried on with him (Hitler), and that there was a general suspicion that 'Herr

Hitler had in mind to make some further move in the near future which would be likely to upset the peace of Europe, either in the Ukraine or by a sudden attack in the West'. Chamberlain asked if Mussolini would do something to mitigate his anxiety. Mussolini replied that Germany had rearmed and was still rearming, but said he was

> . . . convinced that this was only for defence purposes and that Hitler desired a long period of peace in order that he might fuse together the component parts of the expanded Reich and develop its productive forces; in his view these stories about a move eastward by Germany or an attack in the west were absolutely out of the question; Hitler would never send the youth of Germany to fall on the frontier which he regards as already decided.

It is unlikely, if just possible, that Mussolini believed his own words. We shall never know. However, he said nothing further to encourage Chamberlain to feel complacent about Hitler's intentions.

Chamberlain was again greeted by cheering crowds as he went to the station for his journey home. In a speech he declared that the object of the visit had not been to reach specific arrangements, 'but to produce through personal contacts a more intimate comprehension of the respective points of view of the two countries. This object has been achieved. We leave more than ever convinced of the good faith and the goodwill of the Italian Government.' In his report to the Cabinet on his return from Rome Chamberlain described Mussolini as 'a charming host and a man of peace'.

The government-inspired Italian press became virulently anti-British as soon as the warmth inspired by Chamberlain's visit had cooled. Many articles alleged that war was likely if Italian aspirations were not met. On 17 February Vansittart minuted that Mussolini's own paper was using language so intolerably offensive as to expose the whole Anglo-Italian Agreement to ridicule, and Perth was instructed to protest to Ciano. The Foreign Office considered – correctly – that the Ambassador was far too weak in his dealings with the Italians. As a Roman Catholic with a daughter married into the Roman aristocracy, Perth enjoyed Fascist-dominated Rome society, and was mild in his language to Ciano. Vansittart minuted that 'Perth seems to have failed entirely in backbone' and wanted him to be instructed to 'return to the charge', while Cadogan commented that 'the whole Anglo-Italian Agreement seems to count for nothing in Count Ciano's estimation'. The outlook was unpromising.[25]

CHAPTER 14

Prague, Albania, and War with Germany

DURING THE MUNICH Conference, Mussolini had remarked affably to Daladier, 'I hope that now you will not forget my address.' For two years, since the Abyssinian crisis, France had maintained only a Chargé d'Affaires in Rome; now Daladier reappointed a French Ambassador (7 November), thus granting Mussolini *de jure* recognition of his conquest and arousing hopes of a Franco-Italian accord. Both the French government and Mussolini believed that better Franco-Italian relations would constrain Hitler's aggression. Unfortunately, Mussolini's behaviour towards France was now characterized by brashness and insolence – contradictory, at a time when his approaches to Britain were cordial. He had got it into his head that only a tough approach to France would produce concessions, and played his cards badly.

It might have been expected that after his fair words to Daladier at Munich Mussolini would have given the new Ambassador, André François-Poncet, a good reception. But when François-Poncet arrived from Berlin (he had been Ambassador to Germany), Mussolini ordered a boycott of his arrival at the station; the press were instructed to treat the event as of no importance, while at the same time an anti-French newspaper campaign was initiated, condemning the Laval–Mussolini agreement of 1935 as unfair and re-affirming Italian claims against France, especially in respect of Tunisia and Corsica. Mussolini made François-Poncet wait three weeks before he would receive him, and in a speech at Genoa emphasized that France and Italy were on the opposite sides of the barricades in Spain.

Worse was to come. As previously noted, Ciano's office invited the new Ambassador to be present at a parliamentary session on 30 November where Ciano was to make an important foreign policy statement. When Ciano said in his speech that Italy was pursuing her 'natural aspirations', fifteen deputies jumped up crying 'Tunisia! Corsica!' It was clearly premeditated, and François-Poncet left in protest. He and Ciano met again three days later; when the Ambassador observed that relations between the two countries rested on the Laval–Mussolini agreement of 1935, Ciano – to François-Poncet's surprise – denied it; he also failed to apologize for the incident in parliament; a fortnight later, on the Duce's instructions, he officially denounced the Laval–Mussolini agreement. These incidents of course angered the French government, whose Premier, Édouard Daladier, was in any case strongly anti-Fascist (the Foreign Minister, Bonnet, was less so). Ciano's Note denouncing the agreement was indignantly contradicted by the French, and an offer by Ciano to conduct fresh negotiations to revise the Laval–Mussolini agreement was refused. During a visit to Corsica Daladier proclaimed that France would never give up 'one inch of territory' which belonged to her.[1]

Mussolini's attitude to France became increasingly hostile and insolent after Chamberlain's visit to Rome in January 1939, and François-Poncet was ostracized and humiliated by prominent Fascists. Daladier forbade any discussion of their claims with the Italians, and relations became icy. The Duce both inspired and wrote hysterical anti-French articles, including one in the *Tevere* two days after Chamberlain had left Rome in which he went so far as to say, 'I spit on France'.

Then, out of the blue, Daladier sent Paul Badouin, a distinguished banker and director of the lucrative salt lakes in French Somalia, secretly to Rome. It was an odd ploy: François-Poncet was completely bypassed, not even told of Badouin's visit. Badouin met Ciano on 2 February and told him in strict secrecy that Daladier was ready to open talks about the cession to Italy of a large 'free zone' in Djibuti and a share in the administration of the port, support of Italian demands over the Suez Canal, and revision of the status of Italians in Tunisia, provided that 'Tunisia is not made into an Italian Sudetenland'. According to Badouin's report to Daladier, Ciano agreed when he (Badouin) insisted there could be no discussion of frontiers or territorial concessions.

Ciano reported this talk to Mussolini, who said there were only two alternatives – either to make a deal on this basis, 'postponing a final solution', or to force the issue now, which would mean war; but he agreed that negotiations could be opened on Djibuti and Tunisia. Ciano informed the German Ambassador of the French approach, on Mussolini's instructions, and von Mackensen reported to Ribbentrop that Daladier and Mussolini would negotiate, but that Italy's claims for territorial concessions (Corsica and Tunis) would be 'entirely excluded'.[2]

It scarcely seems possible that Mussolini should have really believed France would either cede Corsica to Italy or give up part or all of her mandate in Tunisia; such concessions could only be achieved by an

Italian attack on France, and Mussolini had no such intention. It was bluff on Mussolini's part, to indicate that Italy still regarded herself as an unsatisfied power who had been insufficiently rewarded for coming in on the Allied side in 1915. Yet Mussolini pushed his claims relentlessly. He was disturbed by the advances to France made by Germany which had culminated in a visit to Paris by Ribbentrop and the conclusion (6 December 1938) of a pact of friendship with the French government which also confirmed the existing French–German frontier as final (thus renouncing any German claims to Alsace-Lorraine), and undertook that the two nations should consult together over any future differences – all blatant deceit on Hitler's part, as events were to show. Unfounded rumours circulated that France had also secretly promised Hitler a free hand in Eastern Europe.[3]

Nothing came of the Badouin talks; they were maliciously leaked by Ribbentrop, which fomented hostile publicity in the French press and embarrassed Daladier. With their failure, Mussolini stepped up his anti-French press propaganda and ostentatiously reinforced his garrison in Libya, thus threatening Tunisia.

In a speech to the House of Lords on 23 February, Halifax disclaimed any intention of acting as mediator between France and Italy (as Chamberlain also had, in Rome in January); but then, contrarily, on 28 February he asked the British Ambassador in Paris to suggest to the French government that France should use Britain's 'good offices' *vis-à-vis* Italy. Writing from Rome on 22 February, Perth had suggested that, as it was almost unthinkable that the whole world should go up in flames over the status of Italians in the French colony of Tunis, Britain should thrash out the whole matter with the French government.[4]

On 14 March 1939, without consulting Mussolini, Hitler breached the Munich Agreement and sent his troops across the Czech frontier to occupy Prague: the independent state of Czechoslovakia disappeared. Mussolini was furious; Ciano wondered, in his diary, 'What weight can be given in future to German declarations and promises?' He also recorded that the Duce had ordered troop concentrations on the Austrian border north of Venice, and now wanted to come to an understanding with the Western powers.

Bernardo Attolico, the Italian Ambassador in Berlin, told Ribbentrop that reaction in Rome to the Prague coup was 'tremendous' and relayed Mussolini's complaints that, despite having at Munich espoused Germany's cause 'to a degree which could not be surpassed', he had not been informed until the last minute.[5] On the basis of the good relationship with Mussolini which Chamberlain felt he had established in January, he wrote a personal letter to the Duce on 20

March in an attempt to enlist his help over the Prague crisis. He reminded Mussolini that he (Mussolini) had said in January that Hitler wanted peace

> ... in which to fuse together the Greater Reich, and that you did not believe that he had new adventures in mind ... Does this mean that events in Czechoslovakia are only the prelude to further attempts to take control of other states? ... I do not seek to interfere with the Rome–Berlin Axis. You told me that your policy was one of peace and that you would at any time be willing to use your influence in that direction. I earnestly hope that you may feel it possible, in any way that is open to you, to take such action as may allay present tension and do something to restore the confidence that has been shattered.

The Foreign Office had urged Chamberlain to stress Anglo-French unity, but the Prime Minister would not do so. The letter was drafted in Downing Street with the help of Sir Horace Wilson, and so keen was Chamberlain for Mussolini to receive it at the earliest possible moment that the Rome Embassy was ordered to pursue the Duce to the south of Italy with it.

Mussolini delayed his reply until 1 April, and his reply was a snub: he declared that while he wanted a long period of peace, he could take no initiative 'before Italy's rights have been recognized (*prima che i diritti dell'Italia siano riconosciuti*)';and that in his speeches he had specified his colonial claims against France.[6]

Meanwhile there had been further sinister developments. On 21 March Ribbentrop told Lipski, the Polish Ambassador in Berlin, that the Danzig Corridor dispute must be solved; this amounted to a threat that Germany would invade Poland unless Danzig and the Corridor were ceded to Germany. In a panic lest the threat should be realized, the British Cabinet guaranteed military help to Poland if she were attacked by Germany – regardless of the fact that Britain had no means of access to Poland in the event of war. This fateful decision was taken at a meeting of the Foreign Policy Committee on 27 March. The lack of any access to Poland produced strong disagreement in Cabinet over whether Britain should try to include Russia in a pact for Poland's defence, but Chamberlain was against it, and no approach was made.[7]

On 31 March Chamberlain made the dramatic statement in the House of Commons that if Germany were to attack Poland, Britain and France would go to war against her. Yet Germany had a better claim to Danzig, a German town, than to the Sudetenland, while the Polish government was oligarchical and Poland militarily indefensible, whereas democratic Czechoslovakia, if supported by other western powers, would probably have been too hard a nut for the German armies to crack. The worst feature of the guarantee was that it put Poland into the position of being able to force Britain into war by refusing to negotiate a settlement with Hitler, at the same time as it strengthened Polish determination to concede nothing. Another ominous consequence was that Russia interpreted the guarantee as a declaration that Britain would deny Soviet claims to former Tsarist territory within the Polish frontiers, and it thus facilitated agreement between Hitler and Stalin; clearly, no suspicion of this possibility had occurred to Chamberlain or Halifax.[8]

Mussolini, angered by Hitler's failure to consult him before moving into Czechoslovakia and by the consequent downgrading of the Munich Agreement (which he looked on as the pinnacle of his career), remained gloomy for a few days, wondering whether he had made a mistake in supporting Hitler and pondering whether he should now make an agreement with France, through London. On 19 March Ciano wrote in his diary that because of the seizure of Prague Mussolini now thought it impossible to present to the Italian people the idea of an alliance with Germany: 'The very stones would cry out against it. The last few days have reversed my opinion of the Führer and Germany . . . from today I am working with the Duce for an agreement with the Western powers.'

Perth reported on 21 March that the extinction of Czechoslovakia had given Italian governing circles a severe shock, and suggested Britain should now show Italy that 'the German method is not the only one that pays, and Mussolini should be given public or private assurances that his claims [on France] would be given fair consideration.'

Perth's belief that Mussolini was now anxious to negotiate with France was doubtless correct, since an Italian diplomat, Vincenzo Fagiuoli, was sent to Paris to reopen negotiations with Badouin; Ciano wondered in his diary, 'Will they have a minimum of good sense in Paris, or will attempts to reach an understanding be once more frustrated by an unwillingness to negotiate concessions?' Fagiuoli informed Ciano that it had been Ribbentrop who leaked the earlier Badouin talks to the press. Ciano commented, 'Is it worth while to deal loyally with such people?'

François-Poncet told Perth that Italian demands regarding Djibuti and the Suez Canal 'would present no difficulties', and that with regard to Tunis they would probably be satisfied with safeguards for the Italian community. A proposed visit by Laval (who was still friendly with Mussolini) might have resolved the Franco-Italian conflict, but it was not proceeded with.[9]

In Spain, Barcelona had fallen to Franco at the end of January, and at the end of February Britain and France had recognized Franco's government; on 28 March the Fascists took Madrid, a victory celebrated in every Italian city with much acclamation for the Duce. In a moderate speech on 26 March Mussolini had said that the barrier between France and Italy represented by the Spanish Civil War had come down; the French reply came in a broadcast by Daladier on 29 March. His intention was to keep the door open for Mussolini, but in deference to opinion within his Cabinet he said harsh things which could be taken as referring to Italy, suggesting that whatever concessions were given to the dictators, they would be followed by fresh demands; he also stated that France would neither cede territory nor give up any of her rights. Mussolini took the speech amiss, but when Sir Noel Charles (second in command at the British Embassy in Rome) saw Ciano on 31 March he told him that Daladier's broadcast showed France to be prepared to listen to Italian proposals if they were reasonably presented. 'France and Italy', he said, 'were behaving like a couple of old gentlemen who got thoroughly on each other's nerves, and neither would make the first step towards reconciliation.' On 4 April Perth confirmed to London that 'if France would take the initiative Italy would not refuse discussions'. It seemed that, temporarily at least, there existed an opportunity for a Franco-Italian *rapprochement*. Unofficial emissaries of the King of Italy and the Prince of Piedmont approached Bonnet, imploring the French government to compose their quarrels with Italy quickly in order that Italy should not be sucked into the German orbit. François-Poncet emphasized to Bonnet that this was the moment to reach agreement with Italy, because the Prague coup had had a deep effect on Mussolini. Bonnet was ready but Daladier, who would never trust Mussolini, was 'extremely opposed'. Had official talks begun, it was on the cards that the Duce, smarting under his humiliation over Czechoslovakia, might have been prevented from moving further into Hitler's camp.[10]

The situation changed completely when Mussolini attacked Albania on 7 April. News of the German occupation of Prague had prompted Ciano to note in his diary for 15 March his conviction that going into Albania would raise Italian morale; he was eager for such an invasion, as a counter-stroke to Prague. Mussolini was initially more cautious, but soon convinced himself that a spectacular Hitler-style coup in Albania would do much for Italian prestige.

Although Albania had been under Italian domination for many years, an Italo-Albanian agreement had now been drafted which in effect gave Italy control of the country; the Italian plan was to present this to King Zog and, if he did not immediately agree, to seize the country. King Zog made difficulties, and on Good Friday, 7 April, Mussolini struck.

News of the Italian occupation of Albania prompted an immediate demand from Halifax for formal assurances from Mussolini that this would not provoke a crisis in Anglo-Italian relations or the international situation in general, and Perth was instructed to demand 'the frankest and fullest explanation [of this] and the future intentions of the Italian Government'.

Because he knew her to be eager for Italian assistance *vis-à-vis* Germany, Mussolini felt he had nothing to fear from Britain, and over Albania he was right. Britain did not even consider denouncing the Easter Agreement, despite its clauses pledging the signatories' respect for the *status quo* in the Mediterranean. In a talk with the Italian Chargé d'Affaires on 9 April Halifax merely criticized Italy's irresponsibility in disturbing the waters, and confirmed that Britain had no intention of terminating the Easter Agreement.[11]

Ciano had wanted the Albanian coup in order to prove to the world that Italy was independent of Germany and a great power in her own right, but it had a very different effect. It caused panic in Paris, Bucharest, Ankara and Athens, where it was believed to be a prelude to joint moves by Germany and Italy in Eastern Europe: Mussolini, like Hitler, was seen as an aggressive disturber of the peace, who would soon strike again.

It also had the effect of turning Chamberlain against Mussolini. He wrote to his sister that Mussolini had behaved to him like a sneak and a cad with his 'completely cynical smash and grab raid', and that he had thereby blocked any chances of a future *rapprochement* between Britain and Italy, just as Hitler had blocked any chance of a *rapprochement* with Germany. When Mussolini sought to reassure the Prime Minister through the secret Dingli–Ball channel, Ball told Dingli that Chamberlain was extremely angry, and that the Italian gestures would not deceive a baby. Through his London Embassy Mussolini sent a message that he considered that a crisis in Anglo-Italian relations would be deplorable, 'a game not worth the candle'. In reply Halifax sent an assurance that he would do everything he could to assist 'the maintenance of good relations between Italy and Britain'. Halifax did not share Chamberlain's resentment against Mussolini; he told a meeting of ministers that he was not about to abandon his pro-Italian policy because of Mussolini's action in a country which had for centuries been an Italian satellite, and moreover almost ceded to her altogether at Versailles.

The British response eventually was an Anglo-French guarantee of the independence of Greece and Romania, announced on 13 April, and an offer to Turkey by Britain of a treaty for military aid in the event of an attack. This latter offer made Mussolini extremely angry, and Hitler described the guarantees as 'an encirclement policy'. As Britain and France had no means of providing direct military assistance the guarantees, as in the case of Poland, amounted only to a general threat.[12]

On 13 April the government had faced a pessimistic and critical House of Commons; the Opposition claimed that the German occupation of Prague and the Italian occupation of Albania made Chamberlain's much-vaunted Munich Agreement seem ridiculous, and his Easter Agreement valueless. In reply Chamberlain said:

> The Anglo-Italian Agreement has been violated in every respect by Italy, but I do not think anything will be gained by disowning it with bell, book and candle at this stage. I am still not convinced that Italy has made up her mind, particularly the Italian nation, to be involved in national conflict with Great Britain and France in the Mediterranean.

Hugh Dalton, the Shadow Foreign Secretary, asked whether the government had had any inkling (in advance) of the invasion of Czechoslovakia or Albania. It was his view that by continuing the Anglo-Italian Agreement Britain was condoning aggression in Albania, while under the terms of the Agreement she was still giving Italy information about Britain's air force, troop movements, etc. Sir John Simon, now Chancellor of the Exchequer, would not reply when Dalton asked him if the government were ready to propose a definite military alliance to the Russians. The Prime Minister noted but dismissed rumours that Italy intended to occupy Corfu, and stated that he did not intend to discuss the Anglo-Italian Agreement, which was 'the right policy'.

The Leader of the Opposition, Clement Attlee, denounced the Anglo-Italian Agreement as mistaken policy – a policy of unilateral appeasement – and declared that what he called the rape of Albania was to the Anglo-Italian Agreement what the destruction of Czechoslovakia was to Munich; in his view, Mussolini had only signed the Agreement to obtain recognition of the Italian Empire of Abyssinia. Archibald Sinclair, the Liberal leader, said that 50,000 Italian soldiers and 400 Italian aeroplanes in Albania were a threat to Greece and Yugoslavia. In the course of the debate the Government, although pressed on this point by the Opposition, gave no hint that they were considering a military alliance with Russia. Before long, however, the Cabinet persuaded Chamberlain to agree – reluctantly – to military staff talks in Moscow with the French and the Russians.

Hopes of a Franco-Italian *rapprochement* did not lapse even now, following Italy's invasion of Albania. On 9 April Perth noted that Mussolini, believing he had been rebuffed by the French, would not use his influence to check Hitler until the French showed their willingness to talk. In his reminiscences, François-Poncet wrote that in numerous letters and telegrams he had urged talks on Bonnet, the French Foreign Minister, but obtained no response. He argued that after the shock to Italian opinion of the Prague coup, this was the moment to seek an honourable and moderate agreement: his arguments were ignored. He told Perth that Bonnet was convinced talks were desirable, but that Léger (the Permanent Secretary) and Daladier were 'immovable'. Halifax urged Phipps, the British Ambassador, to press the French Premier to resume contact with Mussolini with the least possible delay.[13]

Mussolini was very cordial when Perth called to take leave on 21 April, his term as Ambassador having come to an end. To his surprise, when Perth suggested Mussolini should communicate details of his claims to the French government, the Duce replied that Badouin's emissary had already been to Rome to set out in detail what France was prepared to offer, and that the Italian government was ready to accept this as a basis for negotiation. Mussolini had considered the French proposals so genuine that, he told Perth, he had informed Berlin that negotiations would shortly begin between France and Italy; but since then, they had heard nothing. Ciano, who was present, confirmed to Perth that Italy had been quite ready for talks in February, but now considered that the next move must come from the French side. Later, on 1 May, Halifax told the French Chargé d'Affaires in London that he hoped Daladier would make some move; in Paris, on 23 May, the French Premier informed him that Italy was asking for two posts on the Suez Canal Board, a free port at Djibuti, control of the Abyssinian part of the Djibuti railway, and a guarantee of rights for Italians in Tunisia. These, according to Daladier, represented four important concessions by France to Italy, who would give nothing in return:

> . . . it was impossible[he considered] for France to make such concessions in present circumstances, especially at a time when Italy had 1,900,000 men under arms. To agree to the Italian demands would be damaging to the prestige and interests of France. The Moslem population in North Africa would think that France had capitulated, and that Mussolini was the stronger.

As part of the 1935 Laval–Mussolini agreement, Daladier continued, Italy had promised to defend the independence of Austria and to resist German aggression, thereby enabling Laval to make concessions to Italy; but Daladier was convinced that sacrifices now would not bring Mussolini into a better frame of mind. Halifax pressed Daladier 'not to lose the present opportunity', but Daladier was adamant in refusing to make any move towards Mussolini.

Thus Daladier, rejecting the advice not only of Britain but of his own minister and ambassador, Bonnet and François-Poncet, turned his back on Mussolini. The diplomatic documents of Britain, France and Italy indicate that Ciano and Mussolini wanted negotiations with France, and the Romanian Foreign Minister, Grigoire Gafencu, visiting Rome, was left with the very clear impression that the Italian government was anxious for a *rapprochement* with the western powers. The failure of Paris to respond was an important factor in Mussolini's decision in May 1939 to enter into a military pact with Hitler.[14]

Other factors also influenced Mussolini's decision: he had taken due note of the abject weakness of Britain and France when Hitler occupied Czechoslovakia; he was unimpressed by the guarantees given to Poland, Greece and Romania, which were obviously incapable of fulfilment; and he was genuinely irritated by the proposed Anglo-French Treaty with Turkey. Greed decided him: regardless of his dislike for Hitler and for Nazi methods, he thought that Italy would obtain more from a German alliance than from friendship with Britain or France. In addition, Mussolini intensely disliked the idea of any involvement of the Russians in a military pact with France and Britain, as was now being proposed from London and Paris.

On 6 May Ciano and Ribbentrop met in Milan – a city with a strong residue of anti-German feeling dating from sufferings under Austrian occupation during the Risorgimento – to discuss a military pact which came to be known as the 'Pact of Steel'. On Mussolini's instructions, Ciano insisted that Italy could not go to war until after 1942. Ribbentrop said that Germany must have Danzig and the highway across the Corridor soon, but it was his opinion that France and Britain would lose interest in preventing this. Deceitfully, he told Ciano that Germany needed a period of peace for not less than four or five years, although she could be ready for war much sooner (in fact, Hitler had already given orders to his generals to prepare an attack to occupy all Poland in August). Hitler thought a pact with Italy would frighten France and Britain and prevent their military intervention on behalf of Poland.

Ribbentrop soft-pedalled on any anti-Soviet motives for the pact; unknown to France and Britain, Germany had already been seeking a détente with Russia. It was significant that Litvinov, the Soviet Foreign Minister, pro-France and pro-Britain, had fallen from power on 3 May. Hints of this change in Hitler's policy towards Stalin had been given to Ciano, but neither he nor Mussolini had taken them seriously enough. Indeed, Ciano even considered the Pact of Steel to be directed against Russia. In the strictest secrecy Ribbentrop told Attolico, the Italian Ambassador in Berlin, that he hoped the Italian Ambassador in Moscow would tell Mussolini that there were signs of a 'natural evolution', with Molotov (Litvinov's replacement) making an approach to the German Ambassador, Schulenberg. This was a strong hint that Germany was making a political approach to Russia.[15]

Both Ciano and Ribbentrop have left detailed accounts of their conversations at Milan on 6 and 7 May. Ciano felt that an Italian–French war could be isolated, without involving Britain, but Ribbentrop disagreed. He thought Mussolini was playing with fire, having failed to realize the complete change in Britain's attitude following the Prague coup: Chamberlain's policy of appeasement was temporarily dead, and there was a new climate in the House of Commons and in British public opinion. Mussolini was deluding himself by believing that German military preparations were so incomplete that Germany could not go to war for a considerable period, but Ciano's forthright declaration that Italy could not possibly participate in an early war was disregarded by Ribbentrop; later (16 December 1939), Ciano was to tell the Chamber of Fascists that he had set the minimum period as three years, while Ribbentrop had implied four to five.

Mussolini agreed to Ribbentrop's proposals impulsively, in the course of a telephone conversation with Ciano. A grave weakness of the Pact from the Italian point of view was the lack of any clause binding the two dictators to consult – a surprising omission, when Hitler's move into Czechoslovakia without Mussolini's knowledge still rankled. Further serious defects from Mussolini's point of view were the lack of a secret protocol affirming a reciprocal obligation not to provoke a war for three years, and the failure to define the respective German and Italian spheres of influence in the Danube–Balkan region, to which Mussolini attached great importance.

The Pact of Steel was an important milestone for Italy. Mussolini rushed into it irresponsibly, and Ciano's diplomacy was ham-fisted; the Italians even allowed the Germans to draft the definitive document. However, at Mussolini's insistence Japan was left out of the Pact, which caused the Japanese considerable annoyance.

The Heads of Agreement reached at Milan were signed as the Pact of Steel in Berlin on 22 May. Mussolini had allowed himself to be trapped into pledging Italy to come to Germany's aid if Germany was involved in war: the impossibility of localizing any German attack on

Poland had escaped Mussolini, in his eagerness to flaunt this show of Axis strength before the democracies. Had he been aware of Germany's well-advanced plans to attack Poland in a few months' time, Mussolini must have seen the red light.

From Rome Lord Perth's successor as British Ambassador, Sir Percy Loraine, commented on the 'Pact of Steel':

> It seems highly probable that pressure to conclude alliance came from German side, and that it was very strong; one can guess that the negotiations for an anti-aggression pact between the UK, France and Russia coupled with the foreshadowed conclusion of an Anglo-Turkish agreement furnished Ribbentrop with powerful arguments in urging Italian Government to conclude alliance . . . There is no doubt that although the Italians would obey Signor Mussolini's orders, Italy's participation in a war for the sake of Germany would be intensely unpopular in this country.
>
> To judge by the very cordial welcome extended to myself, by obvious popularity of British jumping team at Rome Horse Show that ended yesterday (and equally obvious unpopularity of German team) and other indications . . . confirm the impression that the Prime Minister and yourself derived here, there is great friendliness and respect here for the UK and a strong desire . . . to let bygones be bygones.[16]

Sir Percy soon found himself in difficulties. Perth, like his predecessor, Sir Ronald Graham, had been uncritical of Fascism and sympathetic to Mussolini: Loraine was not so compliant.

Mussolini was cold although civil at his first interview with Loraine on 28 May. The Ambassador was put out when Mussolini observed that the conclusion of the Anglo-Turkish alliance and the imminent conclusion of an Anglo-Soviet Treaty 'made him reflect whether the Anglo-Italian Agreement possessed any further value; these treaties coupled with the other guarantees given represented a policy of encirclement of the Axis powers'. Loraine's reply was that after the Italian action in Albania 'it was perfectly open to Britain to maintain [that] the Mediterranean status quo which was a basic object of the Anglo-Italian Agreement had been altered, but they had refrained from raising the question', and that neither the Anglo-Turkish Agreement nor the prospect of an arrangement with Russia affected the status quo in the Mediterranean. Mussolini then stated that any act of encirclement directed against Germany was considered by him 'as likewise directed against Italy'. Not until the Duce said goodbye did he reveal to the new Ambassador the charm of his 'famous smile'. Loraine's final comment on his report of the meeting was: 'I fear the die is cast, and that the only argument is the visibility of overwhelming physical strength.'

The official British reply to Mussolini was that Britain continued to attach the same value to the maintenance of the Agreement as when they concluded it, and saw no reason why the Agreement should not be 'the keynote of Anglo-Italian relations for many years to come'; Britain was surprised at Mussolini's attitude in view of her action (more properly it should have been described as 'inaction') over Italy's occupation of Albania, and there was 'not a new line of policy'.

Hitler's stance over Danzig became ever more threatening, and on 5 July, in a personal message to Mussolini, Chamberlain emphasized that if Germany were to attack Poland in order to recover Danzig, Britain and France would fight for Poland and there would be a European war; and that the Poles were convinced that once Danzig was in German hands it would become a military base and used for dismembering the country and destroying its independence. Mussolini's response was that if war came and Britain fought beside Poland for Danzig, 'then Italy would fight for Germany'; but in his opinion Danzig was not worth a world war and Poland should cede it to Germany. Loraine agreed with the Duce that Britain would prefer a direct settlement of the Danzig question between the Poles and the Germans. Mussolini did not himself think that European war over Danzig would result at that time.[17]

In an important letter to Hitler on 30 May (known as the Cavallero Memorandum), Mussolini pointed out that since an eventual war between the democracies and Italy and Germany was 'inevitable', they should therefore make preparations; but there must be a preliminary period of at least three years of peace, to allow for rearmament, and for the Rome exhibition celebrating twenty years of Fascist rule to take place, in 1942. (The importance Mussolini attached to this Exhibition is childish, but endearing.) He also said he needed time to transfer his armament manufactories from the Po valley to the south, out of reach of bombing raids from French airfields. The Duce did not think there would be ground warfare in the west: unrealistically, he forecast that Italy could begin offensive operations against British and French colonies from Ethiopia. (This was absurd: Abyssinia, if the Suez Canal were closed, would fall easy prey to France and Britain.) Finally, Mussolini advocated occupying all the Danube and Balkan basins, so as to put out of action the 'guaranteed states' of Greece, Romania and Turkey; Hungary and Bulgaria would support the Axis.

This memorandum is so ill-argued that it is hard to believe Mussolini really foresaw Italy's entry into a European war, or that he in any way realized he was playing with fire.[18]

Cavallero spent ten days in Berlin after delivering the memorandum which bears his name, during which time none of the German leaders gave him any indication that the Führer entirely failed to share Mussolini's wish to defer war for three years. The German silence on this point was taken in Rome for agreement, but it was mere blatant deceit.

Lord Perth had always been optimistic that Mussolini felt an innate friendship for Britain; Sir Percy Loraine was not. On 21 July he reported that Mussolini had been burning the bridges between the two countries by converting the Axis into an alliance, and that the Italian press was 'venomous' against England. Against this, according to Loraine, Ciano apparently did not want war, had indeed told Loraine that neither Italy nor Germany wished for war, and that he looked forward to a long period of European peace. Loraine thought it impossible to 'wean' Italy from her German partner, and noted that in the light of the Anglo-Turkish Agreement and Anglo-French negotiations in Moscow for a military pact with Russia, Mussolini was accusing Britain of backsliding on the Anglo-Italian Agreement. Good points, according to Loraine, were the discontent among Italians over pro-German and anti-British government policy, and Grandi's influence in Rome (Grandi had left London to become Minister of Justice). Writing on 1 August, Loraine observed that he could see no way of relieving Anglo-Italian tension, and thought it best for Halifax to maintain his '*silence manquant*' in London, while he maintained his own '*silence souriant*' in Rome.[19]

Mussolini began at this time to show concern over Italy's military weakness and the toll the campaigns in Spain and Abyssinia had taken of his forces. He was fearful of British and French naval superiority in the Mediterranean. In addition he was also, as has been noted, absurdly keen on the International Exhibition to be held in Rome in 1942. Furthermore, there remained the problem of the friction between Germany and Italy over the German-speaking South Tyrol area of Italy. In June 1939 an understanding was reached by which the inhabitants could opt to be transferred to Germany, and rumours were fanned by some Germans that the whole area was to be ceded to Germany, with the Italian citizens moved to barren areas of south Italy. Trieste was also a worry: since the *Anschluss* Trieste had become impoverished through the diversion elsewhere of Austrian exports and imports, an agreement making it a free port for Germany having proved an insufficient recompense to the Triestini, who in addition felt themselves to be unpleasantly dependent on Hitler.

Mussolini began to torment himself as to the wisdom of the Pact of Steel, and was greatly disturbed when Ciano was asked to meet Ribbentrop in Salzburg on 11 August 1939. Unknown to Ciano and Mussolini, operational orders to his generals for the forcible seizure of

Danzig had been given by Hitler on 27 July, and organized moves to exacerbate the Polish crisis were being prepared by the Nazis.

As Ciano prepared to leave Rome for Salzburg on 10 August Mussolini ordered him to insist emphatically that all military action must be avoided, and that instead Germany should obtain Danzig through a European Conference. Mussolini told Ciano he 'should frankly inform the Germans that we must avoid a conflict with Poland since it would be impossible to localize it and a general war would be disastrous for everybody'. Ciano recorded: 'Never has the Duce spoken of the need for peace so unreservedly and with so much warmth. I entirely agree with him.'

Attolico, the Italian Ambassador in Berlin, had learnt something of German intentions, and insisted in his reports to Rome that Hitler had made up his mind to attack Poland. He did all he could to make Mussolini and Ciano realize they were being kept in the dark about the Führer's plans.

Ciano's worst fears were corroborated when he met Ribbentrop in Salzburg: Ribbentrop told him Hitler had implacably 'decided to fight', and that Germany was determined to destroy Poland. After ten hours of talking to Ribbentrop, Ciano accepted the fact that Hitler was set on war and would have nothing to do with any peaceful solution of the Danzig problem. Relations between Ciano and Ribbentrop became icy, and thenceforward Ciano was a convinced anti-Nazi.

Ciano saw Hitler on 12 August, and became even more alarmed when the Führer stated his determination to 'liquidate the Polish situation' by 15 October. Hitler's reasons were the 'provocation' given to Germany by Poland and the 'terror' in which the German minority lived there, together with information he had received that on 15 October Poland would occupy the Free City of Danzig and destroy it. Hitler maintained that fighting could be localized; although France and Britain would make anti-German gestures, they would never enter a war because their rearmament was incomplete and their morale low. The next day Ciano saw Hitler again; the Führer told him it would be better not to issue a press communiqué about their talks, in order 'to leave our hands free'. He also said that the Franco-British talks in Moscow were foundering, while the German–Russian talks were going well; this was true.

When Ciano mentioned that a period of peace for two to three years had been agreed, Hitler interrupted him, declaring that the situation had changed because of Polish provocation, but that he was certain Germany would not need to call upon Italian aid because there would not be a general conflict. He tried to allay Ciano's fear that Britain and France would declare war if Germany attacked Poland, saying that Britain would have to keep all her fighter planes at home because the German fleet would attack the British coast; and that Poland would be quickly defeated, whereupon Germany would be able to station a hundred divisions on the West Wall, the line of fortifications Germany had constructed behind the Franco-German border. Hitler maintained that the French would find it no more possible to overrun the Italian fortifications than they would the West Wall. Ciano disagreed, and told Hitler that he did not believe a war could be localized; furthermore, in a general conflict Italy would be short of all kinds of *matériel*; she would have to transfer her industries to the south, out of reach of Allied bombing raids; she had only two battleships, as against the twelve of the British and French; Abyssinia would be likely to revolt, completely cutting off the Italian army there; and the islands of the Italian Dodecanese would be in difficulties because of the attitude of Turkey. He argued that a general conflict should be postponed, and the Danzig question settled at a European Conference. He said that Mussolini wanted a gesture made by the Axis which would reaffirm the peaceful intentions of Italy and Germany; and he submitted a draft press statement.

Ciano was given short shrift by the Germans. Hitler abruptly rejected the idea of a conference, and declared that the problem of Danzig must be settled by the end of August – holding out the bait that Italy should then invade Yugoslavia. The conversation was interrupted by the arrival of a telegram from the German Embassy in Moscow to announce the agreement of the Russians that a political negotiator should be sent to Moscow from Berlin. Hitler was triumphant.

At their farewell meeting the next day Hitler told Ciano that he and Ribbentrop were agreed there should be no press statement; but to add to Ciano's alarm and anger, he found that, while he was flying back to Rome, Ribbentrop had issued a statement which included an assertion that Italy had declared she would always be on the side of Germany.

During these meetings, Hitler left Ciano in no doubt that he was about to invade Poland; in return, Ciano made it clear that Mussolini wanted the problem of Danzig settled by negotiation, and did not want to risk a war.[20]

Back in Rome, Ciano did what he could to arouse 'every possible anti-German feeling' in the Duce, pointing out that the Pact of Steel had been based on a promise of no war for the time being, and that the Germans had 'ditched' this pledge. At first Mussolini agreed with Ciano; he would break with Germany 'brutally and suddenly'.

Because of Britain's guarantee to Poland, he was now sure that Britain and France would fight. But then he began to shift his ground; sometimes he thought that the democracies might not fight, and that Germany 'would do good business cheaply', from which he did not want to be excluded. Within the week, Mussolini had again done an about-turn. In his diary for 21 August Ciano noted that he had said to Mussolini, 'Tear up the Pact, throw it in Hitler's face, and Europe will recognize in you the natural leader of the anti-German crusade.' But his arguments were in vain: Mussolini impetuously decided to go along with the Germans, and wrote to Hitler on 21 August:

1. If Germany attacks Poland and the conflict remains localized we shall give Germany the support that has been requested.
2. If Poland and the Allies attack Germany we will intervene on the side of Germany.
3. If Germany attacks Poland and France and England counter-attack, we will not take any initiative in warlike operations, given the actual state of our military preparations already communicated to the Führer and Ribbentrop.
4. If negotiations fail because of the Allies' intransigence and Germany intends to solve the dispute by arms we will intervene on Germany's side.

With this promise of intervention, with all its risks, Ciano knew that his attempts to keep Mussolini out of Hitler's embrace had failed. Mussolini was flouting the advice, not only of Ciano, but of the King and his military chiefs as well. However, four days later the Duce was to back-pedal yet again, oscillating between greed and fear.[21]

On 23 August Hitler scored a great diplomatic triumph when Stalin cancelled negotiations for a military agreement with France and Britain, and agreed instead to a non-intervention pact with Germany. The Germans had not informed Mussolini of the course of the negotiations in Moscow, so that the news came as a nasty bombshell for the Duce, in view of his hatred of Russia and Communism. Ciano recorded that on the morning of 25 August, by urging on him the King's opinions, he had dissuaded Mussolini from intervention and persuaded him to approve a letter to Hitler to this effect. Later in the morning the mercurial Mussolini changed his mind yet again, summoning Ciano to the Palazzo Chigi to tell him he wanted to intervene after all.

A letter from Hitler arrived at this point, explaining why the Führer had made his pact with Stalin, and why he had failed to keep the Italians informed. Hitler warned Mussolini that the German attack on Poland might take place at any moment, pointing out that the agreement with Russia had created a completely new situation which was 'the greatest possible gain for the Axis', and that Romania and Turkey would no longer be able to come in on the Franco-British side.[22]

Ciano argued successfully with his father-in-law that Italy must not fight; the Duce replied to Hitler late on 25 August that he completely approved of the agreement with Russia because it prevented encirclement of the Axis, but re-asserting that Italy was not in a position to go to war:

> If Germany attacks Poland and the conflict remains localized, Italy will give Germany every form of political and economic assistance which is requested of her. If Poland attacks and her allies open a counter-attack against Germany, I inform you in advance that it may be advisable for me not to take the *initiative* in military operations in view of the *current* state of Italian war preparations [Mussolini's emphases] . . . *Our intervention can take place at once if Germany delivers to us immediately the military supplies and the raw materials to resist the attack which the French and British would predominantly direct against us.*[23] [My italics. R.L.]

Mussolini also reminded Hitler that it had been agreed that war before 1942 was not envisaged, and emphasized that the military measures already taken and about to be taken by Italy would immobilize '*notevole*' (considerable) French and British forces in Europe and Africa. Thus Mussolini sought to evade war without formally denouncing the Pact of Steel.

The author is convinced Mussolini was not sincere when he stated that he 'completely approved' of the German–Russian Pact: he was always vehemently anti-Communist, and anti-Stalin. But at the end of August 1939 he was irrationally angered by the proposed treaty between Turkey and Britain, and this led him to adopt an anti-British stance. The Italian diplomatic historian Mario Toscano has made an in-depth study of this in his book *L'Italia e gli accordi Tedesco-Sovietico dell'agosto 1939*.

On 22 August Hitler had given his generals final detailed orders to launch the invasion of Poland on 28 August; on 25 August he countermanded them. One factor was Mussolini's refusal to go to war; the other was the announcement from London that the Anglo-Polish Treaty had been signed. In fact, the German Foreign Office attached too much importance to this treaty. Its signing was really only a formality, confirming what had been already agreed; but there is evidence that Hitler was considerably shaken by it. By some accounts, he was on the verge of a mental breakdown. Late on the night of 25 August he replied to Mussolini:

> You have informed me that you can enter a major European conflict only if Germany supplies you at once with implements of war and raw materials in order to resist the attack which the French and British would launch predominantly against you. I would ask you to inform me what imple-

ments of war and raw materials you require and within what time, so that I may be in a position to judge whether and to what extent I can fulfil your demands for implements of war and raw materials.

Furthermore, I thank you heartily for Italy's military measures, of which I have been acquainted in the meantime and which I already regard as a great relief.[24]

The next morning, 26 August, Mussolini and his armed services heads drew up a monster list of Italy's minimum war requirements from Germany. Ciano said it would be enough to kill a bull, 'if a bull could read it'; it was certainly unrealistic. It included 7 million tons of petroleum, 6 million tons of coal, 2 million tons of steel, one million tons of wood, and a long list of other colossal raw-materials requirements; additionally, Mussolini demanded 150 anti-aircraft batteries for the protection of the industrial areas of the north, and much machinery. He knew such demands could not be met by Germany. Ciano telephoned the list to the Ambassador in Berlin, Attolico, who immediately delivered it to Ribbentrop. On his own responsibility, without authority and in an effort to preserve peace, Attolico insisted that everything was required 'before hostilities began'.

Hitler replied to Mussolini that he could meet the call for coal and steel but not that for petroleum, and that delivery could not be made at once 'as Attolico asks'; in view of this, he now only requested the Duce 'to achieve the pinning down of Anglo-French forces by active propaganda and suitable military demonstrations'.

In a personal message to Hitler Mussolini cleared up the misunderstanding about delivery dates, saying that delivery within twelve months of everything except the anti-aircraft batteries would be acceptable; but, he noted, 'it is evident that it is impossible for you to assist me materially in filling the large gaps which the wars in Ethiopia and Spain have made in Italian armaments'; during the initial phase, therefore, he would immobilize the maximum Franco-British forces, and speed up his military preparations. He still felt, however, that in the interests of the German and Italian peoples, a 'political solution' should be sought.

Mussolini told von Mackensen, the German Ambassador in Rome, that refusing to go to war was a 'painful matter for him', but that he had no alternative because his country had waged war for five years 'and had been bled white' by the Spanish Civil War, at a cost of over 14,000 million lire, for which there would be little return. He also told the Ambassador he was convinced there could be a peaceful solution because Britain was putting the strongest pressure on Poland to avoid an armed conflict; and that 'the French and British would attack Italy in full force by land, sea and air immediately war broke out'.

These exchanges reveal how anxious Mussolini was to avoid war; he was especially concerned about the danger of bombing raids from French aerodromes on the industrial areas of Genoa, Milan and Turin. Mussolini wrote to Hitler on 27 August that he would keep the world guessing about Italy's attitude to a war; that he had concentrated troops on the French frontier and reinforced Libya; and that he was prepared to send to Germany (as Hitler had requested) 'the greatest possible number' of workers for industry and agriculture.[25]

According to Sir Percy Loraine, Italy was making no preparations for war; he reported to London on 23 August that Italy definitely would not go to war, and that British dispositions could safely be made on this assumption. At this stage Mussolini became far more cordial towards Britain. He welcomed British efforts to preserve peace, and particularly appreciated the way in which the British kept him informed of their negotiations with Germany, when his Axis partner was leaving him in the dark. He let it be known that he wanted to co-operate with Britain in finding a peaceful solution. Worried that his prestige might suffer from his refusal to support his ally, he pressed for another Munich-style conference.

Meanwhile Hitler was on the horns of a dilemma. His orders for the attack on Poland to begin on 28 August had been issued in the belief that Mussolini would also declare war, and the expectation that Britain and France would stand aside. It was a shock to find that Mussolini was ducking, and that Britain and France intended to stand by Poland. Although without Russian support the Poles could offer little resistance, Hitler's generals had warned him that the French would be able to break through the West Wall if they launched a resolute attack *en masse*, and that the French General Gamelin had promised the Poles to make such an attack fourteen days after the outbreak of hostilities. As the German Commander-in-Chief, Field Marshal Keitel, confirmed in evidence at the Nuremberg trials:

> A French attack during the Polish campaign would have encountered only a German military screen, not a real defence . . . We soldiers thought the Western powers had not serious intentions, because they did not take advantage of the extremely favourable situation.[26]

The German armies on the Polish borders could not be kept indefinitely in a state of readiness: they had either to attack, or be withdrawn. Frontier incidents were frequent. In Berlin, Goering tried to persuade Hitler to reach a negotiated settlement, while Ribbentrop and Himmler pushed him towards war. Goering, surprisingly, on 26 August sent a Swedish intermediary, Birger Dahlerus, to London to negotiate. Lord Halifax recalled Sir Nevile Henderson from the

British Embassy in Berlin, who reported that Hitler did not want war, provided he achieved his territorial claims on Poland – these, according to Henderson, were not 'exorbitant'.

Chamberlain and Halifax saw Dahlerus in Downing Street; they then sent a message – unorthodoxly, through Dahlerus rather than Henderson – to Hitler, via Goering, that Britain was ready to agree to the cession of Danzig and the Polish Corridor, and the return of Germany's former colonies. Together with Goering Dahlerus saw Hitler, and reported back to London that an amicable settlement was in sight.

Henderson was then sent back to Berlin with an official message that the British Cabinet wanted German–Polish negotiations started at once. After seeing Hitler, who was in a friendly mood, Henderson believed that if the Poles would negotiate in Berlin, another Munich was a possibility.

As early as 15 August an effort at mediation by Mussolini similar to the part he had played at Munich had been suggested by Henderson to Attolico, the Italian Ambassador, in Berlin. The two ambassadors agreed that neither Britain nor Italy could 'budge' from their proclaimed decisions – that Britain would support Poland and Italy Germany – but Attolico asked Henderson whether Chamberlain would feel himself in a position to make a move in conjunction with Mussolini. In Rome on 18 August, Loraine told Ciano that Britain was not opposed to a direct settlement between Poland and Germany of the Danzig question, and requested that 'if any Anglo-Italian consultation might help to preserve the peace', Ciano should send for him at once. He reported that Ciano was very friendly. Chamberlain had sent a message to Grandi secretly, via Dingli, to suggest that Mussolini intervene: on 27 August Grandi wrote, 'We are suddenly on the brink of Italian–British collaboration; we have at a stroke reconstituted the London–Rome Axis.'

Halifax wrote to Loraine to say he approved of the initiation by Mussolini of a conference in which Russia was to participate and Poland was to be treated on 'an equal footing'; he also sent a message to Mussolini expressing his faith in the Duce's ability to avert catastrophe. Anglo-Italian cordiality was firmly re-established on 23 August when Ciano saw Loraine and produced a plan in which Mussolini suggested that Danzig be returned to Germany, followed by negotiations and a 'great peace conference'. Mussolini had suddenly become warmer to Britain. Loraine was so moved that he nearly fainted.[27]

It was firmly believed in Whitehall that war could be prevented, at the price of the cession of Danzig and the Corridor and the accompanying boost to Hitler's popularity in Germany. The chief worry in

Downing Street was whether the nation would endorse a further surrender to Hitler on the Munich model. As Halifax noted, 'Everybody
felt that if Hitler insists on invading Poland there is nothing to do but
smash him.'[28]

It is possible that on 28 August Hitler – often unpredictable – was
genuinely considering a peaceful settlement, prevailed upon for once
by Goering rather than Ribbentrop. But the next day, 29 August, he
changed his mind and plumped for war. When Henderson set off for
the Chancellery he was confident that 'Hitler was ready to open
negotiations with the Poles'; instead, to his consternation, he found
Hitler cold and uncompromising, stating that the Poles must immediately either sign or reject proposals drafted by the German Foreign
Office for Danzig and the Corridor. The Führer demanded that a
Polish emissary with full powers should arrive in Berlin the next day
(30 August). When Henderson remarked that this sounded like an
ultimatum, the interview became stormy. Ribbentrop, working
behind Goering's back, had persuaded Hitler to insert the demand for
a Polish delegation to come to Berlin within twenty-four hours, cal-
culating that this would make war inevitable because the proud Poles
would not agree. However, Goering now sent a message through
Dahlerus to Downing Street that a peaceful solution was still possible.
From Downing Street Dahlerus had several telephone conversations
with Goering, who insisted that 'it was an absolute condition that
someone should come from Warsaw to Berlin to negotiate'.[29]

In the light of these messages, Halifax and Chamberlain agreed they
must pressurize Poland to send emissaries to Berlin at once.
Chamberlain, ready to force Poland to yield to Hitler's demands, stipulated only that the capitulation must bear the outward appearance of
being the result of diplomatic negotiations, not an ignominious surrender to Hitler's ultimatum. Halifax accordingly instructed Sir
Howard Kennard, the British Ambassador in Poland, to urge the
Polish government to despatch emissaries to Berlin to negotiate with
Hitler, describing the German terms as not the 'minimum', and reassuring the Polish government of British support. Colonel Józef Beck,
the Polish Prime Minister, refused out of hand to go himself to Berlin,
saying he would not put himself in the same position as Emil Hácha,
the President of Czechoslovakia, in March.

On 31 August Henderson was given a copy of what Hitler called
'generous terms' for Poland, which included the cession of Danzig,
and a plebiscite and exchange of populations in the area of the
Corridor. Henderson thought the terms 'sounded moderate'.
However, it is improbable that Hitler was still making a serious effort
to avert war. He took no steps to postpone the invasion he had ordered

to start during the night of 31 August/1 September, and his demand for a Polish plenipotentiary to arrive urgently in Berlin must have been intentionally unrealistic. The Poles declined to respond; Josef Lipski, the Polish Ambassador in Berlin, even declared that he was uninterested in the terms, because if war came the Nazis would be defeated and 'the Polish army would arrive in Berlin in triumph'. He agreed to see Ribbentrop, but the interview was fruitless, since Lipski stated firmly that he had no authority to enter into negotiations. This was exactly what Ribbentrop wanted, and he eagerly reported it to Hitler. Yet it is conceivable that if a senior Polish plenipotentiary had humiliated himself and his nation by coming immediately to Berlin to give Hitler another glittering diplomatic triumph, the Führer might have stayed his hand.

In conversation with Sir Percy Loraine, Ciano made it clear that Mussolini and he were in deadly earnest in their wish to avert war; in his diary for 31 August he paints a dramatic picture:

> An ugly awakening. Attolico telephones at nine saying that the situation is desperate and that unless something new comes up there will be war in a few hours. I go quickly to Palazzo Venezia. We must find a new solution. In agreement with the Duce I telephone Halifax to tell him that the Duce can intervene with Hitler only if he brings a fat prize: Danzig. Empty-handed he can do nothing . . . Lord Halifax asks me to bring pressure on Berlin so that . . . direct contacts can be established between Germany and Poland.

On 29 August Mussolini had strongly advised Hitler to settle the crisis by negotiation; on the morning of 31 August he suggested to Britain and France that a conference be held at San Remo on 5 September to review the Treaty of Versailles in an attempt to prevent war between Germany and Poland. At the same time he authorized Ciano to tell Loraine that Italy would not fight against France and Britain if Germany went to war, thereby confirming Loraine's personal conviction that Italy would not fight, already reported to London. On the morning of 31 August Ciano telephoned Halifax to tell him the Italian Ambassador in Berlin had warned that the situation was extremely serious, and there would be war if it did not take a new turn within a few hours. He went on to tell Halifax that Mussolini felt 'it would be useless' in the present situation for him to intervene again with the Führer unless he had something new to use, but 'if the Polish Government were to inform Italy and Britain that Poland would give up her rights in Danzig he would propose to Hitler a Conference on the other issues in dispute.' Ciano emphasized Mussolini's conviction that he needed something new to offer the Führer.[30]

Halifax's immediate reaction was that it was unlikely Poland would agree to hand over Danzig without knowing what arrangements would be made for safeguarding her interests there, and what other proposals Germany might make; but he promised to make a further communication. During the afternoon of 31 August he replied by telephone to Ciano, explaining that he could not agree to the proposal because, in spite of their 'best desire' to co-operate with Mussolini, he and the Prime Minister felt it would be impossible to ask Poland to give up her rights in Danzig in advance of negotiations. Thus did the Duce's plan for a 'second Munich' to take place on 5 September wither.

Could Mussolini's plan for a conference have saved peace at the eleventh hour? It is surprising that Britain should have rejected it so summarily, since she had already been urging Poland to cede Danzig, which represented a much smaller sacrifice than Chamberlain had demanded of Czechoslovakia at Munich. Probably Hitler had irrevocably decided on war; however, had Mussolini's proposal been made public, to have rejected it out of hand would have stamped Hitler as a blatant aggressor. Mussolini, smarting under the recent shock of the Ribbentrop–Molotov Pact, was anxious to co-operate with France and Britain, regretting his alliance with Hitler.

Unfortunately, on the morning of 31 August the British suddenly cut all telephone communications between London and Rome; quite why is unclear. It occurred just after Ciano had told Loraine Italy would not fight Britain. Ciano was much upset, telling Loraine later that it had every appearance of being the precursor of a state of hostility, and asking if it was possible 'that after these days of close co-operation for preservation of peace His Majesty's Government could have failed to understand Italy's true feelings and attitude?' Fortunately, at Loraine's insistence orders were soon given in London to restore telephone communications.

At 4.30 a.m. on the morning of 1 September 1939 the German army invaded Poland, crossing the frontier in the wake of a fabricated incident at a border railway station in which German criminals in Polish uniform were barbarously murdered by German soldiers, in simulation of a Polish attack. Warsaw, Cracow, Katowice and other towns were bombed: the Polish Ambassador in London immediately asked Halifax for assistance from the RAF. It was not forthcoming. Dahlerus telephoned to the Foreign Office with a curious message to the effect that Hitler's intentions were peaceful, and that he did not want war, but direct negotiations with Britain – a message apparently confirmed to some degree when Henderson telegraphed that a speech made by Hitler in the Reichstag that morning might be the prelude to another effort at peace. When the Cabinet met at 11.30

a.m. and were told of these two messages, they did not at once accept the inevitability of war.

The Cabinet would have preferred another Mussolini-inspired conference to an immediate declaration of war. They had liked Ciano's lunch-time message of the day before, when he told Loraine of Mussolini's calculation that if, when putting the suggestion of a conference at San Remo to Hitler, he could state that France and Britain had agreed in principle, Hitler could hardly refuse 'or the cat will be belled' – although, as Halifax reminded them, this conversation had been overtaken by events. The House of Commons was then told that a 'Note' had been sent to the German government; some MPs doubted the strength of the Note, and there was indeed no mention in it of a time limit, only a demand to Germany 'promptly to withdraw their forces from Polish territory'.

Both Halifax and Cadogan telephoned to Bonnet, the French Foreign Minister, to enquire the French reaction to Mussolini's proposal for a conference. Bonnet personally favoured the idea; when Cadogan asked whether German withdrawal from Poland should be a prerequisite, Bonnet said they would 'deliberate'. Both the French and the British governments lacked resolution. The French Premier, Daladier, showed more courage: at first he said he would rather resign than agree to a conference. He was overruled by his Cabinet, and during the early hours of 2 September the French issued a statement that they were giving a favourable response to the Duce's suggestion of a conference. Hitler had sent a message to Ciano enquiring whether the British and French Notes were 'ultimata'. Loraine assured Ciano that the British Note was only a warning, not an ultimatum, and through Ciano Hitler then asked whether he could have until noon on 3 September to consider the question of an armistice and the Duce's proposed conference. In his diary, Ciano recorded: 'Contrary to what I expected Hitler does not reject the proposal absolutely.' But in fact Hitler was only playing for time, to delay British and French intervention. He had no intention of halting his troops' advance into Poland.

At 2.15 p.m. on 2 September Ciano telephoned Halifax. The Foreign Secretary confirmed Loraine's assurance that the British Note of the previous day was not an ultimatum, but told Ciano firmly that Britain would not agree to a conference unless Hitler withdrew his troops from Polish soil. At the Cabinet meeting following this conversation Halifax put Mussolini's proposal for a conference to the ministers. He stressed to his colleagues, too, that the British Note to Germany was not an ultimatum, and although he pointed out that it would be very difficult to conduct negotiations with Germany while

German troops were occupying Polish territory, he betrayed his personal hankering for the conference when he said he thought Britain 'might be prepared to consider an extension of the time limit until midnight of 3/4 September'. Chamberlain was also weak; he asked, 'Should we give Germany more time to consider the Duce's proposal?' The other ministers, alarmed, objected strongly, over-ruled Chamberlain and Halifax, and decided that Germany should be allowed no longer than until midnight that evening (2/3 September) to withdraw her troops from Polish soil.

At 5.22 p.m. Loraine telephoned to tell Halifax that when Ciano heard that a conference must depend on the withdrawal of German troops from Poland, he (Ciano) had declared there was no chance of the Duce proceeding further. At 6.28 p.m. Halifax telephoned to Ciano and told him the Cabinet would not 'favour' a conference as long as German troops were on Polish soil. Ciano replied that Hitler would not accept this condition. Halifax then 'urged him to try his best – if he could accomplish this it would be possible to get back to the original basis of negotiations', but it was also essential that Danzig should revert to the status quo. Ciano repeated that Hitler would not accept this. Halifax then emphasized that the Note to Hitler was not an ultimatum, but Ciano repeated a third time that the whole scheme was 'impossible for Hitler'. When Halifax told him Chamberlain was about to make a statement in the House of Commons concerning the proposed conference, Ciano remarked that in his opinion it would be better not to mention it. Finally, Halifax asked Ciano again 'to do his best with Berlin'. But as Halifax put down the receiver at 6.45 p.m. on 2 September, it was clear that the conference proposal was dead: as Ciano recorded in his diary, with this conversation 'the last note of hope has died.' Bonnet had asked Ciano if he could not achieve 'a symbolic withdrawal of German forces from Poland'; Ciano recorded that he threw this proposal into the waste-paper basket. So, as Chamberlain prepared his speech for the Commons on the evening of 2 September, Mussolini's conference proposal was still-born, and the British Cabinet had plumped for an immediate declaration of war. Obstinately, Chamberlain refused to accept this. Disregarding the Cabinet decision, 'in limping phrases' Chamberlain explained to the House of Commons that Britain and France were considering what further time limit to give to Hitler:

> Delay may be caused by the Italian proposal that hostilities should cease and there should be an immediate Conference between five powers – Britain, France, Poland, Germany and Italy. If the German Government should agree to withdraw their forces then HMG would be willing to regard the position as being the same as it was before the German forces

crossed the frontier. I am the last man to neglect any opportunity which I consider affords a serious chance of avoiding the great catastrophe of war at the last moment.

An ugly scene ensued in the House. The Labour front bencher Arthur Greenwood summed it up: 'Resentment, apprehension, anger reigned over our proceedings last night, aroused by fear that delays might end in national dishonour and sacrifice of the Polish people to German tyranny.'

Cabinet members were appalled by Chamberlain's speech. In a body they confronted the Prime Minister in his private room in the House of Commons before he went home. Collectively they informed him that he must not face the House again unless he was ready to announce the expiry date of an ultimatum to Germany. Chamberlain then did a U-turn and telephoned the French Premier. He told Daladier there had been an angry scene in the House, and that unless the French agreed to an early time limit 'it would be impossible to hold the situation here'. Chamberlain proposed an ultimatum to be delivered in Berlin at 8 a.m. the next day, 3 September, giving the Germans until noon Berlin time that day to decide. Reluctantly, Daladier agreed. Chamberlain's reputation would stand higher if he had made this call to Daladier before, rather than after, his hostile reception in the House. At an emergency Cabinet meeting held at 11.30 p.m. on 2 September it was decided to instruct Henderson to deliver the ultimatum to the German government the next morning: unless Germany started to withdraw her forces from Polish territory by 11 a.m. on 3 September, a state of war existed as from that hour. The French fell into line. Britain duly declared war at 11 a.m., France at 5 p.m.

Italy stayed neutral. Her declaration of war on France and Britain, so feared during the summer, had been avoided, and the Axis was temporarily broken. Shocked by the unexpected Soviet–German Pact, Mussolini had done his best to prevent the outbreak of the Second World War. Britain and France had agreed with him that Hitler should be appeased by Poland's cession to Germany of Danzig and the Corridor – but Hitler had decided on a military triumph in Poland come what might, and ignored Mussolini's peace efforts.[31]

CHAPTER 15

Mussolini on the Brink of War

MUSSOLINI WAS CALMER after his announcement that Italy would stay neutral. He had become increasingly frightened of a knock-out blow by France and Britain through devastating air bombardment of the industrial zones of Turin and Milan combined with hostile sweeps by the more powerful Mediterranean fleets of the French and British navies. He was right to be apprehensive: a succession of Italian military disasters in the autumn of 1939 and the early months of 1940, before the spectacular German victories in the west of May 1940, would have toppled him and his Fascist regime.

Italy's status was ambiguous, but British Cabinet Ministers were content that she should remain 'non-belligerent', and rejected any thought of an ultimatum. The War Cabinet, meeting on 4 September, complacently concluded that Italy 'had further to go now than she had in 1914 before she would be induced to throw in her lot with us'.

However, Mussolini was concerned lest in the eyes of the Germans he might be considered a traitor; he therefore solicited a formal letter from Hitler releasing him from his obligations under the 'Pact of Steel'. Hitler's reply of 3 September was magnanimous; he thanked the Duce for his last-minute effort at intervention, and claimed he would have been happy to accept if there had been certain guarantees about the successful outcome of the conference Mussolini had proposed; but, he said, he could not put at risk the sacrifices of blood his army had made during their rapid advance into Poland, and because of the British attitude he did not think peace could have been preserved for more than six months or a year at most.

> You recently have amicably assured me of your help in other fields. I acknowledge this in advance warmly. However I believe besides that even if we now march on separate paths our destiny will continue to bind us together. If German Nazidom were to be destroyed by the western democracies Italian Fascism would also have a grim future.

When he read the letter, delivered personally by the German Ambassador von Mackensen, the Duce was apologetic about his peace efforts. He said he had never had even the 'remotest thought' of engaging in any mediation which was in any way conditional on the withdrawal of German troops.

> England's declaration of war which France had followed only with hesitation was positive 'idiocy' hatched by people who evidently had not even studied a map . . . On land, breaking out from the Maginot Line and overrunning the West Wall was a hopeless undertaking which the French were unlikely to attempt. The western powers' challenge to fight was an utterly absurd undertaking.
>
> Where the Führer's message stated that the Führer and Duce were 'now marching on separate paths' he had to disagree quite emphatically . . . agreement was complete as to the road and goal, and he had done everything, especially in the military field, that the Führer now wished him to do, and was continuing his preparations in the most intensive manner. September would still be a critical month for him in Libya but its end would find him prepared for effective defence there also. Already his measures at the Alpine border and in Africa were containing more than 400,000 men on the enemy side.

Had the British Cabinet known of this, they might not have been so complacent. Chamberlain smugly believed that his joint efforts with Grandi to placate Mussolini (against Eden's wishes) in 1938 had prevented Italy coming into the war. On 13 September he wrote to Grandi: 'I know how steadfastly and effectively you strove while you were in London for [the] same ends and without your help I doubt whether I could have achieved anything.'[1]

Mussolini read Hitler's telegram to the Council of Ministers, and emphasized that Italy had in no way betrayed Germany, because no promise had been given to declare war before 1942. To Mussolini's annoyance Grandi, now Minister of Justice, said that Italy was indeed not traitorous, but had herself been betrayed by Germany; Ciano pointed out that the Molotov–Ribbentrop Pact had been made without Italy's knowledge. With applause, the Council approved the declaration of Italian neutrality.

Mussolini was far from giving unconditional support to Germany in what became known as the 'phoney war'; he hoped to resume his role as peace-maker, and meanwhile to make as much commercial profit as possible from Italy's neutrality. Ciano for his part felt he had been grossly deceived, both by Ribbentrop at Milan and by the Molotov–Ribbentrop Pact; he was intensely anti-Nazi, and commented in his diary: 'I acquiesce in war against Germany but not with Germany. This is my point of view. Mussolini's point of view is exactly the opposite. He would never have war against Germany, and when we are ready he would fight.'

The Duce was conscious that in Germany he was being called a traitor, and that his conduct was being compared to Italy's in 1914, when she had refused to honour her alliance with Germany and Austria; he had always liked to pose as a war leader, and he thought 'neutrality' was derogatory to Fascism. However, above all he was an opportunist: vacillating, and unsure on which side his bread was buttered, he had an inflated opinion of the efficiency of the French army and the strength of the Maginot Line, and was far from confident that Hitler would be successful if he attacked in the west. He knew, too, that his popularity and his ability to manipulate Italian public opinion would enable him to retain power even if he changed camps. So he kept his options open.

At times he talked of a 'parallel war' – meaning an Italian assault on Greece and Yugoslavia without engaging in the war against France and Britain; he felt this would give him great influence at the post-war peace conference. In spite of the Pact of Steel, Mussolini also continued with massive new fortifications on his alpine frontier with Austria – surely an expression of his mistrust of Hitler.

For the first two months of the war Mussolini continued to hope for a negotiated peace, in which Germany would establish a Polish government in the rump of the country as a concession to France and Britain. On 23 September he told Fascist leaders at Bologna that 'with Poland liquidated the West had no valid war aims'. When the Fascist Grand Council met on 7 December Mussolini more or less adopted Ciano's anti-German line. He said that a victory by either of the 'two lions locked in the struggle would be a disaster for Italy, and the best outcome would be that the two lions tear each other to pieces until they leave their tails on the ground and we possibly can go and scoop them up'.[2]

With Mussolini taking this attitude, Ciano put before him the draft of a strong anti-German speech he planned to make in the Italian parliament on 16 December. Ciano described it as 'a very insidious speech which if accepted in its present form by the Duce will definitely destroy or at least undermine our relations with Germany, which are materially worsening', and the next day recorded Mussolini's complete approval.

In his speech Ciano reminded parliament that the object of the Anti-Comintern Pact had been to consolidate the anti-Communist bloc; it was the logical consequence of the consistent policy of the Duce, who had been the first man in the world to denounce the peril of Bolshevism, and to combat it not only in the streets of Italy but on the battlefields of Spain. Ciano then explicitly condemned the Molotov–Ribbentrop Pact. He accused Germany of a breach of faith, describing how during his meeting with Ribbentrop in Milan in May they had agreed they must make every effort to preserve peace in Europe for some time, in order to complete their internal reconstruction and their military preparations. This period of time had been defined as three years by the Italians and four to five years by the Germans, and on this premise the Pact of Steel had been signed on 22 May. Shortly afterwards the Polish crisis had arisen and Italy had proposed a settlement through normal diplomatic channels, but Germany would not accept the delays involved in diplomatic negotiations. Ciano concluded:

> It is universally recognized that it is the realistic attitude of Italy which has hitherto prevented the extension of the war; and it is towards our country that the eyes of all states are turning who wish to safeguard, together with their own interests, the peace of the world.

Ciano was delighted with his speech. He recorded that it was 'a great success', with the German Ambassador listening in silence and showing his disappointment, while Loraine was 'highly satisfied'. In his diary he wrote:

> It was difficult formerly to persuade the Italians to march side by side with the Germans; it is impossible now, despite their pledged word, since they know the whole truth . . . They consider my speech to be the real funeral of the Axis.

Mussolini ordered front-page treatment: the speech was acclaimed all over Italy, and the Italian people were delighted with it. The Nazis were angry; Ribbentrop was reliably reported to the Italian Embassy as being in a state of fury. Ciano commented, 'Berlin are swallowing a bitter pill.'[3]

The speech astonished the world. Although Ciano had strongly criticized Britain and France for destroying the Duce's attempts at mediation, the main publicity focused on Germany's treachery in going back on her Anti-Comintern policy, and on how she had jumped into the war despite her undertaking to Italy not to do so for three years. In London, *The Spectator* commented: 'It was a cool, dignified and most adroit statement . . . and significantly frank in its disclosure of certain facts not hitherto made public.'

Loraine saw Ciano on 17 December; he was less enthusiastic about the speech than perhaps he might have been, pointing out that he could not be expected to share Ciano's opinion that the blame for the outbreak of hostilities rested with the Western Powers; however, as he reported, 'on the whole I felt able to congratulate him'. He also reported that when Ciano spoke of Salzburg and of Germany's default on her obligations to Italy, his eyes flashed with indignation. But Loraine also told Ciano coldly that in the light of his speech he felt 'that the moment when he and I could speak intimately about a number of things of common interest was further off than I could have wished'. In the Foreign Office, Sir Andrew Noble minuted that in his talk with Loraine Ciano had skated delicately around the passages that were likely to be 'unpalatable' to Britain, implying that Britain need not take them too seriously because they had only been put in to hold the balance together. Loraine here missed a good opportunity to press Ciano for greater Anglo-Italian friendship.

Strangely Chamberlain, although secretly through Dingli he sent a most cordial message to Ciano that he would in no way interfere with Italy, did not view the speech positively. It was a mistake not to seize the hand held out and assure Mussolini that British friendship was his for the asking.[4]

On 3 January 1940 Mussolini wrote to Hitler, expressing the anti-German feeling prevalent among the Italian people. The letter was not only critical but also a warning, almost hostile in places. Mussolini confirmed that everything Ciano had said in his speech coincided with his own views, although he knew that some parts of it had not pleased in certain German circles.

> The German–Russian agreement has had painful repercussions in Spain. The Civil War is too recent. The earth which covers the dead – yours and ours and the Spanish – is still fresh. The relations of Italy with the French and the British are correct but cool. We are supplying both with goods of various kinds, some of which may indirectly aid the war effort, but all deliveries of a typically military nature have been prohibited. Between us and the British there was a period of strong tension in connection with the blockade [the Allied naval blockade imposed against German shipping], and although the procedures of the British have been modified for the better, things are far from normal.
>
> British propaganda is emphasizing two facts, namely the Russo-German agreements which in practice mark the end of the Anti-Comintern Pact, and the treatment which is said to have been meted out in Poland to the genuinely Polish population. It is my conviction that the creation of a modest disarmed Poland, which is exclusively Polish, liberated from the Jews – for whom I fully approve your project of gathering them all in a large ghetto in Lublin – can no longer constitute any threat to the greater Reich. I believe that the creation of a Polish state under the German aegis would be an element that would resolve the war and constitute a condition sufficient for the peace.

Obviously Mussolini had little faith in Germany's ability to win in the west, because he wrote:

> Great Britain and France will never succeed in making your Germany assisted by Italy capitulate, but it is not certain that it will be possible to bring the French and British to their knees, or even divide them. To believe that is to delude oneself. The United States would not permit a total defeat of the democracies.

Mussolini continued by advising Hitler to solve his *Lebensraum* problem at the expense of Russia, and warned that

> a further step in your relations with Russia would have catastrophic repercussions in Italy where the anti-Bolshevik unanimity especially among the Fascist masses is absolutely solid as a rock and indivisible . . . Until four months ago Russia was world enemy number one; she cannot have become, and is not, friend number one.

Inconsistently, however, Mussolini concluded by stating that 'Italy intends to constitute at this time your reserve', and that he would 'intervene militarily when the aid will not be a burden but a relief to you'.[5]

This letter makes it clear Mussolini had high hopes that Hitler would conclude a peace with the West and then make war on Russia, and seems to indicate too that a generous approach by France and Britain in January 1940 might yet have detached Mussolini from Hitler. While he was undoubtedly antagonized by the Allied naval blockade, he was at the same time having problems with the Germans in the Alto Adige where, without giving the subject sufficient thought, he had agreed that the State would buy the property of anyone of German descent who opted to leave the South Tyrol; now, with German propaganda increasing the number of those going, an almost intolerable burden was being put on Italian finances.

Mussolini's displeasure with Germany had been further fanned by a provocative speech by the Sudeten German Vice-Mayor of Prague, Josef Pfitzner, who had declared that 'not a single Alpine peak should remain in Italian hands. Germany should roll into the Po Valley, seize Trieste and dominate the Balkans and the eastern Mediterranean.' It was typical of his disillusionment with Hitler that on 26 December Mussolini should have ordered Ciano to pass to the Belgian and Dutch ambassadors in Rome news from the German military attaché in Rome that the German offensive in the west was imminent and would include a lightning invasion of the Low Countries. On that day, Ciano recorded, Mussolini 'for the first time' wanted the Germans defeated.[6]

Mussolini was not consistently anti–German; the records of Ciano and Anfuso, the Duce's principal private secretary, show that he was continually changing his mind. An interesting memorandum by Plessen of the German Embassy in Rome, also dated 3 January 1940, reads:

> The question whether Mussolini intends to enter the war actively on our side cannot be answered with a simple 'Yes' or 'No'. It is impossible to see whether it will seem correct to him. If at the given time Mussolini thinks he can achieve his aims by peaceful means, he will not take military measures.[7]

Hitler was put out by Mussolini's letter of 3 January 1940. He read it 'with avidity' and then discussed it for five hours with Ribbentrop and Goering. He concluded that Italy would only enter the war in the event of great German successes, and that in any case there would not be much advantage in Italy taking part because of the strain she would impose on German supplies. Hitler decided to bide his time before replying.

Unfortunately Britain decided that the Allied blockade of German shipping must take precedence over good relations with Mussolini. Italy was acutely short of coal and since Germany could not satisfy her needs by rail overland through Switzerland, she was also supplying her by sea through Rotterdam. In the middle of February 1940 Britain decided to stop the ships carrying German coal from Rotterdam as from 1 March, and instead to offer Italy British coal, to be paid for in guns and war *matériel*. Mussolini reacted angrily, refusing to sell Britain arms, even though this refusal would cause acute trouble for Italy's balance of payments, and sent strong notes of protest to the British Embassy. Loraine was alarmed, and warned that Mussolini could justifiably claim that the blockade would cause serious damage to the Italian economy through shortage of coal, and that if the measures proposed were activated on 1 March, it would make a crisis inevitable. Ciano told Noel Charles, of the British Embassy in Rome, that the measures Britain proposed taking over coal were 'the sort that will push Italy into the hands of Germany'. Mussolini was furious when the British subsequently seized thirteen coal ships leaving Rotterdam, telling Ciano on 6 March, 'It is not possible that of all people I should become the laughing-stock of Europe. I have to stand for one humiliation after another. As soon as I am ready I shall make the British repent. My intervention in the war will bring about their defeat.' To pacify Mussolini Halifax later ordered the ships to be released, but the damage to the Duce's pride continued to rankle.

Profiting from Mussolini's anger, Hitler sent Ribbentrop to Rome on 10 March to lure him into coming into the war. Ribbentrop bore a message from Hitler to the Duce that he proposed shortly to attack in the west. Mussolini told Ribbentrop that it would be impossible for Italy to stay out of the conflict, and at the 'proper time' she would join the war on Germany's side. He was also adamant that any request from Britain for delivery of cannon, armoured cars or bombers would receive a categorical 'No': 'They will not get a single nail for military purposes.' Nevertheless, Ribbentrop wrote from Rome to Berlin, 'I have no indication at all as to what attitude the Duce will take.' In this he showed some perspicuity, for in private Mussolini told Ciano he did not believe 'in a complete German success' and had not come to a firm conclusion.[8]

Ciano told the French Ambassador, François-Poncet, that Ribbentrop's visit 'had not been a success', and D'Arcy Osborne, the British Minister to the Holy See, confirmed to the Foreign Office from his soundings at neutral embassies that Ribbentrop's visit had indeed not been the success the Germans claimed. However, Ribbentrop had invited Mussolini to a conference with the Führer on the Brenner Pass, and against Ciano's advice, Mussolini had accepted.

Meanwhile, Roosevelt had sent his peace emissary Sumner Welles to Europe to talk to the British, French, Italians and Germans. Mussolini was not intent on war: he told Ciano, 'I shall agree to enter the war, but reserve for myself the choice of the moment. I alone intend to be the judge, and a great deal will depend upon how the war goes.' In a significant comment he told Welles that at the Brenner he would try to dissuade Hitler from an offensive in the west, and said that although the Italo-German Pact existed, 'I none the less retain complete freedom of action.' Mussolini wanted to tell Hitler that Roosevelt had offered to mediate, and said to Welles that if he was to be successful in persuading Hitler to postpone his offensive, he must give him some hope that the Western Allies would not 'be completely intransigent' over the German insistence on *Lebensraum*. Roosevelt refused to give Mussolini any mandate for negotiations, and Mussolini did not raise the subject with Hitler.[9]

Hitler and Mussolini met on the Brenner Pass on 18 March 1940, during a snowstorm.

As Hitler's interpreter Paul Schmidt has explained, the Hitler–Mussolini meetings were never discussions in any true sense of the word. Hitler preferred a monologue: he did eighty to ninety per cent of the talking, with Mussolini only getting in a few words at the end. On this occasion, following his successes in Austria, Czecho-slovakia and Poland, Hitler was clearly the dominant partner in the Axis. He gave Mussolini a boringly repetitive account of the Polish campaign, and illustrated the strength of the German army with endless statistics. But he carefully avoided giving Mussolini any details whatsoever of the German plans for attack in the west – knowing too well how everything was leaked in Rome. (The attack on Norway and Denmark was scheduled for three weeks' time, but Mussolini was told nothing.) Hitler emphasized his absolute certainty of an early victory over Britain and France.[10]

Cautiously and tactfully, Hitler indicated to Mussolini that if Italy was content to remain a second-rate power in the Mediterranean, she need do nothing; if, on the other hand, she wanted first-class status, she would always find Britain and France blocking her path. The victory of Germany would be the victory of Italy; similarly, the defeat of Germany would spell the end of the Italian Empire.

According to the German account, the Duce declared to Hitler that as soon as Germany had created a favourable military situation with her attack to the west he would enter the war without losing any time, and if the German advance lost its rhythm he would wait until the moment when his intervention at the critical hour would be of real help to Germany. Still he was evasive when Hitler made suggestions for the Italian army to co-operate in an attack on the Maginot Line. A few days later Hitler followed up this meeting by instructing the German military attaché in Rome to submit to the Italian General Staff a plan for the despatch of twenty to thirty Italian divisions to southern Germany where, with the Seventh German Army, they would cross the Rhine and advance through the Belfort Gap.

The plan was put to Marshal Graziani and General Roatta, who replied that they could not entertain such a proposition. Badoglio, Commander-in-Chief of the Armed Forces, registered strong opposition, as did Mussolini. The evidence is clear that Mussolini had deceived Hitler over Italy's readiness to take part in the war. Indeed, Ciano certainly did not take the Duce's belligerency seriously: he told Loraine that the Brenner meeting was 'no prelude to surprises in our policy'. He recorded in his diary Mussolini's belief that 'Hitler will think twice before he jumps into an offensive', and his conviction that Hitler was 'not preparing to launch his land offensive'. After reading the minutes of the Brenner meeting, Mussolini told Ciano he intended to write to Hitler to dissuade him from attempting a land offensive 'which is equivalent to putting all his money on a single card'. Grandi, who was now President of the Chamber, was sure Mussolini still hoped to organize another peace conference like Munich.

Loraine reported to London on 28 March: 'I do not think there is any immediate danger of a sudden move to war', but that Italian propaganda had taken on 'a seriously anti-Allied complexion . . . few people here think that Mussolini would dare to over-ride the opposition of the King and industrialists unless he felt certain victory was just going to fall into his hands.' On 30 March Charles talked to Ciano, who told him that 'nothing sensational was going to occur' and 'we must keep in close contact', and assured him the attitude of the Italian press mattered nothing. Ciano was determined to keep Italy out of the war, but the mercurial Mussolini was still oscillating.[11]

Suddenly, on 2 April, Mussolini again became intent on war, telling Ciano that the Germans would win. He may have been influenced by the passivity of France and Britain, and by a weak message from Chamberlain through the secret Dingli channel suggesting that Italy should be a mediator in arranging a compromise peace – Mussolini probably interpreted this as indicating Britain's lack of will to fight. According to Ciano, Mussolini now wanted full steam ahead 'to open conflict if France and Britain really intend as they announce to tighten the blockade', and believed blindly in a German victory and in the word of Hitler concerning 'our share of the booty'.

On 9 April Hitler launched his attack on Norway and Denmark, sending the news to Mussolini after the attack had already begun; this was followed by four further messages telling the Duce how well the campaign was going for Germany. Mussolini, although still keeping his options open, became keener on war. The Germans requested the removal of the Italian Ambassador in Germany, Bernardo Attolico, who was a determined opponent of Italy's entry into the war and a source of personal irritation to Ribbentrop; Mussolini acquiesced, replacing him with Dino Alfieri. Yet Mussolini did not sack Attolico: he appointed him to the Vatican – a subtle snub to Hitler.

In Rome, rumours about Italian military preparations were mounting, and the new French Premier, Paul Reynaud, decided to make a personal appeal to Mussolini. In a letter of 24 April he offered negotiations and a summit meeting to solve the disagreements between the two countries. Mussolini's reply was that 'Italy is, and intends to remain, the political and military ally of Germany'; he rejected out-of-hand a meeting to discuss Italo-French differences. Letters came to Mussolini from the Pope, Pius XII, and from Roosevelt, imploring him to keep out of the war. In reply, Mussolini blamed France and Britain in advance for any decision he might eventually make to come into the war, emphasizing the continuous vexation and economic damage of the naval blockade. However, a ray of hope was contained in his letter to Roosevelt: 'Italy is ready to make its contribution to a better world system.'

On 3 May Charles wrote to Halifax describing Italian newspaper claims that Italy was 'bottled up and humiliated' in the Mediterranean;

he queried whether these claims were a sign of an irrevocable decision to enter the war at the side of Germany, or a 'blackmailing attempt to obtain satisfaction of Italian claims'. He emphasized that Italy's mouth was 'now very wide open'. In addition to the claims regarding Tunis, the Suez Canal Board and the Djibuti railway, it was demanded that Britain and France should abandon their patrolling of the gates and vital points of the Mediterranean, and that the British fleet should be withdrawn. However, Ciano had given Charles the impression that he did not want to go to war, and that Mussolini was afraid of war spreading to northern Italy, so that the most probable conclusion was that Italy 'will try to avoid becoming involved for as long as possible'.

Loraine saw Ciano on 8 May. When he remarked that the possibility of war with Italy had 'reappeared', Ciano replied that Mussolini stood by his pact with Germany and would come to his own decision in his own time; for the moment Italian policy was 'unchanged but he could not say for how long – perhaps two months, perhaps four, perhaps six, maybe even two years'; and he hinted that Mussolini's attitude would be determined by what happened when the 'real war' began. Loraine reported to London the next day that 'prospects of Italy joining Germany appear appreciably less immediate and less certain than has recently been feared'. The Foreign Office disagreed, telling Loraine that 'Mussolini is getting very close to the point, if he has not already reached it, where he will decide to enter the war'. Badoglio, strongly anti-German, now tried to frighten Mussolini out of war by sending him exaggerated reports of French and British military superiority in North Africa.

In spite of the German victory in Norway, at the beginning of May Mussolini was still reluctant to take a gamble and throw in his hand with Germany, although his irritation with the naval blockade was strong. Rab Butler (Under-Secretary at the Foreign Office) and Halifax wanted 'laxity', but Cadogan minuted: 'Whatever we give Mussolini we shall only buy him off for a short time after which he will revert to blackmail again.' Nevertheless, on 4 May the War Cabinet decided to go slow on the blockade. It was too late.

In his last letter to Mussolini about the Norwegian operations, on 3 May, Hitler betrayed no hint that an all-out attack in the west was imminent. He was not taking the risk of telling the Italians the date in advance.

Early in the morning of 10 May von Mackensen, the German Ambassador in Rome, informed Mussolini that the German army had attacked Holland and Belgium as part of a mammoth offensive designed to reach the Channel ports. Mussolini was galvanized by this, but still in no mood to enter the war; he doubted whether Hitler could deliver a knock-out blow. On 10 May Loraine saw Ciano, who told him that 'Everything depends on the Allies' ability to beat off the German offensive': Italy was still 'non belligerent', but all depended on Allied military success, about which he was 'doubtful'. He also raised again Italian grievances over the blockade. Five days later, when the German armies had crossed the Meuse and were advancing fast, Ciano told Loraine that some weeks earlier the betting on Italy coming into the war had been fifty:fifty; now it was nine to one on.[12]

News of the German offensive on 10 May had come as a complete surprise to Mussolini; he had been contemplating a compromise peace. For a fortnight he was on the horns of a dilemma, lacking confidence in the possibility of a complete German victory over the French army, which he much admired. As news of continuing German successes poured in, he still believed it might be many months before Hitler prevailed. In addition, he feared, quite unreasonably, that Roosevelt would bring in America to aid France and Britain. Ciano's diary reveals that when Hitler's letter announcing the offensive arrived, Mussolini was sorely tempted to intervene, but his caution prevailed. Yet once the German defeat of the French and British armies was absolute, Mussolini's greed became too great. On 16 May he received an appeal from Winston Churchill, with whom he had once enjoyed friendly relations and who had succeeded Neville Chamberlain as Prime Minister following the ignominious British defeat in Norway. Churchill's message ran:

> Now that I have taken up my office as Prime Minister and Minister of Defence I look back to our meetings in Rome and feel a desire to speak words of goodwill to you as Chief of the Italian nation across what seems to be a swiftly widening gulf. Is it too late to stop a river of blood from flowing between the British and Italian peoples?

Mussolini's reply was harsh although, as Churchill noted, 'it had at least the merit of candour':

> . . . You are certainly aware of grave reasons of an historical and contingent character which have ranged our two countries in opposite camps . . . I remind you of the initiative taken in 1935 by your Government to organize at Geneva sanctions against Italy, engaged in securing for herself a small place in the African sun without causing the slightest injury to your interests and territories or those of others . . . The Italian–German Treaty guides Italian policy today and tomorrow in the face of any event whatsoever.*

---

* The above letters were the only communications exchanged between Churchill and Mussolini during the war, contrary to numerous allegations made by Italian journalists and historians over the last fifty years.

Yet even by 17 May Mussolini had not firmly decided to go to war; on that day he showed Grandi a large-scale map of the Western Front, saying to him, 'Here there will be the new Marne. Here the Germans will come a cropper for the second time, and Italy can stay tranquil.'[13]

Forty-eight hours after the launch of the 10 May attack, German Panzer divisions under General Rommel had smashed the centre of the French armies through a weakly-guarded gap in the Ardennes. On 24 May the Germans broke the Belgian line, and the King of the Belgians, considering his situation hopeless, prepared to capitulate. In desperation, on 25 May the British Expeditionary Force began its withdrawal to Dunkirk; by the 28th the bulk of the BEF were at Dunkirk and the evacuation was in full swing. The German military triumph was complete. The French were hopelessly defeated, and it was a question whether Britain could continue the war alone.

As the German victory became apparent, Mussolini still hankered after a peace conference; there is evidence that he was frightened of Hitler's military strength. However, by 29 May he had decided on war, and with Badoglio held a conference with the service chiefs – Rodolfo Graziani (Army), Domenico Cavagnari (Navy) and Francesco Pricolo (Air Force). Mussolini told them that any day after 5 June would suit him to declare war, though on the land frontiers they could do nothing spectacular, and would remain on the defensive. Badoglio wanted the Duce to procrastinate as usual, so as to have more time to prepare, but the die was cast, and Mussolini was now itching to get his fingers on the booty. However, at the request of Hitler, the declaration of war by Italy was postponed until 10 June.[14]

On 22 May Daladier, now French Foreign Minister, appalled by what war with Italy would mean for France, told Sir Ronald Campbell, the British Ambassador in Paris, that he was thinking of offering immediate concessions to Italy, to bribe Mussolini into maintaining his non-belligerence. In Campbell's view, as he reported to London, Daladier's idea was 'useless', as 'Mussolini could not be bought'. The Foreign Office nevertheless considered it might be helpful to issue a statement that at the peace conference which would follow the war 'Italy would participate with a status equal to that of the belligerents in order that her claims might be dealt with as part of the general settlement of Europe'; it was felt, however, that in view of Mussolini's forthright rejection of both Churchill's and Reynaud's recent friendly approaches, no immediate concessions to Italy should be offered. Instead, the British and French governments agreed on a joint approach to Roosevelt, requesting his mediation with Italy.

In Washington on 25 May the French Ambassador and Lord

Lothian, the British Ambassador, agreed on a communication which Roosevelt incorporated in a telegram to the US Ambassador in Rome, William Phillips, for urgent personal delivery to Ciano. It stated that if Mussolini would inform him of his grievances or claims against the Allies, the President would immediately communicate them to 'the Allied Governments in order to leave nothing undone to prevent an extension of the war'. The President told Mussolini the Allies were aware that Italy 'entertained certain grievances in regard to the Italian position in the Mediterranean, and would welcome Italian participation at the peace conference with equal status to that of the belligerents'; Mussolini was invited to notify Roosevelt of Italian claims which would in his view 'ensure the establishment in the Mediterranean of a new order guaranteeing to Italy satisfaction of Italian legitimate aspirations in that sea'. Roosevelt undertook to guarantee the execution of the agreement, provided Italy did not enter the war against the Allies. To these fair words Mussolini replied with an immediate and unequivocal negative.

After seeing Phillips, Ciano recorded:

> Roosevelt offers to become the mediator between us and the Allies, making himself personally responsible for the execution after the war of any eventual agreements. I answer Phillips that Roosevelt is off the track. It takes more than that to dissuade Mussolini . . . what he wants is war, and even if he were to obtain by peaceful means double what he claims, he would refuse.[15]

As the gap widened between the French and British armies, the French found themselves unable to form a defence line on the Somme; German tanks rampaged unimpeded through northern France, and Paris became indefensible.

At a meeting of the French War Committee in Paris on 25 May General Maxime Weygand, who had replaced General Maurice Gamelin as Commander-in-Chief, mooted the question of an armistice. The next day, 26 May, the French Premier, Reynaud, flew to London – *not* to ask officially for permission to capitulate (Britain and France had made a solemn agreement that neither would enter into a separate peace with Germany), but to obtain the support of the British government for concessions to Mussolini in the hope of keeping Italy out of the war, and to explore the possibility of mediation by the Duce with Hitler. France had ten divisions on the Italian frontier: if she could be certain that Italy would not fight, they would be invaluable against the Germans.

On 24 May the War Cabinet had authorized Halifax to tell the Italian Ambassador in London, Giuseppe Bastianini, that if Italy would remain neutral Britain would take account of reasonable Italian claims at the peace conference which would follow the war and at which Italy would appear on an equal footing with the belligerents. Halifax also told Bastianini that he hoped the 'treatment of contraband under the naval blockade' had been satisfactorily dealt with. After the German breakthrough, the Master of the Rolls had been sent hurriedly to Rome to try to find a formula which would keep Mussolini happy. Halifax wanted to importune Mussolini to persuade Hitler to agree to a peace conference, and went further than Churchill intended, telling Bastianini that 'the Allies would be prepared to consider any proposals which might lead to peace'. Halifax thought his interview with Bastianini had gone well, but Perucci of the Italian Embassy told Gladwyn Jebb that Halifax had made 'a bad impression' on Bastianini by offering no concrete proposals, even though immediate satisfaction of Italian claims was required.[16]

At lunch with Churchill on 26 May Reynaud mentioned the possibility of 'cessation of hostilities'. He received a dusty reply: Churchill told him France must stay in the war. Subsequently Churchill told the Cabinet that he 'doubted whether anything would come of an approach to Italy, but they would consider it after Halifax reported his conversation with the Italian Ambassador'.

During the afternoon of 26 May Halifax saw Reynaud with Churchill, and told the French Premier that if Italy would collaborate in a peace which would safeguard the independence of Britain and France, the Allies would discuss all Italy's claims in the Mediterranean – in particular the outlets of this sea; this would mean the sacrifice by the British of Gibraltar, Malta and Suez, by the French of Djibuti and Tunis. Churchill did not implicitly dissent from this proposal. On his return to Paris Reynaud reported that 'Halifax agreed, but Churchill took refuge behind the War Cabinet'. On 26 May the fate of the BEF at Dunkirk hung in the balance and a ghastly tragedy was still a possibility, so that Churchill felt himself to be vulnerable over buying Italy off and negotiating with Hitler.

On 27 May the Belgian army capitulated: in an emergency session the French Cabinet decided to make a detailed, concrete offer to Mussolini in Rome, and asked Britain to confirm it. There is pathos in the message they sent Churchill:

> Because of the defection of the Belgian army the Council of Ministers met at 10 p.m. yesterday evening. It decided to ask you to examine afresh with the greatest speed possible the offer to Italy made according to the formula drawn up by Lord Halifax in the presence of Paul Reynaud on Sunday. The French Government consider that more details must be inserted. The Council of Ministers has authorised:

a. Cession of the coast of French Somali [land] as well as the railway to Addis Ababa, with a free zone reserved in the port of Djibuti.

b. Rectification of the Franco-Libyan frontier on the sector envisaged by the [Laval-Mussolini] Agreement of 7 January 1935 on the line between Tunno and Hadames.

c. Cession of a very large slice of territory between the hinterland of Libya and Congo coast.

Should this last suggestion not be sufficient to assure our overtures a favourable reception, we would try again and substitute the offer of a reform of the Statute of Tunisia so as to allow a happy collaboration between France and Italy in the Regency. It is useless to draw the attention of the British Government to the gravity of the situation, as well as to the fact that even if the chances of the success of the proposal are not very great we consider it our duty not to neglect anything to prevent a further aggravation which could have a decisive influence on the result of the war.

It goes without saying that an offer by only one of the Allies would reduce its chances of success.

The day before, Halifax had told the French Ambassador in London he was not in favour of any mention of either Suez or Gibraltar being made to Mussolini, for fear that if they did so Mussolini might raise his 'claims still higher and make extravagant demands'. Cadogan minuted, realistically:

Mussolini is not going to, and in fact dare not, make any separate agreement with the Allies – even if he wishes to. He is simply wondering how much of the general 'share-out' he will be allowed by his 'ally' to take, and whether he will ultimately get more or less by spilling Italian blood for it. We cannot tell which way he'll jump, but I hope we shan't delude ourselves into thinking that we shall do ourselves any good by making any more 'offers' or 'approaches'.

However, Philip Nichols (First Secretary in the Foreign Office) took the suggestion of satisfying Italy over the outlets of the Mediterranean more seriously, minuting:

Surely we can envisage now as part of the peace settlement some face-saving device for Italy, viz., directorships on the Suez Canal and possibly the return of Gibraltar to Spain in return for another base such as Ceuta . . . We might ask the Chiefs of Staff whether, British command of the sea being assured, the continued undisputed possession of Suez and Gibraltar are indispensable.

Glittering prizes seemed about to fall into Mussolini's lap if he would shun Germany. However, he realized that Hitler was now the master of Europe: nothing could be done without the Führer's full approval, or the victorious German armies might be turned against Italy to execute the German will.[17]

On 2 June the Duce wrote to Hitler that he would definitely declare war on 10 June, asserting that he wanted at least some part of the Italian army to fight against the French and British in France

> . . . with your soldiers, so as to seal in the field the brotherhood of arms and the camaraderie of our Revolutions. If you accept this offer I will immediately send some regiments of *bersaglieri*, who are tough and courageous soldiers.

The offer was refused; Hitler no longer had any need for Italian help against the crumbling French opposition.

Fateful War Cabinet meetings were held in London on 26 and 27 May, after Reynaud's return to Paris. Over them loomed the fate of the BEF. On the 27th Cadogan noted, 'I see no hope for more than a tiny fraction of them, now that Belgium has capitulated' – a view widely held in Whitehall.[18]

On the afternoon of 26 May Churchill reported his talk with Reynaud to the War Cabinet: according to the French Premier, in return for staying out of the war Italy would ask for the neutralization of Gibraltar and the Suez Canal, the demilitarization of Malta, and the limitation of British naval forces in the Mediterranean. Some alteration in the status of Tunis would also be asked for. The French suggestion was that the offer of such terms might keep Italy out of the war.

Halifax said he favoured an approach to Italy; in his opinion the last thing Mussolini wanted 'was to see Herr Hitler dominating all Europe', and he would be anxious to persuade Hitler to take a more reasonable attitude. Churchill expressed doubt whether anything would come of the approach to Italy, but conceded that the matter was one which the War Cabinet could decide. At a later meeting that day he said Britain must take care not to be forced into a weak position in which she went to Mussolini 'and invited him to go to Herr Hitler and ask him to treat us nicely. We must not get entangled in a position of that kind before we had been involved in serious fighting.' Halifax responded that

> . . . we might say to Signor Mussolini that if there were any suggestions of terms which affected our independence we should not look at them for a moment.
>
> If however Signor Mussolini was as alarmed as we felt he must be with regard to Herr Hitler's power and was prepared to look at matters from the point of view of balance of power, then we might consider Italian claims.

At any rate, Halifax 'could see no harm in trying this line of approach'.

The former Prime Minister, Neville Chamberlain, was a member of the War Cabinet as Lord President of the Council; he said that if Mussolini was prepared to collaborate with Britain in getting tolerable terms, then Britain should be prepared to discuss Italian demands with him.

Churchill, however, with the evacuation of Dunkirk at the forefront of his mind, thought it would be better to decide nothing until 'we saw how much of the Army we could re-embark from France . . . The operation might be a great failure . . . on the other hand, we might save a considerable portion of the force.' But he did not object to some approach to Mussolini.

Arthur Greenwood, a Labour Cabinet Minister in the coalition government, thought that Mussolini would be 'out to get Malta, Gibraltar and Suez'; he felt sure the negotiations would break down; 'Herr Hitler would get to know of them, and it might have a bad effect on our prestige'.

Halifax was defeatist. In his view, if in the course of a discussion of a general settlement Britain found that she could get terms which did not postulate the destruction of her independence, 'we should be foolish if we did not accept them'. The War Cabinet invited the Foreign Secretary to circulate a paper outlining a suggested communication to Italy; the document, titled 'Suggested approach to Mussolini', was discussed in the War Cabinet the next day:

> If Signor Mussolini will co-operate with us in securing a settlement . . . we will undertake at once to discuss, with the desire to find solutions, the matters in which Signor Mussolini is primarily interested. We understand that he desires the solution of certain Mediterranean questions and if he will state in secrecy what these are, France and Great Britain will at once do their best to meet these wishes.

No longer was Halifax arguing only for a means to preserve Italian neutrality; now he wanted Mussolini to be a mediator with Hitler. No doubt he was influenced by a very gloomy report the day before from the Chiefs of Staff which included the opinion that, if Germany attempted an invasion, 'our coast and beach defences would not prevent German tanks and infantry getting a firm footing on our shores', and that night bombing attacks on Coventry and Birmingham would bring aircraft production factories to a standstill.

A row then broke out between Halifax and Churchill after Churchill confessed to feeling increasingly oppressed with the futility of the suggested approach to Mussolini, which in his view the Duce 'would certainly regard with contempt'. Britain must not let herself be dragged down by France: instead, she must fight on, if necessary without France, and 'even if we were beaten we should be no worse off than we should be if we now abandoned the struggle'. The proposed approach to Italy was, he considered, not only 'futile' but involved us in 'deadly danger'. (There were two separate issues under consideration at this meeting – concessions to Italy to prevent her declaring war, and suggesting to Mussolini that he should intercede with Hitler for a generous peace settlement – and the War Cabinet discussion became rather confused.)

Halifax, nettled by Churchill's remarks, stated that he could recognize no resemblance between the action which he proposed *vis-à-vis* Mussolini, and the suggestion that Britain was suing for terms. He is recorded as having said that:

> In the discussion the previous day he had asked the Prime Minister whether, if he was satisfied that matters vital to the independence of this country were unaffected, he would be prepared to discuss terms [with Germany]. The Prime Minister had said that he would be thankful to get out of our present difficulties on such terms, provided we retained the essentials and the elements of our vital strength, even at the cost of some cession of territory. On the present occasion, however, the Prime Minister seemed to suggest that under no circumstances would we contemplate any course except fighting to a finish.
>
> The Prime Minister had said that two or three months would show whether we were able to stand up against the air risk. This meant that the future of the country depended on whether the enemy's bombers happened to hit our aircraft factories. He [Halifax] was prepared to take that risk if our independence was at stake, but if it was not at stake he would think it right to accept an offer which would save the country from disaster.

Churchill then exasperated Halifax by telling him he was talking in 'unreal terms'. Halifax was offended: suppose, he retorted, the French army collapsed and Hitler made an offer of peace terms to France, and the French government said to Germany, 'We cannot deal with an offer made to France only, alone, and you must deal with the Allies together' – would the Prime Minister be prepared to discuss them?

Churchill then came his closest to admitting that he was considering capitulation: he replied that he would not *ask* for terms, but if he was told the terms, he 'would be prepared to consider them'. The discussion was in fact more acrimonious than as recorded in the official Minutes. Churchill and Halifax were poles apart, but fortunately Churchill had the backing of Attlee and Greenwood. Halifax must have come close to tendering his resignation – which would have produced a political minefield for Churchill, since Halifax was extremely popular with the Parliamentary Conservative Party. Halifax noted in his diary:

Winston talked the most frightful rot, and also Greenwood; and after hearing it for some time I said exactly what I thought of them, adding that if that was really their view, if it came to the point our ways must part.[19]

It must have been a close thing whether Halifax or Churchill prevailed. If Halifax had won, the course of history would have been different; unlike Churchill, he was ready for far-reaching concessions to Mussolini, and a peace conference with Hitler.

There was no response from Italy to Bastianini's interview with Halifax, and no British plea for his intervention was sent to Mussolini. Loraine had by now made it clear that Italy was bent on war. The final direct offer by France alone of territorial concessions, made through the Italian Ambassador in Paris, was treated with disdain by Mussolini, who would not even reply. As the French Ambassador in Rome, François-Poncet, observed, even if Mussolini had been offered Tunis, Corsica and Savoy, he would still have gone to war.

Before he could declare war, under the terms of the Italian Constitution Mussolini had to obtain the consent of the King, Victor Emmanuel III. In common with the majority of Italians, the King was opposed to war; although he was anti-French, he had considerable sympathy for Britain. The Crown Prince, Umberto, was also opposed, as were, to the King's knowledge, leading Fascists such as Badoglio and Marshal de Bono, and even the Duce's son-in-law, Ciano; it was probable that a free vote of the Grand Council would produce a majority against Italy's entry into the war.

Alas, Victor Emmanuel was not made of the stuff that produces revolution; and it seems probable that, surprised by the unexpected and to him unwelcome German military victories, he succumbed like Mussolini to greed for the spoils of a quick war: at all events, on 1 June 1940 he gave his consent. To his family the King claimed he was carrying out the wishes of the people, as he had done in May 1915, when he declared war on Germany, and October 1922, when he appointed Mussolini Prime Minister. It was an unpardonable decision: he took a great interest in military affairs and was well aware how unprepared the Italian armed forces were, but he gambled on Allied resistance being short-lived.

Could Victor Emmanuel have prevented Italy's entry into the war? Regular officers, including the top ranks in the Army and the Navy, were more loyal to the Crown than to Mussolini, but it is doubtful whether a revolution against Mussolini would have succeeded at a moment when German triumphs appeared to justify the Duce's action in allying himself with Hitler. Umberto wanted the King to use his royal veto, but this would have meant abdication.

The King later justified his decision on the basis that at the beginning of June 1940 France and Britain had been so defeated that Italy had no option except war if she was to take a share of the booty. He thought, he said, that only a token military demonstration would be necessary, and that if Italy delayed Britain would sign a compromise peace with Germany, who would then obtain French territorial possessions which the King felt should by right go to Italy. Thus, greed prevailed.

On 10 June Ciano summoned François-Poncet and Loraine to inform them that Italy was at war with France and Great Britain. Loraine had with him his bilingual Air Attaché, Commodore Freddie West, VC, who has told the author that Ciano made it clear how much he regretted what was occurring, although Loraine's Italian was not good enough for him to understand properly. François-Poncet told Ciano that Italy had waited until France was down and out to plunge a dagger in her back: 'If I were in your place I would not be proud.' Ciano blushed, and replied, 'My dear Poncet, all this will last only a short time. We will soon be around a table with a green cloth.'[20]

At 6 p.m. Mussolini announced the declaration of war from the balcony of the Palazzo Venezia; his speech was transmitted by radio all over the country and broadcast from all the main squares and Fascist offices. He said:

> This is the hour of destiny for our country – the hour of irrevocable destiny. We are going to fight against the democracies of the West who always have tried to stop our march and often laid traps to threaten the very existence of the Italian people. Run to your arms, show your stubbornness, courage and valour . . .

. . . together with much more in the same vein of Fascist rhetoric. The announcement left the Italian people unmoved. They were apathetic about the war, hoping that it would be short, as Mussolini promised, and that the peace would bring rich rewards. Seldom has a nation been so disappointed.

Roosevelt spoke for the free world when at Charlottesville in Virginia, in an echo of François-Poncet's words, he said: 'Today, the tenth June, the hand that held the dagger has struck it into the shoulders of his neighbour.'[21]

The traditional friendship between Italy and Britain dating from the days of the Grand Tour and the Risorgimento meant nothing to Mussolini; nor did the comradeship-in-arms of the First World War or his friendships with Austen Chamberlain and Winston Churchill matter to him any longer. At one stroke he abruptly severed the ties which bound the two countries together, allying himself in all-out war with Germany – Italy's traditional foe, and soon to be so again.[22]

Paris fell to the Germans on 14 June 1940, and Field Marshal Pétain succeeded Reynaud as Premier of France. The new government immediately asked the Germans for an armistice – too soon for Mussolini, who had hoped for an Italian military success against the French first, so that he could appear at the peace conference as a victor. But his armies on the French frontier could make no progress, while the British bombed Turin and Milan and the French fleet bombarded the Genoa coast.

On 17 June Hitler summoned Mussolini to Munich to agree the terms of the armistice with France. During the train journey Mussolini, Ciano and General Roatta prepared their demands on France. These were far-reaching, and included Italian occupation of France up to the Rhône, together with Corsica, Tunisia and the Somali coast; the military bases in Algiers, Oran and Casablanca were to go to Italy; and Beirut was to be neutralized. The Italians also wanted the French fleet to be handed over to them. Hitler would have none of this. He wanted revenge for the 1918 surrender of Germany at Compiègne and planned to exact it in the form of a similar ceremony there, in reverse; he insisted there should be a separate armistice between Italy and France.

From Munich, Mussolini sent the King a revealing message:

> I draw the conclusion that they desire to finish the war quickly with France and Britain so to avoid the 'tail' of sea and colonial warfare which would make the state of 'war' chronic; even if it was safely conducted on the periphery it carries the risk of a massive intervention by the United States.
>
> At this moment Germany can be compared with a courageous and lucky player of cards who has continually won by doubling his stake. Now they are a little nervous and want to carry home their abundant nest-egg.

To their surprise, the Italians found the Germans moderate in their demands on France; his desire for revenge notwithstanding, Hitler was worried that terms too onerous or dishonourable might drive the Pétain government out of metropolitan France and encourage them to hand their fleet over to the English; at the same time, he was anxious for peace with Britain.

Ciano states that Mussolini wished for total occupation of French territory and demanded the surrender of the French fleet, although he was aware that his opinion had only 'consultative value'. This was correct, and in the end Hitler would only allow Italy to occupy and demilitarize a strip 40 kilometres wide along her European and North

African frontiers with France. Bitterly disappointed, Mussolini had to agree. His main claims against France would have to wait for the eventual peace treaty.[23]

Thus Mussolini had no booty to exhibit to the Italian people, and what spoils would eventually fall to Italy depended on the whim of Hitler. Nor had he a victory in the field to glory over when the armistice with France was signed at Rome on 24 June: no French territory had been conquered by Italy, although many Italian soldiers had been sent to a useless death.

CHAPTER 16

Mussolini at War

MUSSOLINI EXPECTED THE shortest of wars with Britain. He was anxious that Italian arms should attain glory before the peace, and feared at first that Britain might capitulate before he had an opportunity to attack. However, Churchill rejected a peace offer from Hitler out-of-hand, saying that whatever happened Britain could and would continue the war to a victorious conclusion in whatever theatre of war, by land, sea and air. As we have seen, Mussolini contemplated attacking Greece and Yugoslavia, but Hitler dissuaded him; and from North Africa, Graziani warned the Duce that his troops were in no position to launch an attack to reach the Suez Canal.

Frustrated, Mussolini – to his shame, and to the shame even today of most Italians – two days after the French armistice made an offer to Hitler of Italian troops for the invasion of the British Isles:

> Now the problem is to conquer Great Britain. I remind you of what I said at Munich about the direct participation of Italy in the assault on the island. I am ready to contribute ground forces and air forces and you know how much I desire to do so. I ask you to answer me in such a way that it will be possible for me to pass to the phase of execution.

Fourteen days later, in Berlin, Ciano told Hitler that the Duce had ten divisions and up to thirty squadrons of aircraft ready, and requested urgently to be 'honoured' with permission to fight beside the Wehrmacht in the operation against England. Hitler told Ciano that while his decision must await the view of his High Command, he personally favoured the idea; in return, he offered squadrons of bombers for North Africa, capable of reaching the Suez Canal.

The German military chiefs were horrified at the prospect of ill-organized Italian troops participating in the difficult cross-Channel invasion which was being planned under the code name Sea Lion. They told Hitler that under no circumstances would they have the Italian army involved. Hitler's reply to Mussolini on 13 July was polite, but firm:

The demands the first assault imposes upon the various units are too great to be readily met by commanders who have not occupied themselves for months with the preparations . . . My responsible advisers are convinced that it would no longer be possible today to replace any of the units intended for these first assaults, even with another German unit, without giving the latter four to six months of time for preparation. For replacement purposes it is therefore important to use uniform weapons and ammunition as far as possible. The same applies to the accompanying transport vehicles. It cannot be expected that in the country itself any still serviceable automobiles will fall into our hands . . . in the first stage that seems out of the question. Only after a firm foothold has been established permanently and the area of operations secured could this question be taken up again.

Mussolini replied cordially that his offer of Italian army units for the landing in England would be 'mainly of symbolic value', designed to 'express in visible form our comradeship in arms'. Instead, he now offered the Italian Air Force, claiming that 'We now possess units of new very fast and efficient machines', and saying that 'the most important thing is to strike the decisive blow at Great Britain'.[1]

Goering, in charge of the German Air Force, did not want Italian planes for his attacks on London; however, Hitler accepted them. The result was disastrous. The Italian planes were too slow and their own fighter escort ineffectual so, ignominiously, they had to be protected by German fighters. Even then, the losses they suffered proved unsustainable. An ignoble chapter in Italian military history was soon brought to an end, the planes being transferred to the Mediterranean.

Meanwhile, on 3 July the Royal Navy had attacked the French fleet at Mers-el-Kebir, near Oran in North Africa, where much of it was sheltering. Despite assurances to the contrary from Admiral Darlan, the French Naval Minister, Churchill feared (without proper reason) that the Pétain government might surrender their fleet to the Germans. Flouting the War Cabinet and the Chiefs of Staff, Churchill personally sent orders for the French fleet to be bombarded, in spite of promising on-the-spot negotiations between the French and British admirals for it to be either sailed to safety out of German reach across the Atlantic, or scuttled. One battleship and two destroyers escaped to Toulon; the remainder were put out of action, and 1,300 French sailors were killed. This savage attack turned the Pétain government fiercely anti-British overnight, with the result that later the Germans and Japanese were allowed to use French bases in Vichy-held Syria and French Indo-China, to Britain's grave disadvantage. More immediately, the French hostility to Britain caused Hitler to wonder whether he should make an ally of France, whether France might even declare war on Britain. Hitler had already made Mussolini whittle down his demands on France, and the prospect of a German–French friendship horrified the Duce, who feared none of his claims against France would ever be realized.[2]

On 18 August Mussolini told Graziani in North Africa that the invasion of Great Britain had been decided upon 'within a week or a month':

> The day that the first platoon of German soldiers sets foot on British territory you will attack . . . It is not a question of going towards Alexandria, nor towards Sollum; I only ask that you attack the British forces before you. The loss of Egypt will be the *coup-de-grâce* for Great Britain, while this rich country necessary for our communication with Ethiopia is the great prize that Italy expects and which – I am sure of it – you will give to her.

The war went inconceivably badly for Mussolini. The army had been put under severe strain both in Abyssinia and in Spain and nothing approaching enough new *matériel* had been supplied by the armament industry. The Italian Air Force was ineffective, and army equipment was almost all of 1914–18 vintage. There were no aircraft carriers, and no Fleet Air Arm. Mussolini, who had a strong penchant for self-deception, probably did not realize how unprepared Italy was. Any worries he might have had about her military inefficiency were counter-balanced by his confidence that the war would soon be over, as evidenced by his neglect to halt building work on a site extending to several hundreds of acres for the Rome Trade Exhibition proposed for 1942.

Having failed to win glory against France, Mussolini set his sights on a military success against Britain in Egypt, and he was delighted when Graziani's September attack reached Sidi Barrâni on the Egyptian frontier. According to Ciano, he was 'radiant with joy, and had rarely been in such good humour and good shape'. However, Graziani wisely refused to advance any further, despite exhortations to do so from the Duce.

When in early October Hitler unexpectedly occupied part of Romania, Mussolini then decided to trump his cards by a surprise assault on Greece, where British ships and aeroplanes were using ports and bases for supplies and refuge. As Mussolini told Ciano, 'Hitler always faces me with a *fait accompli*. This time I am going to pay him back in his own coin. He will find out from the papers that I have occupied Greece.' Mussolini did not consult his Commander-in-Chief, Badoglio, but the three heads of the armed forces advised him strongly against such a move.[3]

On the night of 28/29 October Mussolini launched a surprise attack on Greece from Albania. Hitler heard the news of the invasion the same day, two hours before his train arrived at Florence for a conference with the Duce. The Führer was appalled: had he known of Mussolini's intentions he would have forbidden the attack, because once Greece was in the war the British would have been able to bomb the Romanian oil fields, vital to the Axis, from bases in Crete and Lemnos.

Within a week of the initial attack, the Greeks had begun to push back the invading Italian units, and Mussolini was forced to fight a purely defensive war; on 11 November, a carrier-based British air attack put half the Italian battle fleet out of action at Taranto. The crowning ignominy came when General Soddu, the Italian Commander-in-Chief in Greece, advised Mussolini to seek an armistice.

Badly as he had fared in Greece, Mussolini met even greater disaster in North Africa. Desperately short of mechanized transport, Graziani made no effort to respond to Mussolini's hectoring and refused to attack the numerically weaker British forces in Egypt; any idea of an Italian advance to the Suez Canal was a pipe-dream. Then suddenly General Wavell's army advanced with amazing speed into Italian Cyrenaica and by 21 January 1941 had taken Sidi Barrâni, Bardia and Tobruk. By 7 February 90,000 Italians had surrendered at Tobruk, and 113,000 at Beda Fomm – more than the attacking British force.

To counter his disastrous defeats in Greece and North Africa, Mussolini hoped to take Malta with German help, once the Germans had seized Gibraltar in an attack from Spain. Both plans came to nothing.

Hitler was deadly earnest in his desire for Gibraltar, knowing that to hold it was to deny the British fleet access to the western Mediterranean. He was prepared to bribe Franco to allow German troops to operate from Spanish soil, but Franco was determined not to allow his country to be involved in another war. Hitler met Franco at Hendaye on the Spanish–French frontier on 23 October 1940. Franco, tendentiously assuring Hitler that Spain would 'gladly fight at Germany's side', then immediately recited a catalogue of demands, and of difficulties which made such a course impossible, impervious to Hitler's blandishments in his refusal to go to war.

Franco demanded the immediate delivery of many thousands of tons of wheat from Germany to alleviate the Spanish famine, together with a large number of heavy guns and anti-aircraft artillery to protect his coastline from the British. He admitted the certain loss of the Canaries to the British, but his trump card was that it would not be consistent with Spanish pride to accept Gibraltar as a gift from Germany: the fortress must be taken by Spanish troops. Hitler was exasperated; he was accustomed to imposing his demands on helpless smaller countries. He explained to Franco that he had made plans for German troops to cross the Spanish border on 10 January and open the assault on Gibraltar at the beginning of February, and assured him that the attack would quickly succeed because the troops had been exceptionally well trained.

As one of his conditions of entry into the war Franco demanded cession by France to Spain of Algeria from Oran to the west frontier, all French Morocco, and French Catalonia beyond the Pyrenees. This put Hitler in a dilemma: although he had managed to improve his relations with Vichy France, he knew there was a grave risk of the French North African colonies changing sides. For fear of alienating Vichy France, he therefore refused Franco's territorial demands. Hitler asserted that the greatest danger was that the part of the French 'colonial empire' now under General Weygand would, with its abundant *matériel* and military reserves, desert the Vichy government and go over to de Gaulle, England or the United States, that 'an attempt must be made to bring France herself to a definite stand against England', and that any immediate cession of French territory to Spain was therefore out of the question. Franco found this a convenient point on which to stand firm. His intransigence was a blessing for Britain, because with Spanish connivance the Germans would have had no great difficulty in assaulting and capturing Gibraltar. The next day Serrano Suñer, the Spanish Foreign Minister, emphasized to Ribbentrop Spain's insistence on acquiring Oran and French Morocco.

After Hendaye, and with a bad grace, Hitler temporarily abandoned his Gibraltar plan; he later told Mussolini that rather than endure such an interview again he 'would prefer to have three or four of my teeth out'. (The German record of the talks, which lasted nine hours, is incomplete.) Ribbentrop cursed the Spaniards and called Franco 'an ungrateful coward who owed Germany everything and now refused to join us'. In his prison camp after the war, Goering declared that it had been Hitler's greatest mistake not to seize Gibraltar and North Africa 'with or without Franco's consent'.[4]

As 1941 opened Mussolini was reeling under Italy's military disasters and fast losing popularity. On 19 January he met Hitler at Berchtesgaden. According to Ciano, Mussolini consented to the meeting reluctantly, not wanting to meet his ally burdened by failures 'until they have been at least part reversed'; he feared that Hitler would deal with Italy 'only on the basis of brutal self-interest'. However, Mussolini returned from Berchtesgaden 'elated' by a promise of massive German military help in Greece; Hitler had also resurrected his plan of attacking Gibraltar through Spain, and this time he proposed to entrust Mussolini with the task of propitiating Franco. The Duce was not optimistic about the outcome of his negotiations with Franco, considering, as he told Anfuso beforehand, that the Italian setback in Greece would make Spain even more reluctant to become involved. Resigned to failure, he felt considerable sympathy with the Spanish dictator's determination to keep out of war.

Without Ciano, the Duce met Franco at Bordighera on 12 February 1941. Delicately Mussolini broached the subject of Spain coming into the war, and said rather lamely that Hitler was only asking for German troops to enter Spain to capture Gibraltar. This gave Franco the opportunity to repeat that for reasons of honour only Spanish troops could be allowed to assault Gibraltar; he then launched into a tirade of complaints against Hitler, declaring that the Führer did not understand Spain and was pandering to France – Spain's main enemy. He declared that Spain must have wheat or starve, and reiterated another of his conditions, that Spain must receive not only Gibraltar but also French Morocco, which Hitler refused to guarantee. In any case, Franco said, Spain was not militarily prepared for war.

Mussolini, according to the transcripts of the proceedings, appeared detached and did not protest. Afterwards he told Anfuso that he could not blame Franco, but Italy could not imitate him: 'You remember 1939.' Meeting Franco must have given Mussolini regrets about abandoning his non-belligerent stance.

Mussolini then wrote calmly to Hitler: he accepted that Franco would not go to war, even if Germany were to give him all the aid he was demanding, which would take 'months and months'; he considered that it would be better in this situation to 'limit ourselves to keeping Spain in our political camp and see if time would solve her problem of shortage of food and her complete lack of military preparation'.

Hitler conceded defeat, writing to Mussolini that clearly Spain did not want to enter the war and would not do so: 'This is extremely tiresome, since it means that for the moment the possibility of striking at Britain in the simplest manner, in her Mediterranean possessions, is eliminated.' He added that Franco's claim that any such attack must be carried out only by Spanish troops was an ingenious excuse, and exaggerated the capabilities of the Spanish army. Mussolini replied that it was useless to put further pressure on Franco, and Hitler said bitterly that Spain had turned out to be a complete delusion: Britain was let off the hook and should be grateful to Franco.[5]

Joint German and Italian plans for the capture of Malta also failed to gel. Mussolini had introduced a comic element by suggesting that water-buses from Venice should be used to transport the invading Italian soldiers. Admiral Raeder, Chief of the German Naval Staff, was convinced that it was vital to eliminate Malta as a British naval and air base, and that Malta was the 'stumbling block to Italy's conduct of the war at sea'.

Raeder revived the project in March 1941, convincing Goering that airborne troops could capture the island. The Italian Chiefs of Staff responded without enthusiasm; Admiral Riccardi, the Italian naval chief, thought the losses sustained would be unacceptable. Mussolini was keen to attack Malta, prompted as usual by his eagerness for a victory which could be exploited for propaganda purposes. Hitler was more cautious. The German landing on Crete, although successful, had resulted in such heavy casualties for his airborne troops that he shrank from a similar attack on another heavily defended island. (This has prompted the military historian Basil Liddell-Hart to consider that General Freyberg – a New Zealander born in London, commander of Commonwealth forces in Crete – and his troops, although they lost the battle of Crete, may well have won the more important battle of Malta.)

Although General Rommel, in command of the Axis troops in North Africa, at first favoured the attack on Malta, the German General Staff (OKW) were unenthusiastic; nevertheless, in April 1942 a joint German–Italian planning staff concocted a plan (Operation Hercules), to which Hitler allocated 50 landing craft, 200 transport aircraft and 50 gliders. In all, 61,000 men were to be landed on the island. Cavallero, Chief of the Italian General Staff, was full of enthusiasm for the assault, and joint German–Italian training took place near Gaeta. However, Hitler was insistent that the offensive in Libya must have precedence, and the Allies sank so many Axis tankers between Italy and Tripoli that the needs of the Italian and German armies on land consumed the petrol designed for Malta. When Rommel reached the El Alamein line in July 1942, he pleaded for priority in petrol and other supplies so that he could overrun Egypt: Hitler, dazzled by the prospect of the glittering prize of the Suez Canal, called off the invasion of Malta.[6]

When the Allies landed in North Africa in November 1942, Hercules was indefinitely postponed and the forces allocated to it were used for the occupation of French Tunisia, to forestall the Allies' seizure. Hitler was right to fear that a joint Italian–German assault on Malta would have produced enormous casualties on both sides. It is impossible to predict what the outcome might have been, but the loss of Malta would certainly have been a dagger-blow to the Allies in the

Desert War, since submarines and aircraft from Malta continuously took a heavy toll of German and Italian shipping, so that shortages of petrol and ammunition adversely affected the Axis performance.

Franco's intransigence came at a bad moment for Mussolini. When Benghazi fell to General Wavell on 6 February 1941, it put the whole of Cyrenaica into British hands. Italian troops had driven the British out of British Somaliland in the early days of the Italian entry into the war, but by February all Somaliland had been lost to Italy, and operations in Abyssinia were going so well for the British that it was clear Haile Selassie would soon be able to return to Addis Ababa; he did so on 5 May. Mussolini commented to Ciano, 'We have lost our Empire while the French still retain theirs.'

Reports reached the Foreign Office from Italy of sinking morale, strong anti-Fascist feeling, and a widespread desire to get out of the war speedily. Dispirited Italian generals, admirals, and other high-ranking officers became disloyal to Mussolini. Churchill was strongly in favour of offering 'soft' peace terms to Italian dissidents if they were to topple Mussolini, and decided on four possible ways of ending Italy's part in the war. These were:

1. Raising a 'free Italian force' (the Garibaldi Legion) to fight with the British;

2. Establishment of Cyrenaica as a free Italian colony to be 'petted' and made prosperous;

3. Bribes to Italian naval officers to induce them to desert Mussolini, and sail their ships to Alexandria to surrender them;

4. A determined search for an Italian de Gaulle.

Neither Churchill nor Antony Eden, who succeeded Lord Halifax as Foreign Secretary on 1 January 1941, has mentioned these ideas in his wartime memoirs. Perhaps this is understandable: all proved abortive, and they reflect little credit on either statesman; yet it is harder to understand why the official historian of wartime foreign policy, Llewellyn Woodward, chose to ignore them. They were important at the time; and two years later, when Italy was at her last gasp, British policy was reversed to become disastrously hard-line, with nothing but unconditional surrender offered to non-Fascists.

Churchill and Eden eagerly greeted a Foreign Office memorandum drawing attention to the low morale among the great numbers of Italian prisoners-of-war captured in the Western Desert, the wish of the Italian people for peace, and their hatred of Germany. In addition Lord Davies, the influential Conservative newspaper magnate, wrote a letter to Churchill (with a copy to Eden) advocating the raising of a Free Italian Army from Italian POWs in Egypt, to be called the Garibaldi Legion, to fight against Fascism. Eden and his advisors likcd the idea, and Sir Orme Sargent, Deputy Under-Secretary at the Foreign Office, minuted that there was much to be said in favour of organizing an anti-Fascist Italian army.

Fortified by his officials, on 6 February Eden minuted 'PM should approve' on a memorandum to Churchill suggesting that SOE (Special Operations Executive, the British organization for operations behind the lines) were preparing leaflets to be dropped on the Italian naval forces, urging Italian captains to sail their ships to Alexandria where they would receive the same treatment and pay as the Royal Navy and no pressure would be put on them to fight against the Germans or Fascists, and similar ones urging Italian airmen to fly their machines to British aerodromes.

On receiving Eden's memorandum, Churchill minuted enthusiastically to the Chiefs-of-Staff on 11 February 1941 that he agreed to the raising of an anti-Mussolini Italian army in Egypt, and also wanted to establish recently-liberated Cyrenaica as a free, non-Fascist Italian colony, to be treated like the French colonies which had swung over to de Gaulle 'but even better'. The minute clearly indicates Churchill's conciliatory attitude to Italian non-Fascists at this period of the war:

General Ismay, for C. O. S. Committee:

I see no reason why you should not consider raising an anti-Mussolini or Free Italian Force in Cyrenaica. Volunteers might be called for from the 100,000 prisoners we have taken. There must be a great many who hate Fascism. We might even rule Cyrenaica under the Free Italian flag and treat it in the same way as de Gaulle's colonies are being treated, subject to our military control.

Anyhow, I wish Cyrenaica to be petted and made extremely comfortable and prosperous, more money being spent upon them than they are intrinsically worth. Can we not make this place a base for starting a real split in Italy and the source of anti-Mussolini propaganda? We might make it a model of British rule, hold it in trust for the Italian people and have 4,000 or 5,000 Italian troops sworn to the liberation of Italy from the German and Mussolini yoke. This could be run as world propaganda. The matter raises wide political considerations and I am sending a copy of this minute to the Foreign Secretary.

Eden favoured Churchill's idea of a Free Italian Army, although he was doubtful about 'nailing the Italian flag to the Cyrenaican mast'. However, the archaeologist Sir Leonard Woolley, a leading expert on Egypt and the Arab world, was then at the War Office: he produced devastating objections to Churchill's scheme, pointing out that an Italian Cyrenaica 'would lose all sympathy from Arabs everywhere, who would regard it as a betrayal of the local Arabs'; his opinion was that Cyrenaica ought to be attached to Egypt, which would satisfy both the Senussi (the main tribe in Cyrenaica) and the King of Egypt and his government. Woolley's opinion was ignored by a high-level joint Foreign Office, Admiralty, War Office, Air Ministry and Treasury Committee, who instead concluded that a Free Italian Cyrenaica would make a voluntary surrender of the Italian fleet easier, and be excellent propaganda. The Committee did however warn that such a development would be looked upon as a betrayal by the Arab population of Cyrenaica, who were extremely anti-Italian, and suggested it might be preferable to set up the Free Italian colony in Eritrea; it was also pointed out that it would in any case be difficult to provide the necessary imports to sustain Cyrenaica, in view of the supply position in the Mediterranean. The War Cabinet approved the Committee's report, and on 7 March a long cable was sent to discover the reaction of General Wavell and of the British Ambassador to Egypt, Sir Miles Lampson (who had an Italian wife). London wanted their opinions as to whether a Free Italy movement could be created in Cyrenaica among the existing civil population, what the chances were of raising a Free Italian force among the Italian prisoners-of-war, and what would be the reaction to these proposals in Egypt, Cyrenaica and the Arab world in the Middle East generally?

Eden arrived in Cairo shortly after the cable; following discussions with Lampson and Wavell, he reported his own view that the existing Italian population in Cyrenaica were not 'promising material' because they had been especially selected as 'promising Fascist colonists', while Wavell felt strongly that as long as there was a possibility of an Axis counter-attack from Tripoli it would be dangerous to experiment with a Free Italian organization in Cyrenaica. In addition, he felt the Arab reaction would generally be 'unfavourable'.

Churchill's enthusiasm for a Free Italian colony soon waned, while high-level argument centred on whether the Egyptians or the Senussi would rule Cyrenaica. In January 1942 Churchill stated in the House of Commons that because of the help rendered by the Senussi against Britain's enemies, Cyrenaica would under no circumstances be placed under Italian rule again.

Churchill's suggestion that an attempt should be made to find 'an Italian de Gaulle' among the generals captured in Egypt and raise a Free Italian Army was taken up seriously by Wavell. Freya Stark, the well-known Arabist, wrote a memorandum suggesting with strange optimism that two-thirds of the Italian prisoners were anti-Fascist and should be put under sympathetic Maltese guards. General Bergonzoli, an ebullient figure known as 'Electric Whiskers' from his enormous side-whiskers, was one of those being considered as a possible leader, until a War Office report condemned him as a 'mountebank'. Little progress was made among the captured Italian officers in Egypt, but there were hopes that a more favourable reaction might be found in those who had been sent on to India. Such hopes proved false, however; nothing materialized from efforts made in India, and the plan for a Free Italian Army soon died.

The bizarre efforts made to bribe the Italian fleet to surrender are well documented in the British archives. They began in November 1940, a period of Italian gloom and disillusion with Mussolini, and indicate how low morale was in the upper echelons of the Italian Navy. The British Legation in Stockholm was informed that anti-Fascist senior naval officers wanted to surrender the Italian fleet to the British to prevent it being turned over to the Germans. Churchill was enthusiastic that discussions should be pursued, minuting his desire to take a personal interest; on 25 November the War Cabinet approved further contacts. After consultation between Churchill, Eden, and the First Lord of the Admiralty, A.V. Alexander, a telegram was sent from the Foreign Office to the British Legation in Stockholm:

> Following message may be given to Swedish intermediary to pass on to his anti-Fascist contacts: 'We re-affirm our previous offer that we shall gladly receive any units of the Italian Fleet that may come to us, and we will do our best to escort merchant ships with families.
>
> 'If a real effort is made by the Italian Fleet to avoid falling under German control and evidenced by the sending of important units to British overseas ports, this fact would undoubtedly weigh with us when considering terms of peace with Italy, and we should do our best to save Italy from German domination both before and after the final peace conference.'

The Swedish intermediary was J.H. Walter, an engineer who had previously negotiated the sale of Italian destroyers to Sweden on behalf of the Italian government. In March the British Minister in Sweden, Victor Mallet, described Walter as a man with 'guts and love of adventure', although the previous December he had told the Foreign Office that Walter was 'a man with the shadiest of reputations'. Walter produced a price-list for the surrenders, showing amounts varying from $15,000 for a torpedo-boat to $300,000 for a battleship; there was also to be compensation for the families of officers from the surrendering ships.

Churchill minuted to the Admiralty that he wanted to accept; the Admiralty replied that in their view the chances of success were slight, but the payments required were so small in relation to the prizes to be gained that the gamble appeared worthwhile. Nevertheless, Churchill seems to have been faintly nonplussed: on 20 March he scrawled, 'This all seems fantastic. WSC.' Walter requested that $60,000 be deposited in a US bank, and this was done.

The secret channel between Stockholm and Italy was suddenly interrupted for three months when the Gestapo and the Italian Secret Police (OVRA) began to subject suspect military and naval personnel – including even Badoglio and Grandi – to rigorous enquiries and controls. The Italian Ambassador in Sweden, Francesco Fransoni (later to play a part in the peace negotiations) must have been aware of the overtures; he was transferred to Lisbon on 19 June 1941.

On 7 April 1941 the Foreign Office instructed: 'Our propaganda should be that Hitler was going to take over the Italian fleet, and spread such rumours and try and make direct contact with officers of the fleet.' The BBC was told that the government strategy was 'surrender of the Italian fleet and air force' and asked to paint the image of a powerful Free Italian movement outside Italy, with the aim of making it easier for Italian officers to surrender without a feeling of treason. Both Sir Peter Tennant (Press Attaché) and Commander Denham, RN (Naval Attaché), who conducted the negotiations with J.H. Walter in Stockholm, have told the author of their conviction that the overtures were genuine.

On 15 July Mallet cabled from Stockholm that owing to the release from prison of 'certain Italian naval officers', 'communication has again been restored', and that an Italian emissary had arrived recently with assurances from 'certain Italian naval officers' that as soon as the time was ripe the surrender of the Italian ships would take place, despite the fact that 'certain Italian naval officers' had been relieved of their posts and reprisals taken against them. The Foreign Office reply was, 'Tell him our side of the bargain still holds.'

Walter claimed that in Rome he had been in contact with Admirals Cavagnari, Riccardi and Parona, the heads of the Admiralty, and learned that German interference with the Italian fleet had almost prompted Riccardi to resign. Professor Alberto Santoni, a leading Italian naval historian who has written about the negotiations in his book *Da Lissa alle Falkland*, has told the author he has no doubt there was a high level plot in 1940–41 to surrender the Italian fleet. Admiral Massimiliano Marandino, Head of the Italian Institute of Naval History, has declared that in his archives there is not a scrap of evidence to support Santoni's claims. The British archives are convincing, but following the interception of a secret signal Walter was arrested by the Swedish police, and that was the end of the matter.[7]

The tale of these negotiations over the Italian fleet, of the 'Garibaldi Legion', a Free Cyrenaica and the search for 'an Italian de Gaulle' belongs to the dustbin of history: all came to nothing. Yet the story is important in revealing Churchill's policy. At the time the Prime Minister was ready for a 'soft' peace with an anti-Fascist Italian government. On Christmas Day 1940 he broadcast to the Italian nation that Mussolini alone was responsible for the war between two traditionally friendly countries, and incited the Italian people to overthrow the Duce. At that time any worthwhile offers from anti-Fascist leaders would have been well received in London. None came, and when they did, two years later, when Italy was down and out, they were ill-received.

Italy's fortunes in war changed dramatically for the better in 1941. Instead of letting her fight her parallel war alone, Hitler threw powerful German troops into the Italian struggle in Greece and North Africa. Greece was soon overrun, and the island of Crete was captured.

In Libya on the last day of March 1941 Rommel, who had taken command of and reinforced the Italians with powerful German armoured divisions, attacked the British forces, much weakened by sending troops to Greece, and in twelve days had recaptured nearly all Cyrenaica (Libya), surrounded Tobruk and reached Bardia. The British position in the eastern Mediterranean had crumbled, and if Hitler had followed up these victories, Cairo and the Suez Canal would have been lost. Fortunately, the Führer was more intent on attacking Russia, and postponed the offensive to oust Britain from the Canal Zone.

As usual, Mussolini was not consulted by Hitler about his plans. At a meeting between the two dictators on the Brenner on 31 May Hitler told Mussolini nothing about his plans for the campaign against Russia, although the flow of German troops to the Russian frontier had been the topic of excited rumours the whole month. Ribbentrop told Ciano the rumours had no foundation – were, at least, 'excessively premature' – and that it was the Russians who were concentrating their forces on the German frontier.

When the two Foreign Ministers met again at Venice on 15 June, Ciano was left in little doubt that a German attack on Russia was imminent; but it was not until after the German armies had crossed the Soviet frontier on 22 June that Hitler informed Mussolini. In his letter announcing the start of the war with Russia, Hitler gave the Duce the unwelcome news that the attack on Egypt must be postponed until the autumn; he claimed he had not told Mussolini in advance because the decision to attack had only been taken on the previous day; this was an outright lie. The day after hearing the news, Ciano recorded in his diary: 'The thing that is closest to the Duce's heart is the participation [in Russia] of one of our contingents, but from what Hitler writes it is clear that he could gladly do without.'

However, by 27 June Italian units were on the way to the Russian front, after being reviewed at Verona by Mussolini.

As usual, the Duce's feelings and opinions were see-sawing. In his reply to Hitler welcoming the war against Russia, Mussolini wrote that any delay in attacking Russia would have been 'dangerous for our cause', yet on 1 July he told his son-in-law that he hoped 'for only one thing, that in this war in the east the Germans will lose a lot of feathers', while on 25 August he offered to bring his contingent in Russia up to more than nine divisions. Hitler received the offer without enthusiasm, pointing out the logistical difficulties, and suggesting that because of the extreme cold it would be better for the Italians to fight in the warmer Caucasus area. As usual, Mussolini anticipated an immediate German victory. The war against Russia was more popular in Italy than the war against Britain; Italians, especially the Church, were anti-Communist, and priests blessed the Italian troops leaving for Russia as if they were embarking on a crusade.[8]

During the summer of 1941 Eden's line towards Italy changed, and on 18 July the Southern Department of the Foreign Office submitted a memorandum ruling out any possibility of a 'soft' peace. The memorandum pointed out that although the Italian people were not particularly heartened by the Axis victories in Libya, Greece and Russia, they now again saw the Germans as the probable victors, thus leaving Italy no choice but to become a vassal of Germany. The heads of the Italian armed forces were 'against both the war and the Fascist regime', but had been 'too permeated by Fascism to take revolutionary action', and there was 'nothing to be hoped for from the King'; Italian morale, however, was much lower than might have been expected after the long series of Axis victories. The memorandum was circulated to the War Cabinet, together with a note from Eden:

> Apathy and war weariness are the salient characteristics of the prevailing mood in Italy. Chances of knocking Italy out of the war (i.e., separate peace) can now be discounted since the Germans would certainly forestall any such move in Italy by converting the present moral occupation into a physical occupation of the country. But the more depressed and restless the Italians become the less effective is the Italian contribution to the German effort, and the greater the Germans' policing responsibilities in Italy become.
>
> The moral of all this is that even though we cannot now hope to knock Italy out, we should not relax efforts to hit metropolitan Italy by air and from the sea whenever opportunity occurs. Each blow against Italy is a blow against Germany.

The note was approved by the War Cabinet, and Eden wrote to Archibald Sinclair, Secretary of State for Air, on 6 August 1941: 'I would like to draw your attention to the desirability of hitting Italy whenever possible.' Fortunately for Italy, the bombing of civilian targets there was a low priority for the RAF. In August Cadogan minuted that 'hopes of a separate peace were moonshine'. Eden agreed, adding: 'We have to win a victory on land in an important theatre before we can catch any of these moonbeams.'[9]

On Sunday 7 December 1941, 363 planes from Japanese aircraft carriers attacked the US fleet at Pearl Harbour, putting out of action nearly all the battleships there and killing more than 2,400 Americans. There were doubts inside the Foreign Office whether the United States would declare war on Germany and Italy; war with Japan was on the cards, but it was thought Roosevelt would have difficulty in persuading Congress to approve a declaration of war on Germany, let alone Italy. However, Hitler made his biggest mistake when on 11 December he declared war on the United States. From the balcony of the Palazzo Venezia Mussolini followed suit, with apparent pleasure. The crowd, apart from an organized claque, received the news badly; the ties between Italy and the large Italian–American population of the United States were too close for such a war to be popular. Mussolini was behaving like a madman.

In the Western Desert, by December 1941 General Auchinleck's attack had pushed a combined German–Italian force to the identical point previously reached by Wavell with the Eighth Army. German reinforcements, including many aeroplanes and much armour, were then sent to Libya, and in place of the contemplated invasion of Malta, Mussolini agreed to an attack designed to reach the Suez Canal. Rommel successfully pushed the British back to a line fifty miles west of Alexandria and reached El Alamein, inside the Egyptian frontier. Rommel's attack on this line was repelled by the British on 1 July 1942, and the Axis troops began to run short of oil and other *matériel*, as so many of their tankers and supply ships were being sunk in Allied attacks.

Mussolini wanted to extract as much glory as possible from the Axis victory in the desert: he planed to enter Cairo riding on a white horse, to ensure that the victory was hailed as an Italian, not a German, triumph – but two days after he arrived in Africa on 29 June, the offensive ground to a halt. Rommel, who did not care for the Duce, never visited him. Mussolini spent three disagreeable weeks behind the lines of the stagnant battlefield, visiting troops and hospitals. He contracted amoebic dysentery, and returned to Rome a sick and disappointed man, aware that lack of supplies made it improbable that the Axis armies would ever reach the Canal. The halt on the Egyptian front and German setbacks in Russia depressed Italian public opinion, and a wave of pessimism swept the country, at a time when Mussolini was too ill to work to remedy the situation by inspired leadership.

On 23 October 1942 the Eighth Army, now under General Montgomery, assaulted the Axis troops at El Alamein, and by 5 November had secured victory. Two days later, on 7 November, American and British forces landed in Algiers and Morocco. Mussolini was proved right strategically in his constant demand to Hitler to occupy Tunis, since it was only the stream of a quarter of a million German and Italian reinforcements sent through the port that enabled the Axis Front in North Africa to hold; but all they achieved was a delay of a few months before their defeat. On 7 May 1943 Tunis and Bizerta fell to the Allies, and on 12 May the Axis troops in Africa surrendered: 240,000 marched into captivity. Until the last Mussolini refused to accept that all was lost in Tunisia; on 30 April he wrote that the troops were fighting 'splendidly', and asked Hitler to send massive reinforcements of aeroplanes to protect the convoys ferrying supplies to them.

As the Axis position in North Africa deteriorated, Mussolini asked Hitler to negotiate peace terms with Stalin so that the Axis could concentrate their military effort on the Mediterranean. Hitler refused, with the consequence that in November 1942 Ciano tried to discover what would be the British response to a request from Mussolini for a separate peace. Fransoni, now Italy's Ambassador in Lisbon, who had already been concerned in the negotiations in Stockholm for the surrender of the Italian fleet in 1941, was instructed to approach London.

One of Fransoni's staff approached the Polish Embassy in Lisbon and asked them to find out whether the British would do anything to make it 'worthwhile' for Italy to pull out of the war. The Italian contact asserted that Fransoni had frequently made overtures to the British Embassy in Lisbon, but they had never told him 'how they viewed the situation'. On receipt of this information in London, Eden minuted uncomprisingly on 11 November 1942:

> I had much rather kill this stuff and tell the Poles to do the same. We don't propose to make peace with Mussolini, and these men are his creatures. The only hope in Italy is a revolution, which is just what these men want to avoid. If a whisper of this reached Russian ears results would be very bad, especially with Poles mixed up. Anyway there can be no advantage. I think Poles should be discouraged, and we at any rate deprecate the whole affair and refuse to deal with the intermediaries.[10]

Fransoni saw Ciano in Rome in early December 1942, and asked the Foreign Minister if he still had hopes of an Axis military victory. When Ciano said 'No', Fransoni sought permission to send messages to Sir Ronald Campbell, the British Ambassador in Lisbon, through a

Romanian intermediary, Jan Pangal; Mussolini approved. Fransoni's messages were relayed to London, and on 18 December Eden sent a message to Cordell Hull, the US Foreign Secretary, that the Italian legation at Lisbon had used a Romanian intermediary to show His Majesty's Embassy and the Polish Embassy at Lisbon their

> interest in a separate peace. We have decided not to pursue this feeler since the Italians in Lisbon are servants of the present regime, and to maintain contact could only serve to throw suspicion on our declarations that we are out to destroy Fascism.

Hull replied to Eden that although the lines of communication might well be kept open, proposals of this nature should not be pursued with such representatives of the Fascist regime as the diplomatic mission in Lisbon.

At the same time, the anti-Fascists also made overtures to Britain: the Duke of Aosta, a cousin of Victor Emmanuel, sent a message through the Italian consul in Geneva to the Foreign Office that he would lead an armed uprising against Mussolini and the Fascist regime in return for certain guarantees, which included the preservation of the monarchy in Italy and an agreed landing in Italy by US and British troops 'on the understanding that they should land as Allies to assist in the overthrow of the regime and not as troops to conquer and occupy Italy'.

In a further letter to Hull, dated 15 January 1943, Eden made clear his 'hard' line over the question of a separate peace with Italy, which was in marked contrast to the 'soft' line both he and Churchill had advocated two years earlier:

> Our aim must be to knock Italy out of the war as quickly as possible, and this could be achieved with almost equal effect whether Italy made a separate peace or whether dissatisfaction and disorder within the country attained such serious proportions that the Germans were forced to establish a full-scale occupation . . . We have considered the possibility of a party arising in Italy which would be willing and able to conclude a separate peace. Before this situation could occur two prerequisites would in our view be essential. The Germans would have to be so weakened as no longer to be able to control events in Italy, and a national leader would have to emerge with sufficient strength to displace Mussolini. Such evidence as we have recently received does not suggest that either of these prerequisites is likely to be fulfilled . . . The King is regarded as a willing tool of Fascism, and the Italian people appear no longer to be looking to him as a leader.
>
> The view of His Majesty's Government is, therefore, that we should not count on the possibility of a separate peace but should aim at such disorder in Italy as would necessitate a German occupation. We suggest that the best means of achieving this aim is to intensify all forms of military operations against Italy, particularly aerial bombardment.

Hull's reply advised that aerial bombardment of Italy 'should be confined to military objectives as much as humanly possible. Indiscriminate bombing will only stiffen Italian morale.'[11]

Eden's judgement was far astray. First of all, he did not realize that the Italian nation, in widespread disillusion with Mussolini and the war, was indeed turning to the King for leadership, and to an extent that would enable him to topple the Duce; secondly, he failed to consider that the worst thing from the Allied point of view would be a German military occupation of Italy; Eden's aim should instead have been to negotiate with the anti-Fascists for an Allied landing as suggested by Aosta, so that the Germans could be kept out. He threw away a great opportunity for ending Italian participation in the war during the early phases of the costly North African campaign; had he seized on Ciano's or Aosta's initiative, a great number of Allied casualties in North Africa might have been avoided. According to Renzo de Felice, at this time Mussolini would himself have considered concluding an armistice, and his own abdication.

In his letter to Hull of 15 January Eden described it as 'useless' to offer tempting peace terms to the Italian people, because the minimum which would attract them would be a guarantee of their pre-war frontiers, and this was not possible because of the claims of Yugoslavia and (surprisingly) Austria. The White House disagreed, but did not try to soften the British hard line.

At the Casablanca Conference in January 1943 the 'unconditional surrender' formula was invented by Roosevelt and Churchill. However, both had qualms about applying it to Italy; Churchill accordingly sent a telegram to the War Cabinet asking for their view whether unconditional surrender should be demanded of Germany and Japan only, and not of Italy: 'Omission of Italy would encourage breaking up. FDR likes idea.' In Churchill's absence, Eden dominated the War Cabinet over foreign affairs, and he and Attlee sent back a tough reply: 'Cabinet unanimous that Italy must be threatened with unconditional surrender. Knowledge of rough stuff coming to them should have desired effect on Italian morale.' So unconditional surrender was demanded from Italy until the bitter end, with disastrous consequences, and when the non-Fascist Badoglio government actually surrendered, there was no plan in place for an Allied military occupation of Italy to forestall the Germans.[12]

Marshal Badoglio now abandoned Mussolini and made a truce with an old enemy, Marshal Caviglia, a legendary figure from the battle of Vittorio Veneto during the First World War. In January 1943 the Foreign Office and the Chiefs-of-Staff were informed by the SOE that secret contacts in Switzerland were claiming Badoglio and

Caviglia had a powerful following in Italy and wanted to seize power and set up a military government supported by an anti-Fascist army. SOE asked for permission to fly the anti-Fascist General Pesenti out from Italy to talk to the British government on the plotters' behalf and start raising an anti-Fascist army from Italian POWs in North Africa. Pesenti had always been anti-Fascist, and as military commander in Somaliland in 1941 had advised the Duke of Aosta to ask for a separate armistice on the Abyssinian front.

On 18 January the War Cabinet decided to postpone any response to these feelers from Badoglio and Caviglia. On 1 February Eden wrote to Hull that the disadvantages of bringing Pesenti out outweighed the advantages, because 'negotiations with him would entail some undertakings being entered into on our side', and it was inadvisable at this stage for the Allies to commit themselves to the support of any individual Italian without more information regarding the backing he commanded inside Italy – this was inconsistent of Eden, as only a fortnight earlier he had written to Hull that only Badoglio could bring Mussolini down. The Americans were in favour of taking a softer line with Italy, and the War Office wanted Pesenti brought out. This pressure on two sides resulted in a memorandum from Eden to the Prime Minister on 17 February, which revealed how the Foreign Secretary's hostility to Italy was preventing agreement with Mussolini's opponents. Eden admitted that:

> If we want to get some group in Italy to co-operate with us we shall have to hold out at least some hope in regard to the future of Italy . . .

but went on:

> We cannot guarantee the territorial restoration of metropolitan Italy owing to the pledge we have given to the Yugoslavs to espouse their claim to Istria after the war . . . I fancy we are most likely to achieve our object of getting Italy out of the war by sticking to our present tough line, reinforced by heavy bombing and the threat of invasion. Premature and unrelated promises would be interpreted by the Italians as a sign of weakness.

No urgency was accorded the matter by the War Cabinet, and when they finally agreed to bring Pesenti out, on 18 March, it was too late: his pilot had been arrested.[13]

With hindsight, it appears that a god-given chance to liaise with Badoglio and the anti-Fascists was thrown away by Britain in not immediately welcoming Pesenti when he was in a position to fly out. Then, without the knowledge of the Germans, plans could have been concerted for an Allied military take-over of Italy. In addition, according to Field Marshal Montgomery, during December 1941 and

January 1942 the Italian army in Tunisia was fighting harder and better than before, and if the Italian soldiers had heard of a move by Badoglio to raise an anti-Fascist army their morale would have been damaged and they might have left the Germans in the lurch.

As it became obvious that the Axis would eventually be driven out of North Africa, and news came of the Russian triumph at Stalingrad and the abandonment of Italian troops in Russia by the Germans, anti-Fascist activity in Italy increased; overtures through Switzerland, Spain and Portugal were made to the British by the influential industrialists Alberto Pirelli and Adriano Olivetti, by Emilio Lusso, a pre-Fascist Sardinian politician, and Ugo La Malfa of the clandestine Party of Action (he became a prominent post war politician), and by Maria José, wife of Crown Prince Umberto. On Eden's instructions they were all met with the Casablanca formula of 'unconditional surrender'. No assurances of any kind were forthcoming from London about the treatment Italy could expect to receive after the war if they succeeded, as they hoped, in displacing the Fascist regime and allying with the Americans and British against the Germans. The King was in close touch with the dissidents, and he and they much resented the Allied intransigence. However, the lack of progress being made in these talks held in neutral countries eventually convinced Victor Emmanuel that he must attempt a coup against Mussolini, even though no alternative to unconditional surrender was being offered.[14]

The anti-Fascists would have done better to make their approaches to the United States, who took a softer line, but Italian memories of the British–Italian friendship of the days of the Risorgimento lingered on. Eden's hostility was demonstrated by his displeasure when he learnt that the RAF had dropped leaflets on Rome at the beginning of June offering 'peace with honour'. In the British Minister's absence on leave in London, Cardinal Maglione, Head of State at the Vatican, sent for the First Secretary at the British Mission, Hugh Montgomery, and read out the leaflets to him. 'How', he asked, 'could Britain reconcile "peace with honour" with "unconditional surrender"?' Montgomery was instructed by Eden not to try to explain the difference, and Harold Macmillan, the Resident Cabinet Minister in Algiers, was told firmly to prevent the repetition of this phrase in future leaflets as it was not to the liking either of Eden or of Brendan Bracken, the Minister of Information. When D'Arcy Osborne returned to Rome, the Pope sent for him and expressed his concern over the difference between the two phrases. Eden was unruffled about this, and when he heard that Cardinal Maglione had also asked what the British were doing to safeguard the art treasures of Italy, he again revealed his anti-Italian feelings, minuting that Maglione was an

Italian and the Italians should have thought of this before they declared war.

After the fall of Tunis in May 1943, relations between Hitler and Mussolini took a turn for the worse. Mussolini knew Italy could not fight on, and with Hitler refusing to make peace with Russia, he (Mussolini) began to contemplate an arrangement with Britain and America to allow Italy to get out of the war. When Hitler offered him five extra divisions to protect Italy from an Allied invasion he refused, and relations between General Ambrosio, the head of the Italian armed forces, and the German High Command became strained. Hitler suspected that Mussolini was not prepared to fight until the end, and in May began plans for a military occupation of Italy if she should try to withdraw from the war. Mussolini, aware of what his ally was up to, requested aerial support only, with no extra German ground troops on Italian territory.

On 10 June the fortified island of Pantellaria (between Tripoli and Sicily) and its garrison of 12,000 men surrendered to the Allies without resistance. For unexplained reasons (which may have been connected with his desire to extricate Italy from the war) Mussolini gave the commander, Admiral Pavesi, permission to surrender on the grounds of lack of water and superior enemy strength; since there was in fact no shortage of water, this episode aroused German suspicions of treachery on Mussolini's part.

On 10 July 1943 an amphibious Anglo-US force (larger than that deployed for the D-Day cross-Channel invasion) assaulted the south coast of Sicily. Of about 230,000 Axis troops on the island, only two divisions were German; the Germans resisted fiercely, but the Italians showed no will to fight. After a short campaign, on 18 August the Germans and a few Italian units evacuated Sicily across the Straits of Messina; the bulk of the Italian troops had largely disintegrated as a fighting force – there were great numbers of deserters, and nearly 150,000 were taken prisoner.

Hitler was livid at the Italians' performance in Sicily, and particularly infuriated by the Italian admiral in charge of the naval base at Augusta in Sicily, who had blown up his guns and abandoned his post so that his men should not be able to resist the Allies. Hitler bitterly rebuked Mussolini over Augusta, and for the fact that in many areas the Sicilian population had welcomed the Allies, even painting messages of welcome on house walls. The Führer told his generals that in supplying and reinforcing the Italian army they must take into account the likelihood of a *coup d'état* in Rome and the eventual use of the Italian armed forces against Germany; he made plans for a military occupation of Italy should she defect from the Axis.[15]

Shocked by the poor performance of his army in Sicily, Mussolini was even more determined to try to end Italy's participation in the war. He was briefly buoyed up, however, by a renewed suggestion from Field Marshal Kesselring of an attack on Gibraltar through Spain; if this were to be accomplished and Spain should enter the war, the whole Mediterranean position would be altered, opening up great opportunities for Axis submarine warfare. Fortunately, by now Franco fully appreciated the way the wind was blowing, while Kesselring's suggestion was an unrealistic one to which Spain was never likely to agree, and Hitler ruled that an occupation of Spain without the consent of the Spaniards was 'out of the question'.

During the winter of 1942/43 Mussolini made overtures to Admiral Horthy, the Hungarian Regent, and to Marshal Antonescu, the Romanian Head of State. Both Hungary and Romania, fighting unsuccessfully against Russia, were as anxious as Mussolini to get out of the war, and the Duce persuaded them that he might be able to negotiate a state of neutrality for their three countries with the Allies. It was an unrealistic idea, but Mussolini felt that the inclusion of Hungary and Romania would make his overtures more attractive to the British.[16]

Mussolini had dismissed Ciano as Foreign Secretary on 5 February 1943 and assumed the office himself, appointing Bastianini, the former Ambassador in London, as his Under-Secretary. Bastianini was not originally a career diplomat but had come up through the Fascist Party; always anti-German, he was eager to get Italy out of the war.

In April Mussolini angrily condemned Hitler to Bastianini:

> That tragic buffoon stubbornly seeks a victory in Russia that is completely out of the question. I have told him this at least ten times but he does not want to know. Goering and Himmler share my opinion, as does Keitel, I believe.[17]

Bastianini briefed Raffaele Guariglia, the Italian Ambassador to Turkey, Renato Prunas, who had succeeded Fransoni in Lisbon, and Giacomo Paulucci in Madrid that Mussolini accepted the war was lost and was seeking an exit; while the Duce preferred peace with Russia, this had been vetoed by Hitler, so that he was ready for an accord with the British and the Americans. Bastianini saw no hope of an end to the Russian war and was desperately anxious to disengage Italy from Germany and, with Hungary and Romania, make a separate peace with the Allies. Paulucci made the most progress, but all he was offered from London was the Casablanca formula of 'unconditional surrender'.

At a secret meeting on 16 July Bastianini's impassioned entreaties persuaded Mussolini to double-cross Hitler. In strictest secrecy Bastianini made a transcript of this meeting for his closest colleagues.

Stressing the Allied success in Sicily, and especially the jubilation with which the Sicilians had greeted the invading forces, Bastianini told the Duce that the gravity of the situation made it imperative to take drastic action to get Italy out of the war; he emphasized the country's ghastly plight and her inability to repel an Allied landing in the peninsula, expressing his conviction that now the United States had set foot in the Mediterranean, the Americans would never leave it; they did not want Italy to fall into the hands of the Bolsheviks, while the British did not want to turn Italy into a cemetery, and the Pope was anxious to prevent a blood-bath. Mussolini at first said he would never consign Italy to the British, who would use her as a base to attack Germany and deprive her of every resource. Bastianini then reminded him that when Bulgaria ceased hostilities in the First World War the German troops had left her territory, so that to all intents and purposes she became a non-belligerent. This was not a valid precedent but it impressed Mussolini, and when Bastianini declared that it was their 'sacred duty' to get Italy out of the war, the Duce agreed to official contacts being made with the British. Bastianini promised that this would be done through Lisbon, in such a way that if the Germans found out it could be claimed that Mussolini himself was in no way involved.

According to the Italian historian Mario Toscano, Bastianini assured Mussolini he would make the British guarantee that Mussolini himself would be 'spared (*risparmiato*)'. This is improbable, as it would have jeopardized any negotiations; more probably, Bastianini meant he would ask that Mussolini should not be put to death.

Bastianini then obtained a passport from Cardinal Maglione at the Vatican for Giovanni Fummi, a well-known banker with British contacts, and at the same time asked him that the Pope should intercede for a separate peace. Maglione agreed to both requests. (At that time Vatican passports were accepted by the Americans and British, but their use was mainly restricted to clerics on Vatican business.)[18]

The Italian monarchy and certain anti-Fascists were simultaneously making advances to the British through neutral embassies, claiming to be about to overthrow Mussolini. Campbell, the British Ambassador in Lisbon, suspected a German plot but reported Fummi's approach, informing the Foreign Office that he had a Vatican passport and wanted to go to London. Fummi had been instructed by Bastianini not to negotiate with Campbell but to insist on going to London, where he was to tell Eden, in person, that Italy, Hungary and Romania were seeking peace terms from Britain and the United States. Fummi was still in Lisbon when on 25 July Victor Emmanuel had Mussolini arrested, whereupon his credentials became valueless.[19]

Following the Italian collapse in Sicily and coinciding with his decision to try to open negotiations with the British, Mussolini was summoned to a meeting with Hitler on 19 July at Feltre, near Treviso on the Austrian–Italian border. Mussolini knew Hitler had made plans to occupy Italy, and was terrified that his own approaches to the British might have been discovered by the Germans.

This was the most bizarre of all the meetings between the two dictators. As usual Hitler dominated the proceedings. He ranted for two hours: 'It is a question of will power; if we are to save the nations from ruin we must shrink from no hardship' and 'the war will be won in the first place by men and then by tanks, anti-tank guns, aircraft and anti-aircraft weapons'. At midday the conference was interrupted by reports that Rome was being heavily bombed from the air. Mussolini, confident of his abilities as a linguist, always refused to have an interpreter during these meetings, but he was already finding it hard to follow Hitler; after hearing the news of the bombing, he was quite unable to concentrate on the Führer's tirade about Italian military inadequacies, particularly their failure to protect German aeroplanes on Italian aerodromes, where three or four hundred had been destroyed on the ground. Now, Hitler said, if Italy was to be defended, all Italian troops must be put under German control. According to the Italian diplomat Dino Alfieri, Mussolini said nothing: 'He never opened his mouth.'

Mussolini was accompanied that day by Alfieri, Giuseppe Bastianini and General Ambrosio, and the two last were already aware of a plot on the part of the King, Badoglio and Grandi to arrest the Duce.

When they broke for lunch Ambrosio, in much stronger terms than he was accustomed to use or Mussolini to hear, reminded the Duce that the military situation was 'catastrophic' and that some solution (for example, a peace, or a massive German intervention) must be found within fifteen days; Bastianini added that Mussolini must put this to Hitler in unmistakable words. This tough talk gave the Duce a shock. He confessed to having been tormented by this very problem; he had been thinking of capitulation to the enemy, but this would be to throw away the work of twenty years; furthermore, if 'we' broke with Germany, Hitler would allow Italy no freedom of action. Surprisingly, in view of this conversation, Mussolini afterwards said nothing of importance to the Führer, and on his return to Germany Hitler wrote to General Warlimont that he had brought Mussolini back into the ranks.[20]

The King had decided that the Axis had lost the war, and felt that it would be impossible to make peace with the Allies if Mussolini remained in power. With him, Grandi concocted a plan to move a resolution critical of Mussolini at a meeting of the Fascist Grand Council called for 24 July; the passing of such a resolution would give the King an excuse to dismiss Mussolini.

Renzo de Felice writes that at Feltre Mussolini hoped to gain time in which to cut loose from the Germans without running the risk of having his country overrun by them. He is almost certainly correct in this, and also in his opinion that at this point Mussolini felt a great hatred for Hitler and rejected out of hand any idea of German protection against his adversaries at home. De Felice also considers, more doubtfully, that Mussolini entertained high hopes of the overtures to London already initiated by Bastianini. In fact there were none. Bastianini had misled Mussolini: his claims to understand the workings of the British government from his days as Ambassador in London were grossly exaggerated.

At the Grand Council meeting on 24 July Mussolini was curiously indecisive. He dared not indicate that he had made a move towards the British, as this would immediately be leaked to the Germans. He justified the belief he expressed in an eventual Axis victory solely by reference to a new secret weapon Hitler had boasted of at Feltre which would devastate Britain (this weapon was the 'flying bomb', the V1); he must have been convinced that Italy had no option but to make peace with the Allies. Grandi's motion was passed with a substantial majority. Declaring the result, Mussolini told the Grand Council, 'You have provoked the crisis of the regime', but did not realize that his own fate was sealed. The next day, 25 July, he went to report the Council's vote to the King; he was taken by surprise when Victor Emmanuel announced that Marshal Badoglio was to take over as Prime Minister, and dumbfounded by his arrest as he left the King's presence. Overnight, the Fascist Party ceased to exist.

Britain and the United States were amazed by Mussolini's downfall. The Foreign Office in London relied on reports from the Minister to the Holy See, D'Arcy Osborne, but he, closeted in the Vatican, was out of touch with Italian opinion. On 24 July, the day before Mussolini's arrest, Osborne wrote to London, 'I do not expect any serious or successful movement from any quarter against the Fascist Government . . . typhus and famine are more probable.' Early in July Alberto Pirelli, with Mussolini's approval, had gone to Switzerland to explore the possibility of the Swiss acting as intermediaries in a peace move from Italy; on 24 July, Eden saw a report that in Switzerland Pirelli had said, 'The King will replace Mussolini within a month', and wrote on the file in red ink, 'Italians of Pirelli's type have a lot to learn.' Yet even as he wrote, the King had finalized his plan to topple the Duce.[21]

CHAPTER 17

Mussolini's End

As FOREIGN SECRETARY, Anthony Eden turned a cold shoulder to several approaches from Italian monarchists and anti-Fascists during the spring and summer of 1943. Through British embassies in neutral countries the Italian emissaries were told that nothing but unconditional surrender would be accepted from an alternative, non-Fascist government seeking a separate peace. 'Absolute silence' was the Foreign Office response to requests from the Italian dissendents for negotiations, a sharp contrast to the soft line taken in 1940–41 (see Chapter 16). In failing to discuss plans for a coup with the anti-Fascists, the Allies threw away the opportunity for an unopposed landing in Italy when Mussolini was arrested on 25 July. At that time the Germans had only one incompletely equipped division in central Italy, plus some paratroopers, two divisions in southern Italy, and four divisions fighting unsuccessfully in Sicily. If Allied and Italian naval and land forces had co-operated immediately after Mussolini's arrest, the German army in Sicily could have been trapped and prevented from retreating across the Straits of Messina. Eden misjudged the strength of the anti-Fascists, and upon him must lie the responsibility for the failure of the Allies to forestall the German occupation of Italy.

Hitler was as surprised as the Allies by Mussolini's arrest. 'Badoglio has taken over – the blackest of our enemies', he declared, and worried that Allied air and sea forces would arrive in Italy unopposed, in collusion with the Italians. His first reaction was to order the single German division in central Italy to occupy Rome and arrest the new government; he said, 'The Fascist party is only stunned at present. We must act at once or the Anglo-Saxons will steal a march on us by occupying the airfields.' He was counting on support from the Fascists, which would not in fact have been forthcoming. Admiral Dönitz, head of the German navy, advised Hitler that an attack on Rome would be hotly opposed by both the Italian army and the majority of the population, so that evacuation of German troops would become almost impossible, and in his book *The Brutal Friendship* Sir William Deakin demonstrates that if the German operation against Rome had been attempted, their army in Sicily would probably have been lost.[1]

Badoglio issued a statement that the war (in alliance with Germany) 'would continue under his government'; in the House of Commons Churchill predicted that 'Italy will be seared and scarred and blackened from one end to the other', and suggested that 'we should let the Italians stew in their own juice'. These two statements convinced Hitler there was no Allied plan to land in Italy, and so instead of making an immediate strike against Rome he sent as many German divisions as possible into Italy to protect the route to Sicily and prevent Italy changing sides. The Allies, meanwhile, continued to bomb Italy.

Without authorization from the Badoglio government, German divisions with 'Viva il Duce' written on their helmets poured into Italy over the Brenner Pass and German military currency was issued, as if Italy was already an occupied country. Badoglio made no effort to stop these German reinforcements, and his inertia was responsible for the loss of any chance Italy might have had of escaping from the war without having to fight the Germans on Italian soil.

On 17 August the Germans evacuated Sicily; the Allies made plans to invade southern Italy early in September. Although the Badoglio government made abortive attempts to contact the British through Tangiers on 3 August and through Lisbon on 14 August, it was not until 18 August that serious talks took place. Then General Castellano, Badoglio's emissary, conferred in Lisbon with General Bedell Smith (second-in-command to General Eisenhower, GOC Mediterranean). At first Castellano was met with a point-blank demand for surrender, but negotiations were opened after he passed on valuable information about German troop dispositions in Italy. The upshot was that a short surrender document was signed by Castellano and Eisenhower in Sicily on 3 September. The Italians then stupidly refused a generous offer by the Americans to land their crack 82 Airborne Division on the Rome airfields.[2]

With some hesitation Badoglio announced the armistice on 8 September, and on the night of 8/9 September the Allies invaded at Salerno, south of Naples, in the wake of Montgomery's Eighth Army, who had crossed the Straits of Messina six days before. Around Rome, Italian troops outnumbered the Germans and were superior in fire power. The Italian High Command in Rome had been expecting the Allies to land nearer the city, and panicked when some weak Italian units surrendered: the generals advised the King and Badoglio to flee Rome to escape capture. In the early hours of 9 September the King, Badoglio and some heads of departments left for Pescara on the Adriatic and escaped by sea to the port of Brindisi, which the Eighth

Army were now approaching. Abandoned without orders, the Italian army on the mainland disintegrated under brutal German attack. Many Italian soldiers were shot, or sent to Germany in cattle trucks; others took the announcement of the armistice as a signal to go home as quickly as possible, by train, bicycle, or on foot. Within a week the Germans had entirely disarmed fifty-six Italian divisions and taken 700,000 soldiers prisoner. The Italian army in Italy had disappeared. The comment at Eisenhower's HQ was, 'They can be written off.'[3]

Amid the confusion of their unplanned departure from Rome, Badoglio and his ministers overlooked the clause in the armistice agreed with Eisenhower which stated specifically that Mussolini was to be handed over to the Allies. He was being held in a mountain hotel on the Gran Sasso d'Italia, 120 kilometres north-west of Rome, and there would have been no difficulty in taking him under guard to join the royal convoy at Pescara, but no orders about him were given: he was forgotten in the panic. The Germans were soon in full control of central Italy, and could easily have brought him by road to Rome. Instead, Hitler dramatized his rescue. He ordered the flamboyant SS officer Otto Skorzeny to land with gliders on the Gran Sasso and fly Mussolini out in a small aeroplane. This was successfully accomplished, a considerable number of photographs were taken, and the event was celebrated in a blaze of publicity.

Mussolini was flown first to Rome, then on to Vienna. By letting him escape, Badoglio gave Hitler the chance to create a new, puppet Fascist government, subservient to the Nazis. At first Mussolini was reluctant to assume leadership again, but he was persuaded by Hitler to broadcast to the Italian people from Munich on 18 September. Overcoming his hesitancy and putting on a brave front, he proclaimed that he had created a new Fascist state in German-occupied Italy, and announced that Italy would take up arms again 'alongside Germany' to exact revenge for the treachery of 25 July. Mussolini was determined to buttress his position by raising a new Fascist army, believing that this was the only way to gain both respect from Hitler and some standing at the peace conference, if the war should end in stalemate (he no longer hoped for an Axis victory).

All would have been very different if Mussolini had carried through the decision he had made on 18 July to negotiate Italy's exit from the war with the Allies. It would then have been much harder for Hitler to occupy Italy. However, the evidence indicates that Mussolini was under no illusions, and feared at Feltre that Hitler would take drastic action to make the Italian army impotent to resist the Germans. This 'might-have-been' of history has not been explored by historians because too little importance has been given to Mussolini's decision on 18 July to authorize Bastianini to negotiate with the Allies. After his rescue, Mussolini dreaded lest Hitler should discover this attempt to betray Germany by seeking a separate peace with the Allies.

On 23 September Field Marshal Graziani agreed to be War Minister in Mussolini's new government, installed at Salò on Lake Garda. On 3 October Mussolini sent Graziani to Germany to negotiate with Hitler the forming and equipping of a new Fascist army. The Führer agreed to a modest force, but sternly refused to allow recruitment among the more than 600,000 Italian soldiers who had been interned in Germany after the collapse on 9 September. Hitler told Graziani that in principle he would consider finding equipment for four new Italian divisions, to be trained in Germany, but recruits must come by conscription and not from the internees. By the spring of 1944 the four new divisions were in training at Paderborn and Grafenwöhr, in comfortable German army barracks with good rations, clothing and German arms.

In May, Mussolini went to Bavaria to inspect his new divisions and present colours. He was warmly received by his troops, and entertained false hopes that he once again had an effective force with which to fight the Americans and British. He was to be disappointed: as soon as the divisions returned to Italy, desertions became rife and morale dropped. One of the Italian Fascist divisions, Monte Rosa, went into the line in December 1944 in the Serchio Valley northwest of Florence and launched a successful attack in company with German troops, capturing the town of Barga against weak American resistance.

This was the limit of the new Fascist army's success, however, and the four divisions were subsequently considered by the Germans to be fit only for use as garrison troops, or against the partisans who with British and American liaison officers were harrying the German lines of communication. Mass desertions ensued, and ultimately the new Fascist army had almost no effect on the Italian campaign.

Rome fell to the Allies early in June 1944 and their advance continued, so that by September Mussolini knew days of despair when it seemed to him that the Allies were about to break through the Gothic Line north of Florence, overrun the Lombardy Plain and capture Milan, Turin and the industrial north. The Allies had already occupied France and Belgium, and the German army in Russia was in full retreat. However, desperate resistance by the Germans halted the Allies in Italy, and with the failure of the airborne operation at Arnhem in Holland the Germans were able to stabilize the Western Front in the autumn of 1944. Mussolini once again began to believe there was a possibility of a negotiated peace. By now his hatred of Hitler was intense: German secret police and SS units had carried out mass murders of anti-Fascist Italians, and sadistic reprisals were being taken by the German army against civilians wherever the partisans had inflicted casualties on German troops. Mussolini complained bitterly about these atrocities to Hitler, but his complaints were ignored.[4]

Mussolini visited Hitler at his headquarters on the afternoon of 20 July 1944, shortly after the explosion of the Stauffenberg bomb which nearly killed the German dictator. Still shaken, Hitler promised Mussolini that he would improve the lot of the great numbers of Italian soldiers who were being kept in appalling conditions in prison camps in Germany for forced labour, without any Red Cross benefits; he soon reneged on this promise. Mussolini was also angry about the deportations of Italian Jews to the death camp at Auschwitz. Despite the anti-Semitic laws passed in Italy in 1938 in emulation of Hitler's, Mussolini was not himself anti-Semitic: when in April 1944 Hitler ordered the Salò Republic to pass much more vindictive laws with the intention of completely exterminating the Italian Jews, Mussolini allowed the newspapers to leak the story, giving the Jewish community twenty-four hours' advance notice of what was planned. Thus countless lives were saved as the Italian people took Jews into their homes and hid them; for this Mussolini has been given little credit.

Mussolini's dislike of Hitler was further fanned by the way in which Italian local government officials in the Alto Adige and the Trieste area were dismissed and replaced by Austrians; he realized that after the war Hitler intended to annex all those parts of Italy which had been Austrian until the end of the First World War. Another shock was the information he received in July 1944 from the Archbishop of Udine and the Prefect of Trieste that the Friuli area was being occupied by a Cossack army complete with the soldiers' families, whom the Nazis had promised a new homeland in this beautiful part of Italy. Again Mussolini's protests to Hitler were ignored. This was perhaps his lowest moment; he recorded: 'I have already made plain to the Führer the extent of the cruelty, violence and robbery. It is too late. I have drained the poisoned chalice to the dregs.'[5]

However, in December 1944 Mussolini's spirits revived as the war ground to a standstill on all fronts in bitter winter conditions. He hoped that Hitler might make peace with the Russians, or alternatively that German flying bombs and other secret weapons (which Hitler had promised the Italians) might bring the Allies to the conference table, where Britain and the United States might consider him an ally against the spread of Communism.

Mussolini decided on a final effort to reassert himself; on 16 December 1944 he made his first speech in Milan for seven years (and his last), at the Lyric Theatre. He still enjoyed a good rapport with the Italian people, and his audience overflowed into the streets, delighted with his speech. An ebullient Duce persuaded his listeners that he could lead Italy out of her slough of despond. The Milanese were desperately worried by their position between the Allied armies occupying the south of Italy and the Germans in the north: they feared the imposition of harsh retributive penalties by the Allies, while the horrors and barbarities of Nazi occupation were well known. Somehow, Mussolini made them feel that he was the only man who could extricate Italy unscathed from her sad plight. There is little in the written record of the speech to justify such euphoria; yet, for the last time, Mussolini's charisma worked on the Italian people.

Bombastically he talked of 'secret weapons which would certainly win the war', and in his final peroration he asked for the 'supreme sacrifice', saying: 'We want to defend the Po Valley tooth and nail; we want to remain Republican while waiting for the whole of Italy to be Republican . . . and it is Milan which must give the men, the arms, the will and the signal of insurrection.' This was laughable, as it was well known that the fighting army which the Salò Republic could field was tiny, ill-armed, ineffective and disloyal. 'Frenetic applause' greeted his speech, however, and was repeated outside in the streets as he waved to the crowds. The Duce enjoyed three brilliant days in Milan, received everywhere with crowds and cheers. There was no public sign of hatred of him, yet within five months the Milanese were spitting on the corpse of the man they had fêted. It is one of the mysteries of Italian history. Mussolini's elation over these successful days in Milan quickly vanished, however, and during the early weeks of 1945 he sank into depression again.[6]

As a last resort, he determined to move his government to Milan and from there push on with a programme of socialism and nationalization of industry. He believed that by introducing socialism he would obtain the co-operation of the left wing of the Resistance, and also deluded himself into thinking that it would make a bridge for him with the British Labour Party and the trades unions. Nicola Bombacci, a close friend of the Duce, had been an active international trade unionist and socialist before the days of Fascism, and had had strong ties with the British Trade Union movement. Mussolini asked him to contact the British Labour leader Ernest Bevin, a member of the War Cabinet, and ask if some exit from the war could be arranged for his government, on the basis that he would make Italy socialist. No response was received: Churchill's instructions were 'absolute silence' and 'unconditional surrender' only, and Bevin obeyed them.

By early March 1945 it was evident that the Allied victory could not be long delayed. The Russians were pushing deep into Germany, and in the west the British and Americans were approaching the Rhine; in Italy, the Germans clearly had insufficient strength to repulse the British and Americans once the winter ended. Mussolini knew the game was up, and decided on a direct approach to the Allies: he sent his son Vittorio to Milan to ask Cardinal Schuster, the Archbishop of Milan, to approach the Allies on his behalf, a move prudently kept secret from the Germans.

When Vittorio met Schuster he told the Cardinal his father expected that both Germany and the Fascist Republic would soon change sides and 'move into the Anglo-American camp' in order to block the spread of Communism and the Bolshevization of all Europe, and said the Duce hoped for the help of the Vatican in contacting the Allies.

Schuster informed the Vatican of Mussolini's approach, and on 13 March Monsignor Tardini, assistant to Cardinal Maglione, the Vatican Secretary of State, minuted to Pius XII:

1. It is absolutely astonishing that Mussolini expects the Anglo-Americans to enter into an alliance with him and Hitler at a moment when they refuse any sort of negotiation.
2. In my view the Holy See should NOT try to act as a go-between because the response must be 'No' and then the Russians will seize on it as an excuse to fulminate even more fiercely against us.
3. The situation will become embarrassing if Mussolini does send written proposals because we can hardly refuse to pass them on . . . We must not at any time give the impression that the Holy See is trying to divide the Anglo-Americans from the Russians.

The Pope agreed Mussolini should be told that the Holy See was working for a just peace, but that 'recent authoritative information convinces us that the Allies will not depart from their "unconditional surrender" formula'.

At the same time Mussolini sent Abbot Pancini, a close friend, to visit Monsignor Bernardini, the Papal Nuncio in Switzerland, with instructions to discuss his absurd proposal of an alliance between Germany, Fascist Italy and the Allies. Pancini gave Bernardini details of Mussolini's plan, which was that when the German army left Italian soil Republican troops should keep order, and the Allies should promise to prevent the partisans looting, while both the partisans and the Fascist forces would lay down their arms. News of this overture was leaked to the Russians, who suddenly attacked Switzerland on Radio Moscow for being a party to peace negotiations. The Pope, on the point of consulting with D'Arcy Osborne, British Minister to the

Vatican, decided on hearing of the Radio Moscow denouncement not to discuss Mussolini's approach with him. Instead, without any communication from the Vatican to Britain, Bernardini was informed that he must tell Mussolini there was no alternative to 'unconditional surrender'.[7]

Mussolini's last-minute efforts to contact the Allies are of historical interest only, as indicating his state of mind as he realized that the total defeat of the Axis was close at hand. Some Italian historians allege, without proper evidence, that Churchill himself was in contact with Mussolini in March 1945. This is wildly improbable. If Mussolini had had a direct link with Churchill, why should he have needed to use the Vatican, or Bombacci, or his Lisbon Embassy for Bastianini's approach in 1943?

On 19 April 1945, when the Allies had broken through the winter line and were about to advance through the Po valley, Mussolini moved from Salò to Milan, where he installed himself in the Prefecture. He was furious when an Italian journalist telephoned from Bologna to tell him that the city had fallen, and the Allied soldiers were being received with flowers and enthusiastic cheers. 'Impossible!' declared Mussolini. 'Bologna is the most Fascist of all Italian cities.' The journalist was both right and wrong: Bologna was liberated by the Royal Italian Army, who had changed sides and at this stage of the war sported British battledress.

Mussolini arranged to meet the Resistance leaders at the Cardinal's palace, and was ready to order his Republican army to lay down their arms provided his own safety and that of the other Fascist leaders and their families was guaranteed. However, behind Mussolini's back and unknown to him, at Caserta in southern Italy the German generals were negotiating for an armistice with the Allies. When Mussolini was told of this at the palace he became agitated, declaring that '. . . the Germans have stabbed Italy in the back. The Germans have always treated us as slaves.' In a wild rage he stormed out of the Cardinal's palace. It was a fatal mistake: had he stayed where he was, he would have been safe until Allied troops arrived, when he would have been arrested to face trial as a war criminal.[8]

Instead, Mussolini went to Como on Lake Maggiore where he found the Republican troops melting away in the face of the imminent arrival of the Allied forces. On 27 April he joined a German convoy proceeding up the west bank of Lake Como. They were halted by partisans, and Mussolini was taken. The next morning, on the orders of Communist resistance leaders and strictly against instructions issued by the Allies, Mussolini was shot, together with fourteen Fascist ministers who had been accompanying him. The bodies were taken to the Piazzale Loreto in Milan, where Mussolini's was hung upside-down. There the corpses were insulted and spat upon by the citizens of Milan, who only five months before had hailed Mussolini as a hero.

When he was captured, the Duce had with him bags containing thirty-seven files of documents. A theory popular with the Italian press is that one of the bags contained letters from Churchill to Mussolini, written during the hostilities, which the Duce thought would be useful if he were tried as a war criminal, but this is not correct. Recently released documents in the Public Record Office show that three of the partisans present when Mussolini was captured carried off his 'famous bags' and sold the contents to the British secret service in Milan ten days later. On 25 May Harold Macmillan, British Resident Minister in the Central Mediterranean, cabled to Anthony Eden, the Foreign Secretary, that a suitcase of documents contained in thirty-seven folders removed from Mussolini's possession by Italian partisans had been received by the British Embassy in Rome. According to Macmillan, they were concerned with the international crisis of 1939, Italy's entry into the war in 1940, military operations in Egypt, the Italian attack on Greece, the *coup d'état* which overthrew Mussolini in July 1943, the Verona trials where Mussolini's son-in-law Ciano was sentenced to death, and the Duce's plan for a redoubt in the Alps where he could hold out. Furthermore, nowhere in the Foreign Office correspondence between Rome and London is there any reference to letters from Churchill to Mussolini, either during the war or before it. It is inconceivable that, if any previously unknown letters from Churchill to Mussolini were among the documents in the thirty-seven files, Macmillan should not have reported this to Eden at once.

The documents from Mussolini's bags were eventually handed to the official British and American war historians, together with a cache of documents captured at his final headquarters on Lake Garda, plus documents captured by the Polish Army at Mussolini's country house (Rocca del Camminate) near Forli in October 1944 and others found in the Rome ministries when the Allies occupied the capital in June 1944. Until the recent Public Record Office releases there was no indication of how the Mussolini archives had come into Allied hands. They were returned to the Italian government when the Peace Treaty was signed in 1946, but photocopies were kept in Washington, DC and also at St Antony's College, Oxford. The British photocopies were sent from Oxford to the Foreign Office Library a few years ago, where the author worked on them, and they too are now in the Public Record Office.

For fifty years sensational rumours have periodically surfaced in the Italian press to the effect that Churchill wrote letters to Mussolini in the concluding stages of the war which Mussolini kept to use in his defence if he was tried. This is untenable: Churchill would never have written to Mussolini at this stage without informing Stalin, who would have reacted furiously. Stalin was already angry because the Allies were negotiating in Switzerland with the German generals in command in Italy, and he feared this might be the prelude to a separate peace between the USA, Britain, Hitler and Mussolini, but excluding Russia. In such a climate, Churchill was too good a statesman to risk any approach to Mussolini.

In his book *Rosso e Nero*, published shortly before his death, the late Renzo de Felice claimed that a chapter in his final volume on Mussolini would clear up rumours surrounding the Duce's assassination 'which had lasted for fifty years'. According to de Felice, the Americans wanted to capture Mussolini alive and have him stand trial as a war criminal, while the British wanted him put to death at once. Roosevelt had insisted that the war trials must not be confined to Germans; he considered Mussolini to be the father of every aspect of Fascism, and for this reason had insisted on the clause in the Armistice (overlooked by Badoglio) which stated that Mussolini was to be handed over to the Allies. According to de Felice, the British definitely did not want Mussolini at Nuremberg; it would be too 'embarrassing' because he had in his 'famous defensive bag' letters from Churchill – correspondence de Felice describes as likely to be 'surprising' – which the British Prime Minister would not wish revealed.

De Felice was a fine historian with a large following in Italy, and his claim that Britain wanted Mussolini to be executed out-of-hand is widely believed there. In *Rosso e Nero*, he states that a British secret service agent gave orders to the partisans to execute Mussolini as soon as he was captured, because the British did not want him to remain alive as a prisoner. Christopher Woods, former SOE advisor at the Foreign Office, has told the author that there are no papers in the SOE archives to suggest this, and he is positive it is untrue. De Felice had not seen the Public Record Office papers concerning the fate of Mussolini's famous bag; he wrote that all the documents in it had disappeared – indeed, the Italian press has frequently carried stories that Churchill used to holiday in Italy after the war because he wanted to recover the letters from the partisans who had stolen them – and had no idea that they had been returned to the Italian State archives, nor that there were photocopies in Oxford, later in London. The recently released Public Record Office documents prove his theories to be false.[9]

On his final day in Milan (24 April 1945) Mussolini is alleged to have written a letter to Churchill, to be despatched by Special Messenger: it is probably a forgery.

Eccellenza,
Events are hotting up. It is pointless for me to ignore the peace efforts which are taking place between Great Britain and the United States and Germany. In the conditions in which after five years of war Italy is left, the only thing left to me is to wish success for your personal intervention. Overall I want to put on the record your very words: 'Italy is a bridge. Italy cannot be sacrificed', and also that your own propaganda has included an exaltation of the courage of the unfortunate Italian soldier.

It is useless to remind you of my position before history. Perhaps you are the only one today to know that I need not fear a trial. So I do not ask for clemency, only a reasonable judgement and the chance for me to justify and defend myself . . . And besides, now unconditional surrender is impossible because it would sweep away the vanquished and the victors.

Send me now a trusted emissary. You would be interested in the documentation with which I can provide him about the need to deal with the danger from the East. The future lies mainly in your hands. May God help you.

Yours,
(signed) Benito Mussolini[10]

If it is genuine, this letter shows Mussolini's desperate state of mind. It was certainly never delivered: Mussolini is alleged to have tried to send it by hand to the British Legation in Geneva – perhaps his emissary was captured by partisans. The 'peace efforts' referred to were Himmler's in Sweden, not the negotiations to surrender the German army in Italy. As there is no reference to any previous correspondence, this letter indicates that none exists.*

---

* Writing to Neville Chamberlain or Winston Churchill before the outbreak of war between Italy and Britain, Mussolini always began 'Caro Mr Chamberlain', or 'Caro Mr Churchill', and signed himself 'Mussolini', without the 'Benito'. According to a desk diary reputed to be his, on 24 April 1945 Mussolini made an appointment with Franz Spoegler, a German SS officer. After the war Spoegler claimed that Mussolini had asked him to take this letter to the British Consulate in Lugano for onward transmission to Winston Churchill, but that he was unable to cross the frontier. The story is unlikely to be true, because it would have been far easier for Mussolini to contact the British Consulate in Lugano through the Spanish Consulate in Milan. Spoegler is a doubtful character, and there is doubt also whether the desk diary is genuine. The letter is in the Mondadori Archive, and it is known that Arnaldo Mondadori was sold documents that were forgeries.[11]

Notes

Initials and numbers refer to classification in the Public Record Office.

DBFP: Documents on British Foreign Policy (London, HMSO, 1947–)
DDI: I Documenti diplomatici italiani (Rome, Libreria della Stato, 1952–)
DDF: Documents diplomatiques français (Paris, Ministère des Affaires Etrangères)
DGFP: Documents on German Foreign Policy (London, HMSO, 1951–)
IMT: International Military Tribunal: Trial of the Major War Criminals before the International Military Tribunal (Nuremberg and London, 1947–1949))
FRUS: Foreign Relations of the United States Diplomatic Papers (Washington, DC)

Italian Collection: Captured Italian documents formerly at St Anthony's College, Oxford, then in the Foreign Office Library, and now in the Public Record Office. Duplicates are in the Archivio Centrale del Stato in Rome. These are documents captured by the partisans who arrested Mussolini, and by the Allies in June 1944 in the ministries in Rome, at Mussolini's home near Forli in August 1944, and at Salò in May 1945.

CHAPTER 1: EARLY DAYS AND RISE TO POWER

1. Kirkpatrick, *Study of a Demagogue*, pp. 25–33; Balabanoff, *My Life as a Rebel*, pp. 57–61.
2. Barzini, *The Italians*, p. 136.
3. FO 371/7660; Varè, *Laughing Diplomat*, pp. 213–14; Mack Smith, *Mussolini*, p. 25.
4. Hoare, *Nine Troubled Years*, p. 154; Cannistraro & Sullivan, *Il Duce's Other Woman*, p. 176.
5. Gallo, *Mussolini's Italy*, pp. 55–56.
6. Mack Smith, *Mussolini*, pp. 33–6; Seton-Watson, *Italy from Liberalism to Fascism*, pp. 317–19.
7. Seton-Watson, op. cit., pp. 594–627; De Felice, *Il Duce*, pp. 354–80; Cannistraro & Sullivan, op. cit., pp. 259–64.
8. DDI 7.1, pp. 18–19.

CHAPTER 2: LAUSANNE, LONDON AND THE RUHR

1. DBFP 1.XXIV, p. 1.
2. Ibid, p. 4.
3. Ibid, p. 23.
4. Ibid, pp. 1–117.
5. Seton-Watson, op. cit., p. 667; DDI 7.1, pp. 118 *et seq.*
6. FO 371/7600.
7. FO 371/7659.
8. DDI 7.1, pp. 70–1, 87–8.
9. DBFP 1.XXIV, p. x.
10. Nicolson, *Curzon, The Last Phase*, pp. 289–90; Kirkpatrick, op. cit., p. 195; Gilmour, *Curzon*, p. 557.
11. Gilmour, op. cit., p. 160; Nicolson, op. cit., p. 314; Seton-Watson, op. cit., p. 670; DDI 7.1, pp. 565–68.
12. DDI 7.1, pp. 145–51; Lamb, *Drift to War*, pp. 11–12.
13. DDI 7.1, pp. 198–204, 218–19, 227, 240, 272; FO 371/8505.
14. DDI 7.1, p. 219.
15. Blake, *Unknown Prime Minister*, p. 487; FO 371/8818; FO 371/8625; FO 371/8505.
16. DBFP 1.XXI, pp. 27–32, 37, 39.
17. Lamb, *Drift to War*, pp. 18–19; D'Abernon, *Diary: Ambassador of Peace*, Vol. II, p. 262.

CHAPTER 3: CORFU AND ABYSSINIA: 1923

1. FO 371/8898
2. Seton-Watson, op. cit., p. 670.
3. DBFP 1.XXIV, pp. 695–700; FO 371/8898.
4. FO 371/8898.
5. DBFP 1.XXIV, pp. 770–1; DDI 7.2, pp. 91–5.
6. DBFP 1.XXIV, pp. 790–3.
7. DDI 7.2, p. 149; DBFP 1.XXIV, p. 952.
8. DBFP 1.XXIV, pp. 951–7
9. DBFP 1.XXIV, pp. 952–60, 972–3.
10. DBFP 1.XXIV, pp. 972–80, 1002.
11. DBFP 1.XXIV, pp. 1046–7; Dell, *Geneva Racket*, p. 53.
12. FO 371/8900.
13. DBFP 1.XXVI, p. 1092; DDI 7.2, pp. 283–5, 428–30.
14. FO 371/9952.
15. DBFP 1.XXVI, pp. 29, 52–6, 121–2, 167.
16. FO 371/9951; FO 371/9952.
17. FO 371/8410.
18. DDI 7.2, pp. 114–15, 123–4.
19. FO 371/8410.
20. Cecil, *A Great Experiment*, pp. 145–6.
21. FO 371/8410.

22. FO 371/8409; FO 371/8410.
23. DDI 7.2, pp. 256–7.
24. FO 371/8410.
25. FO 371/11561.
26. DDI 7.4, p. 159.
27. Salvemini, *Prelude to World War Two*, p. 75; McCartney & Cremona, *Italy's Foreign and Colonial Policy 1914–1937*, pp. 291–5; *The Times*, 30 July 1926.

CHAPTER 4: THE MATTEOTI MURDER AND DICTATORSHIP

1. FO 371/7659; Kirkpatrick, op. cit., pp. 192–3; Waterfield, *Castle in Italy*, p. 189.
2. De Felice, *Mussolini il fascista*, Vol. I, p. 393.
3. De Felice, ibid., p. 581.
4. FO 381/9940.
5. Seton-Watson, op. cit., pp. 660–3; *New Statesman*, 10 Jan. 1929.
6. Waterfield, op. cit., pp. 197–206; Seton-Watson, op. cit., p. 663, FO 371/9940.
7. DBFP 1A.II, pp. 186–94.
8. DBFP 1A.III, pp. 455–7.
9. DDI 7.4, pp. 341–6; Lamb, *Drift to War*, p. 94; Petrie, *Life and Letters of Sir Austen Chamberlain*, p. 296; FO 371/10688; Gilbert, *Winston Churchill*, Vol. V, pp. 224–5.
10. *Daily Herald*, 17 Nov. 1925.

CHAPTER 5: LOCARNO AND THE BRIAND PLAN

1. DBFP 1.XXVII, pp. 371, 448.
2. Ibid, pp. 726, 738, 741, 809–10, 820; DBFP 1A.I, pp. 27–9.
3. FO 371/10784.
4. FO 371/10743; DBFP 1.XXVII, pp. 819, 874, 883, 1174; FO 371/10743.
5. DBFP 1A.I, p. vii; FO 371/9940.
6. Mack Smith, *Mussolini's Roman Empire*, p. 10.
7. Kirkpatrick, op. cit., pp. 241–3; FO 371/10743; DDI 7.4, pp. 129–32; *Daily Chronicle*, 17 Oct. 1925.
8. Petrie, op. cit., pp. 295–6.
9. DBFP 1A.II, pp. 413, 439; Petrie, op. cit., p. 306; FO 371/11330.
10. DDI 7.4, pp. 340–3, 355–7; DBFP 1A.II, p. 413.
11. DBFP 1A.II, pp. 925–9.
12. DBFP 1.XXVII, pp. ix, 87–8; Cannistraro & Sullivan, op. cit., p. 356.
13. FO 371/11234; DBFP 1A.II, pp. 314–5.
14. *The Times*, 29 Jan. 1926; FO 371/11234; DDI 7.4, p. 181.
15. FO 371/15157; FO 371/14980; FO 371/14981; Cab 27/624; DBFP 1A.II, pp. 248, 401, 521.
16. FO 371/15158; FO 371/15199; FO 371/15160; Cab 23/671; Cab 24/62.
17. Guariglia, *Ricordi*, pp. 80–92.
18. Mosley, *Beyond the Pale*, p. 32; FO 371/49934; Cross, *Sir Samuel Hoare*, pp. 56, 91–2.

CHAPTER 6: DISARMAMENT AND THE FOUR POWER PACT

1. T 160/450; F 130501; T 160/436; F 12630 (Treasury files, PRO).
2. DBFP 2.III, pp. 337–9.
3. Von Papen, *Memoirs*, p. 186.
4. DBFP 2.III, pp. 188–241; Lamb, *Drift to War*, pp. 60–8; Cab 25/505.
5. DBFP 2.III, p. 589; DBFP 2.IV, pp. 105, 173–4, 199, 373, 377.
6. Von Papen, op. cit., p. 206.
7. Cab 27/505; DBFP 2.V, pp. 56, 67–81.
8. Italian Collection, 025783; Northedge, *The Troubled Giant*, p. 390; DBFP 2.V, pp. 358–73.
9. Avon, *Memoirs*, p. 47; DBFP 2.V, p. 702.

CHAPTER 7: MUSSOLINI AND AUSTRIA: 1934

1. FO 371/11638; FO 371/11639.
2. FO 371/11646; DBFP 2.V, pp. 534–5; DBFP 2.VI, p. 245.
3. Cab 27/506; DBFP 2.VI, pp. 395–427.
4. Selby, *Diplomatic Twilight*, pp. 16–17; Kindermann, *Hitler's Defeat in Austria*, p. 44; DBFP 2.VI, p. 589.
5. Monelli, *Mussolini*, pp. 129–30; Hibbert, *Benito Mussolini*, p. 78; Starhemberg, *Between Hitler and Mussolini*, p. 150; Cannistraro & Sullivan, op. cit., pp. 451–2; DBFP 2.VI, pp. 762–4; Adam Archive, Institut für Zeiteschichte, Munich.
6. DGFP Series C, Vol. III, pp. 268 *et seq.*; De Felice, *Mussolini il Duce*, Vol. I, p. 301; Kindermann, op. cit., p. 100; Mosley, *My Life*, p. 359.
7. Kindermann, op. cit., pp. 113–15.

CHAPTER 8: STRESA AND ABYSSINIA

1. Cab 23/81.
2. DBFP 2.XII, pp. 919, 921; FO 371/18560.
3. FO 371/18560; FO 371/18836.
4. DBFP 2.XII, pp. 910–22; MacCallum, *Public Opinion and the Lost Peace*, p. 150; FO 371/18836.
5. Gibbs, *Grand Strategy: Vol 1: Rearmament Policy*, pp. 155–69; FO 371/18845; FO 371/187340; FO 371/18832; Churchill, *Gathering Storm*, p. 111.
6. Adamthwaite, *The Making of the Second World War*, pp. 133–4; De Felice, *Il Duce*, Vol. I, pp. 606–8.
7. Cointet, *Pierre Laval*, pp. 155–9; Avon, op. cit., pp. 122–3; Adamthwaite, *France and the Coming of the Second World War*, p. 32; Duroselle & Serra, *Italia e Francia*, pp. 197–210.
8. Avon, op. cit., pp. 232–4; DDI 8.2, pp. 888, 890, 899, 903.
9. FO 371/19184.
10. *The Times*, 10 May 1933; PRO 30/69/7.
11. Carr, *International Relations since the Peace Treaties*, p. 224.
12. FO 371/19105; DBFP 2.XLV, pp. 110, 176–7.
13. Cab 23/82; FO 371/19105.
14. Thompson, op. cit., pp. 80–95; DBFP 2.XIV, pp. 220–8; FO 405/5.

15. Dell, op. cit., p. 111; Roskill, *Hankey, Man of Secrets*, Vol. III, p. 191; Gladwyn, op. cit., p. 48.
16. Cannistraro & Sullivan, op. cit., p. 467; PRO 30/69/7.
17. DBFP 2.XIV, pp. 281, 309, 311–12.
18. Cab 23/81.
19. DBFP 2.XIV, pp. 318, 323–6, 329–34; Cab 23/82; Avon, op. cit., pp. 451–5.
20. DBFP 2.XIV, pp. 318–34; Cab 23/82; De Felice, ibid., pp. 668–71.
21. Avon, op. cit., pp. 221–9; Rhodes James, *Anthony Eden*, p. 149.
22. M. Toscano in Sarkissian (ed.), *Studies in Diplomatic History and Historiography*, p. 126.
23. FO 371/19163; FO 800/307; Rhodes James, op. cit., p. 149.
24. Griffith, *Fellow Travellers*, p. 25 *et seq.*; Waley, *British Public Opinion*, p. 292 *et seq.*
25. Cab 23/82.
26. Rhodes James, op. cit., p. 150; FO 371/18515; Cab 23/82.
27. FO 401/35; Aloisi, *La mia attività*, pp. 57–60.

CHAPTER 9: ABYSSINIAN WAR AND SANCTIONS

1. DBFP 2.XV, pp. 264–8; Rhodes James, op. cit., p. 152.
2. Cate, *André Malraux*, pp. 217–18.
3. Cab 23/83; DBFP 2.XIV, p. 688; Aloisi, op. cit., pp. 346, 349; Mack Smith, *Mussolini*, pp. 195–6.
4. Cab 23/82; Cab 48/38; FO 371/19155; FO 371/19159; Italian Collection, 02785.
5. PRO 30/69/71.
6. Cab 23/82; Cab 48/38; FO 371/19155; FO 371/19159.
7. DDI 8/2, pp. 359, 447.
8. FO 401/35; Cab 16/136; FO 371/18159; Cab 16/136; DDI 8.2, pp. 334–5.
9. DBFP 2.XI, pp. 117–18, 133–5; DDI 8.2, pp. 367–8.
10. FO 371/19157; Cab 16/136; DDI 8.2, p. 367.
11. FO 371/19164; FO 371/19186; DBFP 2.XV, p. 197; DDI 8.2, pp. 478–80.
12. DBFP 2.XI, pp. 210–13, 264–8; FO 371/19160; FO 371/22560.
13. FO 371/19165; FO 371/19164; Jones, *Diary with Letters*, Vol. III, p. 159.
14. Cab 16/136; Cab 11/420.
15. FO 371/19163.
16. FO 371/19164.
17. FO 371/19163; Cab 23/82; FO 371/19165.
18. FO 371/19164.
19. FO 371/19164; FO 371/19165; FO 371/19168; Cab 23/82.
20. Cab 23/82; Avon, op. cit., p. 286.
21. DBFP 2.XI, pp. 425–7; FO 371/19168.
22. Avon, op. cit., p. 301; FO 371/19168.
23. R.A.C. Parker in *English Historical Review*, Vol. 89, 1972; Avon, op. cit., p. 301; Rhodes James, op. cit., p. 154.
24. Cross, op. cit., p. 249; Cab 23/82.
25. DBFP 2.XV, pp. 449–50.
26. Cab 23/82.

27. FO 371/19168; Cab 23/82; DBFP 2.XV, p. 748.
28. DBFP 2.XV, p. 445.
29. FO 371/19168; Cab 23/82.
30. DBFP 2.XV, pp. 498–520; Cross, op. cit., p. 249; Jones & Monro, *A History of Ethiopia*, p. 246.
31. DBFP 2.XV, pp. 448, 462, 482.
32. DBFP 2.XV, pp. 746–61; Avon, op. cit., p. 307.
33. DDI 8.2, pp. 838–41, 846–53.
34. Cross, op. cit., pp. 251–3; Cab 23/82; DBFP 2.XV, pp. 748–61.
35. Cab 23/82; Cross, op. cit., pp. 251–3.
36. Cross, op. cit., pp. 257–8.
37. Guariglia, op. cit., p. 67; DDI 8.2, p. 875; Barnes & Nicholson, *Empire at Bay*, p. 409.
38. DDI 8.2, pp. 888, 890, 899, 901; FO 371/20159; Cab 23/83.

CHAPTER 10: MUSSOLINI REJECTED BY EDEN

1. DBFP 2.XV, pp. 540–1, 570–2.
2. FO 371/20159; DDI 8.3, pp. 354–62.
3. Cab 23/83.
4. DBFP 2.XVI, pp. 3–7, 36–8; DDI 8.3, p. 424.
5. Cab 27/599; Cab 23/83.
6. DBFP 2.XV, pp. 624, 769–91.
7. DBFP 2.XVI, pp. 8–14, 36–8.
8. DGFP Series C, Vol. IV, pp. 36, 123.
9. DDF Vol. 1, pp. 15–19; Adamthwaite, *Making of Second World War*, pp. 154–5.
10. Cab 24/261; Cab 23/83; DBFP 2.XVI, pp. 59–76, 82–9.
11. Cab 23/83; DDI 8.3, pp. 515, 549–50; DBFP 2.XV, pp. 69–171.
12. DBFP 2.XVI, p. 237; DDI 8.3, pp. 526, 561; DDF 2, Vol. 1, No. 526.
13. DBFP 2.XVI, pp. 108, 111, 316–29; Cab 23/83.
14. DBFP 2.XVI, pp. 403–4; Cab 23/84.
15. DDI 8.3, pp. 170–4, 626 *et seq.*, 864–6, 873; Barnes & Nicholson, op. cit., p. 415; DDI 8.4, pp. 170–4.
16. DBFP 2.XVI, pp. 215, 461.
17. FO 371/20181; FO 371/31363; DBFP 2.XVI, p. 457.
18. DBFP 2.XVI, pp. 460–5; DDI 8.3, pp. 152–7, 215.
19. Avon, op. cit., p. 385; Rhodes James, op. cit., p. 16; Cab 27/622.
20. DDI 8.4, pp. 292–3; 296–7, 501; DBFP 2.XVI, pp. 486–91.
21. Cab 23/84; DBFP 2.XVI, pp. 512, 538–41.

CHAPTER 11: THE SPANISH CIVIL WAR

1. DBFP 2.XVII, pp. 136–9, 151–8.
2. Cab 23/89; FO 371/20534; DBFP 2.XVII, p. 192; Jones, *Diary with Letters*, Vol. III, p. 23.
3. DBFP 2.XVI, pp. 446, 504, 570; DGFP Series C, Vol. V, p. 1125–6.
4. Avon, op. cit., pp. 425–6.

5. DBFP 2.XVII, pp. 513–14, 519, 523, 550; De Felice, *Mussolini il Duce*, Vol. II, p. 352.
6. DBFP 2.XVII, pp. 645, 677–84, 698, 754–5; Seton-Watson, 'The Italian Gentleman's Agreement of January 1937', in Mommsen (ed.), *Fascist Challenge*.
7. DBFP 2.XVII, p. 752; Coverdale, *Italian Intervention in the Spanish Civil War*, p. 113.
8. DBFP 2.XVIII, p. 589.
9. Coverdale, op. cit., p. 175; DBFP 2.XVIII, p. 554.
10. DBFP 2.XVIII, pp. 513, 530–2, 705–7, 724–6, 877, 941–53.
11. Avon, op. cit., p. 451; De Felice, ibid., pp. 419–25; DBFP 2.XIX, pp. 107–8, 118–19; DDI 8.4, pp. 118–19, 218–19.
12. DBFP 2.XIX, pp. 107–8, 119–20, 144–7; Feiling, *Life of Neville Chamberlain*, p. 330; Avon, op. cit., pp. 451–2, 456.
13. DBFP 2.XIX, pp. 147, 152; De Felice, ibid., p. 371; Prem 1/276; FO 800/309.
14. FO 954/13; Prem 1/276; Cab 23/93.
15. DBFP 2.XIX, pp. 155–66.
16. FO 800/309; DBFP 2.XIX, pp. 23–30, 155–66, 207–9, 225–30, 235–6; De Felice, ibid., p. 426.
17. Ciano, *Diary 1937–1938*, p. 8; DBFP 2.XIX, pp. 219–25, 237–8, 252–61; Cab 23/89; Avon, op. cit., pp. 461–3.
18. Ciano, ibid, p. 15; DBFP 2.XIX, pp. 107, 301–2, 490–1.
19. DBFP 2.XIX, pp. 359–60, 372.
20. De Felice, ibid., p. 415; Ciano, ibid., p. 27.
21. Italian Collection.
22. Schmidt, *Hitler's Interpreter*, pp. 76–7; DBFP 2.XIX, pp. 540–55.
23. DBFP 2.XIX, pp. 590–623.
24. DBFP 2.XIX, pp. 639–42.
25. De Felice, ibid., pp. 452–3.
26. Coverdale, op. cit., p. 97.
27. Dilks, *Diaries of Sir Alexander Cadogan*, p. 33; DBFP 2.XIX, pp. 718–20, 723; Prem 1/276; FO 954/13.
28. Prem 1/276; FO 954/13; DBFP 2.XIX, p. 433.
29. FO 371/22395; Dilks, op. cit., pp. 34–5; DBFP 2.XIX, pp. 696–7, 735–7.
30. DBFP 2.XIX, pp. 677–80; Prem 1/276; FO 954/13; DBFP 2.XIX, pp. 677–80.
31. Prem 1/276; Harvey, *Diplomatic Diaries*, p. 83.
32. Prem 1/276; DBFP 2.XIX, pp. 865, 1140; Avon, op. cit., p. 573.
33. FO 954/13; DBFP 2.XIX, p. 915.
34. Ciano, ibid., p. 100; De Felice, ibid., pp. 452–6.
35. Dilks, op. cit., p. 50; DBFP 2.XIX, pp. 946–51; Harvey, op. cit., p. 93.
36. DBFP 2.XIX, pp. 145 *et seq.*; De Felice, ibid., pp. 457–8; Ciano, *L'Europa verso la catastrofe*, pp. 249–78; Cab 23/90; Ciano, *Diary 1937–1938*, p. 78.

CHAPTER 12: EASTER AGREEMENT: 1938

1. Cab 23/90; Cab 27/623; DBFP 2.XIX, p. 910.
2. Kirkpatrick, op. cit. quoting from von Schuschnigg, *Brutal Takeover*, pp. 42–3.
3. DBFP 3.I, pp. 9–33.

4. De Felice, *Mussolini il Duce*, Vol. II, p. 472; Ciano, *Diary 1937–1938*, p. 90.
5. Feiling, op. cit., pp. 341, 348.
6. Cab 27/623; Dilks, op. cit., pp. 63–4.
7. Cab 27/623; DBFP 2.XIX, pp. 1021–31.
8. DBFP 2.XIX, p. 1067.
9. Ciano, ibid., pp. 99–100; DBFP 2.XIX, pp. 1074, 1081.
10. Barnes & Nicholson, op. cit., pp. 501–3.
11. FO 371/22438; De Felice, ibid., p. 471.
12. Ciano, ibid., p. 113; Schmidt, op. cit., p. 83; De Felice, ibid., pp. 480–3.
13. De Felice, ibid., pp. 483 *et seq.*
14. Cab 26/324; DBFP 2.XIX, pp. 1124–5; Ciano, *L'Europa verso*, p. 32; Harvey, op. cit., p. 154; Ciano, *Diary 1937–1938*, p. 129.
15. DBFP 2.XIX, pp. 1127–33; Ciano, *L'Europa verso*, pp. 343–54.
16. Ciano, *Diary 1937–1938*, p. 114–15.
17. DBFP 2.XIX, pp. 1131–4; Dilks, op. cit., p. 85; Harvey, op. cit., p. 161.
18. DGFP Series D, Vol. I, p. 1078; De Felice, op. cit., pp. 468–70.
19. Ciano, ibid., pp. 40, 52, 135; De Felice, *Storia degli ebrei*, p. 251.

CHAPTER 13: MUNICH: 1938

1. Magistrati, *L'Italia a Berlino*, p. 200; Ciano, *Diary 1937–1938*, p. 150.
2. DBFP 3.I, pp. 327, 342; Ciano, ibid., pp. 135, 145.
3. Prem 1/266/A.
4. Ciano, ibid., p. 155; De Felice, *Mussolini il Duce*, Vol. II, p. 513.
5. DBFP 3.II, p. 653; Dilks, op. cit., pp. 96–7; Anfuso, *Da Palazzo Venezia*, p. 68; Cab 23/95.
6. De Felice, ibid., pp. 523–4; Ciano, ibid., p. 156.
7. Cab 23/95; Prem 1/266A.
8. Kirkpatrick, op. cit., p. 560; Ciano, ibid., p. 163; De Felice, ibid., pp. 524–5; DGFP Series C, Vol. IX, p. 77.
9. DBFP 3.II, p. 571; Schmidt, op. cit., p. 105; De Felice, ibid., p. 525.
10. DBFP 3.II, pp. 561, 587–8, 643–5.
11. Shirer, *Rise and Fall of Third Reich*, p. 408; De Felice, ibid., pp. 526–7.
12. Anfuso, op. cit., pp. 734; Kirkpatrick, op. cit., p. 364.
13. Prem 1/266/A; Shirer, op. cit., pp. 415–18.
14. Kirkpatrick, op. cit., p. 354.
15. Prem 1/266/A; Cab 23/95.
16. IMT Vol. X *et seq.* for Keitel's evidence; ibid., p. 361 *et seq.* for Jodl's evidence; General Adam's unpublished Memoirs are in the Institut für Zeitgeschichte, Munich; Taylor, *Munich*, p. 600.
17. Churchill, *The Gathering Storm*, pp. 263–5.
18. DBFP 3.III, p. 319.
19. Anfuso, op. cit., p. 84; De Felice, ibid., p. 529; DBFP 3. III, pp. 319–20.
20. DBFP 3.III, pp. 322–3; Ciano, ibid., p. 172.
21. DBFP 3.III, pp. 323–62.
22. De Felice, ibid., pp. 544–5; Mack Smith, *Mussolini*, pp. 224–5; Ciano, ibid., p. 203.

23. FO 371/22417; De Felice, ibid., p. 569; DBFP 3.III, pp. 473–8, 496–502.
24. DBFP 3.III, pp. 496, 552; Gladwin, op. cit., pp. 83–8; Harvey, op. cit., p. 231.
25. DBFP 3.III, pp. 525–34; FO 371/32793; Cab 23/97.

CHAPTER 14: PRAGUE, ALBANIA AND WAR

1. François-Poncet, *Au Palais Farnese*, pp. 9–15, 22; FO 371/22428; DDF Vol. XIII, p. 69.
2. DDF Vol. XIV, pp. 75–82; DGFP Series D, Vol. IV, pp. 575–6; Ciano, *Diary 1939–1943* (ed. M. Muggeridge), p. 21.
3. Lamb, *Drift to War*, pp. 285–92; Mack Smith, *Mussolini*, p. 225.
4. DBFP 3.IV, pp. 324, 329.
5. Ciano, ibid., pp. 45, 51; DGFP Series D, Vol. VII, p. 175.
6. Prem 1/327; DBFP 3.IV, pp. 402–3, 572–4.
7. Cab 27/624.
8. Aster, *Making of the Second World War*, pp. 112–13.
9. Ciano, ibid., pp. 50–1; DBFP 3.IV, pp. 350, 359.
10. De Felice, *Mussolini il Duce*, Vol. II, pp. 604–6; DBFP 3.IV, p. 358; DBFP 3.V, pp. 122, 127–8, 130; François-Poncet, ibid., pp. 96–110.
11. Ciano, ibid., p. 46; DBFP 3.V, pp. 131–55.
12. Watt, *How War Came*, p. 214; Roberts, *The Holy Fox*, p. 150; DBFP 3.V, pp. 147, 186.
13. François-Poncet, ibid., p. 95; DBFP 3.V, pp. 237, 252–9.
14. DBFP 3.V, pp. 237, 252, 259, 262–4, 386, 611–14.
15. FO 800/315; Toscano, *Origins of the Pact of Steel*, pp. 61 *et seq.*; DDI 8.12, p. 44.
16. Toscano, ibid., p. 325; DBFP 3.V, p. 474.
17. DBFP 3.V, pp. 704–6; DBFP 3.VI, pp. 15–17, 257–8.
18. DDI 8.12, pp. 49–50.
19. DBFP 3.VI, pp. 443–5, 556.
20. Wiskemann, *Rome–Berlin Axis*, p. 149; Ciano, ibid., p. 123; Ciano, *L'Europa verso*, pp. 426–36, 453–9; DGFP Series D, Vol. VII, pp. 47 *et seq.*; DDI 8.13, p. 47.
21. Ciano, *Diary 1939–1943*, pp. 127–30; DDI 8.13, p. 92.
22. Ciano, ibid., p. 134; DGFP Series D, Vol. VII, pp. 281–2; DDI 8.13, pp. 161–4.
23. DGFP Series D, Vol. VII, p. 285; DDI 8.13, p. 165.
24. DGFP Series D, Vol. VII, p. 289; DDI 8.13, p. 170.
25. Ciano, ibid., p. 135; DGFP Series D, Vol VII, pp. 309, 323, 325, 353–4; DDI 8.13, p. 218.
26. DBFP 3.VII, p. 57; IMT, Vol. IX, p. 465; Vol. X, p. 422.
27. DBFP 3.VII, pp. 7, 59–60, 71–2, 75–6, 93–5, 144; Ciano, ibid., p. 132; De Felice, ibid., p. 665.
28. FO 800/317; FO 371/22981; FO 371/22982; DBFP 3.VII, pp. 385–98; Dahlerus, *Last Attempt*, pp. 72–96.
29. FO 371/22982; DBFP 3.VII, pp. 432–3, 440.
30. Ciano, ibid., p. 140; DBFP 3.VII, pp. 432–40; FO 371/22982.
31. Ciano, ibid., p. 143; FO 371/22980; FO 371/22981; Cab 23/100; DBFP 3.VII, pp. 391–535.

CHAPTER 15: MUSSOLINI ON THE BRINK OF WAR

1. Cab 65/12; DDI 8.13, pp. 385 *et seq.*; DGFP Series D, Vol. VIII, p. 182.
2. De Felice, *Mussolini il Duce*, Vol. II, pp. 670–3; Ciano, *Diary 1939–1943*, p. 177; Knox, *Mussolini Unleashed*, p. 62.
3. Kirkpatrick, op. cit., pp. 415–17; Ciano, ibid., pp. 177, 184–5; Mack Smith, *Mussolini*, p. 243.
4. FO 371/23788; Hibbert, op. cit., p. 547; DDI 9.2, p. 547; De Felice, ibid., p. 748.
5. DGFP Series D, Vol. VIII, pp. 604 *et seq.*; DDI 9.3, pp. 19 *et seq.*
6. Mack Smith, ibid., p. 242; Ciano, ibid., p. 188; Knox, op. cit., p. 63; DDI 9.2, p. 705.
7. DGFP Series D, Vol. VIII, pp. 609–13.
8. De Felice, ibid., p. 758; Knox, op. cit., p. 74; Ciano, ibid., pp. 215–17, 219; Cab 65/12; DDI 9.3, pp. 475–6; DGFP Series D, Vol. VIII, pp. 895, 901; Hibbert, op. cit., p. 118.
9. De Felice, ibid., p. 766; FO 371/24937.
10. Schmidt, op. cit., p. 172.
11. DGFP Series D, Vol. IX, pp. 1–16; Kirkpatrick, op. cit., p. 430; De Felice, *Mussolini l'Alleato*, Vol. I, pp. 91–4; Ciano, ibid., pp. 224–5, 230; FO 371/24937.
12. Ciano, ibid., pp. 230–3; De Felice, *Mussolini il Duce*, vol. II, pp. 780–8; FO 371/24943; FO 371/24944; FO 371/24937; Cab 65/12; DDI 9.4, pp. 181–213, 286, 412.
13. Churchill, *Their Finest Hour*, pp. 107–8; De Felice, ibid., p. 823.
14. DDI 9.4, p. 495; De Felice, ibid., pp. 834–5.
15. FO 371/24958; FRUS 1940 Vol. II, pp. 712–15; Ciano, ibid., p. 255.
16. FO 371/24958; FO 371/24943; Dilks, op. cit., pp. 289–90.
17. Cab 65/13; FO 371/24959; Churchill, ibid., pp. 207–9.
18. DDI 9.4, p. 542; Dilks, op. cit., p. 291.
19. Birkenhead, *Halifax*, p. 456; FO 371/24959; FO 371/24958; FO 371/18457; Cab 34/67; Cab 69/1; Cab 63/13.
20. François-Poncet, *Au Palais Farnese*, pp. 173–9; Mack Smith, *Italy and its Monarchy*, pp. 287 *et seq.*; conversation of West with author.
21. De Felice, ibid., pp. 841–3; Ciano, ibid., pp. 256–8.
22. Guariglia, op. cit., p. 453.
23. Ciano, ibid., pp. 266–70; De Felice, *Mussolini l'Alleato*, Vol. I, pp. 122 *et seq.*

CHAPTER 16: MUSSOLINI AT WAR

1. Lamb, *Churchill as War Leader*, pp. 67–9; DGFP Series D, Vol. X, pp. 27, 157, 210–11, 242–3; Ciano, *L'Europa verso*, p. 568; FO 371/99936.
2. FO 371/24967; Lamb, ibid., pp. 67–9.
3. Ciano, *Diary 1939–1943*, pp. 297–8; FO 371/99936.
4. Ciano, *L'Europa verso*, p. 606; DGFP Series D, Vol. IX, pp. 371 *et seq.*; Preston, *Franco*, pp. 393–400; Schmidt, op. cit., p. 197; Kirkpatrick, op. cit., p. 463; *Hitler e Mussolini lettere e documenti*, p. 185.
5. Ciano, *Diary 1939–1943*, p. 325; Anfuso, op. cit., pp. 153–5; Kirkpatrick, op. cit.,

pp. 467–9; Preston, op. cit., pp. 422–3; *Lettere e documenti*, p. 91; DGFP Series D, Vol. XII, p. 197; DDI 9.6, pp. 568–83.

6. Paper given by J.D. Brown at Anglo-Italian Conference, Imperial War Museum, September 1990; Butler, *Grand Strategy*, Vol. III, p. 172.

7. Denham, *Inside the Nazi Ring*, pp. 132–40; Santoni, *Da Lissa alle Falkland*, pp. 194–200; FO 898/16; FO 898/14; FO 371/24936; FO 371/24937; FO 371/29958; FO 371/29940; FO 371/32218; FO 371/37069; FO 371/43522; Prem 3/234.

8. Ciano, *L'Europa verso*, pp. 660–74, 683; *Lettere e documenti*, pp. 101, 105; Ciano, *Diary 1939–1943*, pp. 360, 363–4.

9. FO 371/29922.

10. Toscano, *Dal 25 luglio*, pp. 7–9; Varsori in *Journal of Italian History*, Vol. 1, No. 3, 'Italy, Britain and a Separate Peace, 1940–1943'; *Lettere e documenti*, p. 154; FO 371/33240.

11. FRUS Vol. II, pp. 318–22; FO 371/33240.

12. Howard, *Grand Strategy*, p. 283; De Felice, *Mussolini l'Alleato*, Vol. I, p. 1317.

13. Prem 3/242/9; FRUS, ibid., pp. 320–1.

14. FO 371/33240; FO 371/37260; FO 371/37265; FO 371/37264; Toscano, ibid., pp. 171–81; Lamb, *Ghosts of Peace*, pp. 169–90.

15. Kirkpatrick, op. cit., p 508; Deakin, *Brutal Friendship*, pp. 359–67; FO 371/37265.

16. Deakin, op. cit., p. 287.

17. Bastianini, *Uomini, cose, fatti*, p. 159; De Felice, ibid., p. 1301.

18. Bastianini, op. cit., p. 118; Ortona, *Il 1943 da Palazzo Chigi*, pp. 1123 *et seq.*; De Felice, ibid. pp. 1315–16.

19. Toscano, ibid., pp. 157 *et seq.*

20. Alfieri, *Due Dittatori di fronte*, pp. 312–31; DDI 9.10, pp. 685 *et seq.*; De Felice, ibid., pp. 1333–8.

21. De Felice, ibid., p. 1350; FO 371/37289; FO 371/37265.

CHAPTER 17: MUSSOLINI'S END

1. Deakin, op. cit., pp. 475–90; Lamb, *War in Italy*, p. 53.

2. Garland & Smyth, *Sicily and the Surrender of Italy*, pp. 467–505.

3. WO 204/7301.

4. Deakin, op. cit., pp. 715–26; Lamb, ibid., pp. 111–24.

5. Mellini, *Guerra diplomatica a Salò*, pp. 94–100; Lamb, ibid., p. 284.

6. Deakin, op. cit., pp. 742–4.

7. Vatican, *Actes*, Vol. II, pp. 703–4, 708–9, 723.

8. Cadorna, *Riscossa*, pp. 251–7.

9. FO 371/49932; De Felice, *Rosso e Nero*, p. 148.

10. Fondazione Mondadori archive.

Bibliography

Actes et documents de Saint Siège relatifs à la seconde guerre mondiale (Rome, 1967–81)

Adam, General —, unpublished Memoirs in Institut für Zeitgeschiete, Munich

Adamthwaite, Anthony, *The Making of the Second World War* (London, 1977)

——, *France and the Second World War* (London, 1977)

Alfieri, Dino, *Due dittatori di fronte* (Milan, 1948)

Aloisi, Pompeo, *La mia attività a servizio della pace* (Rome, 1946)

Andriola, Fabio, *Mussolini-Churchill: Carteggio segreto* (Casale Monferrato, 1996)

Anfuso, Filippo, *Da Palazzo Venezia al Lago di Garda, 1936–45* (Bologna, 1957)

Antonicelli, Franco, *Trent'anni di storia italiana, 1915–45* (Turin, 1961)

Aster, S., *The Making of the Second World War* (London, 1963)

Avon, Earl of, *Memoirs – Facing the Dictators* (London, 1962)

Balabanoff, Angelica, *My Life as a Rebel* (London, 1938)

Barnes, John and Nicholson, David, *The Empire at Bay: the Leo Amery Diaries, 1929–45* (London, 1988)

Barzini, Luigi, *The Italians* (London, 1964)

Bastianini, G., *Uomini, cose, fatti: memorie de un ambasciatore* (Milan, 1959)

Birkenhead, Earl of, *Halifax: The Life of Lord Halifax* (London, 1965)

Blake, Robert, *Unknown Prime Minister: Bonar Law* (London, 1955)

Bocca, Giorgio, *La repubblica di Mussolini* (Bari, 1977)

Bonnet, Georges, *Vingt ans de vie politique, 1918–1938* (Paris, 1969)

Bottai, Giuseppe, *Vent'anni e un giorno* (Milan, 1949)

Brown, J.D., Paper given at Anglo-Italian Conference, Imperial War Museum (London, September 1990)

Butler, J.R.M., *Grand Strategy*, Vol. II (London, 1957); Vol. III (London, 1964); Vol. IV (London, 1972)

Cadorna, Raffaele, *La riscossa: dal 25 luglio alla liberazione* (Milan, 1983)

Cannistraro, Philip V. and Sullivan, Brian R., *Il Duce's Other Woman* (New York, 1993)

Carlton, David, *Macdonald versus Henderson* (London, 1970)

Carr, Edward Hallett, *International Relations since the Peace Treaties* (London, 1940)

Carr, Raymond, *The Republic and the Civil War in Spain* (London, 1971)

——, *The Spanish Tragedy* (London, 1977)

Castellano, Giuseppe, *Come firmai l'armistizio di Cassibile* (Milan, 1945)
——, *Roma Kaputt* (Milan, 1963)
——, *La guerra continua* (Milan, 1967)
Cate, Curtis, *André Malraux* (London, 1995)
Cecchi, Donatella Bolech, *Non Bruciane i Ponti con Roma* (Milan, 1986)
Cecil, Viscount, *A Great Experiment* (London, 1941)
Churchill, Winston S., *The Gathering Storm* (London, 1948)
——, *Their Finest Hour* (London, 1950)
Ciano, Count Galeazzo, *L'Europa verso la catastrofe* (Milan, 1947; English translation
    Ciano's Diplomatic Papers, London, 1948)
——, *Diary 1939–1943*, ed. Malcolm Muggeridge (London, 1947)
——, *Diary 1937–1938*, intro. M. Muggeridge (London, 1952)
Cointet, Jean-Paul, *Pierre Laval* (Paris, 1993)
Collier, Richard, *Duce: The Rise and Fall of Benito Mussolini* (London, 1971)
Colvin, Ian, *Vansittart in Office* (London, 1971)
Coverdale, John F., *Italian Intervention in the Spanish Civil War* (Princeton, New Jersey,
    1975)
Cross, J.A., *Sir Samuel Hoare: a political biography* (London, 1977)
Cucco, A., *Non volevamo perdere* (Rocca S. Casciano, 1950)

D'Abernon, Viscount, *Diary: An Ambassador of Peace* (London, 1929)
Dahlerus, Birger, *The Last Attempt* (London, 1947)
Deakin, F. William, *The Brutal Friendship: Mussolini, Hitler and the Fall of Italian Fascism*
    (London, 1962)
De Felice, Renzo, *Storia degli ebrei italiani sotto il fascismo* (Turin, 1952)
——, *Mussolini il Fascista, Vol. I: La conquista del potere 1921–1925* (Turin, 1966)
——, *Mussolini il Fascista, Vol. II: L'organizzazione dello stato fascista 1925–1929*
    (Turin, 1966)
——, *Mussolini il Duce, Vol. I: Gli anni del consenso 1929–1936* (Turin, 1974)
——, *Mussolini il Duce, Vol. II: Lo stato totalitario 1936–1940* (Turin, 1981)
——, *Mussolini l'Alleato, Vol. I: Italia in guerra 1940–1943* (Turin, 1990)
——, *Mussolini l'Alleato, Vol. II: Crisi e agonia del regime* (Turin, 1990)
——, *Rosso e Nero* (Milan, 1995)
Dell, Robert, *The Geneva Racket* (London, 1940)
Denham, Henry, *Inside the Nazi Ring* (London, 1984)
Dilks, David, *Diaries of Sir Alexander Cadogan, 1938–1945* (London, 1971)
Documents on British Foreign Policy (London 1947–)
Documents diplomatiques français (Paris, 1968–1970)
Documenti diplomatici italiani (Rome, 1952–)
Documents on German Foreign Policy, Series C and D (London, 1951–)
Duroselle, Jean-Baptiste and Serra, Enrico, *Italia e Francia dal 1919 a 1939* (Milan,
    1981)
Dutton, David, *Simon* (London, 1992)
——, *Anthony Eden* (London, 1996)

Feiling, Keith, *The Life of Neville Chamberlain* (London, 1946)
Foreign Relations of the United States: Diplomatic Papers (Washington, DC)

François-Poncet, André, *The Fateful Years, 1931–1938* (London, 1949)
——, *Au Palais Farnese* (Paris, 1961)

Gallo, Max, *Mussolini's Italy* (London, 1974)
Garland, Albert and Smyth, Howard McGraw, *Sicily and the Surrender of Italy*
     (Washington, DC, 1965)
Gibbs, Norman, *Grand Strategy: Vol. I: Rearmament Policy* (London, HMSO, 1976)
Gilbert, Martin, *Winston S. Churchill, 1922–1939* (London, 1976)
Gilmour, David, *Curzon* (London, 1994)
Gladwyn, Lord, *Memoirs* (London, 1972)
Grandi, Dino, *25 luglio quarant'anni dopo* (Bologna, 1983)
Griffith, Richard, *Fellow-travellers of the Right* (Oxford, 1983)
Grimaldi, Alfassio, *Deici guigno 1940 il giorno della follia* (Rome, 1974)
Guariglia, R., *Ricordi, 1922–1946* (Naples, 1950)
Guerri, Giordano Bruno, *Fascisti – gli Italiani di Mussolini il regime degli Italiani* (Milan,
     1995)

Hardie, Frank, *The Abyssinian Crisis* (London, 1974)
Harvey, John (ed.), *The Diplomatic Diaries of Oliver Harvey, 1931–1940* (London,
     1970)
Hassell, Ulrich von, *The von Hassell Diaries, 1938–1944* (London, 1948)
Hibbert, Christopher, *Benito Mussolini* (London, 1962)
Hitler e Mussolini: lettere e documenti (Milan, 1946)
Hoare, Samuel, *Nine Troubled Years* (London, 1954)
Hollis, Christopher, *Italy in Africa* (London, 1941)

James, Robert Rhodes, *Anthony Eden* (London, 1986)
Jones, A.H. and Munro, Elizabeth, *A History of Ethiopia* (Oxford, 1966)
Jones, T., *A Diary with Letters, 1931–1950* (Oxford, 1954)

Kindermann, Gottfried-Karl, *Hitler's Defeat in Austria, 1933–34* (London, 1988)
Kirkpatrick, Sir Ivone, *Mussolini: a study of a demagogue* (London, 1964)
Knox, Macgregor, *Mussolini Unleashed, 1939–41* (Cambridge, 1982)

Lacouture, Jean, *Léon Blum* (New York, 1982)
Lamb, Richard, *The Ghosts of Peace* (Salisbury, 1987)
——, *The Drift to War* (London, 1989)
——, *Churchill as War Leader* (London, 1991)
——, *War in Italy: 1943–1945* (London, 1993)
Ludwig, Emil, *Talks with Mussolini* (London, 1933)

Macartney, Maxwell and Cremona, *Italy's Foreign and Colonial Policy 1914–1937*
     (London, 1938)
McCallum, R.B., *Public Opinion and the Lost Peace* (London, 1944)
Mack Smith, Denis, *Mussolini's Roman Empire* (London, 1976)
——, *Mussolini* (London, 1981)

——, *Italy and its Monarchy* (Avon, G.B., 1989)

Magistrati, M., *L'Italia a Berlino (1937–1939)* (Milan, 1956)

Mellini Ponce de Leon, A., *Guerra diplomatica a Salò* (Bologna, 1950)

Michaelis, Meir, *Mussolini and the Jews* (Oxford, 1978)

Monelli, Paolo, *Mussolini, an Intimate Life* (London, 1953)

Montanelli, Indro and Cervi, Mario, *L'Italia della guerra civile* (Milan, 1984)

Mosley, Nicholas, *Beyond the Pale* (London, 1983)

Mosley, Sir Oswald, *My Life* (London, 1968)

Mussolini, Benito, *Opera omnia di Benito Mussolini* (eds E. and D. Susmel) (Florence, 1951)

Nicolson, Harold, *Curzon: the Last Phase, 1919–1925* (London, 1934)

Noël, L., *Les illusions de Stresa: L'Italie abandonnée à Hitler* (Paris, 1975)

Nordio, Mario, *Inviato speciale in europa* (Trieste, 1992)

Northedge, F.S., *The Troubled Giant, 1916–1939* (London, 1966)

Ortona, Egidio, 'Il 1943 de Palazzo Chigi: Note di Diario', in *Storia Contemporanea*, December 1983.

Papen, Franz von, *Memoirs* (London, 1952)

Parker, R.A.C., in *English Historical Review* Vol. 89, 1972

Peters, A.R., *Anthony Eden at The Foreign Office, 1931–1938* (London/NY, 1986)

Petrie, Sir Charles, *The Life and Letters of the Rt Hon. Sir Austen Chamberlain* (London, 1940)

——, *Twenty Years: Armistice and After* (London, 1940)

Preston, Paul, *Franco, a Biography* (London, 1993)

Puntoni, P., *Parla Vittorio-Emanuele III* (Milan, 1956)

Reynaud, Paul, *Mémoires* (Paris, 1963)

Roberts, Andrew, *The Holy Fox* (London, 1991)

Roskill, S.W,. *Hankey, Man of Secrets* (London, 1974)

Salvemini, Gaetano, *Prelude to World War II* (London, 1953)

Santoni, Alberto, *Da Lissa alle Falkland* (Milan, 1987)

Schmidt, P., *Hitler's Interpreter* (London, 1951)

Schuschnigg, Kurt von, *Brutal Takeover* (London, 1971)

Selby, Sir Walford, *Diplomatic Twilight 1930–1940* (London, 1953)

Seton-Watson, Christopher, *Italy from Liberalism to Fascism, 1870–1925* (London, 1967)

——, 'The Italian Gentleman's Agreement of January 1937', in Mommsen (ed.) *Fascist Challenge* (London, 1983)

Shirer, William, *The Rise and Fall of the Third Reich* (London, 1959)

Simoni, Luigi, *Berlino: Ambasciata d'Italia* (Rome, 1946)

Spitzy, Reinhard, *So haben wir das Reich verspeilt* (Munich, 1986)

Starhemberg, Prince Ernst Rudiger, *Between Hitler and Mussolini* (London, 1942)

Stille, Alexander, *Benevolence and Betrayal* (London, 1992)

Tamaro, Attilio, *Due anni di storia 1942–45* (Rome, 1948–50)

Taylor, Telford, *Munich, the Price of Peace* (London, 1979)

Thompson, Geoffrey, *Front-Line Diplomat* (London, 1959)

Toscano, Mario, *L'Italia e gli accordi Tedesco–Sovietici dell'agosto 1939* (Florence, 1952)

——, *Una mancata intesa Italo–Sovietica nel 1940 e 1941* (Florence, 1953)

——, *Dal 25 luglio all' 8 settembre* (Florence, 1953)

——, *The Origins of the Pact of Steel* (Baltimore, 1967)

——, in Sarkissian (ed.), *Studies in Diplomatic History and Historiography* (London, 1979)

Trial of the Major German War Criminals before the International Military Tribunal, Nuremberg (Nuremberg and London, 1947–1949)

Varè, Daniel, *Laughing Diplomat* (London, 1939)

Varsori, Antonio, 'Italy, Britain and the Problem of a Separate Peace, 1940–1943' in *Journal of Italian History*, Vol. 1, No. 3, 1978

Vatican Documents, see *Actes et documentes*

Waley, Daniel, *British Public Opinion and the Abyssinian War 1935–6* (London, 1975)

Waterfield, Lina, *Castle in Italy* (London, 1961)

Watt, Donald Cameron, *How War Came* (London, 1989)

Wiskemann, Elizabeth, *The Rome-Berlin Axis* (London, 1949)

Zampaglione, Gerardo, *Italy* (London, 1956)

Zangrandi, Ruggero, *1943: 25 luglio-8 settembre* (Milan, 1965)

Index